Dawn of a New Era

Krishnamurti and the wisdom explosion
in the American Age

Aryel Sanat

An imprint of
Paradigm Shift Network

TABLE OF CONTENTS

PROLOGUE   v

PART ONE — KRISHNAMURTI
    Chapter 1,   *Unprecedented*   1
    Chapter 2,   *The Analytical Fallacy*   7
    Chapter 3,   *The American Age*   21
    Chapter 4,   *K's Inner Life*   33
    Chapter 5,   *"Masters"*   41
    Chapter 6,   *Disclosure*   67

PART TWO — THE PERENNIAL WISDOM
    Chapter 7,   *Perennials*   83
    Chapter 8,   *Evidence*   93
    Chapter 9,   *Nietzsche*   121
    Chapter 10,   *The Perennial Explosion*   131
    Chapter 11,   *The Perennial Wisdom*   149
    Chapter 12,   *"Authorities"*   159
    Chapter 13,   *Revolution*   167
    Chapter 14,   *"Mysteries"*   175
    Chapter 15,   *HPB, K, and Perennials*   189

PART THREE — A NEW PERSPECTIVE
    Chapter 16,   *A New Language*   197
    Chapter 17,   *Chinese Energy Wisdom*   203
    Chapter 18,   *American Agers*   213
    Chapter 19,   *Victorian Exoterics*   221
    Chapter 20,   *A New Perspective*   229
    Chapter 21,   *Discovery*   249
    Chapter 22,   *TS Mission*   259

PART FOUR — MUTATION
    Chapter 23,   *Unlikely Yogi*   265
    Chapter 24,   *The Process*   271
    Chapter 25,   *Mutation*   281
    Chapter 26,   *Aurobindo*   297
    Chapter 27,   *American Age*   325
    Chapter 28,   *The TS*   353
    Chapter 29,   *Skeptics*   363
    Chapter 30,   *Education*   369
    Chapter 31,   *World University*   375
    Chapter 32,   *Paradigm Shift*   387
    Chapter 33,   *Dying to the Known*   405

EPILOGUE   413

PROLOGUE[1]

WE ALL LIVE IN THE MIDST OF WHAT IS—by far—the most comprehensive and pervasive revolution in the known history of mankind.

At heart, the present is a *wisdom* revolution—a veritable explosion against the me-centered values that have always dominated, everywhere. Since wisdom has no bounds, it is a *borderless* revolution that we are all in the midst of.

As documented here in part, there is and has been an explosion of wisdom going on in our times—in every aspect of human life, everywhere on Earth.

Despite intense and passionate resistance from those who are still attached to the old ways of engaging in conflict and confusion at every level, the wisdom explosion continues to gain impetus. It is as if the present wisdom blast were an unstoppable juggernaut.

* * *

In the twenty-first century, we find ourselves in the midst of the most severe expression ever of an age-old conflict—the clash between borderlessly wise universal morality on one hand, and intelligence-challenged and provincial, me-centered prejudices on the other.

The universally acknowledged and most respected leaders of culture everywhere and everywhen—among them the founders of the great religions—have always spoken of a borderless wisdom-compassion as the universal solvent for all human woes, clashes, and confusions. All religions and ideologies based on

---

[1] For a comprehensive bibliography of all books mentioned, cited, or quoted, please see REFERENCES at paradigmshift.network.

universal morality have appealed, since time immemorial, to that unconditioned and unconditional wisdom-compassion.

Unfortunately, those borderless insights have uniformly been transmogrified into prejudicial group-thinks—thereby creating "new and improved" conflicts between us, and within us.

That ancient war between "the good" and "the bad"—within and without us—has been gaining momentum in our times.

The boom of that grand battle has been creating a sense of urgency—personal and planetary—in our times, in a number of important ways. For one thing, the group-think provincial forces have been successful in creating a multidimensional planet-wide calamity, the likes of which humanity had never witnessed before. There are obvious political aspects to that tragedy. But there are also equally evident environmental, ethnic, economic, social, and numerous other components to it.

Our very survival—as individuals, and as a species—is at risk, in ways that didn't even exist before.

No matter where on Earth one lives, catastrophe of one sort or another seems to be either present or impending—as if it were breathing down one's neck.

* * *

Will borderless wisdom help us and guide us in our present plight, despite its numerous past failures, due to its having been transmogrified by the provincial-minded? Only you and I can answer that *existential* question. We each answer it by the way in which we conduct our lives.

Despite borderless wisdom having failed in the past to touch us to the point of helping us be wiser and more compassionate, the wisdom explosion of our times perhaps justifies some of us in being hopeful, this time.

Perhaps the wisdom explosion turns out to be successful, this time—successful enough to make at least some of us snap out of our atavistic dogmatic slumbers, and awaken us into actually engaging in more sensible ways of being in the world.

In the end, what matters is what you and I *actually* do, in the midst of the conflagration—despite this unprecedented world-wide situation being truly bewildering, perhaps even over-whelming, for many of us.

As you are about to see, a good place to start an exploration into all that—and much more, all related to the present disaster-in-the-making, with its chaos and dangers personal and plane-tary—is to look into J. Krishnamurti's (K) borderless insights, researches, and observations.

* * *

Krishnamurti (1895-1986) addressed the present chaotic and threatening planetary situation in a unique, unprecedented way.

For one thing, he made no appeals at all to a particular religion, or culture, or ideology. Before K, it had been common to address human problems by making such provincial appeals. Unfortunately, appeals to a particular group-think are bound to alienate all those who don't belong to the group in question—and that means alienating the rest of humanity. Provincial appeals *always* make a bad situation worse.

Instead, K appealed directly to our wisdom-intelligence—which is borderless and does not "belong" to any particular group on Earth, while yet being potentially present everywhere.

Simple—and perhaps even simplistic, as that may sound to some—K's approach is in perfect consonance with what the great moral geniuses of the past had proclaimed. It also reso-nates with borderless wisdom-intelligence, which is within every single one of us—if we would only allow it to manifest itself in our lives.

* * *

In many ways, it is surprising that K should have come upon such world-transforming insights. He was born in what was then a small town in southern India, and didn't know any language other than the Telugu of his family. In addition, he grew up being sick all the time, and not expected to live long. Apart from that, his family and acquaintances perceived him to be "very slow and dreamy," possibly "retarded."

How could such a boy come into worldwide prominence? That is in itself a fascinating and intriguing story. I addressed that story in *The Inner Life of Krishnamurti* (1999)—a second edition of which I intend to publish soon after the present exploration.

In fact, *Dawn of a New Era* is—in many important ways—an introduction to *The Inner Life of Krishnamurti*. The latter stands on its own. But unfortunately, I have been able to see that some of its readers have misunderstood some aspects of what I thought had been said rather clearly. *Dawn of a New Era*—which also stands on its own—adds depth and clarity to the earlier work. It is my hope that it also answers some lingering questions, at least for some readers of *The Inner Life of Krishnamurti*.

* * *

My intent now is to "put K on the map" of worldwide culture, in the context of the present planetary wisdom revolution and the catastrophe-in-the-making that we're all witnessing. That takes us into looking carefully at what I have called "the wisdom explosion" of our times—and what I have called "the American Age" in which that explosion has been taking place.

As you are about to see, putting K on the map of worldwide culture within the wisdom explosion in the American Age has profound and multidimensional implications.

Among other factors, it implies taking a serious second look at what is generally understood by words such as "philosophy" and "religion" and "education," and the significance of the institution of the university.

This exploration also addresses the prominent significance of America, in the midst of the planetary chaos and dangers that we can see, all around us.

In addition, this is a novel and focused look at what has generally been called "the New Age movement"—and its significance for gaining a better understanding of the unquestionably unique *planetary* times we're living in.

* * *

None of what you are about to read is "a theory" presumably meant to provide a particular "view" of our admittedly strange times. Our times are "strange"—but only when looked upon in the light of any previous age and time in history.

Part of that strangeness is the now possible realization that theories don't work at all when it comes to us living sensible lives. This limitation of theories is also addressed in this inquiry. So I'm not proposing a theory regarding the unique times we're living in.

I am merely sharing with you here some insights I have gained over the past six decades of intense and extensive research into all of the above. This exploration is meant as being just a single person's contribution to an immense reality.

Others will help to clarify and expand what is being merely *described* here. This exploration is just a pioneering attempt at showing how the many factors involved in the present wisdom explosion are indeed but components of a much larger, planetary grand event.

All of it is inexorably about you.

PART ONE

KRISHNAMURTI

CHAPTER 1
Unprecedented

THE PRESENCE OF J. KRISHNAMURTI in the twentieth century is a phenomenon the likes of which had never taken place before, anywhere in the world. I document this in part in the present exploration. Among other factors:

- Krishnamurti (K) is the only truth-researcher in history who addressed directly the whole world, and not just one region, guild, or culture. In the midst of dangerous disorder everywhere, K addressed everyone on Earth regarding the urgent need for compassionate borderlessness—and *that* is unprecedented.
- K is the only truth-researcher in history who did not appeal to any accepted mores in a particular region, or culture, or guild.
- K is the only truth-researcher in history who did not appeal to an ideological system, to scriptures—to "authoritative" writings of any kind—nor to a methodology.
- K is the only truth-researcher in history who addressed the world crisis in a compassionate, borderless, non-culture-non-ideology-non-guild-oriented context of individual human transformation leading to reconstructing beneficially all societies, everywhere.
- K is the only truth-researcher in history who addressed clearly and directly our psychological states as the beginning point for engaging in any real investigation into *what is*, without appealing to ideological, guild-related, nor culture-committed factors.
- K is the only truth-researcher in history who conflated psychological factors and love-of-wisdom research, while yet not appealing to any form of conditioning.

- K is the only truth-researcher in history who addressed the urgent need throughout the world for a compassionate, caring, comprehensively borderless education—which requires a borderless psychological-moral transformation in teachers and students—in order for any of us to have any possibility for creating a good society.

- K's insights, researches, and observations provide the most clear, thorough, and powerful exposition of the borderless, universal morality that America's founding documents are centrally about. Yet those documents merely *mention* the necessity for such a borderless morality. K's insights, researches, and observations lay out *specifically* what is required of us to be able actually to create a good society.

- K achieves this unprecedented feat. But he does so with no partisanship nor any form of politics or ideology. Practically all would-be borderless organizations today (such as the United Nations), as well as most countries in the world—which are constitutional democratic republics—are based on America's founding documents. So, K's powerful clarifications are immensely and powerfully relevant to our times, everywhere.

- In sum, K is the only truth-seeker-truth-finder in history who did not commit the analytical fallacy—as shown thoroughly in *The Analytical Fallacy* (2002), and more briefly in Chapter 2, "The Analytical Fallacy," and in the book *Insights for a New Era*.

- K is also the only truth-researcher in history who taught only the esoteric component of all the great religions and systems, while excluding any and all exoteric distractions—which usually involve "teachings," or "myths," or "practices." Some have come to worship such distractions—as in conventional religions and ideologies.

Others, more recently, have referred to that process collectively as "the Perennial Tradition," or simply "Traditionalism."[1]

Unprecedented

One way of addressing the astonishing, historically-prominent and unique phenomenon that K is, is to point to the fact that he is the quintessential iconoclast of all times. The importance of K being such a profound iconoclast becomes obvious, when one realizes that previous iconoclasts have been among the great revolutionaries in history. These are individuals who changed importantly the way we all see and understand the world around us. In many ways, those skeptical revolutionaries made it possible for all of us to see the world the way we now see it.

Some of the most influential iconoclasts known in history have been called "philosophical skeptics."[2] Their presence throughout the ages reads like a Who's Who of wisdom lovers and wisdom revolutionaries. The list includes: Socrates (470-399 BCE), Nagarjuna (250-150 BCE), Sextus Empiricus (160-210), Adi Shankaracharya (8th century), Immanuel Kant (1724-1804), Friedrich Nietzsche (1844-1900), the pragmatists, Ludwig Wittgenstein (1889-1951), the deconstructionists, and Richard Rorty (1931-2007).

As shown in *The Analytical Fallacy*, all of those skeptics (and others) questioned—each in his own way—the generally

---

[1] The tandem issues of Traditionalism and the esoteric are addressed succinctly in what follows and in the soon-to-be-published books *Insights for a New Era: Krishnamurti, Blavatsky—and human mutation in chaotic times,* and more thoroughly in *Transformation: The foundation for H.P. Blavatsky's Insights,* and also in *Muse: H.P. Blavatsky's insights for a new era of chaos, revolution, wisdom—and Krishnamurti.*
[2] Skepticism is addressed more fully in Chapter 29, "Skeptics."

presumed relevance of ideologies in general, and analysis in particular, for the purpose of understanding *what is.*

This is really important, because the vast majority of us make the assumption that the one and only proper way of understanding anything and everything is to analyze it. Yet—as you are about to see—analysis is grossly inadequate for understanding deeper issues. So, the fact that the greatest wisdom revolutionaries in history denied analysis where it doesn't belong, is something we all need to pay close attention to.

More poignantly, philosophical skeptics have always noted the limitations of analysis for understanding what matters most to all of us. "What matters most to us" is anything having to do with universal morality, with inquiring borderlessly—and with the perennial dimension in general. The perennial dimension is addressed in what follows.

All that skeptical questioning on the part of previous geniuses is truly excellent. But unfortunately—and given the bewildering number of systems and methods everywhere—such critiques have not been nearly sufficient for holding back the provincial and the intelligence-challenged, throughout the planet.

At the heart of the problem is a deeply concerning reality: In the process of showing the inadequacies of analysis, every single one of the previous critics of analysis and ideologies—without exception—have been simultaneously beholden to analysis.

In world history, K is the only skeptic who has questioned the relevance of analysis itself, when addressing deeper matters.

In doing that, he was questioning any and all analysis-based values-related systems and methodologies—and that includes all previous skeptics, including those just mentioned.

That had never been done before, anywhere on the planet. K's insights, researches, and observations are unprecedented *in world history.*

All previous iconoclasts had mistakenly assumed the primacy of the analytical mind—and their would-be "questioning of analysis" came largely from that tainted source. That source is tainted because all analysis is me-centered—and a me-centered perspective is intrinsically provincial, and ignorant of that which is borderless.[3]

K, however, showed instead the primacy of unconditional and non-conditioned compassion as the most formidable form of intelligence. He showed the primacy of intelligence in the process of revealing the bankruptcy of any and all analyses for the purpose of addressing what matters most to all of us. What matters most to all of us are factors such as justice, love, beauty, truth-seeking-truth-finding, joy, freedom, awe, and, in general, understanding everything that touches all of us more deeply.

Importantly, K achieves this without ever committing the analytical fallacy, and that is an unprecedented, truly astonishing feat. This is especially amazing, when one considers that the greatest geniuses in human history had failed to see this insurmountable difficulty in their otherwise excellent insights.

Perennial Wisdom

Another way of pointing to K's uniqueness in history, is to note his similarity in depth of content to some of the wisest leaders of the past—such as the Buddha, Lao Tse, and Jesus—though one can also note some important differences.[4]

Like all the most influential humans in history (such as the ones just mentioned), K was passionate about contributing to the beneficial transformation of human life—from being me-

---

[3] The intrinsic me-centeredness of all analysis is shown in Chapter 2, "The Analytical Fallacy."

[4] The perennial wisdom—which is what all of those great leaders of culture were inspired by—is the subject of Part Two.

centered, provincial, agonistic, and confused, to being more loving, compassionate, all-embracing, empathic to others, and enlightened.

Yet here also K set a new, unprecedented standard, as well: All the previous great presenters of the universal wisdom, while pointing in different ways towards a more caring and intelligent way to be human, simultaneously appealed to the particular cultural limitations of their respective audiences. Plato was a Greek's Greek, Jesus quoted Hebrew scriptures, Lao Tse was beholden to Chinese culture, Mohammed focused on the Middle East, and the Buddha was clearly addressing and critiquing the cultural background of the Indian subcontinent.

There is absolutely no such concession to people's ideological and regional and cultural attachments and expectations and atavisms—which used to be common among such historically-prominent presenters of the universal wisdom—in K's unprecedented, borderless, purely esoteric presentation of the very ancient perennial wisdom.

No one had ever done that before.

As the rest of this exploration shows, K's radically new approach to borderless morality, to psychological transformation, to education, and to truth-seeking-truth-finding, is indeed a unique phenomenon in human history.

What K did had never been even tried, let alone achieved, before.

CHAPTER 2
The Analytical Fallacy

AT THE CORE OF THE HISTORY-MAKING primacy of K's uniqueness are the two factors bulleted last on the list in Chapter 1. These two factors—the analytical fallacy and the esoteric—summarize all the others, in important ways.

First, K never committed the analytical fallacy—as everyone else before him had done, either by commission or by omission.

Furthermore, in presenting the timeless wisdom, he was only interested in its more relevant dimension—which is the esoteric. As a result, K's insights, researches, and observations addressed the esoteric and only the esoteric, while simultaneously excluding everything that was more superficial—and exoteric. By addressing wisdom in such a way, he was doing something that was contrary to the practice of all the eminent teachers who had preceded him.

I address more thoroughly and substantially these two comprehensive and intimately related issues in *Muse* and in *The Analytical Fallacy*, and also provide some preliminary background for them in *Insights for a New Era*. But for the sake of clarity, a briefer, more succinct statement about this is made here.

To begin with, what is "the analytical fallacy," and what is its significance?

Whenever anyone uses analysis assuming that it is a proper tool to use for the purpose of exploring anything at all about the dimension of values, she is thereby committing the analytical fallacy.

The dimension of values

The dimension of values is very familiar to all of us. It includes, among many other factors:

- Our sense of right and wrong—our sense of justice and fairness.
- The tenderness (call it love, empathy, compassion, or what you will) that we all have experienced at one time or another. Examples are what happens within us upon even just seeing a baby, or when we empathize with a person who is suffering, or the kind of tenderness that a loving mother feels for her child (the actual feeling, not some analysis of it).
- The sense of awe that all of us have experienced at one time or another, either by being faced with the immensity of the starry sky, or with the beauty of a flower, or with the staggering impact on us of an unusual sunrise or sunset.
- The act and process of engaging in *borderless* truth-seeking-truth-finding, in which all me-centered conditioning and expectations (all prejudicial analyses) are absent. It is exclusively in the absence of prejudicial analysis that it is possible for any of us to seek out what is "the truth of the matter"—regardless of what "the matter" happens to be. Without that *borderless* truth-seeking attitude, true scientific research is impossible.

There are other aspects to the dimension of values—such as courage, goodness, and joy. But for our purposes here, what has just been said should be sufficient for conveying the fact that it is in that dimension that "the better angels of our nature" have their being.

We are all well acquainted with the dimension of values.

The problems implicit in committing the analytical fallacy may be expressed succinctly by noticing that the analyzer (any analyzer) is so full of what he *assumes* is "right" according to his unquestioned conditioning, that he cannot see what is universally *good*.

There is, of course, a great deal more implicit in what I have called "the dimension of values." That dimension stands for the factors in our lives that, at the end of the day, are truly the most important to us and that we care most about, in our most attentive and less immature moments.

For instance, everything in the dimension of values is ineffable: It can, of course, be *talked about*—and Lord knows that we all do, as I am doing right now. But *engaging* in the dimension of values is an ineffable process. Using words and concepts—using analysis—confuses and transmogrifies that process into something that is no longer of the dimension of values, no longer ineffable: The mother's intense love for her baby is ineffable—but talking about it is unrelated to her actual experience.

This is only one of many more factors implicit in what I am referring to as "the dimension of values." That dimension of our experience might just as well be called "the ineffable." Without the intrinsically ineffable dimension of values, we're reduced to being brutes—savages such as our cave-dwelling or jungle-denizen prehistoric ancestors, such as we tend to deem them to have been.

Without the dimension of values, we are bound to create criminal-minded societies everywhere, such as the worldwide monstrosity that we are in fact all living in the twenty-first century.

Academia analysemia

In my experience, the people who teach what they call "philosophy" in universities around the world tend to make the never-questioned and never-demonstrated assumption that analysis is the one and only tool at our disposal for addressing any and all issues. According to such "philosophers," analysis is the tool *de rigueur* for addressing anything and everything having to do with the dimension of values.

The act and process of having a lively expectation that assumes unquestioningly that analysis is somehow omnipotent in that way is committing the analytical fallacy.

Importantly, no one has ever demonstrated the necessity for analysis when addressing the dimension of values. Academics and others who hold on to such a belief do so without any evidence whatsoever. They accept this dogma on pure blind faith.

Such academic true believers in analysis are exactly like fire and brimstone preachers, who believe in "the Book" because "it came from God." If anything, preachers are not as intense as the academics in their devotion to their respective militantly-held beliefs. Preachers at least point to there being a source for their unquestioned faith—scriptures.

Academics and others who have blind faith in analysis have no such "authority"—nor do they feel that they need to have any authority. Their overcredulousness in and militancy for analysis is so complete, that they make the fateful assumption that no demonstration is necessary.

It is alarmingly important to point out the immense disaster that has come about—everywhere in the world—by having such blind faith in analysis. For this reason alone, it should be obvious to everyone that blind faith in analysis *must be justified and demonstrated*, before we destroy each other and the planet (such as we now know it) for the sake of defending some purely provincial and never-questioned analysis or another.

The time has come for stopping that insanity. The time has come for us to see the analytical fallacy for the tremendously dangerous monster that it is.

The academic blind faith in analysis is deeply worrisome, because the university as an institution is devoted to following "philosophers." In the act and process of committing the analytical fallacy, it is as if "philosophers" have transmitted a highly contagious disease—a disease that might be called *"analysemia"*—to all other university faculties, and through them to the whole of society.

That is, the university as an institution—everywhere on Earth—is made up of faculties (such as history, psychology, and so on). All such faculties—without exception—are deeply committed to engaging in the analytical fallacy.

But alarmingly, committing the analytical fallacy is at the very heart of immorality, since the prejudices implicit in committing the analytical fallacy are intrinsically me-centered, and have no regard whatsoever for the welfare of all living entities, including human beings.

Analysis is thoroughly unconcerned with the dimension of values.

This shows that—for as long as institutions of higher learning are dedicated militantly to committing the analytical fallacy—such institutions are teaching their students to be immoral.

Obviously, this is an extremely serious matter—and is briefly addressed further in Part Four, "Mutation."

Dangers of analysis misused

Please resist the temptation to misunderstand what the analytical fallacy actually is—and what it isn't. The fact is that I have no interest in engaging in analysis-bashing across the board, and have never been involved in such a silly and reckless enterprise. This is addressed more thoroughly in *The Analytical Fallacy*.

Analysis is wonderful, and even essential. But let's be clear: Analysis truly shines when it's used primarily for the purpose of understanding better that which is physical-mechanical-material-measurable-time/space-bound.

Unfortunately, the moment one takes analysis out of those analysis-defining aspects, the result is "a fine mess," if I may borrow a catchy phrase from yesteryear's comedian Oliver Hardy (1892-1957). When analysis is taken out of its area of expertise and excellence—which is the physical-material-mechanical-measurable—the result is much like what one would expect to see in a sausage factory.

The result is immorality—and the consequent chaos that immorality always brings in its trail.

This transmogrification of analysis is not the private domain of academics. The analytical fallacy is also committed daily by used-car salesmen, televangelists, marketing "wizards," and politicians. All of them make the laughably yet morally lethal assumption that analysis is *the one and only* tool to use in order to understand anything and everything related to the dimension of values.

The morbid obsession with (mis)employing analysis where it clearly doesn't belong is the foundational reason why our societies everywhere are in chaos. All the religions and ideologies that claim to be based on universal morality commit the very same analytical fallacy. This is as serious as it can get.

Our society in general—our institutions everywhere, such as our religions, our ideologies (political, health-related, and others), our very cultures (with their implicit hubris and divisiveness)—is based, in fact, on people everywhere cavalierly committing the analytical fallacy.

That, my very dear friends, is at the core of why we have created such me-centered—and therefore immoral, even criminally-minded—societies, everywhere.

Analysis and morality

One factor that may explain in part why analysis is accepted so widely, is that analysis is—in itself—amoral.

2+2=4 can be said to be an elegant, correct piece of analysis—like many other mathematical and logical arguments and procedures. That much should be obvious to everyone. Such analysis is squeaky-clean. It can be said to be "clinically antiseptic."

But there is at least one thing that no logical argument or mathematical formula can ever be—however elegant or "correct" it may be within its own universe of discourse.

No mathematical formula or logical argument can ever be moral—at least not in the universal sense of goodness and right-and-wrong that universal morality and the whole dimension of values consist of. In fact, one main reason why analysis is so highly lauded is that it is, in itself, so very "clinically clean" and devoid of any personal, psychological prejudgments.

So far, so good.

But there are serious problems with using analysis in order to convert that which is whole into that which is fragmented. All analysis is a form of fragmentation—and universal morality is whole, in itself.

Universal morality is the act and process of caring for and empathizing with all living things—and there are no "parts" or "components" to that existential activity. Simultaneously, universal morality comes from the fact that our personal life is intertwined with and dependent on the whole universe.

Unfortunately, analyzers prefer to ignore the inconvenient but obvious fact that universal morality is transmogrified into something else, the moment it is included as a mere component within an ideological system.

This fact is inconvenient because ideological systems is what all religious and political and all other ideologies are based on, at the end of the day—and most devotees to ideologies are usually quite unwilling to question the object of their deeply-felt affections.

All ideological systems—including religious ones—are logical constructions, analytical constructions. As such, they are intrinsically amoral.

But whenever a system devotee declares that his system is "the best," or even "the only one" that matters, the intrinsic amorality of the system is turned into outright immorality. It turns into an excuse for creating divisions among human beings—and that is an important aspect of what immorality is all about.

The urgent importance of this is that analysis is amoral. This means that analysis is not and cannot ever be related at all to universal morality.

Analysis me-centered

Analysis is *always* me-centered—it exists for the benefit of a particular person or group-think. When I use analysis for some carpentry or road-building project, I am using analysis *for my own benefit*—and that is a good, and even an excellent thing, obviously. That is exactly what analysis is so very good at. We all need analysis for our physcal survival and comfort, precisely because analysis is intrinsically me-centered.

But the moment a person uses this intrinsically amoral tool for the specific purpose of dictating that some ideology in question is "the one and only" way to express universal morality, all hell breaks loose. That's the point at which analysis is transformed from being "clinically clean," to being more like a sausage factory—and alarmingly dangerous to our welfare and to the welfare of all that is.

Universal morality is whole. It is non-provincial and borderless in its very nature. So using analysis—which is intrinsically me-centered and amoral—for the purpose of determining the nature of universal morality is outrageously absurd. It is simultaneously dangerous—and even lethal—to our very existence.

The analysis in question (whether called "Christianity," or "Islam," or "Buddhism," or "allopathic," or "Conservative," or "Liberal") then takes a quantum leap from being amoral—and therefore morally neutral and unrelated to universal morality—to being outright immoral, and sometimes even criminally immoral.

Universal morality needs no help from analysis, and is always diminished and transmogrified by analysis into dangerous immorality.

It is critical for all of us to be at least aware of the implicit inappropriateness and inefficiencies of committing the analytical fallacy. There are highly destructive implications and dangers that *gowith* committing the analytical fallacy. In fact, this may well be, by far, the most important insight any of us are ever likely to face.

At present, we—as a species—are on the brink of bringing about a worldwide calamity of unprecedented proportions, and we're doing it for the sake of continuing to uphold some me-centered perspective or another, based on immoral and even criminally-minded ideologies. We are on the brink of doing our best to destroy ourselves and the planet, and we are doing it for the sake of committing the analytical fallacy.

K

Enter Krishnamurti: K never committed the analytical fallacy.

That is a monumental achievement, because no one else in history had ever been able to do that, although Lord knows that many had tried, as spelled out in *The Analytical Fallacy.* Real *philosophers*—such as Plato, Nagarjuna, Lao Tse, Shankaracharya, Kant, Nietzsche, and Wittgenstein—had tried what only K got to achieve.

K's venerable predecessors—try as well as they could—all pointed to the inefficacies implicit in analysis. Unfortunately, none of them realized that they were themselves committing the analytical fallacy, even in the process of pointing out the bankruptcy of analysis.

The failure of all these previous geniuses came about because—in the process of pointing to the limitations of analysis—they (or, more often, their followers) were still using analysis as their tool de rigueur. Among other factors, they all identified with a particular culture, or region, or ideological milieu—thereby committing the analytical fallacy. K never once was guilty of committing that blunder.

K's venerable and most worthy predecessors (such as those just mentioned) ended up, in every single instance, making *analyses* of why analysis is incompetent for true *philosophical* investigations or for true *religious practice*—let alone for universally moral commitments.

Words fail me, in pointing out the astonishing uniqueness with which K researched into so many issues, without even once ever committing the analytical fallacy. I know, because I deliberately looked meticulously for such gaps in K—and have never been able to find any.

To boot, K achieved this while using very simple language—so simple that often even children could understand what he was saying, which was always jargon-free.

That is part of why I say that K is the first *transanalytical philosopher* in history, and why I suggest that he was "the philosopher of the future" that Friedrich Nietzsche (1844-1900) had presciently referred to.[1]

The esoteric

Another major, comprehensive way of expressing K's singularity in history, is to note how he taught the esoteric—and only the esoteric—as briefly noted in the last of the bullets opening Chapter 1.[2]

As fully documented in *Muse*, the esoteric dimension of the borderless wisdom is that which happens in theosophical (divine-like) states of awareness—*according to H.P. Blavatsky and her borderless wisdom mentors.*[3] Those states of awareness are an intrinsic and even central component of the ineffable dimension of values.

Let's keep in mind that the word *"esoteric"* is a synonym of the word *"philosophy"* in the respective origins of those two

---

[1] For Nietzsche, see Chapter 9, "Nietzsche."
[2] I address this more fully in *Muse* and in *Insights for a New Era*.
[3] The subject of Blavatsky and her mentors is central to this exploration, and so it is addressed in a number of different ways throughout much of what follows.

words in Pythagoras. This insight is found profusely also in Plato—who was the most famous and influential Pythagorean in history. To both of them, these words refer explicitly to engaging in human transformation—which they both also referred to as what happens at "initiation." For both of them, that word implies the death of the me and the *initiation* of the borderless dimension of values.

Just moments before he was executed, Socrates affirmed that being a *philosopher* means that you die every single day of your life.[4] Unlike—and even contrary—to today's "philosophers," Socrates characterized analysis as *doxa* (opinion). Analysis, then—according to Socrates—is the committed enemy of true love-of-wisdom, which he called, with Pythagoras, *philosophia* (the love of wisdom).

In saying this, Socrates was obviously not talking about committing suicide every day—which is an absurdity. He was clearly referring to the daily death of one's conditioning. This death of one's conditioning is the death of the me—the me that you and I and all of us identify with as being "who I am" (or rather, who we *assume* we are).

That daily death of the me—and not analysis—is what real philosophy consists of, according to Pythagoras (who coined the word "philosophy") and Plato, who went on to clarify its meaning as referring to psychological transformation, not to theories and analyses.

Importantly, this transformation is precisely what K often referred to as "dying to the known."

This daily act and process of dying to one's conditioning is what all esoteric schools throughout history (and not only Pythagoras' and Plato's) have referred to as "initiatory"—as

---

[4] Plato, *Phaedo* 64a (Thomas Taylor translation).

Blavatsky (1831-1891) documented throughout all of her writings.[5] This initiatory act and process of dying to the known, which *defines* what the esoteric is, is precisely what K was addressing in everything he said and wrote, for more than seventy years.

Quintessential iconoclast and *philosopher*—in the purest, transformative, original sense of the word—and educator *par excellence*, teacher of the esoteric to the exclusion of any and all exoteric distractions, K steadfastly denied identification with any particular "philosophy" (read "opinion"), religion, or school of psychology.

Further, K's *transanalytical*, transformative insights, researches and observations have deeply influenced huge numbers of intelligent people from numerous disciplines and walks of life, everywhere on the planet—as is partly documented in what follows.

---

[5] See the paper "Transformation: Central Teaching of H.P. Blavatsky's *Secret Doctrine*," which was read at the third symposium on *The Secret Doctrine*, held in Oklahoma City in May 1998. The issue of the initiatory tenor of all of HPB's writings is addressed more thoroughly in the upcoming *Muse*, which incorporates and expands on that paper, and *Insights for a New Era*, and more briefly here, in Part Four, "Mutation."

CHAPTER 3
The American Age

WE ARE INDEED AT THE BEGINNING OF A NEW ERA—a planetary era. But what makes it a new era is totally unrelated to believing in this or that—as so many fervently and recklessly assume. In fact, believing in this or that—and identifying and being attached to that which one believes in, is precisely a perfect way to characterize the old.

What makes this a new era is that it is the first time in history when the borderless wisdom has ever had an opportunity to manifest itself much closer than before to what it actually is—and done so throughout the whole planet.

That is, it is a new era only if and to the extent that you and I undergo a major psychological-spiritual transformation. Anything short of that is unrelated to creating a new era.

Perennial America

The oneness of all humanity had been expressed prominently at the foundation of all the great religions and philosophies based on universal morality, for millennia.

Poignantly, this oneness is also what the founding documents of America clearly and unambiguously are based on, and refer to—to the point that the new era can most accurately be called "the American Age." The new era could be said to be "the age of America's founding documents."

Given the propensity among many to politicize everything, it must be clarified that—in that historically critical and poignant sense—"America" is a new borderless wisdom paradigm, not a country, nor an ideology.

Unfortunately, it is a fact that all previous efforts to manifest the universal wisdom have failed in their attempts to create an actual fraternity of all humans—truly worthy as those efforts have been, in many ways, towards helping create a grand fellowship of all the peoples of Earth.

The United States of America (the country, which I call here "the US") is no exception to such failure, so far—despite having had the benefit of being educated by past achievements in universal morality.

Lamentably, all religions and philosophies of the past have been transmogrified into hierarchies of authority and me-centered rigid systems of thought and practice. So, while they unquestionably have been and are inspired by the borderless and timeless and intrinsically non-partisan and non-prejudicial love-wisdom, they have also largely turned into various forms of group-think at war with one another.

Thus—in the very act of being the particular religion or philosophy that they are—they deny their pedigree and foundation in the universal, borderless wisdom.

Like all previous attempts through religions, philosophies, and other means, the US—despite its achievements, which admittedly have been quite considerable—has largely followed along the same lines of previous failures, at least so far.

It is true that some of its citizens—including a few public servants—have done their best to live their daily lives in the inspiring context of the perennially-sourced founding documents. But for the most part, a significant number of US citizens—including those in government—have tended towards being partisan, racist, and divisive.

Such sectarianism—whether religious, ethnic, or ideological—blatantly contradicts the founding documents. Wrapping oneself in the American flag while being divisive in any way is a slap in the face of America's Founding Fathers—and their documents. Such behavior betrays its origin in the old, non-

American (and even anti-American), conflict-ridden, tribalist ways.

More importantly, schismatic and partisan attitudes are a blatant violation of the borderless morality, whether expressed in America's founding documents or in those of all the great religions and philosophies based on that self-same universal wisdom-compassion that informs those documents. This means that anyone who is prejudicially partisan, in any way, is thereby violating the perennial canons of religion and universal morality, as well—regardless of how loyal to a particular ideology or "church" they may be.

Divisive and partisan attitudes are clear violations of all universal values.

Schizophrenic dichotomy

However understandably, people everywhere have made the grossly mistaken assumption that the America of the founding documents was meant to be "just another country."

The US *is* a country, obviously. As such—as an institution that even necessarily must have borders—it has never come even close to achieving the borderless values that its founding documents declare. So, the clear dichotomy there is between the America of the founding documents and the country called "the US" needs to be spelled out.

Clearly, there is a profound difference between the US and America's founding documents. In fact, it even makes sense to speak of "the US versus America"—rather than "the US of America."

This schizophrenic dichotomy is much like that found in all previous attempts at emplacing the borderless wisdom in the history of mankind.

Why has there always been such a dichotomy within each and every one of the great religions and philosophies of the past? Why is there such a dichotomy now, throughout the planet, despite the universal acknowledgment of the primacy of America's founding documents, everywhere?

After all, the planet is now made up almost totally of democratic republics (or dictatorships that pretend to be democratic republics), all with constitutions based on the American constitution. Why should there be such a dichotomy, everywhere?

I submit to you, attentive reader, that this dichotomy describes to a T the way you and I are put together.

Each and every one of us is a conditioned, me-centered entity—an entity full of assumptions based on our very personal background and expectations.

Simultaneously, a universally moral dimension expresses itself through each and every one of us; each of us is an inescapable expression of all that is, and each of us responds morally from the depths of all that is. As one of the pioneers of quantum physics, Erwin Schrödinger (1887-1961) put it, showing his deep interest in Indian thought, "There is obviously only one alternative, namely the unification of minds or consciousnesses. Their multiplicity is only apparent, in truth there is only one mind. This is the doctrine of the Upanishads."[1]

Despite that oneness, it is a fact that we all have to deal with the split nature of our beings. These two elements that we are made up of—each and all—is what makes us be the way we are. That is, each of us is a walking, talking, living dichotomy. As a result, all institutions that we create will reflect that dichotomy.

All the religions, the philosophies, the ideologies—including the United States of America—reflect that very personal yet widely pervasive dichotomy.

---

[1] Schrödinger, Erwin, *What is life?* Epilogue.

For as long as one is primarily beholden to the me-centered side of us all, we are bound to live in a world of confusion, violence, stress, and conflict. All the major religions and philosophies based on universal morality have been telling us precisely that. America's founding documents tell us precisely that. Our own intelligence tells us precisely that—but only if we'll look intently and carefully at the psychological-spiritual landscape we find ourselves in—which includes our personal inner being, as well as our relationships, and what we do planetarily.

It is true that America's founding documents provide a level of worldwide reference that could not have been achieved before. The present is a planetary world, and such a world had never existed before—so far as we can collectively recall.

Yet our intrinsic problem has not changed. Each of us is still charged with undergoing a major psychological transformation, whereby the universal morality within us will have the upper hand, for the first time ever. Such is the grand challenge of the American Age—a challenge that is addressed directly to each and every one of us by all the great religions and philosophies, including America's founding documents.

America

America's founding documents tell us clearly and unambiguously—from the moral perspective—that we are all "equal" before the law. They make it clear that there must be "justice for all."

In other words, in America, *justice* is not just for a particular group, as had always been the case in societies everywhere, before and outside of America. Justice for only a specific, privileged group—whether religious, ethnic, or ideological, or gender-related—is obviously the denial of actual justice. After all, justice is borderless—being as it is part and parcel of the universal wisdom-compassion. In order to have a better sense of what is being said here, it is critical to look sensitively at these factors—implicit as well as explicit—in America's founding documents:

- Those documents tell us that America (which includes the whole planet) is meant to be *"A pluribus unum"*—a unified plurality, a pluralistic whole, a pluralistic brotherhood: out of one, many; out of many, one.
- They exhort us to see and acknowledge that all religions and ideologies must be respected, while not favoring any one in particular. In other words, America's founding documents are telling us—clearly and unambiguously—that the same universal morality is present in all religions and ideologies based on that self-same universal morality.

   America's founding documents are telling us that universal morality comes first. Only then—starting out from universal morality—can we have truly universally moral ideologies and religions.
- This critical founding principle of those documents declares unambiguously that it is the universal wisdom-morality in all the differing expressions of it that we all need to aspire to, primarily—if we are ever to create a good society.

Being a practicing American, then, means living daily life in terms of universal morality. If any citizen wishes to continue being a member of a specific religion or a believer in a specific ideology, America's founding documents have no objections.

The only thing that matters is that a practicing American is someone who lives daily life in terms of universal morality, as much as possible.

Evidently, by practicing in earnest one's religion or ideology, one is thereby practicing the universal morality that informs and inspires all such religions and philosophies—and that is why all religions and philosophies are to be respected in the America of the founding documents. That is why America's founding documents declare, unambiguously, that no particular religion or ideology is to be upheld above all others.

America is not for partisans. It is for planetary citizens.

Anyone in the world can be a practicing American. So long as a person is a practicing American—someone who lives daily life according to universal, borderless morality—it makes no difference whether that American chooses to be a Hindu, or a Muslim, or a Christian.

We can all see this for ourselves. What matters is that one put into daily practice the universal wisdom, whether it comes from Christianity, Hinduism, atheism, Islam, Buddhism, Platonism, Taoism—or America's founding documents. The only thing that really matters is that one live one's daily life, as much as possible, in terms of universal morality.

We are—each and all—charged by America's founding documents to practice the borderless wisdom-compassion that is at the core of all the great religions and moralities. We are charged with engaging in such a practice, rather than adhering prejudicially to one's chosen group-think, which is what has always been done in history, before and outside of America's founding documents.

Freedom

America's founding documents tell us that we must have freedom in our daily lives. But freedom cannot be "given" to you by anyone else—as power-hungry demagogues of all types have always cynically and self-servingly claimed. Freedom can only come from your own heart.

But what is freedom? Here—as in so many other instances— K provides an American Age insight not to be found anywhere else. The fact is that only someone who is free from me-centeredness is truly free—as K spelled out numerous times, in various ways.

All other "freedoms" are ancillary to that foundational freedom. The assumption that "freedom" means freedom for the me to do "whatever I want" is a me-centered misunderstanding and transmogrification of what the freedom of America's founding documents truly means. Such a misunderstanding is clearly pregnant with divisions and conflicts—since "my" freedom is bound to clash with "yours," sooner or later.

It is only when we mature that we realize that all freedoms will necessarily come as a result of me-centeredness not being present in the way we conduct our daily lives. It is only when the slavery that always *goeswith* me-centeredness ceases to be, that actual freedom can come into being. It is only with the ending of me-centeredness in oneself that one is in a position to appreciate more fully other expressions of what freedom truly is.

Importantly, every single major religion or philosophy based on the borderless wisdom has entreated us to end me-centeredness in ourselves. In America's founding documents, that self-same insight emphasizes the freedom aspect of the universal wisdom-compassion.

K and America

K clarified with great power all of the above, and much more that is relevant to America's founding documents—and he did so in an unprecedently clear way, using simple language. He achieved this in such a way that his insights make it possible for all of us to have a much clearer understanding of what America's founding documents are merely stating—but without the kind of clarity that K's insights are brimming with.

It is in K's insights, researches and observations that we can all have a truer understanding of the immense and transformative wisdom implicit and explicit in America's founding documents.

Yet K achieved this without ever making a single reference to America's founding documents—just as he did not rely on any specific religion or philosophy, or any other form of group-think. He always appealed to the intelligence within each and every one of us, as individuals—exactly as America's founding documents do. Both K and America's founding documents appeal to the intelligence in us, not to a doctrine promoting some form of group-thinking.

What makes it possible for K to achieve this, is that his explorations are the borderless wisdom-compassion itself. It is that wisdom-compassion, exactly, what the great religions and philosophies of the past are centrally about—and that is what America's founding documents are centrally about, as well. That self-same wisdom-compassion is within "you," and within "me."

The only difference is that K managed to express this in astonishingly clear and simple and borderless, non-sectarian language—and that had never been achieved before. As he put it, in the context of addressing a deeper meaning of freedom and responsibility—both of which are at the very core of America's founding documents:

Freedom is one of the most important factors in life. Man has fought politically for freedom all over the world. Religions have promised freedom, not in this world but in another. In the capitalist countries, individual freedom exists to some degree, and in the communist world it has been denied.

From ancient times freedom has meant a great deal to man, and there have been its opponents, not only political but religious—through the Inquisition, by excommunication, tortures and banishments, and the total denial of man's search for freedom.

There have been wars and counter-wars fought for freedom. This has been the pattern of man's endeavours for freedom throughout history.

Freedom of self-expression and freedom of speech and thought exists in some parts of the world, but in others it does not. Those who have been conditioned revolt against their backgrounds, and react in immature ways. This reaction, which takes different forms, is called "freedom." The reaction to politics is often to shun the field of politics. One economic reaction is to form small communities based on some ideology or under the leadership of some one person, in which authority is denied and an attempt is made to be self-supporting, but these generally disintegrate.

The religious reaction against established organizations of belief is to revolt, either by joining other religious organizations or by following some guru or leader or by joining some cult. Or one denies the whole religious endeavour. Don't all these indicate mere outward movements toward freedom?

One thinks of freedom only as freedom of movement, either physical or the movements of thought. It appears one always seeks freedom on the surface, the right to go from here to there, to think what one likes, to do what one likes, to choose, and to seek wider experiences. Surely this is a rather limited freedom, involving a great deal of conflict, wars and violence.

Inner freedom is something entirely different. When there is deep, fundamental freedom, which has its roots not in the idea of freedom but in the reality of freedom, then that freedom covers all movement, all the endeavours of man. Without this freedom, life will always be an activity within the limited circle of time and conflict.

So when we talk of freedom we are talking of the fundamental issue. It is not a freedom from something, but the quality of a mind and heart that are free, and in which direction does not exist. Freedom from something is only a modified continuity of what has been, and therefore it is not freedom. When there is direction, and therefore choice, freedom cannot exist; for direction is division and hence choice and conflict.

The responsibility of a conditioned mind is irresponsibility, which can be perceived in the present cultures of society, whether of the East or of the West. This irresponsibility is shown in education, in social injustice, in national divisions with different ideologies leading to competition, wars, starvation, affluence and poverty. The irresponsibility of organized religions is shown in their support and maintenance of these cultures. These religions preach morality, but sustain corruption. They are at war with each other, asserting that they alone have the truth, that their gods and saviours are the real. This irresponsibility is shown when an intermediary is placed between the real and the human. This irresponsibility is shown when temples, mosques and churches become a power in the land.

Responsibility has quite a different meaning when there is freedom. Responsibility does not deny freedom, they go together. When there is the deep fundamental reality of freedom, responsibility is concerned with the whole of life and not with one fragment of life; it is concerned with the whole movement and not with some particular movement; it is concerned with the whole activity of the mind and the heart and not with one particular activity or direction.

Freedom is the total harmony in which responsibility is as natural as the flower in the field. That response is not induced or imposed; it is the natural outcome of freedom. Without responsibility, there is not freedom. To respond to every challenge out of freedom is responsibility. It is the inadequate responce that is irresponsibility.

The mind that is dependent in attachment becomes irresponsible to the whole.

So freedom is love, which in its very nature is responsible to the flower by the roadside, and to the neighbour—whether the neighbour is next door or a thousand miles away.

Compassion is the very essence of freedom.[2]

---

[2] Krishnamurti, *The Whole Movement of Life is Learning* (n.d.), chapter 66, j.krishnamurti.org.

CHAPTER 4
K's Inner Life

TRYING TO WRITE A BIOGRAPHY about such a monumental phenomenon as K was, is bound to be an exercise in futility—particularly considering the many dimensions of human experience that he addressed, in one person's short lifetime.

In every critique or criticism made by me of authors who have engaged in such an exercise, please understand, caring reader, that with every such remark on my part goes an acknowledgement of immense gratitude to these authors for their valiant and worthy, if quixotic efforts. Critical statements made in this chapter are documented and further clarified in subsequent chapters.

While *The Inner Life of Krishnamurti* is not a biography of K, it does address primarily one aspect of his multidimensional life, which I have called his "inner life." It deals particularly with aspects of his private life that most of us would identify as having to do with what many would call "the psychic." I intend to publish a second edition of it soon after the present exploration.

One of the main factors that compelled me to address first this aspect of K's persona, is the confusions and misdirections I perceived in published works that addressed his life. I have already dealt to some extent—in *The Analytical Fallacy*, as well as more briefly in papers at paradigmshift.network—with the leading-edge historical significance of K's insights, researches, and observations. The present exploration goes more in depth into that aspect of K's presence in the twentieth century. But in writing *The Inner Life of Krishnamurti* initially, it seemed to me that it was important to do my best to point out a number of misconceptions that I perceived in all extant biographical attempts.

I feel that even if I have misperceived this—and given the relevance that K's work is bound to have, at least over the next few centuries—the present is a worthy endeavor. What I am sharing with you here may turn out, of course, to be just as quixotic as previous efforts by K's biographers—and just as forlorn in its quest.

After all, I am using words, and words are bits of analysis—which is the enemy of wisdom, as noted in Chapter 2, "The Analytical Fallacy." In any case, what I tried to do in *The Inner Life of Krishnamurti* is investigate a few previously unexplored (or inadequately explored) pieces of the puzzle implicit in K's life and work—particularly his inner life, a subject that had largely been kept under wraps for most of K's life.

I should clarify that the present exploration is largely a much revised and expanded version of the first three chapters of the first edition of *The Inner Life of Krishnamurti*. So, this is intended to supersede and further clarify what was said in the earlier work.

"The occult"

Part of the reason for the hushed attitude surrounding K's inner life is that most of those who have been interested in his life and work—including writers on those subjects—have perceived him as being opposed, across the board, to anything and everything having to do with psychic matters. Indeed, in many of his talks and writings, K insisted emphatically that "occult" mystifications were frivolous and sometimes dangerous ways of wasting energy.

He often suggested that such energy would be best directed instead to the arduous, energy-intensive task of understanding oneself—of understanding *what is*—without filtering it through any of the many screens and expectations coming from our me-centered conditioning.

K stressed repeatedly that if humanity is to have a spiritually meaningful future—or perhaps even any future at all—the radical psychological-biological mutation that such understanding implies *must* take place. Further, throughout more than six decades of sharing his insights with others, K earned a reputation as a result of his scathing exposés of the shallowness and danger implied in all belief systems and methods—including those based on psychic or "occult" teachings.

A K ideology

In light of this public stance, many who are familiar with K's insights have found it surprising that his private life was rich in "occult" happenings, from early childhood until his death. As *The Inner Life of Krishnamurti* documents, these happenings were very real.

More significantly, it is in-your-face obvious that these experiences were of immense importance to K himself.

Yet despite that reality, it is also a fact that would-be K followers—even when they cleverly identify themselves as being "non-followers"—tend to deny the existence of his very rich psychic life. Unfortunately for them, anyone who denies the existence of the facts of his life is doing so arbitrarily—and based on provincial conditioning, not on what actually is the case.

Apparently, such would-be K "non-followers" deny certain realities in his life for the sake of defending what turns out to be *a K ideology*—much as these would-be non-followers may protest or deny it. But it is what it is.

As the following research fully documents, it has become imperative to lay all of this out as clearly as possible, so as to try to prevent the creation of a cult based on what turns out to be a monstrosity—a K ideology. That ideology—which arbitrarily and immorally denies the reality of K's inner life—creates a great danger. Despite its presumable "good intentions," such a belief system will create a new group-think based on misunderstandings of various sorts regarding who the actual K was.

In order to understand the truer meaning of what K said, it is essential *to accept* the whole reality *of who he was. Denying the centrality of K's inner life is one and the same with creating an unacceptable and dangerous "K ideology"—an ideology that clearly denies thoroughly the borderless nature of his insights.*

There is no question but that K's insights and observations are ultimately what matter, as he himself emphasized—and as is emphasized in this exploration. Nevertheless, the fact that his personal life was so saturated with the psychic is intriguing, at the very least—particularly since he seemed to be so vigorously opposed to anything "occult" in his public pronouncements. Also, K's insights, researches, and observations were never a form of analysis—as is believed arbitrarily by many, including his non-followers—as I document more fully in the works cited, especially *The Analytical Fallacy.*

The message

Even more important, however, is the fact that an understanding of K's inner life is *essential* for anyone to have a clearer grasp of the deeper aspects of his open-ended, borderless investigations. K himself suggested such an investigation of his inner life is essential, as the explorations in Parts Two and Three reveal.

Anyone sympathetic to K's insights, researches, and observations, but who simultaneously rejects or ignores his inner life in any way, is thereby placed in an unenviable position:

Rejection or non-acknowledgment of his inner life as the product of some vision, delusion, or hallucination means accepting a break in the integrity of what he said in his talks and writings.

Yet most authors who have written about K explain away the psychic elements present in his life by relying exclusively on their personal conditioning. Based on that opinionated provincialism, they proceed to attribute arbitrarily K's psychic experiences to hallucinations, delusions, visions, or inventions on the part of the witnesses—and often of K himself. These would-be "explainers" thereby assume that they knew and understood better than K and other witnesses what happened in his inner life. They thus assume that their very personal and provincial K ideology trumps many fully documented facts in his life.

This is hubris, at its best.

Clearly, analysis-based attempts to insist on a separation between K and psychic elements in his life—such as those made by some of K's would-be biographers in the process of *rejecting the evidence* that was right in front of them—give the strong impression of being based on a misunderstanding of the nature and purpose of such elements. In any case, these denials of facts related to K's inner life are arbitrarily based on a critics'-created K *ideology* that is incompatible with K's open-ended, borderless researches into *what is*.

Even more damning is the reality that such opinionated denials are not based on any facts or documentation. Such analyses depend—unfortunately for the perpetrators—on ignoring or repressing the actual facts and documentation that are available.

Analytical fallacy

My perception is that many K followers—and other K inter-preters—commit the analytical fallacy in the process of invent-ing an analytical way of perceiving and understanding K.

That is, they *analyze* the well-documented psychic elements in K's inner life from a perspective given by their insufficiently-questioned conditioning—which assumes that "surely" there "must" be "something wrong" with any and all things psychic, and that one "must *therefore*" extract it altogether from K's life, and shove it under the rug as if it never had happened.

However mistaken, this attitude is quite understandable. As noted in Chapter 2, "The Analytical Fallacy," almost everyone on Earth has been committing the analytical fallacy, and assuming that analyzing all events and happenings from the perspective of one's conditioning is "quite proper." Such an assumption is made possible by the more deep-seated, never-questioned as-sumption that analysis is the proper tool to use whenever one is delving into truth-seeking-truth-finding. Yet truth-seeking is but one of many facets of the borderless, *non-analytical* dimen-sion of values.

The attitude of K interpreters (both "pro" and "con") is quite understandable, because—before K came along—the vast ma-jority of us had made the fateful and grossly mistaken and dan-gerous assumption that analysis is indeed a proper tool to use for understanding that which is clearly outside the scope of anal-ysis.

Also, it never even occurred to most of us that analysis—whenever (mis)used in aspects of our lives in which it does not belong, such as the dimension of values—is *always* me-cen-tered. That is, analysis in and by itself is "clinically clean," and not related to borderless morality in any way: There is obviously nothing "right" or "wrong" (in the moral sense) with anyone declaring that two plus two equals four. Such an assumption is, in fact, at the core of the wonderfulness and the beauty and the importance of analysis in the physical-material-measurable aspects of our lives.

But when a Roman in early Christian days declared that "Christians are bad," he was using analysis in an altogether different, non-clinical way. He was *assuming* that "being Roman" was equivalent to "being logically true" (as in 2+2=4). Such an ancient Roman—coming as he did from that self-serving "Truth"—believed mistakenly that he was "therefore" in a position to analyze anything and everything and *everyone*, from that putative "given."

That ancient Roman was assuming that a "Roman" way of analyzing "Christians" had the "logical elegance" of a statement such as "2+2=4"—even though he was taking a quantum leap from mathematics to a conditioning-based, purely provincial, self-created "reality." The Roman assessment of Christians, in actuality, did not have the "clinical cleanliness" associated with mathematical and logical statements and propositions. It was more like the gross mess that one would expect to see in a sausage factory.

Of Romans and K-ites

That Roman was committing the analytical fallacy. It's instructive to look at how he arrived at his moral indictment of Christians.

First, he noted with pride how analysis had been so wonderful for building the great roads that Rome is still admired for, more than two thousand years later. Analysis had always made it possible to create the great Roman cities. It is analysis that had made it possible to organize Rome's unstoppable armies. All of those Roman achievements, and more—such as its form of government and its laws—had been made possible by using analysis.

Less obvious, but just as real, was the fact that the Roman was assuming that analysis is the end-all and be-all *for any conceivable circumstance*. Rome's many analytical successes had made it "obvious" to him that "therefore" he was "in the right" when he similarly analyzed another human being from the perspective of the "order" created by the implicitly and explicitly brutal Roman society.

That Roman could not see that he was crossing an important line that divides *the moral* (the dimension of values) from *the amoral*—which analysis and logic clearly are. He was assuming that it is correct to use the amoral (analysis) specifically for the purpose of determining what is "right" and what is "wrong"—which are the domain of the analysisless dimension of values.

The moment that that Roman made such an assumption, his analysis had thereby ceased to be clinical and amoral. His assumption—his analysis—had actually taken a quantum leap across the line. That fateful assumption had turned into the foundational tool for all universal *immorality*—in all times and places.

Something strikingly similar—while less dramatic, on the surface—takes place when an unwitting K-ite ideologue makes all sorts of assumptions regarding K's inner life. Such assumptions—exactly like those of the ancient Roman—have never been questioned by their asserters. At best, they have been insufficiently questioned. Yet it is based on such an opinionated ignorance that K non-followers make their unsupported assertions.

Thus, because of deeply entrenched prejudices regarding what the psychic implies and what K said regarding it, I begin Part Two with a look at it, especially as it relates to K's life and work.

CHAPTER 5
"Masters"

PROBABLY THE MOST INTRIGUING ASPECT of a description of K's inner life has to do with "the Masters." Those "Masters" are said by K and by numerous witnesses to have been in charge of his life-long psychic experiences.

Would-be "friends" and "foes" of K alike—as the analyzers that they clearly are, by their own self-definition—have had a field day with the notion of "Masters." It has been an all-out, reckless food-fight kind of Masterfest, ever since H.P. Blavatsky (1831-1891) brought up "the subject" of "Masters."

I put the word "subject" in quote marks, because the word "Master" was never meant by her to be "a subject" for people creating beliefs out of it—both "pro" and "con." Such beliefs turn out to be based on people's me-centered, provincial conditioning—as addressed with full documentation in *Muse* and elsewhere.[1]

HPB on "the Masters"

Regardless of opinions, one thing is certain: The word "Masters"—much as Blavatsky (HPB) seems to have meant well by using it—is a most unfortunate one, as even she eventually came to see.

HPB had been the senior founder of the Theosophical Society (TS)—the organization within which K flowered as a child and as a young man. HPB's deep and passionate regret regarding her ever having brought up the "subject" of "Masters" is addressed most poignantly in an article titled "It's the Cat!" which she published in her journal, *Lucifer*, in June of 1889. As she put it,

---

[1] For this and related subjects, please consult paradigmshift.network.

[T]he reader must realize that the present writer entertains no desire to force such a belief on anyone unwilling to accept it. Let him be a layman or a theosophist. The attempt was foolishly made a few years back in all truth and sincerity, and—it has failed.

More than this, the revered names were, from the first, so desecrated by friend and foe, that the once almost irresistible desire to bring the actual truth home to some who needed *living ideals* the most, has gradually weakened since then. It is now replaced by a passionate regret for having ever exhumed them from the twilight of legendary lore, into that of broad daylight.

The wise warning,—

"Give not that which is holy unto the dogs. Neither cast ye your pearls before swine . . ." (Matthew vii; 6) is now impressed in letters of fire on the heart of those guilty of having made the "Masters" public property.

Thus the wisdom of the Hindu-Buddhist allegorical teaching which says, "There can be no Mahatmas, no Arhats, during the *Kali-yuga*," is vindicated. *That which is not believed in, does not exist.* Arhats and Mahatmas—having been declared by the majority of Western people as nonexistent, as a *fabrication*—do not exist for the unbelievers.[2]

The word "Masters" began to come into wide misuse and abuse as a result of HPB referring to her borderless wise-compassionate mentors using that word—and its synonyms, such as "Mahatmas," and "Adepts."

My take on this issue—based on reports on HPB's life-long association with such wise-compassionate individuals—is that even just being in their presence evoked a sense of awe, a sense of being loved and understood deeply, a sense of experiencing with one's whole being the profound wisdom and compassion flowing out of them. No verbal expression could ever do justice to the reality of what HPB meant by that word. This happens to jibe perfectly with K's very similar experiences with perennials,

---

[2] Blavatsky, *Collected Writings,* vol. XI, pp. 292-293.

as related by him—and as fully documented in *The Inner Life of Krishnamurti.*

Despite the impossibility of conveying in words to conditioned people what she had experienced, HPB wanted desperately for others to be able to have an understanding that resonated with her experiences. She thought that by referring to them, and by stating that one could get near them through the ending of the me—which act and process she often called "initiation"—a few might understand, at least a little bit, what she was referring to. She thought that even a relatively imperfect understanding would be a justification for even speaking of their existence.

"The word is not the thing"

But what should anyone call such exemplars of the universally moral dimension? Words such as "saints" and "angels" were in the process of going out of fashion in the Victorian Age—except among an ever-diminishing number of group-think worshippers.

HPB thought that the word "Teachers" would be appropriate—given that, in her own experience, she had always learned even by just being in the proximity of such individuals. Also, the word "Teachers"—capitalized, as German Idealism had taught Victorians how to express themselves—was meant by her to come closer to the "Jesus" that "Christians" widely believed in. Such associations would make words like "Teacher" come closer to the transformative nature of her actual encounters with them. Since the word "Masters" was widely in use at the time, she used both words—and others, as just noted—interchangeably.

Lamentably, to those who identify with their conditioning—which were (and still are) the vast majority of her audience—the word "Masters" has numerous connotations that convey meanings that actually tend to *deny* what the word was meant by HPB to refer to. She had hoped that at least a few would see that her reference would inspire them to cease to live self-centered lives.

Instead, it only served to stimulate their me-centeredness further, by creating absurd hierarchies of authority and related beliefs—in which the believers arrogantly saw themselves as being somehow "privy" to "knowledge" that "others" did not have.

In any case, the 1880s marked the time when that word first began to come into wide use, to refer to her wise-compassionate mentors—at first only among members of the TS, which she had helped to establish in New York City in 1875.

Victorian hegemony

The 1880s and 1890s could be said to have marked the peak of the Victorian era. It was a time when Europeans *knew* themselves to be "Masters" of the universe. The rest of the planet (and perhaps even the universe itself)—including "of course" all other humans—were assumed by Europeans to exist for the exclusive purpose of being at Europeans' beck and call. In their minds, if you were not a European "Master," you were *inevitably* and "obviously" *a slave* of the "Master."

Apart from that sense of it, "Master" was the word used to refer to a teacher in Victorian period schools—and all such schools were beholden to the brutally imperialist and colonialist mainstream.

The school Master would regularly whack "unruly" children, sometimes savagely. Any child who dared to display any originality away from the very strict and rigidly prescribed Victorian norms and expectations, was considered "unruly" and therefore "unfit" to be part of "the empire." Such a brutal "educational" blueprint was followed all over Victorian Europe, and in its colonies throughout the world—where children were basically considered to be the "slaves" of their "Masters"—and were treated accordingly.

Nietzsche

The implicitly colonialist-imperialist-racist sense of the word "Master" was further complicated in the HPB milieu, with the unintended help of Friedrich Nietzsche (1844-1900). His is a fascinating and relatively unknown story, in its own right—a story that happens to be eminently relevant to the present discussion, as briefly addressed in Chapter 9, "Nietzsche." The gist of it is that Nietzsche made a crucial distinction between what he called "Master" versus "slave" morality.

It is important to note that Nietzsche was thoroughly unknown in his lifetime—even in the 1880s, when all of his major works were produced, published, and went largely unread. Intriguingly, the only known demographic group interested at all in what he was saying seems to have been made up of HPB's followers, beginning in the 1880s.

Eventually, the best known and influential among these HPB-related Nietzsche enthusiasts were Rudolf Steiner (1861-1925) and A.R. Orage (1873-1934). Both of them had a large following in their respective circles—Steiner mainly in the German-speaking world, and Orage largely in the European and American political, artistic, and literary arenas. Both of these Nietzsche admirers would eventually develop a worldwide following of their own, so their interests were to have major repercussions.

When these two highly influential leaders of culture wrote books on Nietzsche in the 1890s and early 1900s, they created an environment in which Nietzsche began to be taken extremely seriously planet-wide, for the first time ever. Though—to my knowledge—the present exploration is the first time that this is revealed to later generations, it is a fact that it was HPB colleagues who first "put Nietzsche on the map" of worldwide awareness.

Both Steiner and Orage were prominent members of HPB's TS. Steiner had been the head of the German TS Section, and Orage had been an international TS lecturer.

Both of them left the TS, eventually—Steiner to found his own Anthroposophical Society in 1912, and Orage in 1907, to focus on heading the internationally influential journal *The New Age* (1907-1922). Later on, Orage was to join "the Work" of G.I. Gurdjieff (1872?-1949).

Importantly, the diverse groups that came out of Gurdjieff's work all had a significant background and even foundation in HPB's insights.[3] Intriguingly, at least part of Steiner's justification for leaving the TS in 1912—twenty years after he'd been the TS's most prominent leader in the German-speaking world—was that he decried the TS's promotion of "that dark boy," Krishnamurti.

The issue of "Master morality" versus "slave morality"—which is prominent in Nietzsche's work—turned out eventually to be grossly misunderstood by Adolf Hitler (1889-1945). Hitler's genocidal proclivities were justified by him in part through his defense of what he called "the Master race." Hitler's wild misunderstanding and misrepresentation of what Nietzsche had actually said is yet another negative dimension of the word "Master."

Given these bizarre associations, the word "Master" is clearly incompatible with HPB's experiences—which unambiguously

---

[3] For HPB's strong influence on all the main leaders and strands of the Gurdjieff work, see James Webb. *The Harmonious Circle*: *The Lives and Work of G.I Gurdjieff, P.D. Ouspensky, and Their Followers* (1980).

referred to her wise-compassionate mentors, not to a brutish and blood-thirsty tyrants' insane notions.

Part of the relevance of this fact in the present context is that Hitler's Nazi ideology and dreams of creating a Third Reich had been informed and inspired in crucially important ways by Ariosophy—a German ideology that was an intensely racist, transmogrified version of HPB's theosophy.[4]

Steiner and K

Despite his very many beneficial contributions to world culture—which contributions were important aspects of the wisdom explosion in the American Age—Steiner had a central place in this very dangerous transmogrification of the borderless wisdom that HPB exemplified.

I consider it extremely important to address this issue here—however briefly—because I have personally met or known about New Agers (including TS members and K-ites) who hold racist views, and who in many ways are following in the footsteps—or who are locked in goosestep—with Ariosophists, Steiner, and Hitler.

The presence of such elements—who see themselves as being *central* to the wisdom explosion—creates confusion not only among New Agers, but also among those in the mainstream. So this needs to be addressed squarely, in the hope of helping to clarify this nasty issue.

In making this clarification, I have found the work of Peter Staudenmaier (b. 1965) to be extremely helpful. He is professor of modern German history at Marquette University in

---

[4] For Ariosophy and Hitler, see Nicholas Goodrick-Clarke, *The Occult Roots of Nazism: The Ariosophists of Austria and Germany, 1890-1935 (1985);* see also Peter Staudenmaier, *Between Occultism and Nazism: Anthroposophy and Politics of Race in the Fascist Era* (2014).

Milwaukee, Wisconsin, and his work as a historian focuses among other things on Nazism and Fascism, the history of racial thought, and the political history of environmentalism. His professional and personal interests have led him to address the issue of racism in Steiner's perspectives—and that has earned him a prominent place in this highly sensitive discussion.

Staudenmaier encapsulates some of the wisdom explosion issues involved in a brief contribution he made to the online Waldorf Critics discussion list. In his comments, he makes reference to "Steiner's reaction to the Theosophical Society's anointment of Krishnamurti as the new World Teacher and reincarnation of Christ."

I consider this such a critically important issue in everyone's understanding of what the borderless wisdom is actually about—as opposed to what so very many mistakenly believe that it is—that I quote him at great length, with his permission, and with your indulgence. Also, Staudenmaier provides further documentation for his statements—and that makes the following long quote all the more important and clarifying. As he says,

> The standard anthroposophical position that Krishnamurti's "racial" background played no role in Steiner's rejection of his status as the next messiah is historically naive.
>
> The fact that Krishnamurti was not white was a stumbling block for many people at the time who took theosophical race theory at face value; for a very revealing background on precisely this question, see Jill Roe's study *Beyond Belief: Theosophy in Australia* 1879-1939.
>
> Steiner's own stated position on the racial-spiritual status of Asians, including South Asians, explains much about his own stance, though his rivalry with Annie Besant and the India-based leadership of the Theosophical Society played a crucial role as well.
>
> Making sense of Steiner's indignant attitude toward the Krishnamurti affair requires taking seriously Steiner's statements about the racial character of Asians, the future direction of racial evolution, the spiritual significance of skin color, the obsolete and inferior nature of Eastern spiritual traditions, and other factors.

While Steiner did hold that no living person could be the reincarnation of Christ, he did not leave the matter at that. He pointedly ridiculed the notion that this "Hindu lad," as Steiner called Krishnamurti, could embody the Christ.

According to Steiner, Hindus had long since played out their evolutionary function and were now leftovers of former spiritual grandeur, an anachronism trapped in decline. Krishnamurti was neither white, European, nor Christian, and thus failed Steiner's test of adequacy for cosmic leadership. At the same time, according to reports from his theosophical associates, Steiner may have encouraged his own followers to think of Steiner himself as the new appearance of Christ.

More important still, the Krishnamurti affair was the occasion for Steiner's final break from the mainstream theosophical movement, which was headquartered in India, and this break, the founding moment of the anthroposophical movement as such, did indeed involve racial ideology.

In the midst of the acrimonious split, in 1911, a close colleague of Steiner, anthroposophist Günther Wagner, wrote that both Steiner himself and his followers believed that "since we are the most advanced race, we have the most advanced religion" (1911 letter from Wagner quoted in Norbert Klatt, *Theosophie und Anthroposophie: Neue Asekte zu ihrer Geschichte*, 102). That is an important part of why it was such an affront to the anthroposophist mindset when the rest of the theosophical movement cast its lot with Krishnamurti, who was neither racially nor religiously suited to the role, in their eyes.

Steiner's general statements on the significance of race can also help illuminate the incident. His basic stance was straightforward enough: "One can only understand history and all of social life, including today's social life, if one pays attention to people's racial characteristics. And one can only understand all that is spiritual in the correct sense if one first examines how this spiritual element operates within people precisely through the color of their skin" (Steiner, *Vom Leben des Menschen und der Erde,* 52). This criterion was of particular importance when Steiner addressed the ostensible spiritual-racial contrast between Europeans and Asians.

Steiner claimed that it was the special destiny of the Germanic peoples to fulfill the "mission of white humanity" by integrating the spiritual and the physical, and that this integration of the physical and spiritual is what accounts for white skin. This integration has failed in non-white peoples, Steiner explained, referring specifically to "the Asian peoples." In Asians and other non-whites, according to Steiner, the spirit "takes a demonic character and does not completely permeate the flesh, there white skin does not appear. Atavistic forces are present which do not let the spirit come into complete harmony with the flesh" (Steiner, *The Christ-Impulse as Bearer of the Union of the Spiritual and the Bodily*, 8).

Steiner was explicit about this fundamental contrast: "How could one fail to be struck by the profound differences in spiritual culture between, let us say, the peoples of Europe and Asia! How indeed could one not be struck by the differences connected with the colour of the skin?" The purportedly different levels of development were central to this contrast: "How can we fail to realise that the Asiatic peoples have retained certain cultural impulses of past early epochs, whereas the Euro-American peoples have advanced beyond them?" (ibid., 6).

Steiner further held that it is the task of "the German people" to spread "spiritual life," which "the Oriental" has lost; the Oriental must now receive spiritual guidance from the Germans (Steiner, *Gedankenfreiheit und soziale Kräfte*, 141.) Steiner taught that "the soul life of the Orient" is not fully part of "normal human life," explicitly equating "normal human life" with "our own, in the West"; the spirituality of the East in contrast is "decadent" and "certainly in decline" (126). He faulted English-speaking Theosophists for looking to India for "ancient oriental wisdom" and for "borrowing completely from the Oriental Indians," whose springs of wisdom had long since run dry (130).

The problem, in Steiner's eyes, was not merely an Asian lack of originality and creativity; for Steiner, "the Oriental thinker" is not at the same level of development as "European spiritual culture"; it is only in the West that the seeds of the future are to be found (132). The decadent and declining features of Indian spiritual life, he insisted, are wholly inappropriate for Europeans (133). "And it is an example of decadence in the West, of abandonment of all the good spirits of European humankind, that there are many people today who seek to shore up their European spiritual life by absorbing the Oriental essence" (137). Steiner attributed "the purest and cleanest form of thinking" to "the Germans," who are indeed the carriers of "the future of humanity" (142); but this future can only be realized by "our own spiritual striving, not by borrowing from the Oriental" (141).

Steiner sharply contrasted "the Eastern school" from his own "western school" of esotericism, presenting the difference in racial terms: "But this oriental form of truth is worthless for us western peoples. It could only obstruct us and hold us back from our goal. Here in the West are the peoples who shall constitute the core of the future races" (Steiner, *Aus den Inhalten der esoterischen Schulen*, 221). "The dying races of the East still need the Oriental school. The Western school is for the races of the future" (ibid. 227).

In his book *Christus und die menschliche Seele*, Steiner discusses the role of "racial evolution" at length, particularly the cosmic differentiation of humankind into racial groups representing varying stages of spiritual progress. The book's second chapter, a lecture from May 1912 (in the midst of the heated intra-theosophical dispute over Krishnamurti), includes a three-page disquisition on the relationship between "race development" and "soul development," explaining that more advanced souls incarnate in "higher races," while less developed souls incarnate in "subordinate races." This process of continual racial-spiritual progress eventually results in "the dying out of the worse elements in the population" (93). Steiner then segues into a comparison of Indian and European spiritual traditions, emphasizing the differences in the "physical incarnation" between these two streams; the "Christ impulse," he explains, played the central role in differentiating the European from the Indian orientation (98).

Then there's Steiner's lecture "The peoples of the earth in the light of spiritual science," published shortly after Steiner's death in the anthroposophical journal *Die Drei*, vol. 5 no. 9 (December 1925). Here Steiner has quite a bit to say about "the Oriental peoples" and their spiritual practices, which pale in comparison to the spiritual culture brought forth by "the German nation" (651). According to Steiner, the Germans already possess, as part of their "ordinary characteristics," those spiritual achievements that "the Indian strives toward as his ideal of the superhuman." Hence "the European," with his "natural endowment," stands "a stage higher" than "the Oriental" (652).

Taken together, such sources and the numerous others of comparable content carry a consistent message. This lengthy list of assumptions about Indian spiritual traditions, combined with the presumption of European superiority, helps explain anthroposophy's origins in the dispute concerning Krishnamurti and the proper direction of the worldwide theosophical movement. These teachings, which Steiner repeated many times, indicate that aside from his reservations about a physical reincarnation of Christ, he could not conceive of a new

"World Teacher" who did not emerge from the German people, heralds of the new age.

In Steiner's view, Krishnamurti was racially, culturally, and spiritually ineligible for the role assigned to him by Besant, et. al. When it came to discerning the appropriate form for advancing the Christ Impulse, anthroposophical race doctrine was a decisive factor. For further examples of Steiner's negative assessment of Asian spiritual traditions in European contexts, see among others Steiner, *Luzifer-Gnosis*, 370-71, Steiner, *Grundelemente der Esoterik*, 108-115, and Steiner, *Westliche und östliche Weltgegensätz-lichkeit*, 226-39.[5]

I have quoted Professor Staudenmaier at such great length partly because of its obvious relevance to the intimately intertwined issues of K in the history of the borderless wisdom and in the wisdom explosion in the American Age—primarily as it all concerns the TS and its innumerable spinoffs, such as the highly influential Anthroposophical Society.

But in addition, I find this thorough dismantling of Anthroposophy as a racist enterprise to be importantly clarifying, while simultaneously making clearer the vital role of *borderlessness* in the universal wisdom throughout the ages—but especially right now, when racism and other forms of me-centeredness are attempting to set back all the gains achieved by the wisdom explosion that has come to all of us in the American Age.

Of races, Hitler, and "Theosophy"

Hitler's messianic assumptions regarding the Third Reich came straight out of an "occult" milieu created by proto-Nazis—such as the composer (and racist) Richard Wagner (1813-1883), the Ariosophists, and others. For this reason alone, the

---

[5] Staudenmaier, "Steiner's reaction to the Theosophical Society's anointment of Krishnamurti as the new World Teacher and reincarnation of Christ," in Waldorf Critics discussion list, on January 23, 2009, waldorfcritics.org.

relevance of Steiner's spelling out his own very personal racist take on "the Perennial Tradition" cannot be exaggerated.

Like devotees of "the Perennial Tradition" (which is generally identified as being a *European* Tradition), Steiner insists on the "Western superiority" over all other human groups. So bringing this up points to a serious problem implicit in the notion of "the Perennial (presumably "Western") Tradition" as it is now understood, largely—though not exclusively—by academics.

In addition, numerous other groups and authors have endorsed the notion that what matters most is the "Western" approach—which often incudes "Christian" undertones. The best example of this may be Alice Bailey (1880-1949)—as exemplified in works such as *The Reappearance of the Christ* (1947), *which directly contradicts the evidence*, which I share briefly in Parts Two and Three. In claiming that "the Christ" would reappear in the twentieth century, she is in perfect harmony with Steiner, *et al*—but in total disagreement with the available documentation, as laid out in this exploration.

Many others have followed this "Western" *interpretation* of the *borderless* wisdom that had been promoted by Richard Wagner, the Ariosophists, and Hitler. But that is clearly a subject for a different venue.

In any case, the long quote also helps enormously to clarify why and how prominent twentieth century leaders of what its devotees call "Traditionalism" have been defenders of racist fascism. Julius Evola (1898-1974) and Mircea Eliade (1907-1986)—both of them excellent scholars in their respective disciplines—are prime examples of this extremely dangerous, misguided, fact-poor trend.

The "Theosophical" understanding of (and obsession with) "races" tends to be pregnant with racist implications—at least as it was presented by those who followed HPB. The long quote above shows, quite clearly, the reality of this aspect of Victorian

Theosophy. While I'm not aware of any other major TS leader expressing such transparently racist opinions, I have witnessed TS members proposing racist notions—which are profoundly incompatible with the actual *borderless* wisdom.

But a careful reading of discussions on race outside of HPB (including some of her contemporaries) will show a similar racist tendency, though expressed in more careful—or perhaps more hypocritical—tones.

This latter attitude is much like that of many mainstream Europeans and their descendants—including those outside of the European continent—who have been accustomed to accepting and putting into practice their furtive racism, often in their "Christian" churches. The main difference between Steiner and others is his in-your-face highly irresponsible recklessness in expressing such views, where other HPB followers who have also been racist have tended to be more tame—or even hypocritical—whenever expressing themselves on the subject.

This racist attitude—regardless of who holds it, whether furtively or openly—is in stark opposition to the first object of the TS, "To form a nucleus of the universal brotherhood of humanity, without distinctions of race, creed, sex, caste, or color." There is zero place for any kind of racism in such an organization or in its many spinoffs, in the wider wisdom explosion in the American Age.

Traditionalism

This is a severely serious issue for all "Traditionalists"—those who mistakenly interpret the *borderless* wisdom to be, instead, a mainly "Western" Tradition. Anthroposophists are not the only ones in this camp.

Highly influential groups, such as the followers of Alice Bailey in the Arcane School and elsewhere (including the TS), and followers of René Guénon (1886-1951)—who do refer to themselves as "Traditionalists"—hold to the strange and mistaken belief that the *borderless* wisdom actually consists of having borders.

In my experience of six decades and counting, the borderful attitude of Traditionalists of any kind is that of erecting a wall far thicker and formidable than the proverbial Wall of China— and this is immensely concerning, and recklessly dangerous.

True wisdom is thoroughly borderless. It is *never* regional nor ideological—as the central belief of Traditionalists *requires*. That should be obvious to anyone who even cares to look at this fact in the eye. It is alarmingly concerning that Traditionalists beg to differ.

Before leaving this necessary subject, it is relevant to clarify that—despite Steiner being a major contributor to the foundational ideology of Nazi Germany—he did make important beneficial contributions to the American Age wisdom explosion.

Though Steiner made other important contributions, I consider the most valuable of these to be the Waldorf schools, the promotion of eurythmy in the arts (primarily dancing), and biodynamic farming. Among other contributions is, for instance, his Western bias itself. While being at least worrisome (if not outright dangerous), as just noted—that bias has had the major benefit of inspiring numerous scholars and others to look into the universal wisdom as it has expressed itself in Western societies. Other Traditionalists—including those just mentioned— have also made this beneficial contribution.

It seems as if nothing is ever purely black nor purely white. Grey seems to rule.

"Masters" and the will to power

It should be noted that Nietzsche became—in the minds of cult-following Nazis, if nowhere else—"*the philosopher*" who presumably promoted "the will to power" so dear to devotees of the notion of *"the Master race."* Given his very high standing in German culture immediately prior to Hitler's rise to power, Steiner may have been Hitler's main inspiration—or at least importantly instrumental—in this gross misunderstanding of Nietzsche.

Nazis in general tended to misunderstand Nietzsche's "will to power" to refer to promoting "Masters" over "slaves." So the word "Masters" figured prominently in the Nazis' bewilderingly mistaken assessments of what Nietzsche actually said. This gross and tragic misunderstanding—among many others—was clarified magnificently by Walter Kaufmann (1921-1980), particularly in *Nietzsche: Philosopher, Psychologist, Antichrist* (1950)—a post-World War II masterpiece that marked the beginning of a deeper and more sane understanding of Nietzsche, in the mainstream.

In summary—and "to make a long story short"—the word "Master" is not a good word. Not in itself—and most assuredly not to refer to HPB's mentors in the universal wisdom-love that all of her insights were actually referring to. For these and other reasons, the word "Masters" appears in all of my writings—including the present exploration—almost exclusively in the process of quoting or referring to Victorians (and their replicants, in the form of later generations), who were either following or attacking HPB.

To this day, such HPB "friends" and "foes" alike have turned out to be passionate Victorians at heart in numerous important ways, as documented in what follows. Further documentation of the otherwise puzzling phenomenon of Victorians assuming themselves to be "borderless" is addressed more in-depth in *Muse*.

"Mahatmas," et al.

Many words other than "Masters" have been used, to refer to exemplars of the universal wisdom that HPB was the first to refer to—at least publicly. Unfortunately, all of these alternatives to the word "Masters" are also lacking—or even concerning—for differing reasons, in their respective intentions to refer to those perennial exemplars.

The word "Mahatmas" is an excellent example of this difficulty. "Mahatma" is a Sanskrit word, which has been translated as meaning "great soul"—"maha" being translated as "great," and "atma" as "soul." This word has clearly different connotations from the word "Masters," and at first gives the impression of being a clear improvement on it. The word "Mahatma" refers to the fact that exemplars of the universal wisdom are unusually wise and compassionate—with no necessary implications of their being "superior" or "controlling," the way the word "Masters" does.

But despite its benefits, the word "Mahatma" brings with it other concerns. To begin with—because of its Sanskrit origins—it mistakenly assigns subliminally the notion that universal wisdom exemplars come *exclusively* from the Indian subcontinent, or that in any case such exemplars have a strong association with that region of the world, *and "therefore" with its cultures, beliefs, and practices.*

So the word "Mahatma"—while it avoids some of the pitfalls of the word "Master"—has problems of its own. Anyone who refers to "Mahatmas" is thereby insinuating that universal wisdom exemplars are somehow importantly associated with cultures, beliefs, and practices from the Indian subcontinent. This is much like saying that "gravity" must be British, since it was "discovered" by Sir Isaac Newton (1643-1727).

In addition, the Sanskrit word "atma" (which is part of "Mahatma") refers to something far more comprehensive than the word "soul" conveys in the various European vernaculars. In Hinduism—particularly in the Advaita Vedanta, where "atma" (or "atman") is explored intensively and extensively—a distinction is made between the conditioned "me" that most of us identify with, and "atman."

In Advaita Vedanta—which is considered almost universally as being the most philosophically sophisticated school in all Hinduism—"atman" is but a hologramic instantiation of "Brahman," which stands for *all that is*. According to this perception, atman comes into its own only in the process of the me (*ahankara*) ceasing to be: When the me is not, atman is. In that context—while understandable—the word "Mahatma" is an imperfect way of saying that an exemplar of the universal wisdom is someone who has actually gone very deeply into that process of ending the me.

Lamentably, many who have used the word "atma" (or "atman")—especially in the New Age environment, and particularly in the TS—astonishingly equate that word with what they call "the higher self"—a "self" that is assumed to be a kind of "next stage" or "alter ego" of the personal "me." Everyone I have met, and most books I have read on this subject, suggest that "atman" refers to such a "higher self."[6]

This belief in a presumably "higher self" takes us back to problems implicit in using the word "Masters." The moment one makes a distinction between the "higher" and the "lower" self (as in the word "Mahatma"), one is inadvertently, yet firmly, promoting a more subtle version of me-centeredness—and me-

---

[6] An important exception to this grossly mistaken notion is *Advaita Vedanta: A Philosophical Reconstruction* (1969) by Professor Eliot Deutsch (1929-2020).

centeredness is what needs to go *irrevocably*, in order for there to be universal wisdom, such as the wisdom present in its exemplars.

So the word "Mahatma"—however surreptitiously it may do so—suggests that such an individual is an expression of "the higher (or 'greater') self." That will not do—especially when that word is further attached to a particular culture and region of the world, thus denying the implicit and explicit borderlessness of the perennial wisdom and its exemplars. An exemplar of the universal wisdom is someone in whom there is no me-centeredness of any kind—let alone a presumably "higher" form of me-centeredness.

The word "guru"—which has also been absorbed into popular culture, worldwide—actually incorporates problems present in the words "Master" and "Mahatma." Like "Master," the word "guru" (as it is commonly used) implies that one is referring to someone who is an authority in moral and "spiritual" matters— and that has been shown to be problematic, in various ways, as discussed in this exploration.

In addition, the word "guru" shares with "Mahatma" its association with Indian cultures and expectations. Such an association with a particular culture and region denies—or tends towards denying—the *universal* wisdom, which is *borderless* and not regional, much like gravity.

The word "Teachers" avoids the regional issue—but it does so in the process of taking us back to the word "Masters," and some of its problems. The issue here has been addressed throughout the ages by actual exponents and exemplars of the universal wisdom.

For instance, in almost all of his *Dialogues*, Plato (428-348 BCE) was showing how "virtue" cannot be taught. In the Pythagorean milieu—of which Plato was the most influential exponent—the word "virtue" stands for all aspects of Pythagorean *philosophia*.

Among Pythagoreans and Platonists, *philosophia* included love, justice, courage, beauty, goodness, and the like, as an intrinsic aspect of its meaning. Plato's *Meno* addressed squarely this very issue. But if the universal wisdom that "virtue" stands for in the Platonic dialogues cannot be taught—as shown explicitly in Plato's *Meno*—that means that he is saying that there cannot be "Teachers" of it. Plato was not the only one who pointed this out.

As the Buddha expressed it, in his ever-so-brief description of all of his insights, given as his last words on Earth, "Seek out your own salvation, with diligence: Buddhas do but point the way."

Clearly, this is stating unequivocally that there cannot be any "Teacher" of the borderless wisdom, and that it's only by each of us searching borderlessly for ourselves, that any wisdom can be found. All of Buddhism—despite numerous differences between the sects—is about that insight. Like gravity, it is a *borderless* insight.

So the word "Teachers" is grossly inappropriate, if one wants to refer to exemplars of the borderless wisdom.

Perennials

The universal wisdom is not bound by time nor by space. It refers to insights that take place to the extent that there is an act and process of being open to *that which is*.

Being open to *that which is* may express itself as borderless truth-seeking-truth-finding.

It may express itself as unconditional love.

It may express itself as actually experiencing borderless fairness and justice—and living daily life in a way compatible with such borderlessness.

It may express itself in the form of art, or science, or *philosophia*, or social justice—or in practices such as meditative gardening, carpentry, or engineering.

I feel that the word "perennial"—which suggests timelessness and borderlessness—is a much better word to use, to refer to the universal wisdom. So I call its exemplars "perennials," and the wisdom itself "perennial wisdom"—though other qualifiers are applicable, such as "universal" and "timeless" and "borderless." Importantly, perennials have never considered themselves to be "authorities" in the moral realm—and the word "perennials" has no connotation of authority at all.

Perennials have always claimed to have as much authority as perennial flowers.

Perhaps better words could be found. If so, I'll be the first to use them—but only if they prove to be an improvement over "perennials." So for now, it is "perennials"—a word that avoids all the problems and concerns of other words, and that does refer fairly well to what it intends to refer to.

Words

The words that one uses matter.

As I showed in *The Analytical Fallacy*, words are but bits of analysis—and analysis is a dangerously inappropriate tool to use, when one is addressing issues related to universal morality.

The present exploration uses words. But words are being used here—*with a hope and a prayer*—as *incomplete descriptions* that transcend the words, somewhat like poetry. Words are not being used as standing for "the Truth"—whatever that unfortunate word may refer to, especially when capitalized.

Truth-seeking is profoundly different from "the Truth." Truth-seeking is the act and process that comes from not knowing—from emptiness of content—and that tries passionately to see or understand better.

The expression "the Truth" denies true inquiry, by its apparent and recklessly silly finality. It is a pretentious expression that could only come from me-centeredness—and therefore from profound ignorance.

Analysis is magnificent—but exclusively when it is kept in the areas of our experience that are appropriate to it and congenial with it. Anything that is physical, or material, or mechanical, or measurable, or in time-space—is the proper setting for using analysis. *That* is where analysis excels. Analysis excels in those areas of our experience, to the point that it has provided for all of us a level of safety and comfort that might not have been possible, otherwise.

In fact, it is precisely because analysis has been so very wonderful for all of us, in so many ways, that we have come to rely on it for addressing *everything*—and *that* is where analysis gets to be transmogrified, and turned into our very worst enemy.

It is analysis that has invented all sorts of me-centered and prejudicial divisions between races, nationalities, religions, genders, ideologies, "philosophies"—and everything else in the kitchen sink of all of our experiences. It is from our prejudicial attachment to those and all other forms of group-think—which all come from the dangerous *misuse* of analysis—that all human problems stem.

Whether it is personal, or in relationships, or in communities, or planet-wide—all of our problems come directly from our otherwise understandable yet lethal, recklessly cavalier (mis)use of analysis in aspects of our lives in which analysis clearly and dangerously does not belong.

Words are but bits of analysis. They are always loaded with our very personal and provincial ways of seeing everything. So if and to the extent that one truly cares about clarity of perception, one has *the obligation* to look as carefully as one can at how or why words get to have the kinds of meaning that we get to ascribe to them. That, precisely, is what I have tried to do, in speaking of "Masters," "mahatmas," "gurus," and "teachers"— among other words that have been misused in the process of trying to refer to *perennials*.

In a book in which K figures centrally—such as this is—it is essential to clarify what words such as "Masters" refer to, especially given the outrageously off-the-mark assumptions that so very many have made, regarding that and related words. As noted, that and similar words, whenever used, are kept here exclusively in the context of period quotes and of how people spoke and wrote in the past—or even in the present, in the case of those who have regressed to Victorian times through a kind of time warp.

This is important, in itself—given the commonplace assumptions that tend to be made by so many, regarding moral or "spiritual" authorities. But it becomes critical in any discussion related to K, because there have been severely serious misunderstandings regarding what he meant by "Masters" and related matters.

I am not claiming any special wisdom about any of this. In fact, I'm just a borderless researcher. I am totally open to anything newly presented to me that contradicts *with documentation* anything I have said. The very changes in the present exploration—which started out being the beginning of a second edition of *The Inner Life of Krishnamurti*—are proof of that.

But there is a catch to this: Any criticism to what is being said here *must* come with actual evidence, documentation, and borderless truth-seeking. Anything else is silly and not worthy of consideration by anyone who is serious about these matters.

Philosophy

Parts Three and Four consider some of the deeper, implications of K's psychic-transformative experiences, particularly as they relate to the future of humanity. K had no system, no method, no metaphysics. He was most emphatically not "a philosopher" in the narrow, analytical, *superficial*, academic sense of that word. Yet his work represents the best and deepest that actual *philosophy* has achieved to date, as discussed thoroughly in *The Analytical Fallacy*.

Like Socrates, K was a pure investigator into *that which is*.

Importantly, K's researches were always free from a "point of view," and came from the kind of emptiness from conditioning that Patañjali, Nagarjuna, and numerous other perennials everywhere in the world explored at great depth.

Interestingly, Socrates' explorations—which are generally identified as being iconic of the philosophical enterprise itself—were often limited by his identification with Greek culture. K, on the other hand, had no such identifications with any culture. Cultures implicitly assume me-centered presuppositions and display a lack of emptiness of content—which is a requirement of the borderless wisdom.

That fact—in and by itself—is clearly telling us that K was a deeper investigator into what is *than Socrates ever was, or could be.*

Please take a moment or two, to digest that fact.

K was unambiguously and absolutely a *borderless* investigator into *what is*. Such a borderless investigation is universal—not Greek, nor Indian, nor German, nor Paraguayan. Yes, a careful reading of Plato shows that Socrates was unquestionably addressing *that which is* universally and borderlessly so. But unfortunately, that universality got to be masked and even watered down by his constant appeals to Greek culture and by an ancient Greek way of looking at everything.

There is no such *confusion* or *distraction* in K—and that is a major difference between K and Socrates, though not the only relevant one.

Exactly the same can be said about all other previous investigators into *that which is*. While many of them seem to have had truly good intentions whenever they explored *that which is*, the fact is that they all ended up being beholden to the cultures and group-thinks that they were immersed in, and surrounded by.

There is never once a single instance of K committing that blunder—which is one of many ways of committing the analytical fallacy, by getting distracted away from the universal by being attached to the particular culture or ideology of one's contemporaries.

K never once committed the analytical fallacy—and that *makes him the most accomplished true and pure* philosopher *in history.*

For instance, Nagarjuna is widely acknowledged to be the champion of Buddhist sunyata (emptiness). But as a Buddhist, he shared the same kinds of culturally-based atavisms that Socrates suffered from. Not K. Not even once. K is a unique phenomenon in the history of humanity, and not just in the history of "philosophy" or in the history of "human thought"—or in the history of the perennial wisdom.

I address more fully the relationship between philosophy and K in *The Analytical Fallacy*, wherein I document how his insights, researches, and observations mark a radically new beginning in what philosophy means and is—while yet being in complete agreement with the inmost insights of the likes of Pythagoras, Plato, the Buddha, Nagarjuna, Shankaracharya, the skeptics, Immanuel Kant, Friedrich Nietzsche, and Ludwig Wittgen-stein, just to mention a few of the truly *philosophical* research-ers in history.

K's presence in the twentieth century tells us—clearly and unambiguously, indeed—that "we are at the dawn of a new era," as HPB poignantly and presciently expressed it.

What K did is, in itself—as just noted—an astounding achievement, particularly considering that K had no academic training and had no personal knowledge of any previous re-searchers—except by acquaintance with students and professors who consulted him throughout his life.

CHAPTER 6
Disclosure

AT THIS POINT, ATTENTIVE READER, I FEEL COMPELLED to share with you a little bit more about where this whole exploration is coming from. This is particularly relevant in regard to comments I make in reference to the perennial wisdom and its present explosion everywhere—and with K as its centerpiece.

Revenant

When I was a baby (just a few months old), my physical body died in a pediatric clinic, and was dead for several minutes. While the little body lay dead, awareness continued, in a state of shock and surprise—and some events took place, psychologically. That near-death experience set the tone for how I have lived my life. It set the tone for the borderlessness explicit and implicit in everything I have been sharing with others for years, including this exploration.

Since then, death has been my constant companion—not in a morbid sense, but in a way that implies living life more abundantly, more richly, at greater depths.

The constant sense of imminent death throughout my life has made me practically impervious to the many overwhelmingly many peddlers and lobbyists soliciting for various "camps," or "ideologies," or "points of view." Such pestering is something we all have to suffer through as we live our lives—even if we haven't been dead before.

In general, it's always been intrinsically foreign to me, to be partisan for "the blue team" or "the red team." That has been especially true when it comes to anything having to do with the moral dimension of our lives.

So, crude as it may sound, it is nevertheless true: That aspect of my nature has made it irrelevant to me personally whether K was "the World Teacher," as some have claimed—or a monkey's uncle (as many have thought, though usually not expressing it verbally in such an etiquette-violating manner).

I feel exactly the same way about the perennial wisdom, and about its explosion in the twentieth century and beyond. I have never wanted nor not wanted for there to be a perennial wisdom, nor a perennial explosion. Yet there they were.

You see, this daily living-with-death thing has made me into something that is anathema in the society we have all come to build: I am "an outsider"—an expression made famous by Colin Wilson (1931-2013) in *The Outsider* (1956).

However, I should clarify that I use the expression in a different sense than Wilson does. For one thing, his "British existentialist," me-centered use of that expression is incompatible with being a true outsider—in my sense of the expression. Also, I am a borderless truth-seeker-truth-finder, someone who is ever curioser and curioser about anything and everything, while yet being continuously skeptical about anything I think I know. I just don't have the capacity to belong to "the red team" or "the blue team"—as someone who identifies himself as being "British" or "existentialist" obviously does.

That general attitude has made me be an outsider, in a society in which it seems as if "everyone" gives the impression of making the assumption that every one of us "surely" *must* identify with some ideology, or background, or group, or set of beliefs.

Unfortunately for those who have such lively me-centered expectations, ever since I came "this close" to dying—and then living with death throughout the rest of my life, including having several other "close shaves"—I lack severely where those around me have had more than plenty: I can't recall a single instance in my life when I identified with an ideology or with a group, or with any me-centered expectation based on conditioning.

"Nice" as that may sound to some, the fact is that it has put me at odds with all sorts of true believers—and that includes practically everyone I have encountered in almost eight decades, as of this writing.

Being an outsider can be a foolhardy way to be. This is especially the case when one grows up in a place, Cuba, made famous by its dictatorships and totalitarian regimes and would-be "revolutionaries"—all of them being most enthusiastic at the prospect of making everyone behave and think and wear their hair in ways that the tyrants considered "normal." Being "abnormal" in any way in such a venue can be dangerous to one's health and welfare. I attest to that, most emphatically.

Watershed

I began to become externally aware of the existence of the perennial wisdom in 1958, when I was thirteen, and still in Cuba. But a deeper awareness of it—and its twentieth-century explosion—only came in New York, in 1963. That was the watershed year in which I first encountered the Theosophical Society (TS)—and as a result of it, discovered yoga, Buddhism, Asian cultures (particularly Indian, Japanese, Tibetan, and Chinese)—and K. Taoism I had encountered as a child, but deepening into it came later.

From the time of my near-death experience, I had lived my life in the context of knowing that I had "a mission"—but not knowing initially, and for many years, what that mission was. In fact, my life could be said to have consisted centrally and passionately of figuring out what my life mission was, for many years.

Until the age of four, and as a consequence of the near-death experience, I was a hard-core meditator living in a Third World country—a place where there was no tradition or even any acknowledged awareness of meditation, let alone of its immense value.

Sitting daily in my little rocking chair for hours on end every single day made me a strange infant and child in the 1940s— especially to my bewildered parents and others who witnessed what to them was a worrisome "condition." I grew up with my family members referring to me behind my back as "El Loquito" (the little crazy one). For me, it meant—at least in part—that I grew up being an alien in my own family and a foreigner in my own country, if you will.

I grew up being an outsider.

But the New York summer of 1963 clearly marked an important new beginning in my life. The new vistas opened up by the TS, Indian culture, opera and concerts, Columbia University, Buddhism, mythology, and K—and a great deal more—led to a focusing of my energies, at the age of 18.

In those days, I referred to New York as "a spiritual gym"— given its bewilderingly many attractions and distractions. For someone on a mission quest, that place *required* moment-to-moment alertness.

I studied voraciously, and practiced what to me were the newly-discovered forms of Asian meditation. Up to that point, I didn't even know there was a word for what I'd been doing, since babyhood. This led me, if anything, to practice meditation even more intently than before—much like a child discovering a new, fascinating toy.

Also, as I began to discover connections between major cultural developments and the theosophical movement, I started to write down my observations. These writings were often at odds with received dogmas in the milieu I was surrounded by—I was

an outsider, perhaps still "El Loquito." After all, people do identify with "the red team" and "the blue team"—so my perceptions
were qualitatively different from everything and everyone I was
exposed to.

I was an outsider and borderless researcher, not a joiner. So
the many notes and observations I made led to more serious research, over the many subsequent years, and to this day. I have
been writing about all this since 1963, and have many boxes full
of unpublished manuscripts, going back to those early days.

Fritz

In the 1960s in New York, I was extremely fortunate. Importantly, I got to meet and befriend Fritz Kunz (1888-1972)—
who became my mentor in much that is covered only ever-so-
briefly in this book.

In his youth, Fritz had been the right-hand man of C.W. Leadbeater (1847-1934)—who is a central figure in the present exploration and in *The Inner Life of Krishnamurti*. Fritz had had an
intimate connection with Leadbeater (CWL), from the time
when Fritz was in his twenties and through his early forties. This
in turn led to Fritz being also personally acquainted with K,
when K was a child and a young man.

In addition, Fritz—whose parents had been TS members—
had met Mrs. Annie Besant (1847-1933) at the First Parliament
of World Religions. That took place in Chicago in 1893, when
Fritz was five years old. Mrs. Besant (AB) shook his little hand.
AB later became international President of the TS, from 1907
until her death in 1933.

Later in his life, Fritz married Dora van Gelder Kunz (1904-
1999). Dora had been one of "the Leadbeater girls" as a child and
adolescent. She is referred to in K's biographies, and eventually
became President of the TS in America (1975-1987). I was also

extremely fortunate to get to befriend Dora, whom I got to see at least once a week throughout the 1960s, when I participated in various lines of work—including healing and meditation sessions—that she was conducting.

Statements and perceptions about CWL and AB that I share with you here, dear reader, are at least partly based on first-hand information I received directly from Fritz and Dora. As the following narrative shows, it was CWL who "discovered" K clairvoyantly, and AB was the closest person to K—who called her "Amma" (mother).

Also, Fritz had been the founder of the pervasively influential Foundation for Integrative Education—which he started in 1940. He was also the editor of the Foundation's equally influential journal, *Main Currents in Modern Thought*.

To my knowledge, Fritz was the originator of the now commonly accepted insight that there is an intimate relationship between the very ancient perennial wisdom, and leading-edge developments in contemporary perceptions, particularly in the sciences. This is an insight that Fritz had originally had in 1922, and which eventually led to his intimate acquaintance and friendship with numerous pace-setters at the leading edge of research in various areas, especially in physics.

Long before there was a David Bohm, or a Fritjof Capra, or a Ken Wilber, there was Fritz Kunz—an unsung and largely unknown hero of the twentieth century, though he was born in 1888.

My very intimate mentoring friendship with Fritz led to my developing personal acquaintances with a number of such leading-edge luminaries as philosopher F.S.C. Northrop (1893-1992), geneticist and evolutionary biologist Theodosius Dobzhansky (1900-1975), physicist John A. Wheeler (1911-2008), and German-born Lama Anagarika Govinda (1898-1985), among many others who were at the avant-garde in their respective fields at the time. Earlier in life, Fritz—who was a Buddhist—had been the head of the Buddhist Colombo College in Ceylon (now Sri Lanka).

Much of what I say in these pages about the perennial explosion in the American Age comes from direct, personal experience, or from accounts sourced from actual "players."

Fritz and K

Having shared with you briefly my very rich relationship with such a cultural pace-setter—as Fritz clearly was—I would be remiss if I fail to show also the main factor that led to our eventually moving in separate directions, especially since it touches importantly on much of what is said in this exploration.

Fritz had an unquestionably genius-like prescience regarding the importance of the very real, intimate relationship there is between the ancient perennial wisdom and contemporary science.

I still find it astonishing that he had this insight *in 1922*—so many decades ahead of everyone else. Please take note of the fact that Fritz had this insight before quantum physics was a factor, even among most physicists, let alone the mainstream. The connection between contemporary science and ancient perennial wisdom—which is now taken to be "common knowledge"— began to be pervasively popularized only after Fritz's death, in the 1970s.

The main difference between Fritz and I is that he failed to see the immense significance of the presence of K in the twentieth century, whereas K became the center of my attention, even from my very first acquaintance with him. As I saw it then (and still see it now), Fritz failed to see K's importance, despite the fact that he had known K personally throughout K's youth and early manhood, and that he had been personally and intimately involved in K's work for two decades.

So even though I admired and loved Fritz to no end; and even though I was (and still am) immensely grateful to him for the opportunities he opened up for me; and even though I was deeply touched by his proposing to pass the baton of his work to me despite my young age and lack of academic credentials at the time, the fact is that the life-defining mission I'd been entrusted with as a baby was related to K's work.

I saw clearly then—as I see it now—that Fritz's major insight, to which he dedicated most of his adult life, was of critical importance for human culture, worldwide. But I could also see that K's insights, researches, and observations implied a world of being that transcends the limitations of the academic world in general—and reforming the academic world was at the core of Fritz's efforts.

I feel that if Fritz had seen the immensity of what K was doing—if Fritz had incorporated K's insights into his work (as David Bohm came to do)—it is almost a certainty that I might have considered staying in New York. It's difficult to say for sure, because there were also personal factors involved in my making that fateful move away from New York—which had been so very enriching, educational, and good to me in so many ways.

My feeling then and now has been that what is required in education is not a reform of the university as an institution, which is what Fritz was partly after, largely by proposing more substantial cooperation and communication in universities between the sciences and the humanities.

In fact, so far as I know, it was Fritz who first addressed the dire need in universities for interdisciplinary collaborations—which are now common, especially in the more prominent institutions of higher learning. But for fully a quarter of a century—beginning in 1940—Fritz had been the lone voice that cried in the wilderness, regarding the need for interdisciplinary studies in institutions of higher learning, at least to my knowledge.

Insofar as anything having to do with universities is concerned, what I felt then—and feel now, even more intensely—is that what is required is the creation of an altogether different kind of institution. What is required is a university based on truly philosophical, esoteric, transanalytical perceptions and values—a radical revolution, if you will.[1]

So despite my deeply-felt appreciation and love for Fritz and for the work he was doing, I ended up moving away from New York—from Fritz, from Columbia University, and from New York culture.

I was an outsider—yet again.

Before moving on from speaking of Fritz, I feel compelled to share with you something I consider important, in the present context.

In 1976—when she had just been elected president of the TS in America, and I was a volunteer at its headquarters in Wheaton, Illinois—Dora communicated to me that when Fritz died in 1972, she was deeply touched by the fact that K contacted her personally, to express his condolences to her, and that they spoke for quite a while.

As she was telling me this, she was overwhelmed with emotion, because neither she nor Fritz—nor anyone else in their inner circle—had been in personal touch with K for decades. The last contact she and Fritz had had with K had been more than forty years before.

Also, this was the only time I ever saw Dora get sentimentally emotional about anything at all. She was proud of being a very "practical" person and "a tough cookie" (as she might have

---

[1] The urgent need for a revolution in education is addressed more carefully in Part Four, "Mutation."

expressed it) and—apart from having a joyful personality—was never someone who displayed sentimentality, in any way.

How did K know that Fritz had just died? Dora couldn't figure that out. So far as she knew, there was no way that he could have known, through the few who knew of Fritz's death.

Dying to the known

Speaking of this parting of the ways with Fritz—which was then a surprising and unexpected development in my life—gives me the opportunity to clarify something that might otherwise be misunderstood. Whenever I refer—in this book and elsewhere—to "dying to the known" and related expressions, I am *never* speaking of a repeatable practice or methodology. Nor is this intended as a "subject" for chit-chat at a party or at a K discussion group.

Dying to the known is not about talking, nor about one's opinions—however "right" they may seem to be.

When I left New York, I was leaving behind—and doing so with full awareness—a whole world of untold, unique opportunities. I was leaving behind a world and possibilities that were very easy to be attached to. In retrospect, walking away from it can be seen as dying to it, without ever looking back—perhaps wondering "what if."

Dying to the known is not so much about "choosing" to do "X" in order to feel good about yourself. It is more about having the general attitude in life of *doing the right thing*, even when it means irrevocably losing something or someone dear to you.

Can you live that way, dearest reader? I am asking you, personally. This is not a rhetorical question. I ask you to ask yourself this question deeply, meditatively, in part because if you can't live that way, then you would have no interest in being free, psychologically—and therefore free in every other way that matters.

Freedom from the fear that you might "lose" this or that can only come from the ever-fearful me. This is not meant as a theory that you might accept or reject—which is the refuge of those who are fickle and can't go very far from the shallows of their own conditioning and related fears. That deeper freedom—which is the source for all other freedoms—can only take place in oneself when one is free from attachments to this or that.

If one cannot live like that, then one has *chosen* to be a slave. In such a case, one makes it *impossible* to research deeply into the truth of anything—including everything addressed in this book.

Dying to the known is not some bumper-sticker catchphrase. It is the way one lives when there is seriousness about *actually* dying to one's predilections and proclivities. It is not about pursuing pleasure or pain. Pursuing pain or discomfort can be just as much a me-centered attachment as pursuing pleasure and what's comfortable.[2]

Dialogue

I should make clear that I am not "a devotee" of K, if by that expression is meant deifying him or his insights, or assuming that he can do—or say—no wrong. In spite of the nature of much of the material in this book, I believe that, while exceptional, K was a human being—and as such was subject to failings common to all humanity. Nor do I identify with, or have a predilection for, any particular school, organization, or teachings.

---

[2] I have addressed some aspects of this in the paper "On Dying to the Known," available at paradigmshift.network. Initially, I had written that paper as my introduction to the book *Dying to the Known* (2004), authored by my very dear friend Arturo Moldéz-Pérez—a professor of philosophy at the University of the Philippines.

You may take this exploration as part of an ongoing, friendly dialogue on who J. Krishnamurti was, and on the nature and sources of the very ancient yet ever new perennial wisdom—and its present explosion, which is touching every one of us, as we speak.

Nothing I have said about K—here and elsewhere—is meant to be "an interpretation" of what K said or did. I am merely sharing my perceptions with you—and I am not attached to any of those perceptions. If you see "an interpretation" in any of it, please look within yourself. That is the only place where such an "interpretation" is likely to be found.

I ask you—as is often recommended in courts of law, and as the most serious skeptics throughout history have done: It is wisest to *suspend judgment* until the whole case has been heard. Please keep in mind that "the whole case" is not about opinions—not at all. "The whole case" implies *looking* at all of this— and doing so *borderlessly*. Like it or not, that is easier said than done.

K's inner life is a very strange story, not the least because he largely kept it a secret for over six decades. Yet—as you are about to see—that inner life has critical implications for our understanding of both his life and his insights.

Equally important is the fact that K's inner life is essential for our understanding of the New Age movement, as well as all the major approaches that have been developed throughout the ages, everywhere on the planet, in the process of us—each and all—trying to come upon a better understanding of *what is*.

That means that this exploration is meant to be relevant to such diverse group-thinks as Buddhism, philosophy, psychology, America, the teachings of Gurdjieff, socio-political developments, and other factors—not to mention the perennial wisdom itself. In fact, what is addressed here involves the contemporary milieu in its entirety. I address these connections more carefully in the works and papers already mentioned, as well as in others in preparation.

With that preamble, let us begin to look at the perennial source for the wisdom explosion—that phenomenon which is impacting all of us immensely at present.

While it is a fact that the world is in chaos as never before, it is also true that the wisdom explosion is all around us, in many brand new, unprecedented ways—and there's more to come.

Let's then proceed with the inquiry by looking into the borderless wisdom—what it is, and why it is so important for each and every one of us.

PART TWO

THE PERENNIAL WISDOM

CHAPTER 7
Perennials

J. KRISHNAMURTI ARRIVED FOR THE FIRST TIME in California's Ojai Valley in the summer of 1922, when he was twenty-seven. Shortly thereafter, he went through highly unusual and transformative experiences of a psychological and psychic nature, which included visible physical signs and manifestations.

As documented in the second edition of *The Inner Life of Krishnamurti*—and to some extent in what follows—K's experiences seem to be unprecedented. Despite this, some elements of these experiences give the impression of sharing at least some similarities with practices associated with so-called "higher yoga." Because of these similarities, some authors have attributed K's experiences as being "the same" as yoga or tantra.

At the time, K referred more simply to what was happening to him as "the process"—an expression that has subsequently been used by everyone who has spoken or written of these experiences—though he also sometimes used yogic terminology to refer to some aspects of it. In her memoir of K, Pupul Jayakar (1915-1997) described the events this way:

> In August 1922, Krishnamurti was to be plunged into the intense spiritual awakening that changed the course of his life. In the Indian tradition, the yogi who delves into the labyrinth of consciousness awakens exploding kundalini energies and entirely new fields of psychic phenomena, journeying into unknown areas of the mind. A yogi who touches these primordial energies and undergoes mystic initiation is recognized as being vulnerable to immense dangers; the body and mind face perils that could lead to insanity or death.
>
> The yogi learns the secret doctrines and experiences the awakening of dormant energy under the instruction of the guru. Once the yogi becomes an adept, these transformations of consciousness on the playground of consciousness are revealed in a mystical drama. The body and mind must undergo a supremely dangerous journey. The

adept is surrounded and protected by his disciples; secrecy and a protective silence pervade the atmosphere.[1]

There are several points worth looking at carefully in Pupul Jayakar's comments and assessment. However, in order to understand more clearly her remarks—and their implications—it is important that we explore first the background and context in which K's experiences took place. In order to at least try to do justice to this context, one must address directly the nature of the borderless wisdom—which is the source of these developments, according to K and other relevant witnesses.

That universal wisdom and way of being—which is (at least potentially) within each and every one of us—has often been referred to as "the perennial philosophy." But as addressed in Part One, I call this deeper dimension of our being "the perennial *wisdom*"—which strikes me as a far more proper expression. A look at this ancient yet ever new approach and its historical background will help us put K's inner life in a more proper perspective. That is the central subject of this Part Two.

K's "Teachers"

First of all, it's important to note that Jayakar's remarks betray her personal identification with Indian culture. By making such an assumption, she subliminally seems to imply the non-existence of a borderless, universal, perennial wisdom. In all of her writings, she never once refers to the existence of borderless wisdom-compassion.

Yet that *borderless* dimension is clearly and unambiguously what K's life and insights were all about, according to overwhelming evidence, as documented in *The Inner Life of*

---

[1] Jayakar, *Krishnamurti: A Biography* (1986), 46-47.

Krishnamurti, in this exploration, and elsewhere.[2] Unfortunately for her assumptions, Jayakar offers no evidence at all in defense of such a provincial assessment—neither in her biography of K nor anywhere else.

For instance, Jayakar's comments are made in general about any yogi, and gives the impression that K was an "Adept" and "a yogi" who had "a guru"—in the sense that the word "guru" has in Indian culture. She further assumes that this "guru" was in charge of all the proceedings connected with the process.

As shown in this exploration and in *The Inner Life of Krishnamurti*, "someone" was indeed in charge of the process, according to K and other witnesses. But all the evidence shows that there were *several perennials* involved, not *one* "guru," as the Indian understanding *requires*. Clearly, her statement that it was a single "guru" is arbitrary, false, and unrelated to K's actual experiences. She offers no evidence for such a claim, and there is no evidence at all in favor of making such a provincial assumption.

Contrary to Jayakar's *analysis* based on her conditioning, the fact is that—whenever the process was taking place—references made by K and other witnesses in this regard were not to one "guru," but to *several perennials*. Let's recall that perennials are never authorities, the way gurus are always assumed to be. So this clarification is critical for having a better understanding of what was going on in K's process.

As noted in Part One and in what follows, perennials are most emphatically not "gurus"—a word that is loaded with a particular culture's expectations and with an authoritarian spirit that is profoundly foreign to, and absolutely incompatible with the borderless perennial wisdom.

For reasons addressed in Chapter 5, "Masters," K and others in the theosophical milieu called these perennials "Masters."

---

[2] Consult paradigmshift.network.

These perennials were said by K and others to have been the same who had inspired the foundation of the Theosophical Society (TS)—as addressed briefly in what follows.

The TS had been devoted—from its start in 1875—primarily to the creation of a nucleus of the universal brotherhood of humanity. It was also founded for the purpose of promoting the study and deeper understanding of comparative religion, philosophy, and science, and of investigating unexplained laws of nature and the powers latent in humanity.

The TS is said by an increasing number of scholars to have been the springboard for what has come to be called "the New Age movement," and for numerous other cultural developments of the twentieth century.[3] I call this grand phenomenon "the perennial explosion," for reasons discussed briefly in Part One, and more thoroughly in *Muse.*

Some students of K, including Jayakar, have asserted recklessly and mistakenly that the perennials—who were a constant in K's whole life—were "visions," or even "hallucinations." Lamentably, she offers no evidence for her *assertions.* The fact that she was making such claims without any evidence whatsoever gives a strong impression that it is Jayakar who was hallucinating and having visions, not K.

The explanations offered in many books about K—and not just Jayakar's—concerning the perennials are unfortunately puzzling, in that they contradict everything K himself said on the subject. For instance, Stuart Holroyd (b. 1933) asserts as gospel truth that K must have been wrong in what he perceived regarding these perennials. Holroyd says about K's more explicit pronouncements regarding the perennials *in his personal experience*:

---

[3] See, for instance, the numerous and excellently-researched works by authors like James Webb and Gary Lachman.

> One cannot but wonder whether there was not, perhaps at a sub-conscious level, an element of role-playing and even self-deception in the way that Krishnamurti was speaking at this time.[4]

For her part, Pupul Jayakar characterizes K's connection with these perennials as "visions," without ever providing any evidence for her unresearched and provincial *opinion*. As she put it:

> [K] beheld visions of the Buddha, Maitreya, and the other Masters of the occult hierarchy.[5]

Given the fact that K himself never described his encounters with perennials as having been "visions," and that his whole life was about *not* being deceived—and especially given his unprecedented uniqueness in world history, as addressed in Part One—opinions to the contrary would seem to require a great deal more than unsupported assertions based on someone's conditioning, such as those made by Jayakar, Holroyd, and other authors.

A wiser course, I suggest, and one that I try to follow, is to *look at the evidence* concerning how K himself viewed these experiences and how witnesses described the events in question. Looking at the evidence also implies seeing and acknowledging the reality of the many perennials in history, and doing one's best to understand what a perennial is. Furthermore, this evidence-seeking approach turns out to be far more fertile, at least in the sense that it makes it possible—among other factors—for all of us to see more clearly the unique place that K has in history.

It strikes me as profoundly odd that the experiences of such a historically unprecedented worldwide phenomenon—as K clearly was—should be based on "hallucinations" and "visions"

---

[4] Holroyd, *Krishnamurti: The Man, The Mystery, and the Message* (1991), 18.
[5] Jayakar, *Krishnamurti*, 57.

and confusions or "deceptions" on K's part. That might be possible, of course. I'm merely saying that the hallucinations theory—like the "yogic" *opinionated, provincial theory*—needs to be looked at carefully, since it contradicts all the evidence available, as documented in the present exploration, and in *The Inner Life of Krishnamurti*.

In subsequent manifestations of the process that took place in the late 1940s, in the presence of Pupul Jayakar and her sister Nandini Mehta (n.d.), K always spoke in the plural when referring to those who were in charge of the psychic proceedings.

Who, we must ask, were "those in charge"?—and what part (if any) did they play in his life and in his insights in particular, and in the inception of the perennial explosion in general?

These are the kinds of questions that need to be addressed squarely and borderlessly by critics such as Jayakar, Holroyd, and others. Otherwise, one is merely playing with oneself, and not researching at all.

It seems clear—from what K himself stated numerous times—that the perennials involved in K's process were the same as those identified by HPB and others as being connected to the explosion and dissemination of the perennial wisdom at this time in human history.

If we accept that K was stating the simple truth about who these perennials were, a great deal can be explained about his experiences that otherwise remains "mysterious." More importantly, pivotal elements in K's insights can be clarified by recognizing their connection to the very ancient yet ever new perennial wisdom—and therefore to the fountainhead of the most transformative and influential insights throughout the ages, everywhere on the planet.

That needs to be explained credibly and borderlessly by any critics of the actual presence of perennials in K's life, in TS history, and in the history of mankind. Anything else is just regurgitating their never-questioned conditioning—and that will not do. This is much too serious.

All of this makes it critical for anyone who wishes to comprehend K's life and work to have as good an understanding as possible of who these perennials were—according to K and to those who first brought their non-provincial, borderless wisdom-compassion to public attention.

"Teachings" and "Masters"

Helena Petrovna Blavatsky (HPB) said numerous times that she started the theosophical movement at the behest of her perennial mentors, who she said were the living exponents and custodians of the very ancient (yet ever new) perennial wisdom.

When her Victorian audiences heard and read what HPB said about her perennial mentors, they began a trend that continues to this day. HPB had said from the beginning that the only proper way to understand what she was saying was also the only proper way even to have an inkling of who or what her perennial mentors were. She said that in order to understand any of it properly, one must first undergo a *perennial* "initiation."[6]

A perennial initiation involves, first of all, *actually* realizing that me-centeredness wreaks havoc with one's life—and thereby with the life of the community one lives in. This realization leads to seeing that me-centeredness *must* come to an end—if there is to be any substantial peace, insight or love in one's life. Only after one has been engaging in the act and process of perennial

---

[6] The requirement of initiation in order to understand the perennial wisdom as well as its exponents and exemplars is documented fully in the two-part paper "Transformation: Vital Essence of H.P. Blavatsky's *Secret Doctrine*." This paper—which is available at paradigmshift.network—was read at the Third Symposium on *The Secret Doctrine*, held in Oklahoma City in May, 1998. I have incorporated and expanded that paper as part of the text of the soon-to-be-published *Muse: H.P. Blavatsky's Insights for a New Era of Chaos, Revolution, Wisdom—and Krishnamurti*.

initiation is one in any position to understand any of it, or even to have an inkling of what any of it is about—*according to HPB and her perennial mentors.*

Otherwise, one is bound to interpret everything one experiences in terms of one's clearly limited, provincial, and me-centered conditioning.

Unfortunately, HPB's Victorian audiences were impatient—just as humans everywhere have always been impatient, when it comes to the borderless wisdom. The vast majority assumed that their Victorian savvy was far more than sufficient to "know" and understand *all of it.* It is as if, as a group-think, they decided that they were somehow privileged and knew better, and that HPB *and her perennial mentors* didn't know what they were talking and writing about. The hubris of those Victorians was colossal, and was exceeded only by their actual provincialism and ignorance.

It was in this way that a cult began to be created—a cult based not on what HPB and her perennial mentors said, but on Victorians' interpretations and assumptions based on their very limited and limiting conditioning.

This cult *assumed* that any Tom, Dick, or Harriette could "easily" understand the "teachings" that they took for granted is "what it was all about." This me-centered assumption included what they presumed was a "teaching" about the existence of "Masters" that any of them could relatively easily have *physical* access to.

Claiming to have access to these Victorian fantasy "Masters" became, in fact, the springboard for numerous authors writing yarns about "Them"—with a capital T, since that made the "Masters" somehow more "important" to the ears of Victorians. A number of those authors and other HPB readers created organizations, where people would erect new subcults based on the original Victorian cult. It is largely in such a way that the so-called "New Age movement" had its inception.

If it were not for its truly tragic consequences, this fantasy "Masters" worship cult based purely on Victorian perceptions is a rather amusing comedy of errors.

A main feature of all the many New Age cults has always been that everyone involved made the crucial assumption that *evidence is never required.* "If you believe"—assume the cultists— "then it is so. If you don't, then there is 'obviously' something wrong with you."

That main feature has been at the very heart of most New Age teachings and organizations—including the TS. If someone claims that they had breakfast this morning with a "Master," there will be many who will believe it. Those followers would also believe as "authoritative" whatever "teachings" were said to come from the "Master" *du jour.*

I fully realize that numerous New Agers would balk at such a description. Unfortunately for them, that description is based on extensive experience with numerous such groups and their followers. To them I would say now what I have said to many others like them, for six decades. Show me actual evidence that the teachings you believe in came from a "Master."

In sixty years of asking earnestly for such evidence, I have not encountered a single follower of "Masters" who could show even one single speck of evidence. Hence the vigorous way I express this. If anyone doesn't like it, it is very easy to make me change my perception, and the way I express it.

All you have to do is show me the evidence.

HPB's perennial mentors described themselves as being *borderless researchers*—not Victorian know-it-alls. These wise-compassionate researchers were inviting all of us to do the same kinds of researches that they had been involved in, for millennia.

According to actual perennials throughout history, they have always been looking for *humble researchers*. They have always been looking for the more morally serious among us.

They have *never* been looking for gullible followers—who are, by their very nature, me-centered.

Unfortunately, this fact has been widely ignored—and it is on such ignorance that the lion's share of New Age beliefs and attachments and practices has come from, including in the TS. This is addressed more fully in *Muse*.

CHAPTER 8
Evidence

THERE IS AN IMPASSABLE CHASM between actual perennials—including HPB's and K's mentors—and the numerous "Masters" that New Agers have come to believe in and have been devoted to.

Of "Masters" and *perennials*

First of all, the would-be "Masters" subsequent to HPB are always presented as authority figures who give out "teachings." In contrast—as addressed in Chapter 5, "Masters," and more thoroughly in *Muse*—perennials absolutely *never* present themselves as authorities. Instead, they exhort each of us to "seek out your own salvation, *with diligence,"* as the Buddha—who was a seminal perennial—put it.

The "authority" invariably invested by would-be "followers" on perennials throughout history has always come from theologians and other group-thinkers. New Age fantasy "Masters" are beliefs held by what turns out to be just the most recent crop of me-centered analyzers in a very long history of wanton and dangerous misrepresentation of perennials.

One of many differences between actual perennials and fantasy "Masters" is directly related to the level of evidence there is for the existence of each.

There is quite a bit of evidence for the physical reality of perennials in history—as witness the Buddha, Pythagoras, Jesus, Shankaracharya, Plato, Lao Tse, and numerous others. There also have been numerous anonymous perennials, who have done their work less visibly, but often just as powerfully—as anyone can discover, by researching this borderlessly and with serious intent.

Among the anonymous perennials are those who inspired HPB and K—for the existence of whom there is a great deal of evidence, as shown briefly in this chapter, and more thoroughly in other writings.[1]

On the other hand, "Masters" invented subsequently to those actual perennials seem to have come out of very thin *hot air*. Among these are the plethora of fantasy "Masters" saturating the New Age movement—including the TS—following the presence of actual perennials in HPB's lifetime, and later in K's, as documented partly in this exploration, and more so in *The Inner Life of Krishnamurti*, and in *Muse*.

It is a fact that after HPB, many other writers and group-thinkers have attributed "spiritual teachings" to her perennial mentors, despite the fact that they specifically referred to themselves as being *borderless researchers*—not propaganda spinners.

Instead of speaking of perennials being the researchers that they say they are, these Johnny-come-lately group-thinkers would often refer to those perennials using self-created, bombastic-sounding expressions to presumably refer to their fantasy "Masters"—such as "Ascended Masters," or "the Great White Brotherhood," and the like.

Authors such as Alice Bailey (1880-1949), Guy Ballard (1878-1939), and Elizabeth Clare Prophet (1939-2009)—a.k.a. "Guru Ma" and "Mother of the Flame"—for example, stated that their books and accounts were actually authorized—and even authored—by some of these same perennial *researchers*, who had inspired the founding of the TS.

Unfortunately for their many followers, the fact is that there is absolutely zero evidence for the reality of such subsequent fantasy "Masters." Such later excrescences contradicted egregiously the writings of actual perennials—which anyone can

---

[1] Consult paradigmshift.network.

consult, thanks to their voluminous correspondence being in print now.

A baroque *Kapellmeister?*

All of these subsequent New Age developments seem to have had their start in C.W. Leadbeater's (CWL) elaborate schemes of "levels of initiation" and other hierarchical notions.

In many ways, CWL could be said to have been something like the Pied Piper of Hamelin for his many followers in the New Age movement. Unfortunately for all such schemes (his as well as theirs), the fact is that *all hierarchical notions are obviously analytical*—as documented fully in *The Analytical Fallacy*, and as addressed more succinctly in Part One of the present inquiry.

Since all analysis is me-centered, hierarchical schemes are blatantly, in-your-face me-centered—which makes them anti-perennial, since the perennial wisdom is centrally about the ending of the me, in any of its forms. As *The Voice of the Silence* put it, *as preliminary to perennial candidates*, and in the process of making specific reference to the analytical mind,

> The mind is the great slayer of the real. Let the disciple slay the slayer.[2]

Such hierarchical and similar schemes had a tendency to evolve into ever-increasing analytical complexity. A lot of CWL's readers lapped it all up, and would engage in presumably "erudite" discussions regarding each of the many levels and sub-levels and super-levels. Bailey even spoke of *Initiation Human and Solar* (1922)—the title of her first major work, in which she was clearly elaborating further on CWL's already complex enough hierarchical models.

---

[2] H.P. Blavatsky, *The Voice of the Silence*, I, 2-3.

It makes one wonder how Bailey came upon the alleged "information" that the sun gets to be "initiated"—and what does that mean? And what does it matter, if the sun does get "initiated"? Furthermore, what business is it of ours? How does that presumable "knowledge" free anyone from me-centeredness—which is the foundational *cancer* within *that each of us* must *deal with?*

The answer to those and similar questions is that—so far as devotees of such systems are concerned—it doesn't matter. What matters to them is to be devoted to the labyrinthine, convoluted scheme. One might as well ask—as *erudite* medieval "philosophers" and "theologians" did, in a now mostly forgotten time and place—"how many angels can stand on the tip of a pin?" It's not the question itself that matters. It's the scheme—and its implications to its devotees—that matters.

CWL—who was a passionate monarchist and priest, and loved the bright colors, pomp, and circumstance that *goeswith* priestly and monarchical hierarchies—wrote and behaved as if he'd been obsessed with such elaborate, Byzantine schemes.

All such schemes were built up much in the manner of Johann Sebastian Bach's (1685-1750) canons. For instance, CWL also used to speak of "the races of mankind," which included very complex divisions into "planetary chains," and "rounds," and "root races," and "sublevels" and "superlevels" of "planes of existence"—from the "physical" to the "atomic," and their numerous sublevels and superlevels.

There were also the "rays" and "sub-rays" to presumably describe the specific number of temperaments—"seven," if you must know—that classify all humans, as well as all other entities. The "heads" of rays provide a kind of "platinum standard" for the way in which people under each of the "rays" are supposed to behave.

All such schemes—which were lapped up by a large congregation of New Agers—were much like the "voices" in Bach's canons, which related intimately with each other by somehow resonating with one another. This was a take-off on the ancient "Law of Correspondences" that HPB had referred to. But in its New Age incarnation, it was developed to a point that made it seem as if it had been teratologically transformed—as if it were on steroids.

There seemed to be no end to such purely analytical (and therefore me-centered and non-perennial) schemes in the very many group-thinks that were invented out of whole cloth, in the process of creating the New Age movement.

Such purely analytical devices give the impression of being a regression to the (now mostly considered) absurd complexities of the baroque period that had been the rage all over Europe after the Renaissance, and for about three centuries.

CWL's passion for providing hierarchical schemes and sub-schemes and super-schemes—all "wonderfully" interconnected with one another—could be described as "baroque."

But if CWL's multi-level harmonies could be described as "baroque," the amazing nuances of his intellectual heirs (people like Bailey, Ballard, and Prophet) were the epitome of rococo. They unquestionably took CWL's baroque presentations to ever more intriguing levels of complexity, confusion, magic, and sometimes nearly incomprehensible excess.

Unfortunately for these authors and their many followers—despite the baroque "elegance" and "subtleties" of their schemes—no one has ever provided a single piece of physical evidence for the existence of the fantasy "Masters" these authors and other New Age leaders have spoken of, through today.

This is important. After all, it is their precious fantasy "Masters" who occupied "places of distinction" in the rococo hierarchies and "initiations" (including those of the sun and the planets) that generations of scheme followers pondered over intently, to this day—much like their intellectual medieval ancestors had scoured their minds over the number of angels standing on pin heads.

All of this does make it look like CWL may have been—unwittingly and unbeknownst to him—much like a Pied Piper for his followers, a baroque *Kappelmeister*.

Of real and false coin

Before moving on to other related issues, I feel compelled to clarify three things related to what I just said. First of all, I love baroque music, and actually have no objections to a lot of rococo art. But my point is that there is such a thing as taking things to extremes—and people can get caught up with and sucked into the internal logic of systems, often forgetting to look out the window, to determine whether it's sunny or raining outside.

My point is that scratching an itch can give some pleasure, but excess scratching can land you in the ER.

Second, there is sufficient physical evidence to show that CWL had a very real relationship with the actual perennials who inspired HPB and Olcott (HSO) to found the TS. CWL was a very serious individual who served the perennials in a number of important ways. For instance, even though he was a committed Anglican priest, he helped HSO in his courageous and difficult *and illegal* work of establishing Buddhist schools in Sri Lanka (then Ceylon)—over the passionate objections of the ruling British government.

Also, a letter that CWL received from one of the perennials was materialized in front of several dozen witnesses, on the outstretched hand of HPB. The contents of that letter happen to be one of the most formidable expositions of what it means to be a perennial.

Apart from those factors, CWL was the creator of a brand-new language for expressing the perennial wisdom—a language that had never existed before, but which is now widely in use, even in mainstream culture, including films and ads. This latter contribution by CWL is addressed more thoroughly in Part Three, "A New Perspective."

I say this, because it is important to take note that there is a profound chasm between CWL and the New Agers who have copied him relentlessly, to this day—but without ever giving him credit. Those copyists proceeded to invent their own personal, me-centered systems of thought and methodologies, claiming that it all came from their fantasy "Masters."

Ad hominem?

Pointing out how CWL was misinterpreted and misused by others has another purpose—which I feel is at least just as important. Having a relationship with perennials is no guarantee that one understands *everything* relating to the universal wisdom. This is key for anyone trying to understand better the borderless wisdom—at least that is my impression, at present.

In CWL's case, it is most poignant to take note of the fact that he stated in the late 1920s that he didn't understand what K was saying. Yet at the same time, he continued to say, till the end of his life, that K had indeed been the blueprint exemplar for the new era at this sensitive transition point in human history.

Subsequent New Age authors and group-think leaders never had such a close relationship with perennials as what CWL has been shown to have had—at least so far as evidence is concerned. The evidence for CWL having had such a relationship is there for anyone to see.[3] The evidence for fantasy "Master"-mongers having had such a relationship shines for its absence.

---

[3] This evidence is addressed more thoroughly in *Muse*.

So when CWL creates a language that includes levels and hierarchies, he was putting his own personal touch on insights he'd first gotten from HPB—and from the perennials directly. In fact, HPB herself—and even her perennial mentors—spoke of cycles and levels and hierarchies. But one has to read what they say *very carefully.*

HPB and the perennials provide us with themes for us to meditate on and to research. They are not telling anyone to accept what they say at face value, and then elaborate on it according to one's conditioning.

The perennials are not giving us rigid mental pictures for us to elaborate on, based on our me-centered conditioning. On the contrary, they always emphasized that first there must be a transformation away from me-centered conditioning and towards the borderless and universal, before one can even *begin* to understand any of what they said. This has been fully documented in the soon-to-be-published *Insights for a New Era*, and gone into further in the upcoming *Muse*.[4]

As HPB put it to a private *Secret Doctrine* study group shortly before she died, as relayed by one of the participants (emphasis added),

> Exoteric interpretations are all very well, and she does not condemn them so long as they are taken as pointers for beginners, and are not accepted by them as anything more.
>
> Many persons who are in, or who will in the future be in the TS are of course potentially incapable of any advance beyond the range of a common exoteric conception. But there are, and will be others, and for them she sets out the following and true way of approach of the *SD*.
>
> Come to the *SD* (she says) without any hope of getting the final Truth of existence from it, or with any idea other than seeing how far it may lead TOWARDS the Truth.

---

[4] See Sanat, "Transformation: Central Teaching of H.P. Blavatsky's *Secret Doctrine*"; see also the article *"The Secret Doctrine,* Krishnamurti, and Transformation," downloadable at paradigmshift.network.

See in study a means of exercising and developing the mind never touched by other studies.[5]

A "mind never touched by other studies" is a mind empty of content, a *borderless* mind, a mind in meditation. Such a mind is not full of "knowledge" and cleverness—ever ready to "elaborate" on what HPB (or CWL) said. Yet HPB is saying here that only such an empty mind is in a position to study anything truly—but especially "the *secret doctrine.*"

Group-thinking contrarians

More recently, a new crop of group-thinkers, mostly scholars of early TS history, have questioned the reality of the perennials, altogether. These contrarians—like the New Agers just addressed ever-so-briefly—also took seriously the notion of purely analytical Victorian fantasy "Masters." In that respect—and regardless of what century they happened to be in—they are most properly identified as "Victorian-minded contrarians." Like many Victorians, these contrarians are so convinced that they know "so much," that they can't be bothered with the facts.

A major difference between these scholars and their Victorian-minded New Age intellectual cousins is that they would often start out their "investigations" by making the unsupported assumption that the Victorian fantasy "Masters" came strictly from HPB's imagination.

These contrarians are so deeply faithful devotees to that unsupported assumption, that they do their very best not to let any "pesky" facts get in their way. Some of these time-warped people claim that, if the "Masters" were real in any way, they "surely" must have been ordinary people who HPB had met in the course of her life and about whom she presumably "exaggerated."

---

[5] Robert Bowen, *Madame Blavatsky on How to Study Theosophy*, 8-9.

Perhaps the best known of these relatively recent "researchers" is K. Paul Johnson (b. 1953).[6] Johnson and his intellectual kin claim that the perennials—whom they call "Masters," following the lead of Victorian group-thinking—are fictional.

In an important way, the contrarians are right, of course, since their complaint is about *Victorian fantasies*—not about HPB's *perennial mentors*. The trouble for "researchers" like Johnson is that their obsession with the false coin implicit in the Victorian notion of "Masters" blinds them to the existence of real coin—which are the perennials, in this case.

Both Victorian-minded "Masters" devotees and Victorian-minded contrarians express themselves as if they seem to be unaware of the huge mastodon in the little room—the actual perennials. Such writers are of course entitled to their *unsupported and unresearched opinions*. But unfortunately for Johnson and kindred authors and similar contrarian worshippers, there is a chasmic difference between opinions and facts.

People are entitled to their opinions—but not to their self-created "facts."

Facts require documentation. Opinions don't. Like New Age devotees of Victorian "Masters," Johnson offers no evidence at all for his claim that there's no such thing as *perennials*. Instead, what he does do is that he documents in part the error in something that previous HPB attackers had claimed—incidentally, also without evidence. He documents the fact that HPB had met in her worldwide travels with explorers, scholars and other people on a quest for deeper understanding.

In fact, Johnson has done us a great service by documenting that HPB had indeed been involved in such soul-searching worldwide travels, and that she did indeed meet with many fascinating and some influential and/or well-informed people,

---

[6] Johnson, *The Masters Revealed: Madame Blavatsky and the Myth of the Great White Lodge* (1994).

throughout the planet. Johnson's documentation of this fact demonstrates that previous authors who had claimed that HPB had not engaged in any such travels—that she had "invented" her journeys—had been completely wrong in their claims. We all need to thank Johnson for helping to clarify that. I certainly do.

But when Johnson says that HPB was *inventing* the physical reality of her perennial mentors, and that they were, instead, composites of ordinary people she had met in the course of her intense soul-searching world-trotting, he's crossing the rigorous line there is between fact and fiction.

Johnson never once offers any evidence that his conspiracy theory is a description of what actually was the case.

In that respect, Johnson only succeeds in letting us all know what his very personal beliefs and predispositions regarding HPB had been, all along. He's letting us know that he is no researcher. Rather, he is a group-thinker—a conspiracy theorist with an axe to grind against HPB—*and zero facts to support his conspiracy theory.*

Johnson's lack of interest in facts—and his passion for his preconceived notions—is revealed transparently by Daniel Caldwell (b. 1949), who is an actual researcher into anything related to HPB.

Caldwell has addressed, point by point, the various erroneous claims made falsely and recklessly by Johnson.[7] Further, Caldwell shows how Johnson—even when faced with documentation the impossibility of at least some of his claims, persists on adhering to them. Caldwell's work is must reading—especially for anyone foolish enough to turn into an enabler, let alone being a devotee, of Johnson's conspiracy theory.

We now know that—when dealing with the question of *HPB's perennial mentors*—a large body of evidence and quite a

---

[7] Daniel H. Caldwell, *K. Paul Johnson's House of Cards? A Critical Examination of Johnson's Thesis on the Theosophical Masters Morya and Koot Hoomi,* blavatskyarchives.com.

number of reputable witnesses documented their physical reality.[8] Group-thinking conspiracy theorists (such as Johnson) avoid mentioning this evidence. When they do refer to it, they always do so by selecting carefully—cherry-picking—what agrees with their preconceived theory, while ignoring the facts of the case.

Importantly, that evidence is truly overwhelming, and *must be addressed* in any serious discussion or consideration of the presence of perennials in early TS history. Yet Johnson writes his books as if he were unaware of any of this extensively published material.

In fact, in some instances, Caldwell shows how *Johnson actually acknowledges the reality of HPB's perennial mentors,* though he does so only privately. Yet even then, he persists in holding on with both hands to his pet preexisting *unresearched* conspiracy theory—*but only in his published writings.*

Evidence

To my knowledge, some of the most valuable evidence for the reality of perennials in TS history comes from Colonel Henry Steele Olcott (1832-1907), who was the founding international President of the TS (1875-1907). Olcott (HSO) wrote a massive, six-volume history of the early years of the movement, based on his diaries—which he kept faithfully, for years. In those six large volumes, he reported numerous instances of the physical reality and presence of the perennials.[9] HSO's evidence is of special interest for a number of reasons.

To begin with, he was himself an eyewitness: He reports having met the perennials many times in their physical bodies, both alone and in the presence of others—including, on a few occasions, HPB. Of equal importance, his background as an internationally-renowned avant-garde agricultural scientist-research-

---

[8] A good place to start this research, in fact, would be blavatskyarchives.com.
[9] Olcott, *Old Diary Leaves: The True Story of the Theosophical Society*, 6 vols. (1874-1898).

er, and later as an unusually successful investigator of graft in the military during the Civil War, and as a main investigator into President Lincoln's assassination, and then as a lawyer and investigative journalist, must all be taken into account.

All this background enhanced HSO's innate abilities as a borderless researcher and impartial observer. It all also points to his having had an unusual level of integrity and death-defying courage. Further, before his association with HPB, he had been one of the most respected investigators of psychic phenomena in the world.

As a researcher of psychism, he had exposed numerous frauds, to the point that his pioneering work inspired other scientists to explore more carefully the claims made by psychics—and that inspiration contributed importantly to the creation, a few years later, of the Society for Psychical Research, which exists to this day.[10]

In fact, it was in this capacity as a skeptical researcher into psychic claims and as an investigative reporter for the *New York Sun*, that he first met HPB in 1874.

It is instructive to clarify that HSO had earned his rank during the American Civil War investigating graft and fraud in the military. He was so highly respected for his immense courage and integrity, that he was included in the team that investigated President Abraham Lincoln's (1809-1865) assassination. This is relevant, given that there was a fear that Southerners might suspect fraud in that investigation, in order to "falsely claim" that Southerners had been behind the crime.

That is, HSO was highly respected—not only for his scrupulous investigative skills, but also and importantly for his integrity. Even among Southerners, his presence in the investigating team was expected to allay any potential suspicions of government "tipping the scales" in the investigation.

This was a man of unusual integrity and clearly not an ordinary person. His actual success in the investigation of crime

---

[10] For Olcott's work as a pioneering researcher, see Olcott, *People From the Other World* (1874).

throughout the Civil War—when his life was constantly being threatened by powerful criminals, and when he was daily being offered all sorts of bribes—and later as a psychic researcher who uncovered many frauds, tell us that this was someone who was not easily duped or suborned, even when losing his life was a very real possibility.

This is someone whose evidence must be taken very seriously by anyone pretending to *research* into matters having to do with the physical reality of perennials in TS history.

HSO's experiences and statements *must* be assessed with great care, before someone whose courage and integrity have not been tested—as Olcott's were—would jump to conclusions regarding the physical presence of perennials in TS history, without a proper, *borderless* and non-prejudiced investigation. A proper investigation *must* address directly HSO's voluminous, well-documented, and eminently credible evidence. Otherwise, there is nothing proper about "investigations" such as Johnson's.[11]

Given HSO's background, reputation, *and meticulously careful research methods*, his evidence *must* be considered. It *must* be looked at *specifically*, and taken seriously. Books such as Johnson's, which claim arbitrarily and flippantly the non-existence of perennials, ignore the cornucopia of evidence provided by HSO. An actual researcher would unquestionably have gone very seriously into this massive body of evidence. Yet Johnson looks the other way instead, and pretends that none of it ever happened. He fails to tell his readers anything at all of the existence of Olcott's massive evidence—which he obviously must have known.

Books such as Johnson's—since they *deliberately* ignore the evidence as if it didn't exist—must be discounted as a form of yellow journalism supporting a conspiracy theory: Such books say more about the lack of seriousness and lack of integrity of

---

[11] For HSO's amazing courage and integrity, see his biography, Murphet, *Hammer on the Mountain* (1972).

their authors, than they do about the subjects that they flippantly tattle about.

The only reason why I have dwelled so much on Johnson, is that some actual researchers and scholars have taken Johnson's bait by presenting him as a serious investigator, and have thereby become Johnson's enablers.

For full disclosure, I should mention that I addressed this very serious problem personally with Johnson, shortly after his first tattle book came out. The venue was the Washington, D.C. branch of the TS, where he spoke shortly after his first book was published. He did not respond to my questions regarding the overwhelming evidence for the presence of perennials in TS history. Rather than respond to the essential questions regarding his total lack of evidence, he changed the subject and ignored the queries.

A real researcher

Importantly, HSO made careful and thorough notes immediately after each physical encounter he personally had with the perennials. Memorializing notes such as Olcott's are taken seriously in courts of law, even when dealing with capital crimes. If there were others present in the presence of perennials, HSO secured from them affidavits to the effect that they had indeed been part of an experience in which a perennial had been physically present, and to the effect that they had actually seen perennials with their own eyes, and had related to them during the experience.

In addition, HSO always made sure that he had witnesses attesting to the veracity of these affidavits to his very careful notes describing the encounter with perennials. Please keep in mind that, among other things, HSO was a lawyer, who in addition was well aware of the dire need for taking such measures, given his background as a fraud investigator of psychic claims.

A serious problem for would-be detractors, is that HSO's evidence is not limited to one or two meetings. He kept a diary, in which he meticulously described each of such meetings. In addition, he reports dozens of witnessed encounters, with supporting personal notes and affidavits by witnesses. HSO then secured further affidavits from third parties, who testified to the truth of the affidavits having been signed in the presence of the original witnesses. Such affidavits and "super" affidavits—and the experiences they relate—span the period from 1874 to 1907.

Anyone who ignores this formidable body of evidence is thereby informing all of us that he is making unsupported assertions not based on any documentation or facts. Yet such is precisely what authors such as Johnson have done.

Shame on them—*and even more so on anyone who becomes a follower of such conspiracy theories, or a supporter of such outlandish, false claims.*

More importantly, shame on anyone who publishes or in any way promotes this egregious violation of scholarship. This is a very serious matter, and anyone supporting such lies and tall tales in any way is putting himself in exactly the same category, by participating in a recklessly unfounded conspiracy theory. Any actual scholars who have been enablers of this false conspiracy theory have the obligation to retract their support for it publicly. Integrity demands such a course of action.

We are all in the midst of what is, by far, the most formidable effort in history ever made by exemplars of the perennial wisdom. It is of the utmost importance that we all deal with matters such as this with the level of seriousness that the facts deserve. The present as well as the future of humanity depends on our honesty and integrity.

Other witnesses

In addition to the above, the perennials sometimes left a physical personal item behind after these encounters, some of which—including a large body of letters, a perennial's lock of hair, and a turban a perennial was wearing—can be examined, to this day.

Other researchers, such as Geoffrey Barborka (1887-1992), have also investigated and documented very carefully the physical presence of the perennials in the early years of the movement.[12] Barborka provides testimonials of numerous other eyewitnesses, who attest to the perennials' physical reality in the early days of the TS.

According to documented reports, the perennials communicated physically not only with HPB and HSO, but with at least about three dozen other people, most of whom (though not all) were perennial apprentices, and—for that reason alone—individuals of personal integrity (or at least trying to be).

Actually, my very dear friend Ram Kumar Singh—who has himself been a borderless researcher into these issues for many decades, made a list of *105 different individuals* who are documented to have had some tangible contact with the perennials.[13]

Among these others, the most important from the perspective of the present investigation were Annie Besant (1847-1933) and CWL. Besant (AB) had been a major and quite courageous civil rights defender for many years, before (and after) she became the second international president of the TS in 1907, upon HSO's death. CWL "discovered" K in 1909, as laid out in this exploration and in *The Inner Life of Krishnamurti*.

AB's and CWL's respective first physical encounters with the perennials occurred while HPB and HSO were still living, and their relationship with the perennials is said to have continued until CWL and AB died. These encounters with the perennials

---

[12] Barborka, *The Mahatmas and Their Letters* (1973).
[13] Personal communications, including the list with all the names, dates, and the circumstances.

took place at a time that could be referred to as the "early years" of the TS—its most influential period, when CWL and AB were still vigorous presences. That "early" period ended in the early 1930s, upon their deaths—and upon the beginning of K's intense planet-wide presence independently of the TS.

K's evidence

My perception is that—overwhelming as the above evidence is for the physical presence of perennials in early TS history—the "early" documentation is not the most definitive evidence there is. As I see it, the most credible evidence is even far more formidable, and it comes from J. Krishnamurti—much to the chagrin of his non-followers and of many New Agers, who are likely to balk at that *fact*.

As outlined in Part One, "Krishnamurti," K's presence in the twentieth century was unquestionably an unprecedented phenomenon in the history of mankind and in the history of the perennial wisdom's public exposure. Yet K had no schooling, he had no teachers, and was born in what was then a remote Indian village. How can anyone explain this astonishing phenomenon?

Yet it must be explained, if one is honest with oneself—and has integrity.

Apart from that poignant fact about his insights, the "process" that K underwent—from 1922 when it began, until 1986, when he died—was carried out by the perennials as a kind of psychic surgery on his psychic anatomy (though also impacting visibly his physical body), as documented fully in *The Inner Life of Krishnamurti*.

This is important, because "the process" consisted of an extremely sophisticated type of psychic surgery performed on K's body and psyche—to the point that some observers have referred to it as a component of "higher" yoga. So the process—in and by itself—points to the presence of the perennials throughout most of his life. After all, the perennials are the ones properly credited with performing that highly unusual and dangerous form of psychic surgery. The process is gone into at great length in the second edition of *The Inner Life of Krishnamurti.*

From the moment that CWL "discovered" K on Adyar Beach in early 1909, the perennials became and continued to be a constant presence in his life—according to K and many other witnesses.[14] Importantly in the present context—and *according to K*—one of these perennials had been the actual author of *At the Feet of the Master*, which has always been attributed to K.[15] It was precisely at the culminating point in TS history, in the 1920s, that these same perennials began to be a more emphatic and ostensive presence in K's life—in the form of being in charge of the process. Critically, the perennials were also behind K's lifetime of speaking and writing, *according to K.*

For instance, when he was in his deathbed in 1986 (exactly ten days before he died) he specifically requested to make a recorded statement—over the objections of some non-followers who were present. At that poignant moment, he affirmed that,

> [F]or seventy years that super energy—no—that immense energy, immense intelligence, has been using this body. I don't think people realize what tremendous energy and intelligence went through this body . . . and now the body can't stand any more.
>
> Nobody, unless the body has been prepared, very carefully, protected and so on—nobody can understand what went through this body. Nobody. Don't anybody pretend. Nobody, I repeat this: nobody amongst us or the public know what went on. I know they don't.
>
> And now, after seventy years, it has come to an end. Not that that intelligence and energy—it's somewhat here, every day, and especially at night . . . You won't find another body like this, or that supreme intelligence operating in a body for many hundred years. You won't see it again.[16]

---

[14] Hear the audio of the talk, Aryel Sanat, "Krishnamurti on the Masters," paradigmshift.network, also available at the library of the Theosophical Society in America. This was a talk given at the national headquarters of the TS in America in the spring of 2000.

[15] Alcyone (Krishnamurti), *At the Feet of the Master* (1910).

[16] Mary Lutyens, *The Open Door*, 148-149.

Numerous New Age authors and leaders have claimed to have been in contact with fantasy Victorian "Masters." Unfortunately for all of them, the fact is that no one has given any evidence that the perennials communicated with others, once K began his work in stride, beginning soon after the process began in 1922.

It is also intriguing to note that the presence of perennials in early TS history ceased to be a factor, the moment K began his more public work, upon the deaths of CWL and AB. From that point on, their presence came primarily in the form of K's expositions. It was a very different—yet even more poignant—kind of perennial presence.

It should be noted especially in that statement—which K made as he lay dying—that he refers to his having been "protected throughout" his life. He specifically refers to "that intelligence" as being the source for his insights. Regardless of the likes or dislikes on the part of K non-followers and by New Agers (including TSers), there it is.

The Inner Life of Krishnamurti documents fully the very intimate relationship that K had with the perennials who had inspired the foundation of the TS. That very intimate relationship went on at least from 1909 until his death in 1986.

It is what it is.

Claims and blind faith

Authors such as Alice Bailey, Elizabeth Clare Prophet—and many other New Agers—claimed that their work was inspired by the very same perennials who had been responsible for founding the TS. Yet not a single one of them offers any evidence (such as HSO's and that of many others in early TS history) for their claims.

Clearly, in the absence of any physical evidence, there is a severely inconvenient truth that followers of such authors must face:

Anyone who accepts their claims is doing so on blind faith, and nothing else.

It is important to keep this in mind, in light of the fact that the conceptual, analytical, *exoteric* approach and tenor of "teachings" coming from these subsequent sources diverge completely from what the actual perennials had said in their large correspondence, which has been public and published since the early 1920s.

Nor are these Victorian fantasy "Masters" in agreement with K's transformative, *unprecedented* insights and observations—as laid out in Part One, "Krishnamurti."

Collectively, K's insights stand for a watershed moment in the history of philosophy and religion, worldwide—as noted in Part One, and more thoroughly in *The Analytical Fallacy* (2002) and in the soon-to-be-published *The Moral Revolution*. Even more importantly, K's insights are *purely esoteric* in their nature—another word that has been obscenely misused and abused by impertinent New Agers—as addressed briefly in Parts One and Four, and more pointedly in *Muse*.

Unlike the ones mentioned above and other New Age authors—who make claims of association with the perennials, but without offering any physical or *philosophical* evidence for their claims—K turns out to be himself one of many witnesses to the existence of these perennials in TS history.

In fact, K is the most significant witness to the reality of perennials, given the unique, transformative quality of the radically new way of presenting before the mainstream public the very ancient—yet ever new—perennial wisdom, as discussed more thoroughly in the works just cited, and in Part One, "Krishnamurti."

That is, it strikes me that K's insights, researches, and observations are in themselves proof of its unquestionable source—especially given its unprecedented nature, and how it supersedes everything that had previously been thought to be what the borderless wisdom consists of.

K's revolutionary and powerful and eminently clear presentation of the very ancient wisdom is proof of the only place it could have come from—the perennial wisdom and its

exemplars. It is the perennials who have always been the re-
positories and exponents of the borderless wisdom.

The perennials

According to HPB, the perennials were neither "spirits of
light" nor "goblins damn'd,"[17] as authors interested in mystifications and "mysteries"—such as most New Agers, including
TSers—have (mis)represented them to be. Rather, she said—
and her colleagues and other witnesses concurred—that her perennial mentors were human beings who happened to be wiser,
more insightful, and more compassionate than the common run
of humanity. The perennials are also borderless researchers, not
authority figures. Authority figures are always provincial.

Many of these perennials—though not all—had abilities that
are usually considered "paranormal" by people who have not
subjected themselves to the scientific and moral rigors that perennials exemplify.

These abilities made it possible for them to communicate
with people in ways that might be considered "magical" or "supernatural" by someone unacquainted with certain aspects of
the perennial wisdom's scientific dimension. It is as if a remote
tribe somewhere on Earth—whose members are not acquainted
with today's technology—would consider "magical" or "supernatural" (or "nonsense"), what to us are ordinary objects, such
as cell phones, airplanes, and televisions.

Abilities such as those displayed by perennials do not belong
to any culture, school, or region of the world, though they are
often identified at present with places like India, Tibet, or
China—or with extraterrestrials or other-dimensional intelli-
gences. Anyone wishing to speak of these perennials—whether
in the context of writing or speaking about K, or in any other
context—would benefit from reading HPB's own words about
them (emphasis added):

_____

[17] Blavatsky, *Key to Theosophy* (1889), 288.

[The perennials] are *living men*, born as we are born, and doomed to die like every other mortal.

. . . We call them "Masters" because they are our teachers; and because from them we have derived all the Theosophical truths, *however inadequately some of us may have expressed, and others understood, them*. They are men of great learning, whom we term initiates, and still greater holiness of life. They are not ascetics in the ordinary sense, though they certainly remain apart from the turmoil and strife of your western world.[18]

Two of HPB's eminent students, Gottfried de Purucker (1874-1942) and Katherine Tingley (1847-1929), discussed the living presence of these borderless perennial researchers throughout history:

No one who has read history can be oblivious of the fact that its annals are bright at certain epochs with the amazing splendor of certain human beings, who during the periods of their lifetimes, have swayed the destinies, not merely of nations, but of whole continents.

The names of some of these men are household words in all civilized countries, and the most negligent student of history cannot have done otherwise than have stood amazed at the mark that they made in the world, while they lived—yes, and perhaps have left behind them results surpassing in almost immeasurable degree the remarkable achievements of their own respective lifetimes. A few of these are the Buddha and Shankaracharya in India; Lao-Tse and Confucius in China; Jesus the great Syrian Sage in his own epoch and land; Apollonius of Tyana, Pythagoras, Orpheus, Olen, Musaeus, Pamphos, and Philammon, in Greece; and many, many more in other lands . . .

One point of great importance should be noted: that a careful scrutiny of the teachings of these Great Men, the Seers and Sages of past times, shows us that in the various and varying forms in which their respective Messages were cast, there is always to be found an identical [insight] . . . identical in substance in all cases, though frequently varying in outward form: a fact proving the existence all over the world of what Theosophy very rightly points to as the existence of a Universal Religion of mankind—a Religion-Philosophy-Science based on Nature herself, and by no means nor at any time resting solely on the teachings of any one individual, however great he may have been.

---

[18] Blavatsky, *Key to Theosophy* (1889), 288, 289.

It is also foolish, downright absurd, for any thoughtful man or woman to deny the existence of these great outstanding figures of world-history, for there they are; and the more we know about them, the more fully do we begin to understand something of their sublime nature and powers . . .

We introduced these great men in order to illustrate the thesis that the human race has produced these monuments of surpassing genius in the past; and there is not the slightest reasonable or logical argument that could be alleged by anybody in support of the very lame and halting notion that no such men live now, or could live in the future.

The burden of all the evidence at hand runs quite to the contrary. It would be a riddle virtually unsolvable, if one were to suppose that because such men have existed in the past, they could not exist again, or that—and this comes to the same thing—what the human race has once produced, it could never again produce.[19]

After having looked very carefully into the issue of perennials for six decades—and done so (as much as my limitations have permitted) borderlessly and without prejudgment—it strikes me as obvious that the presence of K in the twentieth century provides the most formidable evidence, to date, for the very real, actual presence of perennials throughout the ages.

K and America

As briefly noted in Part One, and in *The Analytical Fallacy*, K was the only person in history who never committed the analytical fallacy, the only truth-researcher ever who taught the esoteric and only the esoteric, and who addressed himself to the planet as a whole, not just to a particular culture or region thereof. These points are intimately related to an additional factor—a factor that puts K at the vanguard of the unprecedented American Age.

K provided an exposition of the importance of the essence of America's founding documents—though he never referred in

---

[19] Gottfried de Purucker and Katherine Tingley, *H.P. Blavatsky: The Mystery* (1974), 12-14.

his public pronouncements to America specifically, let alone its founding documents.

This last point is of particular importance, because America's founding documents were clearly meant to be a kind of charter for helping all of us Earthlings to create a good society, throughout the whole planet. This is in fact what has happened—or rather begun to happen. After all, the vast majority of countries today are democratic constitutional republics—not tyrannies, by whatever name—and their constitutions follow the borderless moral tenets of America's founding documents.

The worldwide relevance of America's founding documents was emphasized most poignantly by President John F. Kennedy (1917-1963) in his inaugural address, in which he famously said, "My fellow Americans: ask not what your country can do for you—ask what you can do for your country."

What is not usually noted is what he proceeded to add immediately after that well-known and much-quoted expression of universal morality. He then proceeded to clarify, "My fellow citizens of the world: ask not what America will do for you, but what together we can do for the freedom of man." In that whole statement, JFK encapsulated the deeper, worldwide significance of America's founding documents.

America's founding documents are not exclusively about the founding of one nation. They are explicitly and thoroughly about the transformation of human consciousness, everywhere on Earth.

Even the few dictatorships that still exist make the claim that they are constitutional democracies—despite the fact that they say so cynically, but out of respect for what could be called "the American mainstream," which has spread throughout the world.

Importantly, the same is true of the Charter of the United Nations, which is also based on the self-same founding documents of America.

This is not a coincidence. America's founding documents did not come about exclusively for the creation of one nation. That much should be obvious to any fair-minded person.[20]

Those main features of K's presentations outlined in Part One point clearly to an inescapable fact: K's insights, researches, and observations reflect seamlessly the clear intentions of all perennial researchers throughout history, and in every region of the world.

A main difference between K's and other presentations is that his approach is tailored to the unique—non-regional, planetary—circumstances brought about by what I call "the American Age," which began with the founding of America, and gained deeper dimensions with the wisdom explosion catapulted by the TS.

As noted in Part One, in *Muse*, and in *Insights for a New Era*, the main difference between "the old" and "the new" is that K never once appealed to existing cultures or religions, never once quoted scriptures, never once committed the analytical fallacy, never once gave in by mixing exoteric components into his purely esoteric insights.

It needs to be kept in mind that factors such as metaphysics, mythologies, methodologies, and other analysis-pregnant approaches are—one and all—purely exoteric notions.

Like America's founding documents, K was appealing to our intelligence, not to our me-centered conditioning.

The main difference between "the old" and "the new," then, is that K was able to express the very ancient yet ever new perennial wisdom in its purest form, ever.

TS members in particular and New Agers in general—and everyone in the world who is seriously interested in democracy—would do themselves the greatest possible favor by looking carefully at these facts.

It is in those facts that can be found the deeper mission of the TS, and of the New Age movement—and of America.

---

[20] I address the very real and intimate relationship between K and America's founding documents in the soon-to-be-published *The Moral Revolution.*

But these facts cut much, much deeper—since these insights affect every nation on Earth that has been influenced by America's founding documents. That includes all democratic republics at present that have a constitution as the law of the land, and it even includes dictatorships that pretend to be constitutional democracies.

It also includes the United Nations, whose charter is based on America's founding documents—which are perennial in their means, intent, and projections for the whole planet.

CHAPTER 9
Nietzsche

ONE OF THE BEST CONTRIBUTIONS to understanding what a perennial might be like, may come not from "Masters"-obsessed New Age devotees, nor from the HPB-contrarian milieu of the twentieth century—both of them inspired by Victorian notions.

Perhaps it may be found in Friedrich Nietzsche (1844-1900)—a prophet from the nineteenth century who broke the Victorian mold while living in that quaint era. He was a precocious prodigy who foreshadowed the perennial explosion that we are all still witnessing.

Nietzsche could correctly be said to have been an enlightened precursor of the twentieth century's momentous developments outlined briefly in Part One—and more thoroughly in *Muse.* His insights shed light on an important dimension of this study—specifically, the urgent necessity for human transformation.

That transformative dimension is central not only to *philosophy* (as understood by Pythagoras and Plato). Psychological-moral transformation has always been the very foundation of the perennial wisdom—and is clearly at the core of insights coming out of both HPB and K. So Nietzsche's take on human transformation provides a fascinating "third way" of looking at the borderless wisdom. He enriched our understanding of what the word "mutation" refers to in a psychological context—as well as lay out some of its larger implications.

Morality

Nietzsche was deeply concerned that humanity had come to an impasse—a point where the old nostrums of conventional religion would no longer serve adequately to rein in the darker side of the human psyche. In this regard, he referred primarily to Christianity and Judaism, which were the dominant religions in Europe in his time. But while he focused on the Judeo-Christian milieu in which he lived, he insisted all along that this religious malaise was a worldwide phenomenon.

Cassandra-like, he predicted that the moralities and religions that the world knew in the nineteenth century would lead to nihilism.

Such provincialist religious "moralities"—he vaticinated—would lead to loss of any sense of a truer, *borderless* morality. Unfortunately, it is this kind of provincial "morality" that most humans believe in, and even worship, to this day. Given that fact, the loss of provincial "morality"—which most people falsely assume to be "the one and only" morality there is—would in turn result in a loss of any sense of communion with something universally good, true, and beautiful. Hence, the hopelessness of nihilism was inevitable.

The old ways—said Nietzsche—had run their course. A new morality—a new way of being—was called for, if the darkest dangers of nihilism were to be avoided.[1]

However, what could such a "new" morality be based on? Even in Nietzsche's time, we already should have known that a borderless morality could not be based on metaphysics nor on conventional religion. Immanuel Kant (1724-1804) and Ludwig Feuerbach (1804-1872), among many others, had led the way in showing why the claims of metaphysics and conventional religion have absolutely no foundation because of their me-centered regionalism and their lack of universality.

It is humans who create what they believe is "reality," by believing in their own flawed analyses—their metaphysics—Kant had shown.[2] It is humans who create what they mistakenly believe is "religion," through their flawed small-town analyses, Feuerbach had laid out.[3]

Nietzsche predicted that as the public became increasingly better educated, their disappointment in the old systems would

---

[1] See Nietzsche, *The Will to Power* (1901).
[2] Kant, *The Critique of Pure Reason* (1781).
[3] Feuerbach, *The Essence of Christianity* (1853).

lead first to cynicism and then to some form of psychological and social chaos. In fact, even the illiterate would be forced to see and experience the bankruptcy of their formerly morally reliable religions.

Psychologically, he said, there would be more depression and more dependence on some form of narcotic—religion having once been the great narcotic. But once religion failed us—as it has—use of chemical narcotics would be widespread, predicted Nietzsche. Socially, there would be more enmity and self-centeredness based on resentment and pettiness.

In other words, in order to see how accurate a prophet Nietzsche was in this respect, all we have to do is look all around us—or read or watch the daily news.

According to Nietzsche, humanity would find itself at a major crossroads, beginning in the twentieth century.

Either humans would discover a new way to be—he warned—or they would be overtaken by social disaster.

As he saw it, these were the only choices. Whichever we "choose" by the way we live our daily lives, that is what we choose for the entire human race. We and we alone are responsible for what happens in our daily lives and for what happens in the whole planet. There are no longer tribalist scriptures nor authorities to appeal to in the moral dimension, as there had been in the past.

If metaphysics and conventional religion—with their provincial, sham, me-centered "morality"—are cast aside, what could be the foundation for a new humanity, a new era? Even by Nietzsche's time, there was awareness of the limitations of the analytical mind for dealing effectively with ethical, aesthetic, and religious questions—yet those are the moral problems that each and every one of us must face, whether we like it or not. Even in Nietzsche's time it could be seen that the formerly successful analytical nostrums would no longer be of value—particularly after the formidable broadsides launched by Kant, Feuerbach, and many others.

If anything, the twentieth century turned that nineteenth-century insight—which then had the markings of a mere intellectual skirmish—into a social-political rout, a veritable nightmare. Today, only the militantly uneducated or the gullible would defend provincial religion and metaphysics, since religion and metaphysics can now be seen as being intrinsically divisive sources of confusion and conflict—much like what Nietzsche had predicted.

Yes—given their perennial origins—religions and ideologies based on universal morality all had and still have a borderless dimension. Unfortunately, borderlessness of any kind is not something that can be captured by an institution. If anyone tries to institutionalize borderless morality—as all the religions and ideologies based on universal morality have done—the result is a me-centered sham. This, anyone can see today.

So while institutions have an immense value in that they do get their source of inspiration from borderless morality, all institutions, in themselves, are me-centered enterprises. Lamentably, the me-centeredness implicit in all such religious institutions is clearly and intrinsically antagonistic to the borderlessness that lays at their source.

Institutions, then, are wonderful—but only if and to the extent that their followers keep in mind daily that it is the borderless morality that matters, not the me-centered externals of the institution in question.

The only true morality there is, is borderless morality. The very same morality must apply to every single human being. Anything and everything else is a pretentious and very dangerous sham, obviously.

This is precisely what the motto of the Theosophical Society had pointed out, even preceding Nietzsche by a few short years. That motto proposed "There is no religion higher than truth."

Mutation

Systems, methods, and institutions—despite their potential value, have failed us. To the extent that we identify with institutions rather than with the borderlessness that gives to institutions their value, to that extent we are bound to feel betrayed by those institutions. It is this kind of collapse that Nietzsche was predicting, and warning against.

What is required, in fact, is not a new *system* of some kind. Creating "new" systems is precisely what had been tried many times over millennia—and it has failed miserably, as we can see, all around us. What is required—pointed out Nietzsche—is *transformation.*

Nietzsche was presciently speaking of the urgent necessity in our lives for what K called "mutation."

K used often the word "mutation" in reference to a foundational psychological switch. He used that word in a manner similar to the way biologists use it, when they intend to refer to major transformations in biological organisms.

Humans must put behind them the resentment, fear, hope, and pettiness that always accompany reliance on the me-centered analytical mind—even within otherwise potentially inspiring institutions. We (especially to the extent that we adhere to institutions) have always depended on *concepts* and *regulations* for solving deeper issues—and deeper issues are not conceptual, nor are they amenable to analysis of any kind, as laid out thoroughly in *The Analytical Fallacy*, and briefly in Part One.

A new kind of human being *must* come into existence, said Nietzsche. What our dire situation requires is an altogether different kind of human being—a human being who is not a follower nor a believer, but an exemplar of borderlessness. What the radically new situation we find ourselves in requires is—in Nietzsche's words—an *Übermensch,* a superman:

> The Superman is one: whose self-mastery yields an abundance of the power to create; who exercises the master privilege of the free spirit—living *experimentally;* who bids farewell to the reverence of

youth and who stands apart from the views and values of the herd; who reverences enemies as allies; who knows how to forget and recuperate from the blows of life; who shakes off with a single shrug the vermin that eat deeply into others; whose overflowing plenitude and gratitude cleanse both body and spirit of all guilt and all *ressentiment*; who perceives that "body" and "spirit" are two names for a single mystery; who calls humankind to return in love to its true home, the Earth; whose every muscle quivers with a proud consciousness of a truly free will and a sovereign individuality that "no longer flows out into a God"; who realizes that creative individuality is indeed the Earth's goal and humanity's hope; who, without metaphysical consolations, affirms life not only in its joy but in all its horror and who, thereby, conquers nihilism.

. . . this "antinihilist; this victor over God and nothingness—*he must come one day.*"

The Superman is shaped in the school of self-overcoming whose curriculum requires both courage and discipline, and above all, the ability to distinguish between an asceticism that denies life and one that stands in its service. The school of self-overcoming gives birth to the creative will.[4]

It should be clarified that there are important differences between Nietzsche's understanding of the superman, and the perennials. However, everything Nietzsche has to say about "the superman" is applicable to and is consistent with things that HPB and K said about their respective perennial mentors.

K's numerous remarks about transformation-mutation point in the same direction—though in his talks and books he never once spoke of "perennials" under any name. But the mutation that K referred to points precisely to what HPB called (perennial) "initiation," which results in "adeptship." It refers, simultaneously, to the kind of human being that an *Übermensch* is.

That is, HPB, Nietzsche, and K were all referring to the same perennial phenomenon, but expressed what a perennial is when looked at from uniquely different perspectives. In the process, they had differing ways of pointing towards what transformation consists of. Therefore, the act of considering all three

---

[4] Novak, *The Vision of Nietzsche* (1996), 18-19. Passages quoted are from Nietzsche, *On the Genealogy of Morality* (1887), 1.10, 2.2, 2.24; and *The Gay Science* (1882), 285.

simultaneously enriches our understanding of who the perennials are, and what transformation is about. Doing so would hopefully help prevent confusions on the part of readers of this exploration.

An important aspect of what all three seem to be saying, is that it is only in the process of us mutating into perennials that there is any hope of creating a more harmonious, productive, caring, and enlightened society. That seems to be no more and no less than what Plato intimated when he proposed that a good society will be created only when only philosophers can be kings, and all kings are philosophers—"philosophers" being the non-analytical, the transformed.

Prescient TSers

Incidentally, this explains in part the high regard in which Nietzsche was held in theosophical and related circles, even while he was living. Such an embracing of Nietzsche was extremely rare at that time, since he was at least a century ahead of his time, and was largely ignored by his contemporaries. Even his closest friends did not understand his books, which went largely unread in his lifetime.

As addressed in Part One, Rudolf Steiner had been a prominent TS member for twenty years (1892-1912). While he was a TS member, Steiner met Nietzsche and wrote a series of articles as well as a book about him.[5]

Given the revolutionary nature of Nietzsche's insights and the fact that the rest of the world largely ignored him for more than half a century—except for Adolf Hitler and his followers, who grossly and even comically misunderstood him—such early interest on the part of TSers is clearly more than a passing curiosity.

In 1920, K—who had never in his whole life been a reader of non-fiction—read Nietzsche's *Thus Spoke Zarathustra* (1883), at the suggestion of friends. This work—which is a major source

---

[5] Steiner, *Friedrich Nietzsche, ein Kämpfer gegen Zeit* (1895).

for the notion of the superman—"impressed" K, according to his biographer Mary Lutyens (1908-1999).[6]

K on morality

It is quite instructive to see what K has to say about morality, in part because it shows his total grasp of what the likes of Kant, Feuerbach, and Nietzsche had been warning against. As K put it,

> To deny all morality is to be moral, for the accepted morality is the morality of respectability—and I'm afraid we all crave to be respected—which is to be recognised as good citizens in a rotten society.
>
> Respectability is very profitable and ensures you a good job and a steady income. The accepted morality of greed, envy and hate is the way of the establishment.
>
> When you totally deny all this, not with your lips but with your heart, then you are really moral. For this morality springs out of love and not out of any motive of profit, of achievement, of place in the hierarchy.
>
> There cannot be this love if you belong to a society in which you want to find fame, recognition, a position. Since there is no love in this, its morality is immorality. When you deny all this from the very bottom of your heart, then there is a virtue that is encompassed by love.[7]

This is an astonishing statement, in many different ways. First of all, there is, of course, the clarity and immense power of the statement itself.

But also, in that thoroughly clear and to the point statement, K was summarizing what Kant, Feuerbach, Nietzsche, and many others had expressed in more convoluted—and perhaps polemical—ways.

In that brief summary, K conveys exactly the same concerns that previous geniuses had tried to express—though no one had done so with K's level of clarity and simplicity. Further, there is absolutely no jargon and no system of thought involved in the

---

[6] Lutyens, *Krishnamurti: The Years of Awakening* (1975), 120.
[7] Krishnamurti, *The Only Revolution, Europe* Part 12, jkrishnamurti.org.

way K expresses this. His statement can be understood by anyone on Earth—which cannot be said about anyone who came before him.

In those simple words, K summarizes all the essential points that had been made by some of the most brilliant minds before him. Yet he communicates it with utter simplicity while very powerfully.

That statement, all by itself, shows—clearly and unambiguously—a level of genius that humanity had never seen before.

CHAPTER 10
The Perennial Explosion

WHAT NIETZSCHE SAID WAS INTRIGUINGLY SIMILAR in substance to the esoteric approach of the perennial wisdom in general, and of K in particular. In addition—and like HPB and K—he was so much ahead of his time, that it is hard not to see his contribution as being integral to the foundations of the grand perennial explosion that is still going on.

In fact, an important telling sign of the decline of the esoteric dimension in the New Age movement—especially in the TS—is its blissful ignorance of Nietzsche, its negation of K, and its misunderstanding and misrepresentation of HPB.

Borderless explosion

Contemporary with and subsequent to Nietzsche, there have been other revolutionary contributors in various fields—participants in the wisdom explosion who seem to have been similarly inspired by the borderless wisdom. Like Nietzsche, a number of them were perhaps peripherally but not necessarily directly connected with the work of the TS.

This non-institutionalized borderless openness suggests strongly that the wisdom explosion in the American Age was to be truly universal for the very first time in the very long (and largely sad) history of its major manifestations. The American Age explosion would be planetary, not regional—as the perennial wisdom had always manifested itself publicly in the past.

In addition, this time the perennial manifestation would not be presented in a way easily amenable to being institutionalized—such as the authoritarianism that had always corroded and diminished its previous expressions.

The closest that the wisdom explosion has come to being institutionalized is in its having manifested primarily through the TS—as well as through the TS's bewilderingly many spinoffs, each of which would claim for itself a kind of hegemony of the *borderless* wisdom.

That process of institutions pretending that they each are in a position to "own" the borderless wisdom, is nothing new. Such a pretension is, in fact, practically identical to what conventional religions and ideologies and "schools" have always done before.

Such misappropriations are a main reason why previous perennial efforts have failed miserably. In fact, this previous failure of institutions was alarmingly revealed by Nietzsche. Even more relevantly to the present exploration, it is precisely this point that was affirmed unambiguously by the Mahachohan in the one letter ever received from him publicly.[1]

As the Mahachohan put it, "[I]t's time theosophy enter the arena."[2] The Mahachohan is stating quite plainly and poignantly that "theosophy" had *never before* been in a position to "enter the arena" of worldwide, mainstream presence.

That ubiquitousness of the perennial wisdom has now been made possible by the American Age presence throughout the planet—and by the borderless message of J. Krishnamurti, which is the keynote transformative approach of the new era. Whatever anyone may believe (or not) regarding HPB's perennial mentors, one thing can be said, irrefutably:

The borderless wisdom has now indeed "entered the arena."

It strikes me that the present non-institutionalized universality of the age-old wisdom goes to the very heart of why America's founding documents were presented to the world at large as giving the (wrong) impression that they were merely components in the mundane process of creating a nation.

That would also explain why the TS was founded as "just another institution," while numerous American Age perennial pioneers were inspired by it while either being outside of it, or

---

[1] The Mahachohan is the most senior perennial known to have been connected with the TS through correspondence.
[2] Chin, *The Mahatma Letters, Chronological* (1993), Appendix II, 477; Jinarajadasa, *Letters From the Masters of the Wisdom, First Series* (1923), 1.

being in it and then leaving it in order to promote specific contributions of their own.

This time, in the American Age, the perennial effort would be delivered worldwide, not regionally.

This time, that effort would be deliberately not institutionalized, as had always been the case before.

This time, the onus would be on transformation at the individual level, not on creating an "authoritative" system that followers would adhere to.

This time, we would all each have to take responsibility for planetary as well as personal welfare, rather than assume that "it's all up to" the presumed "authorities."

The perennial wisdom has, indeed, "entered the arena," finally.

Given the unique nature of this most recent expression of the timeless wisdom, it seems appropriate to speak of the grand historical phenomenon of our times as being "a perennial explosion."

TS decline

Despite the central place conferred upon the TS as a perennial *popularizer*, the expression "wisdom (or 'perennial') explosion" describes the phenomenon more accurately than phrases such as "the theosophical movement" or "the New Age movement" might—especially considering the shallowness that tends to be associated by many with such titles.

The wisdom (as well as the reality) of this insight is borne out by the worldwide decline of the TS—even as a popularizer. It is important to point clearly to that decline—otherwise, "popularizers" are bound to misunderstand.

The beginning of the TS's decline can be dated to the moment when K was kicked out of the TS by its leaders, soon after he had announced in 1929 that "truth is a pathless land."

It is instructive to see how this awkwardly embarrassing and very sad moment for the TS took place. One day, when Krishnaji returned to his room at the TS international headquarters in 1933 (soon after AB's funeral), he unexpectedly found his luggage outside the door. He couldn't get in, because the lock had been changed. That's how K found out that he wasn't wanted or welcome in the TS anymore.[3]

Soon after this shameful event, TS leaders who had taken over after AB's death started the rumor that Krishnaji had "left the TS." Most TS members still believe that Orwellian yarn, to this day.

As noted up to this point in this exploration, TS members had been creating a Victorian-minded me-centered ideology that was profoundly incompatible with the actual borderless wisdom. Comically and tragically, many of them still give those Victorian-oriented me-centered beliefs the name of "Theosophy."

This incompatibility between the cultish belief system created and the actual wisdom was not altogether evident early on—due to a perennial presence in its leadership and in a few of its most attentive and sensitive members, in the first five decades of TS history. But that period crashed into its end upon the deaths of AB and CWL—and the unceremonious ousting of K from its midst.

Those events were centrally responsible for the TS's decline, from that point on. In its beginnings—and up to that inflection point—the TS had been a major and powerful inspiration to numerous leaders of every aspect of culture, everywhere.[4] Though diminishing as time went by, that influence continued even after

---

[3] This detail is not in any of K's biographies, though all such writings document the fact that K never left the TS, and that he continued to be deeply interested in it until he died. I can further attest to K's intense interest in the TS, as told to me in personal communications from Radha Burnier (1923-2013). Radhaji was the seventh international TS President. The specifics of K's unceremonious ousting were related to me by Enrique Orfila (n.d.) a very serious TS life member and engineer who had been the caretaker of the TS Headquarters campus grounds and buildings in Adyar, India, for 25 years (1952-1977). Numerous TS members who had been in Adyar at the time had related the sad event to him. Others confirmed this personally to me, when I was in Adyar in 2002-2003.

[4] The immense influence of the TS, worldwide, is addressed and documented in the upcoming *Muse: H.P. Blavatsky's Insights for a New era of Chaos, Revolution, Wisdom—and Krishnamurti.*

its leadership and many members moved away from its glorious, culture-transforming beginnings. However much it has dwindled, TS influence on culture continues even now, despite its clear decline, as an institution.

New Age heyday

As the TS decline intensified with the passing of years after 1933, the New Age movement that came from it—with its very strong Victorian-minded tendencies—gained momentum. At first, this New Age progress was hardly noticeable by mainstreamers. It was only in the 1960s—mainly (though not exclusively) through the so-called "counter-culture" movement—and in the 1970s, when it really took off. My personal recollection (accurately or not) tells me that it was in the year 1970 that the expression "New Age" began to come into its own, even in the mainstream.

All of a sudden—or so it seemed to some of us who witnessed it, at the time—"New Agey" concepts and beliefs began to become an intrinsic part of the mainstream, everywhere on the planet. A series of ads told us that Coke was the drink "for the new age." New Agey teachings began to be commonplace "everywhere"—even including in major feature films.

Some prominent films—such as *Down and Out in Beverly Hills* (1986), which inspired the creation of a TV sitcom of the same name—were dedicated exclusively to lampooning while describing (and perhaps promoting) New Age behaviors and beliefs. There were many such films—some of them merely descriptive, some of them showing a darker side to the movement, some of them promoting New Age concepts. Most of this kind of New Age promotion took place without ever mentioning the expression "New Age."

Ever since the 1960s—especially in the first three decades or so since that period—it has seemed as if everybody and her sister has had a guru. At the same time, every other guru seemed to claim to be "the avatar of the new era."[5] Victorian-inspired New Agers had come into their own, and there seemed to be no end to what they assumed was their presumably deep understanding of "all and everything" (as in the title of Gurdjieff's book series).

Ever since that time, many New Agers have tended to present themselves as if they knew something—a very important "something"—that mainstreamers didn't know. At the end of the day, New Agers could be said to have been acting as if they were unique revolutionaries—revolutionaries in that they thought they had just discovered latte.

Cool Victorians

Yet despite all the New Age hoopla everywhere, there is at least one intriguing and usually unknown fact about it all: Everything that could be called "New Age" had come—directly or indirectly—from the TS *popularizing* understanding of what "the new era" is about.

One result of this ignorance on the part of New Agers regarding their TS pedigree carries with it an implication bound to be deemed undesirable by any self-respecting New Ager. Allow me to explain.

First off, I should share that, as it happens, all New Agers I have met have assumed that their beliefs and practices make them somehow "cool" and "above the mainstream" and "knowing what no one else knows." Yet there is an inconvenient truth related to such assumptions—an inconvenient truth that New Agers (including TSers) may find very difficult to accept.

New Agers' understanding of "all and everything" is very often actually a comical-tragic rehash of early Victorian TS notions. Such notions were based on severely serious Victorian misunderstandings of what HPB and her perennial mentors actually had shared with all of us.

Lost in the bewildering shuffle of beliefs, gurus, "channelings," practices, and "esoteric (sic) teachings," is the fact that

---

[5] For some specific "avatars of the new era," see Chapter 26, "Aurobindo."

most—if not all of it—came from a Victorian misunderstanding of the very ancient yet ever new perennial wisdom, which is borderless and timeless.

By their beliefs and practices, New Agers are but a reincarnation of Victorians—proud heirs of the Victorian era, and its beliefs and presumptions—despite the pervasive assumption among them that they are unusually "at the leading edge," plus being cool and savvy.

Despite that misstep, there is no denying that the TS's charge to "popularize" the borderless wisdom has been a resounding success, in the form of the amazingly pervasive New Age movement, throughout the planet.

Yet in many ways, this "triumph" of the New Age movement—which we can see all around us, in the twenty-first century—turned out to be a kind of Pyrrhic perennial victory. After all, that triumph has taken place at the expense of participants being profoundly and multi-dimensionally unaware of the borderless wisdom, whence it all came. In addition, what was originally a Victorian attempt at *popularizing* the borderless wisdom has turned into a *vulgarization* of it. Popularization—despite its serious shortcomings—has been good. Vulgarization, not so much.

This pesky problem was there even from the start—beginning in the 1870s, when the TS was being formed and founded. So it is of very great value to bring awareness to the chasm there is between popularized "teachings" and "practices," and the intrinsically unteachable *universal* wisdom.

The theosophical movement is unquestionably the center around which much of the perennially-inspired New Age and other related presentations have turned. But the perennial explosion that we are all witnessing is clearly more comprehensive and more pervasive than what is possible to convey through a single institution. As one of HPB's perennials said in a letter addressed to a British Theosophist in the 1880s:

> Europe is a large place but the world is bigger yet. The sun of Theosophy must shine for all, not for a part. There is more to this movement than you have yet had an inkling of, and the work of the TS is

linked in with similar work that is secretly going on in all parts of the world.[6]

The presence of numerous circles of theosophical influence throughout the world is amply documented, for instance, by James Webb (1946-1980) in his book *The Occult Establishment*.[7] Webb's act of documenting the pervasiveness of "Theosophy" in the grand wisdom explosion is all the more intriguing, given Webb's obvious lack of sympathy for it. He refers to Theosophy sarcastically as being "irrational." So he acknowledges this crucial important TS contribution very much in spite of his personal predilections.

Indian turn-around

Apart from being the main source for the New Age culture—which has spread far and wide, everywhere—there have been numerous other factors related to the perennial explosion. For instance, the work of HPB's perennial mentors has ben instrumental in bringing about major shifts in several Asian cultures. Those cultures have experienced significant transformations as a result of this powerful input—and that in turn has had a great impact on subsequent developments in religion, philosophy, psychology, and social life, all over the world.

Though this influence is well documented, it is unfortunately not generally known—much less acknowledged and incorporated into accounts of this most important historical phenomenon of our times. The wisdom explosion influence that I point to here is but the tip of an enormous iceberg—and the subject of works in progress, beginning with *Muse*.

In that respect, it is intriguing to note the major shift in presentation that the TS underwent when HPB and HSO

---

[6] Chin, *The Mahatma Letters, Chronological* (1993), 133, Letter 48; Humphreys and Benjamin, *The Mahatma Letters* (1962), 267, Letter 47.

[7] Webb, *The Occult Establishment* (1976), 43-46, 53; see also Green, *Prophets of a New Age* (1992), 65; see also Lachman, *Madame Blavatsky* (2012), among many other authors and titles.

transferred the TS headquarters from New York City to India, in 1879. It is only from that inflection point on that the TS began to be associated with "Asian" culture, especially that of India.

Contemporary Victorians—particularly in India—took it for granted that the universal wisdom was "Indian," and that "therefore" most of what HPB was addressing had been "derived from" Indian texts. British citizens and Anglo-Indians who were friendly to the TS, in particular, made the slap-happy laughable assumption that this "ancient wisdom" was thereby somehow "part of the empire."

One result of those early TS clueless and misguided developments has been that countless books have been written about how "Theosophy" came from "Indian scriptures"—ignoring the fact that *Isis Unveiled*, which HPB had published while still in New York, in 1877, addresses primarily Western traditions, religions, culture, and science.

From the beginning, HPB had made it very clear that the "wisdom religion" that she had been referring to was planetary, not regional.

But Victorians never listened. As the Victorians that they were, they assumed that they knew better. Their kindred intellectual heirs and descendants still don't—and their tumor-like group-thinks have metastasized throughout the world, including in the TS.

A major reason for the move to India seems to have been related to India's much richer and older *and living* understanding of the universal wisdom than what was possible in America or even in Europe. There was at least another major reason for the move, but even mentioning it would be more of a distraction than is necessary, in the context of the present inquiry—so I'll leave that for future publications.

It was important to start the movement in America, not only because HSO and HPB were both Americans—HSO having been a "Yankee" born in its heartland, and HPB by choice. After all— as many references in HPB's works point out—it is in America that the great perennial work of our times was to spring from.

For reasons outlined throughout this exploration, the perennial explosion that we're all witnessing can be said to be but a first salvo in what I call "the American Age." But once the move took place, India and all its culture took center stage, in many ways.

What the lion's share of those who have written about this have missed is what strikes me as being the elephant in the room. Most of such authors have made the grossly mistaken assumption that "Theosophy" comes from "Asian sources"— mainly Indian sources. Anyone who makes that assumption is thereby doomed to fail in understanding anything and everything having to do with HPB in particular, and with the American Age in general.

The universal wisdom doesn't belong to any culture or region of the world. It is within each and every one of us. It has expressed itself in numerous ways, throughout the history of every nation and region of the world.

That is a simple yet immensely profound statement. Anyone who ignores it has thereby doomed herself to misunderstand anything and everything having to do with "all and everything." The evidence for this simple yet profound fact is there, for anyone open-minded enough to look at facts while putting aside old nostrums based on me-centered conditioning.

Regarding the TS and HPB, it's not difficult at all to see clearly that the perennial wisdom is prior to all Asian culture— including the Indian. In fact, Indian culture—just like all other cultures—was inspired and came from the universal, borderless wisdom. HPB and her perennial mentors said this till they were blue in the face.

But Victorians weren't listening—and their intellectual descendants still aren't. They assumed—then and now—that they knew and know better. It is based on that simultaneously comical and tragic misunderstanding that the beginnings of the perennial explosion have been tainted by.

Given the gross limitations of Victorian misunderstandings, one thing should be made very clear: Despite gross interference at the hands of "know-it-all" Victorians (old and new), the popularized version that they wrested from the actual wisdom has had an immense influence on all human culture.

Asian renaissance

An example of this profound planetary TS influence is the developments that took place in the so-called Hindu Renaissance in the twentieth century. Mohandas K. Gandhi (1869-1948) is widely acknowledged as a pivotal figure in this historically significant movement. However, it is rarely—if ever—recognized that what started him on his path toward reform and revolution and a deeper understanding of religion was his contact with HPB and her colleagues.

In his *Autobiography*, Gandhi explains how he left India for England in 1888 (when he was 18), yearning to become as British as he could—and leaving behind what he then perceived to be the "superstitions" of Indian culture. His renunciation of everything Indian was so thorough, that he was officially ostracized just before his departure by Hindu religious authorities—in an act that members of the semitic religions might refer to as "excommunication." This was so serious, that it may well have been a main reason—and perhaps the only reason—why when Gandhi left England he didn't return to India, but went to Africa, instead.

In London, however, he met HPB and her students in 1889. They showed him the enormous and very real value of the Hindu scriptures for all humanity—something he had not even conceived before. His main tutors were Bertram (1860-1944) and Archibald Keightley (1859-1930), who were intimate friends of HPB, and were the editors of HPB's magnum opus, *The Secret Doctrine* (1888).

The day he was assassinated, Gandhi was still speaking of how Theosophy is the deeper side of Hinduism.

Importantly, all of Gandhi's biographers—without exception—omit this critical and even life-defining TS background to his work. This means that the only reliable source for this critical starting point for Gandhi's revolutionary and deeply religious life, is Gandhi himself.[8]

It is important to note that there have been at least several other cases just like Gandhi, where biographers fail to reveal the HPB-related sources for the respective influential contributions of the subjects of their biographies. But that, too, is a subject for another time.

It is true that one person does not a revolution make—even someone as influential as Gandhi was. Other salient figures of what has come to be called "the Hindu Renaissance," among many others, include Rabindranath Tagore (1861-1941), Sri Bhagavan Das (1869-1958), Jawaharlal Nehru (1889-1964), and Sarvepalli Radhakrishnan (1888-1975). They all contributed importantly to the twentieth-century Hindu Renaissance and to worldwide culture, and are universally acknowledged as some of the most visible leaders of that aspect of the perennial explosion.

What is not widely known—much less acknowledged—is that they were all members of the TS. Bhagavan Das and Radhakrishnan in particular were following in the footsteps of HPB's perennial mentors in their expositions of Indian culture and philosophy, which have been greatly influential throughout the whole planet.

Another major landmark in the Hindu Renaissance was the establishment of the Central Hindu College (CHC) in Benares in 1898. This was the first educational institution in India where a high level of respect for Indian scriptures and philosophy joined hands with rigorous European scholarly methods.

But there is one fact that is not widely acknowledged in accounts of the unprecedented transformations that ensued in India's cultural and political life as a result of CHC's existence: The College was founded by Annie Besant (AB), who became the second international president of the TS. AB continued to work on the College's behest—and made numerous other seminal

---

[8] See Gandhi, *My Experiments with Truth: Autobiography* (1948), especially p. 68.

contributions to India's culture and political life—until her death in 1933.[9]

Ornithologist Allan Octavian Hume (1829-1912) is well known in India for being the founder of the Indian National Congress Party—which has been the dominant political party in India for most of its independence-related history. The Party goes back to the 1880s, and it's still a major political force—having been associated with the likes of Gandhi, Nehru, and Indira Gandhi (1917-1984).

What is usually either not known or belittled—even in India—is the fact that A.O. Hume was one of the main early correspondents with the perennials who inspired the foundation of the TS, and was a TS member, as well.

There are numerous other references to the very intimate relationship there is between the Hindu Renaissance and the TS, but this is not the place for going any further into this. Hopefully, what has been said is enough to show the very real and palpable nature of that relationship—for anyone who takes facts seriously.

In any case—and even independently of those easily confirmable facts—anyone today who is involved in any practice or approach that came initially from Asia owes a great deal to the pioneering work of the TS and its members. This includes not just elements that clearly came to "the West" from India, such as yoga and meditation: Other elements in worldwide culture today, such as international Buddhism and Taoist practices, owe a great deal to the pace-setting, pioneering work of early TS members—as well as the very many who were influenced by them.[10]

---

[9] For AB's profound and multidimensional influence on Indian culture, see *Annie Besant in India* (2021), compiled by C.V. Agarwal and Pedro Oliveira.

[10] I have addressed this all-encompassing influence of HPB and her colleagues in *Muse;* also see the website, paradigmshift.network. But this has also been documented by an ever-increasing number of researchers. A good place to start looking into this research is HPB's biography, Cranston, *HPB: The Extraordinary Life & Influence of Helena Blavatsky, Founder of the Modern Theosophical Movement* (1993), particularly Part 7, "The Century After"; see also most books by Gary Lachman, especially *Madame Blavatsky: The Mother of Modern Spirituality* (2012), and *The Secret*

The Perennial Wisdom

The perennial wisdom—which HPB often called "Theosophy," among many other names—is borderless, and does not belong to any single culture or regional tradition. It is not strictly Asian, as has been suggested by some writers without any evidence, just as it is not European, African, Australian, or Toltec. It transcends all of these—as well as many other specific traditions. Like gravity, it is everywhere—and nowhere in particular. As HPB put it,

> The Secret Doctrine was the universally diffused religion of the ancient and prehistoric world . . . showing its character and presence in every land, together with the teaching of all its great adepts.[11]

Most importantly, the perennial wisdom is within each and every one of us. In its essence, it is not some "school of thought" or practice. Nor is it a set of beliefs, nor a methodology. The borderless wisdom—by its very nature—is not amenable to being institutionalized.

A wider and truer understanding of the perennial wisdom is more likely to be had by not holding fast to traditional, regional or conceptual interpretations. Particular individuals and even schools dedicated to being as perennial as possible may *incidentally* have beliefs, methodologies, systems, hierarchies, and so on. But the essence of the universal wisdom has its being exclusively when there is no me-centeredness.

If and to the extent that there is me-centeredness, the borderless wisdom is not there. THAT is what matters. All else is unessential—and potentially dangerous, as Nietzsche had warned.[12]

For instance, a fundamental perennial insight is that wisdom is a state of awareness in which insight and compassion pervade. Christians sometimes refer to that all-comprehensive

---

Teachers of the Western World (2015); see also the works of James Webb, *The Occult Underground* (1974), *The Occult Establishment* (1976), and *The Harmonious Circle* (1980).

[11] Blavatsky, *The Secret Doctrine*, I xxxiv.

[12] See Chapter 9, "Nietzsche."

state of being by the name "Christ." Buddhists might call it "Avalokiteshvara," while people in other religions and cultures give it yet other names. The wisdom within us tell us that the names and the cultural trappings that go with them are of little importance.

What is important is daily communion with this insight-compassion.

Many Christians, however, become caught up in the traditional trappings surrounding insight-compassion and insist that it is only accessible through the name and form and concept of "Christ" as "our (only) Lord and Savior."

Communion with universal insight and compassion is thus turned into holding certain beliefs and accepting "authorities," and following hierarchies. This is used by some people who call themselves "Christians" to justify segregating themselves from those who do not share *their beliefs and practices.*

In this way, the universal, borderless, perennial insight is turned into something incompatible with it. The borderless thereby becomes particular, provincial, quarrelsome, and limited. This happens, of course, not only in Christianity but in *all* religions, ideologies, cultures and group-thinks—as K constantly pointed out, from the beginning of his work until his death in 1986.

The Perennial Philosophy

In 1944, Aldous Huxley was the first ever to use the expression "perennial philosophy," in the sense it has come to have.[13] However, he was following HPB's lead in using that phrase to refer to the same body of ancient insights that HPB had written extensively about.

HPB alternately spoke of "occult philosophy," and "the Hermetic teachings," and "*gupta vidya,*" and "occultism," and "the ancient wisdom" and "esoteric teachings," and "the secret doctrine," and "theosophy," among a number of other appellations.

---

[13] Huxley, *The Perennial Philosophy* (1944).

What HPB was referring to by all these various expressions, is much the same wisdom-religion that Huxley would talk about half a century after her death, when he referred to "the perennial philosophy."

Intriguingly, even though HPB was the original author of this insight, Huxley never gave her credit for it—at least publicly. Other scholars who have spoken of "the perennial philosophy" have followed in his footsteps—as if they all belonged to a secret club that takes from HPB but without giving her any credit. As far as these many scholars and their surrogates are concerned, when it comes to HPB, "mum" is the password for membership in the secret club.

As spelled out in Part One and in Chapter 29, "Skeptics," it strikes me as prudent and wise, whenever referring to the perennial wisdom, to depart from any reference to the word "philosophy." That word—which used to be wonderful, when Pythagoras coined it and Plato popularized and gave it visibility—has been transmogrified. That word now has analytical, divisive, exoteric, and intelligence-challenged connotations.

I suggest instead to refer to "the perennial *wisdom*." In doing so, I am also departing from HPB's appellations, which were eminently appropriate in the nineteenth century—and which now sound like they came from . . . the nineteenth century.

Then was then

We have now experienced far more fully the perennial explosion—or whatever else anyone wishes to call the grand phenomenon that we all have been witnessing, often unawares. That massive, worldwide movement includes everything having to do with "the New Age," as well as the many revolutions in different areas of human interest and concern—such as religion, literature, politics, education, cinema, feminism, racial confrontations, and others.

At the center of this grand cultural explosion—as outlined ever-so-briefly in Part One—is J. Krishnamurti. So the names used by HPB to refer to *wisdom* (plain and simple)—useful as they were in their time—now sound like, well, quaint nineteenth century jargon. They are still excellent museum pieces, to be appreciated by scholars and other passers-by. But then was then.

Yet one must ever keep in mind the immense depth and wisdom in K's expression—which he used many times—"the word is not the thing." K was a master at articulating sometimes very deep and highly sophisticated insights by using surprisingly simple language—as noted earlier. "The word is not the thing" is a great example of that. Don't get caught up with the word, K suggests. Look carefully, borderlessly, and intently—and ineffably—at what the word tries fruitlessly to point to.

Does it matter all that much, if one calls this *reality* "occultism" or "secret doctrine" or "theosophy" or "perennial philosophy"—or "perennial wisdom"? Perhaps that is important—but only to the shallow and the intelligence-challenged—who may insist on using a certain specific terminology, and no other.

What matters in this context is for one to realize that there has existed—as far back in history as one can go, and everywhere on the planet—a body of compassionate-insightful human beings, moral geniuses who have shared with the rest of us something of that *perennial wisdom.* According to HPB, such wisdom-intelligence existed throughout the planet even long before the history that we now know of—as affirmed in the *Secret Doctrine,* as quoted at the beginning of this chapter.

If you are not aware of the existence of this borderless perennial wisdom, dear reader, it can only be because you have not researched this subject sufficiently, or at all. Some of those who *have* researched it—sometimes reluctantly—have written books such as this one, which addresses and acknowledges that reality.

The shallow and the unresearchers can reject it—*without evidence, one may add*—till they are blue in the face.

Yet there it is.

CHAPTER 11
The Perennial Wisdom

IT SHOULD BE EXPLAINED THAT the word *occultism* (and its cognates)—which was employed extensively by HPB and her early students—was used by her strictly as a synonym for the perennial wisdom. In her writings, that family of words never has the connotations of evil and the supernatural that they have had in the writings of other authors.

Occultism

After having looked intently and carefully into this for decades, my perception is that the word "occultism" (and its cognates) was used by HPB's perennial mentors *precisely* because it was inevitably bound to provoke negative knee-jerk reactions on the part of the prejudiced, in the nineteenth century and beyond. The word "occultism" was deliberately intended to *provoke* Victorians and Victorian-minded people. That word was not meant necessarily to *define* the perennial wisdom—as many HPB contemporaries *assumed*.

The perennial wisdom has always appealed to truth-seeking-truth-finding faculties in us—*and we all have such faculties*. Its appeal has never been directed at me-centered and never-questioned preconceptions we may have acquired, through our conditioning.

Anyone who wants to understand what HPB and her perennial mentors meant by "occultism"—or anything else they said, for that matter—will have to work at finding out what they meant. Importantly, "what they meant" can only be discovered by intelligence—and intelligence requires the absence of the conditioned me.

By using words such as "occultism," HPB's perennial mentors were winnowing out those who by their very prejudices would exclude themselves even from gaining *knowledge* of the perennial wisdom—not to mention encountering wisdom itself. In any case, in the present context, it is important to keep this in mind whenever references are made (often in period quotations) to K's "occult" or "inner" life, in order to avoid confusion. In *The Key to Theosophy*, which was written in the form of questions and answers on various subjects related to the perennial wisdom, HPB commented *(emphasis added)*:

> . . . The "Wisdom-Religion" was one in antiquity; and the sameness of primitive religious philosophy is proven to us by the identical doctrines *taught to the Initiates during the MYSTERIES, an institution once universally diffused.* "All the old worships indicate the existence of a single Theosophy anterior to them. The Key that is to open one must open all, otherwise it cannot be the right key."
>
> . . . So it is in our day. We can show the line of descent of every Christian religion, as of every, even the smallest, sect. The latter are the minor twigs or shoots grown on the larger branches; but shoots and branches spring from the same trunk—the WISDOM-RELIGION. To prove this was the aim of Ammonius [Saccas], who endeavored to induce Gentiles and Christians, Jews and Idolaters, to lay aside their contentions and strifes, remembering only that they were all in possession of the same truth under various vestments, and were all the children of a common mother. This is the aim of Theosophy likewise.[1]

Please, attentive reader, look carefully at what she says, at the top of that quote: She is telling us in her unique way of addressing such subjects, that you must be an initiate in order to understand any of what she says in her extensive writings. This is not some theory. Rather, it is a description of an actuality— an actuality that one must take seriously, if one is ever to have any hope of understanding properly any of what came out of HPB and her perennial mentors.

Only someone who is transformed—someone moving away from being me-centered and conditioned by a particular groupthink (whether ethnic, or cultural, or ideological), is qualified even to *begin* to understand what the perennial wisdom is about.

---

[1] Blavatsky, *Key to Theosophy* (1889), 4, 5.

The perennial wisdom is not about reading books nor about accumulating knowledge nor about believing in this or that.

The perennial wisdom is about actually undergoing a switch in consciousness—a switch that goes from assuming as "given" that which we learned from our mommies and daddies, and into a mature consciousness. That "new" consciousness *initiates* a new life by taking responsibility for all of its actions, rather than childishly transferring that responsibility to "God" or to "the priest" or to "the guru" or to some never-questioned set of beliefs.

"Initiation"—this major switch in our consciousness, *in your consciousness—must* take place. Otherwise you'll find yourself in the same position as that of a dog chasing its own tail, going round-and-round without ever getting anywhere.

If there is not this major switch—this *"initiation" into intelligence* that HPB refers to throughout her writings—you may become a true-believer belonging to some cult, and call yourself "a Theosophist" on the grounds that you believe in this or that. But if that is what your "Theosophy" is, then, clearly, you are not an esoteric, you are not *a theosophist*, in any truly relevant sense of the word. In the words immortalized by the late great Duke Ellington (1899-1974):

> It don't mean a thing, if it ain't got that swing.[2]

If it doesn't have the vibrancy that only the esoteric life can confer, the "Theosophy" that many still believe in—with its provincial, unhistorical, unphilosophical, unquestioned understanding of "metaphysics" and "mythology"—is but another form of solipsism. There is zero intelligence in *that*. It may be entertaining for the purpose of playing with oneself, but it is clearly irrelevant, at the end of the day, to *the esoteric act and process* of dying to the me, without which no "Theosophical" system has much value—if any.

---

[2] Duke Ellington, lyrics by Irving Mills (of the Mills Brothers), *It Don't Mean a Thing If it Ain't Got that Swing* (1932).

It don't mean a thing, if it ain't got that swing.

HPB also said that the "wisdom-religion," or perennial wisdom, had been taught secretly for millennia in all major cultures of the world. In fact, what she actually said was much stronger than that. She stated that in our prehistory, the "wisdom-religion" was taught and practiced in the whole planet, and that it doesn't belong to any one region or culture. As she put it,

> The Secret Doctrine was the universally diffused religion of the ancient and prehistoric world . . . showing its character and presence in every land.[3]

Importantly, anyone interested in becoming acquainted with the perennial wisdom's insights and practices, she said, would have to be initiated into its "mysteries." Anything else is just grist for the me-centered analyzer, and is unrelated to the universal wisdom.

The word *mystery* comes from the Greek *mysterion*, meaning "secret rite" or "divine secret." This word in turn is related to *mystes*, "one initiated into the mysteries." K's process, as well as several initiations he underwent prior to the process—*according to him*, and as documented in *The Inner Life of Krishnamurti*—were said by him and by his perennial mentors to be part of that perennial practice.[4]

Why, we might ask, do such initiations—*and the lifestyle they imply*—need to be secret? The word *occult*—which means "hidden"—was applied to these experiences and lifestyle in part largely because they were traditionally veiled in secrecy.

More importantly, this is a "secrecy" from the mundane world—the world in which the conditioned me rules.

---

[3] Blavatsky, *The Secret Doctrine* (1888 ed.), I xxxiv.
[4] For Krishnamurti stating in 1979 that he underwent several initiations, see Krishnamurti, *Truth and Actuality*, 86-89; see also Sanat, *The Inner Life of Krishnamurti*, 261-267.

To understand the necessity for this secrecy, it is best to quote HPB at length, since she provides the background for our discussion of the perennial wisdom *(emphasis added)*:

The WISDOM-RELIGION was ever one, and being the last word of possible human knowledge, was, therefore, carefully preserved. It preceded by long ages the Alexandrian Theosophists [Ammonius Saccas (175-242) and his disciples], reached the modern, and will survive every other religion and philosophy.

. . . [*It was preserved*] *among Initiates of every country; among profound seekers after truth*—their disciples; and in those parts of the world where such topics have always been most valued and pursued: In India, Central Asia, and Persia.

. . . The best proof you can have of the fact [of its esoteric nature] is that *every ancient religious, or rather philosophical, cult consisted of an esoteric or secret teaching, and an exoteric (outward, public) worship.* Furthermore, it is a well-known fact that the MYSTERIES of the ancients comprised with every nation the "Greater" (secret) and "Lesser" (public) MYSTERIES—e.g., in the celebrated solemnities called the *Eleusinia*, in Greece.

From *the Hierophants of Samothrace, Egypt, and the initiated Brahmins* of the India of old, down to the later Hebrew Rabbis, all preserved, for fear of profanation, their real *bona fide* beliefs secret. The Jewish Rabbis called their secular religious series the Mercavah (the exterior body), "the vehicle," or, *the covering which contains the hidden soul*—i.e., their highest secret knowledge.

Not one of the ancient nations ever imparted through its priests its real philosophical secrets to the masses, but allotted to the latter only the husks. Northern Buddhism has its "greater" and its "lesser" vehicle, known as the *Mahayana,* the esoteric, and the *Hinayana*, the exoteric, Schools. Nor can you blame them for such secrecy; for surely *you would not think of feeding your flock of sheep on learned dissertations on botany instead of grass?*

Pythagoras called his Gnosis "the knowledge of things that are" . . . *and preserved that knowledge for his pledged disciples only: for those who could digest such mental food and feel satisfied; and he pledged them to silence and secrecy.*

Occult alphabets and secret ciphers are the development of the old Egyptian *hieratic* writings, *the secret of which was, in the days of old, in the possession only of the Hierogrammatists, or initiated* Egyptian priests.

Ammonius Saccas, as his biographers tell us, bound his pupils by oath not to divulge his higher doctrines except to those who had

153

already been instructed in preliminary knowledge, and who were also bound by a pledge.

Finally, do we not find the same even in early Christianity, among the Gnostics, and even in the teachings of Christ? Did he not speak to the multitudes in parables which had a two-fold meaning, and explain his reasons only to his disciples?

"To you," he says, "it is given to know the mysteries of the kingdom of heaven; but unto them that are without, all these things are done in parables" (Mark iv; 11). The Essenes of Judea and Carmel made similar distinctions, dividing their adherents into neophytes, brethren, and the perfect, or those initiated. Examples might be brought from every country to this effect.[5]

HPB is telling us—unambiguously and with absolutely total clarity—that there must be initiation, before anyone is in a position to understand, even remotely, what the perennial wisdom is. If there is no initiation, there is no perennial wisdom.

HPB is saying—with transparent clarity, that if there is no initiation, there is no "theosophy."

It don't mean a thing, if it ain't got that swing.

Wilber, Watts, and the perennial wisdom

HPB was the first person in history to make widely known to the public the existence of the perennial wisdom. She did so *by popularizing its husk*. According to her, a new era—an era in which what used to be hidden would become widely available—was to begin at this time.

If she was right about this, it might explain, for instance, the unprecedented popularity of formerly secret paths, such as the Kabbalah, Tantra, Toltec, Zen, and Tibetan Buddhism. Those schools had been hermetically sealed to outsiders since their inception—until the HPB-inspired perennial explosion brought them out into public notice. HPB's presence and insights at the end of the nineteenth century were said to represent the first salvo of that "new dispensation" or "new age."

---

[5] Blavatsky, *Key to Theosophy* (1889), 7, 8, 9.

Subsequently, numerous scholars and authors—beginning even before Aldous Huxley—have made statements (usually without giving credit to HPB) confirming and expanding upon what she said on the subject. For instance, Ken Wilber (b. 1949), is generally known to be one of the leading contemporary exponents of transpersonal psychology. Without referring to HPB—even though she was *the* source for everything that he and Alan Watts (1915-1973) had to say on the subject—Wilber states that:

> The perennial philosophy is the worldview that has been embraced by the vast majority of the world's greatest spiritual teachers, philosophers, thinkers, and even scientists. It's called "perennial" or "universal" because it shows up in virtually all cultures across the globe and across the ages. We find it in India, Mexico, China, Japan, Mesopotamia, Egypt, Tibet, Germany, Greece . . .
> And wherever we find it, it has essentially similar features, it is in essential agreement the world over. We moderns, who can hardly agree on anything, find this rather hard to believe.[6]

The careful reader will note that Wilber gives the impression that "the perennial philosophy" that he talks about is just "knowledge" that any Tom, Dick, or Harriette can have, and accumulate. In doing so, Wilber puts himself in exactly the same position that the Victorian-minded had been putting themselves in, since the 1870s.

Wilber does not even mention initiation as the starting point. Instead, he continues to promote the well-worn Victorian yarn that the perennial wisdom is "a system of knowledge" for *anyone* to believe in. Wilber makes exactly the same mistake that the likes of Alice Bailey and Guy Ballard had made. Instead of telling the truth by showing how the perennial wisdom is about initiation, not about beliefs, he quotes Alan Watts—who says much the same thing as Wilber:

> But as Alan Watts summarized the available evidence . . . "Thus we are hardly aware of the extreme peculiarity of our own position, and find it difficult to recognize the plain fact that there has otherwise

---

[6] Wilber, *Grace and Grit* (1991), 77.

been a single philosophical consensus of universal extent. It has been held by [men and women] who report the same insights and teach the same essential doctrine whether living today or six thousand years ago, whether from New Mexico in the Far West for from Japan in the Far East."

This is really quite remarkable. I think, fundamentally, it's a testament to the universal nature of these truths, to the universal experience of a collective humanity that has everywhere agreed to certain profound truths about the human condition and about its access to the Divine. That's one way to describe the *philosophia perennis*.[7]

It should be obvious to anyone who can read, that both Wilber and Watts were but rephrasing in their own words what HPB had said a century before. Watts began his perennial learning as a member of the TS in the 1920s, so he was well aware of where his statements were coming from.

Wilber had been inspired by Fritz Kunz—a devoted theosophist whose contributions are addressed in Chapter 6, "Disclosure"—and by HPB's work. Relevantly, Wilber's very first book, *The Spectrum of Consciousness* (1977) was published by the Theosophical Publishing House. So he, too, was well aware of the fact that everything he has said on the subject had been first presented by HPB.

Yet neither Watts nor Wilber ever let their audiences know where their (mis)information came from. Maybe neither of the two knew that only an actual perennial initiation can ever be the proper source for true wisdom, as HPB and her perennial mentors had insisted, all along.

Their silence on this crucial reality seems to be part of what I have called "the code of silence"—which is far more pervasive in every major area of human culture since HPB's time than most people might think.

The code of silence consists of authors—such as Huxley, Wilber, and Watts—basing what they say on HPB's works, but not ever even mentioning her name—let alone giving her the credit that she is clearly due. Some might consider this as a form of

---

[7] Ken Wilber, *Grace and Grit* (1991), 77-78.

intellectual plagiarism. I call it simply "the code of silence." The word is not the thing.

Importantly—and as just noted—both Wilber and Watts steal HPB'S insights without giving her any credit. And they do so in the process of misrepresenting what she actually said. That is, they both fail to state that the perennial wisdom is about initiation, not about "philosophy" (a purely analytical and therefore me-centered enterprise)—as both of them assert, without any evidence—and *against* all the evidence.

Given the very high place in New Age thinking and practice that both of them have, it is of the utmost importance to point out how even they blunder so seriously, on this most foundational of all matters.

Krishnamurti's foundations

If one is to give oneself any possibility of understanding more fully the eminent relevance of all this—as well as of K's insights—it is of critical importance to keep in mind the perennial foundations of K's inner life as well as his insights.

Unfortunately, none of the hitherto available K-related biographical materials make any reference at all to K's borderless foundations—leaving their readers to puzzle over the actual source not only of K's inner life. They create an unnecessary "mystery" and puzzle regarding the source for his insights, researches, and observations.

Even when discussing the TS and its leaders, these "biographers" and other authors either assume that no perennial mentors were involved in the movement's foundation—thereby contradicting without evidence Olcott's thoroughly-documented testimony, among the available sources—or claim arbitrarily and recklessly that such perennials were the invention of TS leaders.[8]

---

[8] For the overwhelming evidence for perennials being present in early TS history, see Chapter 8, "Evidence."

Equally unsupported assertions are often made that, when K stated that the perennials were in charge of the process—which is described briefly in what follows, and more thoroughly in *The Inner Life of Krishnamurti*—he was either "having visions," or was "hallucinating," or was "deluded."

Yet all of these *interpretations* contradict (wantonly and rashly, I may add) what K said consistently over a period of nearly eighty years—from 1909 to 1986—about his relationship with the perennials, and therefore with the timeless perennial wisdom.

CHAPTER 12
"Authorities"

WE HUMANS—EVERYWHERE AND EVERYWHEN—have largely assumed that every aspect of our lives depends on authorities. It is as if we never really grow up—psychologically and morally—and tend to make the assumption that we "need" our mommy or daddy to tell us "what to do," no matter how old we are.

Victorians, if anything, were drunk with the notion of authorities being required for every human task or endeavor. They did not know that we were all entering a radically different, brand new era. So they subscribed to the age-old, seemingly omnipresent notion of requiring authorities—a notion that had actually been with us since time immemorial.

Victorians held on to authorities in every aspect of human life. They did so with a vengeance, by wallowing in the thrill of being part of ruthless empires, fear-mongering, ecclesiastical and scholarly hierarchies, and brutally oppressive male-white domination over everything and everyone that didn't look or think like them.

In a way, it's understandable that they should have made all sorts of flatly false assumptions regarding the ubiquitousness of authorities, in every aspect of their lives. It is as if they were blissfully unaware of Kant, Feuerbach, Nietzsche, and so very many others, who had been sounding the alarm against such a provincial and regressive way of looking at everything.

So when HPB appeared in their midst and began to talk about "Masters," everyone and her sister in the whole planet had a knee-jerk reaction to the word. Fatally, they developed a very high level of certainty about the meaning and significance of that word, without further ado. Their intellectual heirs are still at it—just as blissfully unaware of the very serious plight they find themselves in, and just as clueless.

Enter Krishnamurti.

K

K's take on the issue of moral authorities (under whatever name) was radical, unequivocal, and uncompromising. His acid attacks against following gurus—or following anyone else in the moral dimension, for that matter—are well known. People who have been touched by his expositions tend to share his concerns about authorities in psychological-moral aspects of our lives.

Given K's alarm regarding the dangers of authority, it is understandable that when his listeners are told about the exemplars of the perennial wisdom, they tend to have a knee-jerk reaction, and immediately dismiss *the facts* without further research or evidence.

The misperception of many of K's New Age and similar readers is particularly understandable, especially when one takes into account that New Agers—including many TSers—are unacquainted with the esoteric dimension of the perennial wisdom. Coming as they do from that lack of existential awareness of the esoteric dimension, they miscall its exemplars "Masters." In doing so, they then proceed to create various cults around those "Masters"—using the word much in the sense that Victorians had done.

This odd situation has resulted in many of K's New Age readers throwing away the baby, while *worshipping* the soiled bath water—"the baby" being the actual perennials and the borderless wisdom, and "the bath water" consisting of the Victorian cult of fantasy "Masters," under whatever name.

There are other quandaries involved in this bizarre situation. It pays to go into at least some of those quandaries, in the hope of getting some clarity about it all. First of all, an important distinction needs to be made between the notion of "gurus" or "Masters" on one hand, and perennials on the other, as addressed in Chapter 5, "Masters."

Throughout history, people have always followed moral authorities—thereby assuming themselves to be helpless children looking for guides. In that sense, the mainstream in our times—

as well as New Agers, including TSers—are not very different from our historical predecessors. Such authority-mongering has always done its best to interfere severely with the borderless wisdom within us. Given our collective errant ways, it must be stated again.

Moral authorities—whether in exerting power over others, or in people assuming that there is such a thing—are always me-centered.

Perennials—being as they are exemplars of the borderless perennial wisdom—are thereby exemplars of the act and process of being deeply self-effacing and self-negating, from moment to moment. Perennials are exemplars of the one universal sense of being—which is at one with *all that is*. Their daily lives are about living in the borderless reality—a reality in which there is no conditioned me.

Making this distinction between fantasy "Masters" and perennials might help dispel some of the confusion regarding "spiritual teachers" in general. It is also worth noting that K himself was certainly an instructor, recognized himself as such, and spoke on numerous occasions about the importance of instructors.

For K, however, an instructor of psychological-moral matters has no knowledge to offer and cannot liberate anyone—and he certainly doesn't set himself up as being a moral authority. Rather, such a *perennial* instructor performs the limited yet vital task of *pointing* in the right direction—and does nothing more. You and I still are the ones who have to do the actual work. What perennials can do may consist largely of showing what does not work, what is false. As K put it:

> Can you, if you are the *guru* of so and so, dispel his darkness, dispel the darkness for another? Knowing that he is unhappy, confused, has not enough brain matter, has not enough love, or sorrow, can you dispel that?
>
> Or has he to work tremendously on himself? You may point out, you may say, "Look, go through that door," but he has to do the work entirely from the beginning to the end. . . . You are the *guru* and you

point out the door. You have finished your job. Your function as the *guru* is then finished. You do not become important.

I do not put garlands around your head. I have to do all the work. You have not dispelled the darkness of ignorance. You have, rather, pointed out to me that, "You are the door through which you yourself have to go."[1]

K is pointing out that dismissing *any* authority in the moral dimension does not preclude the existence of and even the necessity for instructors. Pythagoras, the Buddha, Socrates, Jesus, Nagarjuna—and Krishnamurti—were all instructors in the moral dimension. They shared their perennial wisdom in a manner appropriate to their respective circumstances.

Poignantly, when one reads biographical materials on these and other historical instructors in the moral dimension, one almost always finds that they were helped by secret schools and instructors. Often one must turn to original sources—not "commentators"—in order to find this out. K himself is certainly no exception in this regard, as he did make references to his own "secret" instructors and their "school"—as is documented fully in *The Inner Life of Krishnamurti*.

Followers of K who dislike—or who disagree with—this acceptance of his role as an instructor perhaps need to read the complete passage from which the above quote is taken. It comes from a discussion on the role of gurus that he had with Swami Venkatesananda (1921 1982). I should add that this is only one of many similar references in which K addresses the role of a teacher.

Given K's more well-known exposés of the dangers of authority in the moral dimension, a knee-jerk reaction on the part of his readers and listeners is quite understandable. However, there it is: K was saying that there *is* a function for a teacher, and that that function is for that teacher to show the way; what happens next is up to the listener—assuming, of course, that there is someone listening at all.

---

[1] Krishnamurti, *The Awakening of Intelligence* (1973), 140, 141.

This should come as no surprise to Buddhists. As already noted, when the Buddha was about to die—surrounded by a multitude of monks—his closest disciple Ananda asked for him to summarize his message for all, before his passing. The Buddha's last, summarizing words were: "Seek out your own salvation, with diligence: Buddhas do but point the way." That is no more nor less than what K said regarding the function of teachers.

There is no "controversy" here—except in the minds of K ideologues. As ideologues—and unlike K—they have an agenda. That agenda prevents K ideologues from seeing what K is actually saying.

The analytical fallacy

Perhaps at least part of the confusion regarding perennials comes from our more common usage of the word "teacher"—as addressed in Part One. I am returning to this issue—however much I do so from a different perspective—because it is extremely hard for people schooled in Victorian ways of thinking to see the obvious.

Normally, the main sense of the word "teacher" is to refer to someone who can guide us in physical-material-mechanical-time/space-bound-measurable aspects of our experience, as addressed briefly in Chapter 2, "The Analytical Fallacy," and more thoroughly in the full-length book of the same title. The physical-mechanical is the dimension of our experience in which analysis—which is intrinsically me-centered—appropriately reigns supreme. Importantly, there is no morality at all in *that*.

If one is interested in learning or developing skills or knowledge—in carpentry, or engineering, or grammar, or cybernetics, or reading and writing—it is invariably wise to consult someone who has a great deal of knowledge or skill in that discipline, and who sometimes comes from a long line of teachers of the respective subjects. So long as they stay within the comfortable bounds of the physical-mechanical-material-measurable, their function is most important, and is even a critical factor explaining our success as a species.

The confusion comes whenever anyone makes the assumption that because teachers are close to being essential in guild-related activities, "therefore" they are always *essential, in every aspect of our lives—including the moral dimension.*

Unfortunately, the moral dimensions of our existence are not physical-material-mechanical-time/space-bound-measurable. As addressed in Chapter 2, the moral dimensions of our experience are independent of analysis. Analysis is *always* me-centered. When it is misapplied in the moral dimensions, it is based on a person's particular conditioning in and attachment to a culture, or nationality, or gender, or social status, or similar distinctions.

By contrast, the moral dimensions of our experience are borderless and whole—and are thus not analyzable, in themselves. Love, beauty, goodness, and truth-seeking-truth-finding are not "Christian," nor "American," nor "conservative," nor "white," nor "upper class." Anyone who expects "to be taught" in these dimensions of our experience is someone who does not see or understand that the word "teacher" in the more commonly-used sense does not apply at all in the moral dimensions—which are not mechanical in nature.

One important way of distinguishing between the moral dimensions of our experience and those related to the analytical-physical-material-mechanical is to note how they each relate to wholeness or fragmentation.

The analytical—by its very nature—is always implicitly and explicitly about fragmenting and breaking down everything, whereas the moral-spiritual is always implicitly and explicitly about wholeness and integrity.

When you experience tenderness, or beauty, or joy, there are no parts to the experience; the experience is always a whole, and has no "parts." In a way, the word "wholeness" could be used for describing *in words* the nature of the whole dimension of values.

By contrast, anything having to do with analysis—such as any and all activities related to the physical-material-mechanical—is *always* me-centered and always fragmenting. For instance, when you learn carpentry—or any component thereof—you obtain a personal benefit, in being able to construct various things that are useful *to you personally* and to others who may benefit personally, as well.

The activity itself is largely about breaking down and measuring and understanding the mechanical possibilities and limitations of that which you are working with. This means that me-centeredness is an essential component of this physical activity, and you hopefully can become more proficient and better at it, as time progresses. Everything related to the me is time-bound. This is clearly a harmless (and even useful) instance of being me-centered.

In the moral dimension(s), however, everything is different. When you experience a shockingly beautiful sunset, there is no time involved in terms of the experience, in itself. Yes, it takes place at sunset or sunup or noon, and so at a certain "time." But that has nothing to do with the intrinsically timeless "moment" of beauty in itself, with the way in which your whole being is overwhelmed by the touching spectacle.

Victorian-minded, authority-thirsty people would say: "Please, teach me how to be overwhelmed, when I see a sunset. I don't have the capacity to be overwhelmed by beauty. Please, please, be my teacher. I need to be overwhelmed. I need a teacher."

Importantly, there is no me in that experience, in the sense that you don't experience it because you are a Bolivian, or a Hindu, or "lower class," or educated, or black, or any of the myriad things that make up what we call "me," including personal memories. There are no "parts" to the experience. "Parts" do not play any role whatsoever in the moral dimension—at least not in what actually happens whenever such a dimension is in place.

"Parts" and "time" and "me" will only come into play in such experiences the moment that there is an attempt at describing the experience, and impertinently attributing it to "me" (the Bolivian). Anything that happens in the moral-spiritual dimension(s) is whole, and has no "parts."

Parts exist exclusively in the analytical universe of discourse, which is the arena of the physical-material-mechanical-space/time-bound-measurable. In that arena, teachers are indispensable, for anyone wishing to be more efficient and more able.

That which is perennial is one and the same with wholeness. Perennials exemplify that wholeness by the way they are and the way they live. But what they are and what they do—inspiring as it is for anyone with the sensitivity to respond to it—is not a set of procedures for others to follow.

CHAPTER 13
Revolution

WISDOM, LARGELY THROUGH THE TS, is the main source of the revolution in thought and culture that came about in the twentieth century, and beyond—as a springboard of the American revolution of the 1770s. This explosion can be seen as a major force behind a plethora of cultural phenomena that we mostly tend to take for granted today. Among those revolutionary events are these seminal, culture-transforming developments:

- An unprecedented, truly planetary culture.
- The spread of constitutional democracy everywhere—and with it, the expectation of justice for all, planet-wide.
- Major developments in psychology—a discipline that never existed, as such, before our times—exemplified especially in transpersonal psychology.
- Calls for social reform and justice, exemplified by the rise of feminism, a clamoring for basic universal income, and an increasing appreciation for mutual ethnic and cultural respect.
- Deep concerns over the health of planet Earth—and its possible demise as a home for humanity, unless we each do something to help prevent it.
- Educational advances such as those implicit in Summerhill and in the planetary-minded Waldorf, Montessori, and Krishnamurti schools—as well as even conventional schools of higher learning having and promoting an interdisciplinary, internationalist, more democratic intent.
- Profoundly brand new borderless forms of art, such as cinema and the internationalization of music and dance, as well as non-objective painting and sculpture, among other factors.

- A renaissance and internationalization of Asian culture, cabalistic studies, and Traditionalism—making us all more aware of the single common source for all humanity in the very ancient yet ever new borderless wisdom.
- Worldwide popularity of behaviors such as vegetarianism, animal welfare, cremation, aid to victims of catastrophes worldwide, and international travel.
- Space exploration and colonization of other planets.
- Increasing realization that the source of human life is in other celestial systems—as exemplified in major governments, prominent scientists and scholars, and millions of humans testifying to that very ancient yet ever-present reality.

All of the above—and much more, as documented here and elsewhere—is a manifestation of the "rush" towards a much greater visibility of the perennial wisdom in our times, however imperfectly or incompletely it may have been implemented.

Much of all of the above has been spearheaded by the TS, directly or indirectly—however imperfectly or incompletely. We are—clearly and unambiguously—in the midst of a perennial explosion. We are indeed witnessing a revolution in human consciousness such as humans had never seen before. As HPB put it at the beginning of her magnum opus, "We have not long to wait, and many of us will witness the Dawn of a New Cycle."[1]

In addition to the above—lest we forget—anything and everything labeled "New Age" traces its very existence directly back to HPB declaring that the twentieth century would mark "the dawn of a new era" for mankind.

---

[1] Blavatsky, *The Secret Doctrine*, I xliv. For further documentation of these statements, see paradigmshift.network.

Poignantly, HPB and her perennial mentors also stated that at the vanguard of the new era there would be "an avataric manifestation."[2]

As documented briefly in what follows, the "avataric manifestation" that HPB and her perennial mentors were referring to was later declared by C.W. Leadbeater and Annie Besant to refer to the borderless wisdom message that would be given through J. Krishnamurti. CWL and AB said all along that those declarations were made not by them personally, but by the perennials who had been the source for the foundation of the TS. Those same perennials were later to be in charge of K's process, *according to K.*[3]

The perennials involved in this "avataric manifestation" are described as being exemplars of insight and compassion, who are passionately intent on helping to implement highly beneficial transformations in humanity.

Given that the perennials have been inspiring us throughout history—as addressed briefly in Chapter 8, "Evidence," and more thoroughly in *Muse*—would it not be an oversight of colossal proportions on their part, if they were not behind the present perennial explosion—a revolution which is clearly, by far, the most powerful and influential, comprehensive, planet-wide transformation of human consciousness in history?

Moreover, anyone who claims that there were no perennials behind the theosophical movement—thereby ignoring the overwhelming evidence for their physical presence in it, as briefly noted in Chapter 8, "Evidence," and elsewhere—is thereby forced to give to HPB all the credit for single-handedly precipitating the amazing perennial explosion that has come about, largely as a result of her work.

---

[2] For "avataric manifestation," see Blavatsky, *Esoteric Instructions* (1888), 74, 75; see also *Secret Doctrine* (1897, 1971 edition), V, 465, 466; see also *Collected Writings*, XII, 600, 601. The issue of "avataric manifestation" is addressed more fully in *Muse*. Consult paradigmshift.network for further clarification.

[3] For K stating that the perennials were in charge of the process, see, for instance, Krishnamurti, *Truth and Actuality*, 86-89; see also Sanat, *The Inner Life of Krishnamurti*, 261-267, and Chapter 6 of *The Inner Life of Krishnamurti*.

Due credit

History provides examples of a single person being largely responsible for a major social or cultural transformation. Martin Luther (1483-1546), for instance, may be cited as such an example. He is generally credited with starting the religious movement in Europe called "the Reformation," which spawned Protestant Christianity in the sixteenth century. However, one invariably finds other factors contributing to major changes attributed to one person.

In Luther's case, there had been social and political forces conspiring for several centuries, independently of him, to make the Reformation a possibility—and perhaps an inevitability. The rise of mercantilism, the emergence of humanism, the "discovery" of the Americas by Europeans, corruption in the Vatican, and the fact that Germanic and Anglo-Saxon monarchs were about to break away from the abuses of popish Rome—which those kingdoms had been fighting against, for several centuries—are some of the more prominent factors leading to the Reformation.

In other words, the fruit was ripe, and Europe was ready for a major change—and Luther was an excellent catalyst who provided a viable way of channeling something that had been wanted, with urgency, even for centuries before him. History is pregnant with individuals whose indisputably great accomplishments came about—like Luther's—in the context of a milieu and a *Zeitgeist* which carried them and supported them in their efforts and accomplishments.

HPB's uniqueness

In HPB's case, however, there were no readily visible helpers—whether political, economic, or religious—to promote her work. Unlike Luther, she was not attached to any institution nor to institutionalized group-thinking.

As a result—and rather than receiving help from outward sources—she was actually persecuted by those who either envied her or misunderstood her aims and the nature of her borderless work, or who were deeply entrenched in their own conditioning, and felt threatened by the universality that she was speaking and writing about. Unfounded anti-HPB prejudices are alive and kicking, even to this day.

For instance, the British government suspected her of being a Russian spy in India. From the British perspective, such suspicions came about as part of "the Great Game"—which was the nineteenth century ancestor of the "Cold War" between the Soviets and "the West," in the twentieth century.

Official "Christianity" unChristianly financed plots deliberately to smear HPB's character in order to discredit the non-sectarian, borderless nature of the spirituality she was proclaiming to the four corners of the world.

In addition, scientists and scholars snickered at many of her statements, because what she said disagreed with the established "scientific" beliefs of the times.

For instance, her perennial mentors declared through her writings that Earth is about 4.3 billion years old—which is roughly about what is believed today. But the Victorian science of her day was "certain" that Earth could not possibly be much older than 100 million years. Not until three-quarters of a century later did conventional science begin to catch up with this particular perennial scientific gleaning.[4]

There were quite a few such differences between what Victorian scientists and scholars believed and what HPB said. Her statements in this regard were later to be corroborated by non-Victorian conventional scientists and scholars. This is too big a subject to do it justice in the present context. But the evidence is there, for anyone who would bother to research this subject.

---

[4] For the ages of Earth according to HPB's perennial mentors—and to her scientist contemporaries—see Barborka, *The Peopling of the Earth* (1975), 203, 205; see also Blavatsky, *Secret Doctrine* (1888), IV, 264.

As Marilyn Ferguson (1938-2008) documented, persecution of the ideas, practices, and insights that were first made public by HPB—which Ferguson calls "a conspiracy"—continued even more than a century later, despite the fact that the culture created by the perennial explosion is finally making its formidable presence felt, everywhere in the planet.[5]

There is one sense in which HPB was aided by external forces. I'm referring, for instance, to factors such as Nietzsche's insights regarding how the whole planet was ready for a major, comprehensive revolution—given the massive failure on the part of institutions, everywhere. In that respect, it should be kept in mind that—as documented in Chapter 9, "Nietzsche"—the world at large got to know at all about Nietzsche as a result of the work of HPB's colleagues.

In any case, what Nietzsche said in reference to this, is that a major transformation needed to take place. As he expressed it, the need for such a transformation was due to a major yearning—a harrowing cry of all humanity—for all of us to come to our senses, finally.

This yearning has been present throughout human history, and the twentieth century is, in a way, but the watershed moment in history when finally "something" planetary and significant began to be done about it. Yet that yearning—which is very real—is not the same as social pressures—such as those that aided Luther, and numerous others.

In any case, Nietzsche—and many others, then and to this day—strikes me as an important presenter of the borderless wisdom, in his time. It should be kept in mind that the universal wisdom is not an institution made up of authority figures with a me-centered agenda. On the contrary, the perennial wisdom consists of the non-existence of any me-centered agendas, and all of us partake of that wisdom—to the extent that we make such accessibility viable. Nietzsche was such an individual.

The grand revolution that we are all witnessing in the twenty-first century has come about directly as a result of the borderless

---

[5] Ferguson, *The Aquarian Conspiracy* (1980).

wisdom in us manifesting itself in numerous ways and through innumerable agencies and agents. In that sense, HPB and Nietzsche—critical as their contributions were—turn out to be but "fronts" for an immense paradigm shift that has been taking place, all over the planet.[6]

It is proper to acknowledge them and others, especially since doing so makes it possible for us to have a clearer understanding of what the multidimensional revolution is about. That, precisely, is what I am doing my best to do here, and elsewhere.

However, and for whatever it's worth, it strikes me as unlikely that HPB single-handedly spearheaded the colossal, multidimensional cultural revolutions of the twentieth century and beyond—which, as noted, are largely traceable back to her, in many ways.

Despite that, she said all along that she was not only inspired by the perennials and their agents and representatives throughout the world, but was also helped by them in various ways. In fact, the obverse makes a great deal more sense: A more accurate way of describing the relationship would be to say that it was the perennials who inspired the perennial revolution—and that HPB was but one of their outward "fronts." As one of those perennials tersely stated—as noted earlier—in response to one of his "concerned" Victorian correspondents,

> Europe is a large place but the world is bigger yet. The sun of Theosophy must shine for all, not for a part. There is more to this movement than you have yet had an inkling of, and the work of the TS is linked in with similar work that is secretly going on in all parts of the world.[7]

The multidimensional wisdom explosion that came about as a direct result of this work by the perennials is solemn witness to the truth of that simply stated description.

---

[6] For "paradigm shift," see Chapter 32, "Paradigm Shift."
[7] Chin, *The Mahatma Letters, Chronological* (1972), 133, Letter 48; Humphreys and Benjamin, *The Mahatma Letters* (1962), 267, Letter 47.

CHAPTER 14
"Mysteries"

THERE ARE NUMEROUS DOCUMENTED INSTANCES of HPB receiving different kinds of help from the perennials. Countess Constance Wachtmeister, for instance, documented many witnessed instances of HPB's *Secret Doctrine* (her magnum opus) being written by someone other than HPB. HPB had stayed with the Countess for several months at the time HPB was writing that work.[1]

Further, according to those who knew her well—her family and friends for earlier in her life, and later, her theosophical colleagues and students—the wisdom that came through HPB's works was not altogether personally hers.[2]

In this way HPB and K are similar, for he also was not known, as a person, to have anything like the abilities he displayed in his capacity as a speaker and writer.[3] K's personal limitations are addressed further in *The Inner Life of Krishnamurti*, and more briefly in what follows.

Some may choose to see this as "a mystery" at the core of the lives of these two sharers of deeper matters. In HPB's case, a number of books, parts of books, and articles have been written, to the effect that she was "a mystery," or "a sphinx."[4] However, both K and HPB made it very clear that whatever it was that they were sharing with others came from the perennial dimension, not from them personally.

---

[1] Wachtmesiter, et al., *Reminiscences of H.P. Blavatsky and The Secret Doctrine* (1893); for other instances of HPB being helped by perennials, see also Olcott, *Old Diary Leaves* (which is itself a six-volumes-long, well-documented confirmation of such help); see also Barborka, *The Mahatmas and Their Letters* (1973); see also Cranston, *HPB* (1993).

[2] For HPB and others on her limitations, see, for instance, Neff, *Personal Memoirs of H.P. Blavatsky* (1937), as well as the other works cited.

[3] For K and others on his limitations, see Lutyens, *Krishnamurti: His Life and Death* (1991).

[4] For HPB as "a mystery" or "sphinx," see, for instance, Mario Roso de Luna, *La Esfinge (The Sphinx*, 1924); see also Cranston, *HPB* (1993).

References to HPB being "an instrument" of the perennial dimension have been given above, however briefly. K's relationship to the perennials is documented in *The Inner Life of Krishnamurti*, and more briefly in Part Four, "Mutation," but some details of that relationship may be advanced here.

While reading the rest of this chapter, please keep in mind the quaint "coincidence" there is between HPB and K.

The first book K ever published is *At the Feet of the Master*. That small and inspirational book begins with K's statement: "These are not my words; they are the words of the Master who taught me."[5]

Importantly, ten days before he died, K made a statement that he clearly meant to be definitive regarding the source for his inner life, as well as for his insights, researches, and observations. In his deathbed, he declared that "for seventy years that super energy—no—that immense energy, immense intelligence, has been using this body."[6]

Of sacred mysteries

As fully documented in what follows, the authors of books published to date about K cannot make any sense of what K called "the process." So they simply say that it is "a mystery"—as briefly noted in Part One, "Krishnamurti," and in Chapter 24, "The Process." That language—speaking of "mysteries" and of events being "unknowable"—is precisely the one used by the superstitious and the uneducated.

Two authors who write about K even use the word "mystery" in the titles of their books—clearly emphasizing the general and pervasive puzzlement there is over K's inner life.[7] Evelyne Blau, in her exquisitely produced anthology, *Krishnamurti: 100 Years,* states:

---

[5] Alcyone (Krishnamurti), *At the Feet of the Master* (1910), 1.
[6] Lutyens, *The Open Door* (1991), 148.
[7] Holroyd, *Krishnamurti: The Man, the Mystery, and the Message* (1991); Michel, *Krishnamurti—Love and Freedom: Approaching a Mystery* (1995).

There may be elements in this book, as recounted by witnesses to extraordinary events, that may seem incomprehensible, confounding to our linear, rational thinking. But let us not linger too long with this part of the story—it is unknowable.[8]

Some aspects of K's inner life we may never get to understand fully, as Blau suggests. But this can be said to be true of the life of any human being—there always remain aspects of anyone's life that are puzzles, even to the person in question.

I submit that those who have written about K's life may be more willing to accept "mysteries" than is necessary. There was indeed, in one sense, a mystery in K's life—and he spoke to friends about this mystery on various occasions, especially during the last decade of his life. Given the intriguing similarity between K and HPB on their respective relationships with the perennial wisdom in general and the perennials in particular, the following comments on "mysteries" may apply to HPB, as well as to K.

To begin with, the word "mystery"—in both cases—has at least two completely different meanings, and that needs to be spelled out. The sense of the word *mystery* that K spoke of privately to friends, points to *the sacredness* that he referred to often in his talks and writings. This sense of the word is much like the way HPB viewed perennial initiation. In speaking of "mystery" being synonymous with that which is sacred, K was clearly referring to what cannot be known by the conditioned mind—and that is not "mysterious," but a simple statement of fact.

HPB stated many times that in order to understand properly what she was trying to convey, there had to be perennial "initiation" in members of her audience.[9] But she never explained openly and clearly what her own sense of the sacredness implicit

---

[8] Blau, *Krishnamurti: 100 Years* (1995), 270.
[9] For HPB on the absolute requirement of initiation in order to understand what she and the perennials were really teaching, see the upcoming *Insights for a New Era*, which provides full documentation for that fact in all of HPB's major writings.

in perennial initiation was—as K was to do with utmost clarity and power.

The fact is that during HPB's time, the mainstream of humanity—and even those who were somehow attracted to her message—was not yet ready to have even the vaguest understanding of what "the sacred" in this sense might mean. It's only after the foundations that she was laying down were cured enough—beginning in the twentieth century—that there would be a population intelligent enough to grasp this, even if only "through a glass darkly" (if I may borrow from the biblical expression).

The sacredness implicit in the meaning of the word "mystery" is much the same sense of the word (or at least clearly similar) as the sense in which it was used in the ancient Greek initiatory *mysteries*. In such *mysteries*, candidates would find themselves confronted with the unknown, numinous aspect of existence. This sense of the word is also akin to Rudolf Otto's *mysterium tremendum et fascinans*, which became an important concept in twentieth-century Western theology.[10]

This expression conveys the sense of the word *mystery* when used to refer to an act and process of psychological transformation. The individual confronting a deeper level of awareness feels out of depth, unable to rely on the usual human baggage of knowledge, experience, and conditioning—let alone finding the words that would describe it accurately for others.

In such a state of awareness, nothing identified as "me" has any relevance whatsoever. Hence, such a transformation implies a sense of awe that features deeply-felt panic, since it involves the death of the me—with which we all tend to identify very strongly. In the literature, people experiencing this transformative event often speak of their hair standing on end, or experiencing nausea or other physiological reactions. Such is the *tremendum* aspect of this *"mystery"* transformation.

---

[10] For a good discussion of Otto's notion of the *mysterium tremendum et fascinans* in the context of twentieth-century theology, see Westphal, *God, Guilt, and Death* (1987).

The *fascinans* component comes from the other aspect—which is an experience of awe. This other aspect stands for *seeing* with unprecedented clarity and depth—and often sensing oneself as being in communion with all that is.

Of "mysteries" as puzzles

However, what was just addressed is not the sense of the word "mystery" most often used by those who have written about K's life. Instead, they tend to surround K's process and the source of his work with what they call "mystery," in the sense of something that the author in question does not know or understand. For such authors, K's inner life "is unknowable," as Blau put it.

Unfortunately—instead of confessing to their audiences (and to themselves) candidly, and say "I don't know anything (or don't know enough) about this, and so I don't understand it"—they arrogantly proceed to transmogrify their self-acknowledged ignorance by converting it into meaning that this is "not appropriate to be examined further, *by anybody*."

The hubris implicit in such an attitude is truly so astonishing, that it may be said to be more typical of mystery-hungry Victorians—or of superstitious people in medieval times in Europe—than of   anyone acquainted even superficially with K's insights. Lamentably, those who have referred to K's process as "a mystery" or as "unknowable" have embarrassed themselves thoroughly.

Some followers of K have suggested that there is something intrinsically wrong with investigating the source of K's work—as I do here and in *The Inner Life of Krishnamurti*—as such research might "confuse" people's understanding of K's insights and observations.[11]

---

[11] In 1995, at the K centennial celebration held at the University of Miami of Ohio, I had an opportunity to address this issue of "mystery" with two of the people closest to K in the last decades of his life. One of them was Dr. C. Parchure (n.d.), who had been K's friend—and his personal physician whenever K was in India. The other was Mary Zimbalist (1915-2008), who was the closest person to K in the last two decades

In perfect contradiction with his would-be followers, K stated that certain aspects of his inner life *are indeed* amenable to such explorations. Moreover, he stated that it is eminently proper—and perhaps even necessary—to make such explorations. That is precisely what I did in *The Inner Life of Krishnamurti*, and that is what I am doing here.

I feel compelled to point out that—however well-intentioned many of K's followers may be on this subject—their promotion of there being an "unknowable mystery" implicit in his life will definitely be the foundation for the creation of a K cult.

Truth and facts will never be the foundation for a cult of any kind. It is when "well-intentioned" people hide facts and truth that problems of this kind will unquestionably and inevitably arise. I am passionately interested in truth and facts—especially when it relates to what is, by far, the most important event, so far, in human history, as documented here and elsewhere.[12]

K clarifies "mysteries"

In 1972, K told some members of the Krishnamurti Foundation of America (KFA) in Ojai that the source of his work could not be understood by the conscious mind, while at the same time he rejected the idea that it is "a mystery"—in the sense of it being "an unknowable puzzle."

The careful reader will note that in that statement K was trying to clarify the existence of the two very different senses of the word "mystery" just pointed out. Lamentably, authors on K's life—and many K non-followers—have consistently conflated

---

of his life. *The Inner Life of Krishnamurti* had not been published, so I gave them each a copy of the unpublished manuscript, asking them to critique it. After reading it, they both implored me not to publish it. They both said to me—at first independently, and then together—that I had succeeded so well in explaining K's inner life, that "people will misunderstand, and create a religion out of it." They both thought it would be best to let people continue to believe that K's inner life was "a mystery" (in the sense of being "unknowable" and "a puzzle")—even though they acknowledged that such a perception was mistaken.

[12] Please consult paradigmshift.network for further information.

those two intrinsically incompatible senses of the word whenever referring to K's inner life.

In my experience, K non-followers actually tend strongly towards avoiding bringing this up at all—perhaps out of fear that letting it out will spoil their belief in a K ideology that is incompatible with the facts of his inner life.

That dangerously erroneous conflation of the two incompatible meanings of the word "mystery" is at the heart of the confusion that has existed about this issue, in K circles. As K stated to the KFA staff and trustees on that occasion, when the subject of K's inner life came up:

> I feel we are delving into something which the conscious mind can never understand, which doesn't mean I am making a mystery of it. There is something. Much too vast to be put into words. There is a tremendous reservoir, as it were, which if the human mind can touch it, reveals something which no intellectual mythology—invention, supposition, dogma—can ever reveal.
>
> I am not making a mystery out of it—that would be a stupid childish trick. Creating a mystery out of nothing would be a most blackguardly thing to do because that would be exploiting people and ruthless—that's a dirty trick.
>
> Either one creates a mystery when there isn't one or there is a mystery which you have to approach with extraordinary delicacy and hesitancy, and, you know, tentativeness. And the conscious mind can't do this. It is there but you cannot come to it, you cannot invite it. It's not progressive achievement. There *is* something but the brain can't understand it.[13]

Perceptive reader, if you look *carefully* at what K says in that statement, you will notice that he actually makes exactly the same distinction that I am making here, regarding two completely different—and mutually incompatible—senses of the word "mystery." K is telling us that there *are* indeed at least two mutually exclusive and incompatible senses of the word "mystery"—as I am pointing out. He is also warning that confusion *will definitely* be the result of not sorting out these two completely different meanings of that word.

---

[13] Lutyens, *The Years of Fulfilment* (1983), 224-225.

Seven years after he made that statement to the KFA, and in a different context, K indicated that the nature of the source of his insights and observations was something that *could* and *should* be looked into. What he says in the following passage is remarkable because he says that *others* could investigate his inner life, whereas he could not. Presumably this inability of his may have resulted at least partly from the secrecy involved in initiatory oaths that he had taken, as documented in *The Inner Life of Krishnamurti.*

Mary Lutyens, in the company of Mary Zimbalist, probed into the question of inquiry into the source of his inner life with K, in 1979. Please note that when K speaks of "the head starting," he is referring to a very intense pain that he felt in the head whenever the process, or a significant aspect of it, took place. When he speaks of "the boy being vacant," he is referring to the absence, since childhood, of self-centered content in his mind. When he refers to "feeling something in the room," he is referring to the perennial presence, which others could often feel, when in his presence. These subjects are discussed further in *The Inner Life of Krishnamurti.*

> Mary Lutyens: Might someone else be able to find out? And would it be right to inquire?
>
> Krishnamurti: You might be able to because you are writing about it. I cannot. If you and Maria [Mary Zimbalist] sat down and said, "Let us inquire," I'm pretty sure you could find out. Or do it alone. I see something: what I said is true: I can never find out. Water can never find out what water is. That is quite right. If you find out I'll corroborate it.
>
> ML: You would know it if it were right?
>
> K: Can you feel it in the room? It is getting stronger and stronger. My head is starting. If you asked the question and said, "I don't know," you might find it. If I was writing it I would state all this. I would begin with the boy [being] completely vacant.
>
> ML: Do you mind it said that you want it explained?

K: I don't care. Say what you like. I'm sure if others put their minds to this they can do it. I am absolutely sure of this. Absolutely, absolutely. Also I am sure I can't find it.

ML: What if one could understand it but not be able to put it into words?

K: You could. You would find a way. The moment you discover something you have words for it. Like a poem. If you are open to inquire, put your brain in condition, someone could find out. But the moment you find it, it will be right. No mystery.

ML: Will the mystery mind being found?

K: No, the mystery will be gone.

MZ: But the mystery is something sacred.

K: The sacredness will remain.[14]

In the earlier quotation, K seemed to refer, using non-technical words, to "the sacred"—to something akin to Otto's *mysterium tremendum et fascinans*. In this second instance, K has made the subtle distinction—which I am now spelling out— again in simple words, between the "mystery" (in the sense of it being "unknowable") and *the sacredness,* which is akin to the *mysterium tremendum et fascinans*, and is presumably what happens during perennial initiation.

In other words, the mystery that is the core of genuine spiritual experience remains—and is ineffable. But *the mysteriousness* that may surround it can be removed. Because the latter can and should be removed, K felt that it was proper—perhaps even necessary, for clarity—to investigate the source of his inner life.

That is precisely what is being done in the present research, and what is done in *The Inner Life of Krishnamurti.*

In addition, it should be noted that Mary Zimbalist had this conversation with K in 1979. K was telling her that "someone"

---

[14] Lutyens, *The Years of Fulfilment* (1983), 228-229.

would be able to explain all this, and that that would be proper, and perhaps necessary.

Yet when she read the unpublished manuscript of *The Inner Life of Krishnamurti* in 1995, she implored me not to publish it—contrary to K's injunction to her directly—despite the fact that she said to me that I had succeeded in doing what K had suggested would be proper, and perhaps even necessary.

I find it curious that K had made this clear to Mary Zimbalist in 1979 for the first time. That was the same year when I first met both K and Mary Zimbalist in person.

In any case, I point this out in order to make it as clear as possible that K's non-followers—more often than not, in my experience—are true-believers in a K ideology that is incompatible with the facts of his life, and with something even more important:

The ideological attitude that K-ites assume is "the only proper way" to understand K happens to be incompatible with and directly opposed to K's specific statements regarding his inner life. That ideological attitude on the part of K non-followers is absolutely incompatible with his insights and observations.[15]

My concern is that such a purely ideological (and therefore analytical and me-centered) K-ite attitude will unquestionably result in the creation of a K cult—regardless of how well-intentioned the adherents of that K cult may be.

The reality of perennials

The origins of K's inner life touch intimately on the question of the existence and nature of the perennials. That is—*according to K*—it is only after he went through the intense pains and discomforts involved in the process (his "passion") that it became possible for his body to become a vehicle for the universal wisdom to speak through him.

---

[15] For "K-ites," see the upcoming *Insights for a New Era*.

But *also according to him*, it was perennials—exemplars of the borderless wisdom, which is within each and every one of us—who conducted that very delicate and harrowing "surgical operation" (as K called it). And—*again, according to K*—it was "that intelligence" (not him) that was responsible for all of the insights, researches, and observations attributed to him.

Those *facts* go directly to the very heart of why I am going into these issues here, as thoroughly as possible. It strikes me as not seeming possible to make any sense of K's inner life unless the perennials in charge of the process were real flesh-and-blood human beings, though ones with extremely sophisticated, non-culture-bound paranormal abilities.

Anyone wishing to say that there were no perennials involved in K's life, would have to provide evidence for how the process could have happened, if there were no perennials involved.

Such a person would also have to explain why K said all along that the insights came from "that intelligence," not from him as a person.

Such a critic would also have to explain the very real connection there is between the process and the insights. After all, K and those around him could see that Krishnaji the young man did not have the capacity—before the process—for expressing what eventually came out of him. It was only after the process—which began in 1922 in Ojai—that it became possible, for the very first time in his life, for borderless insights to be expressed through him.

Anything short of a full, detailed explanation based on facts—not on speculation and not on opinions—is bound to create a K cult. That, precisely, is what has been happening already. K-ites have been creating a K cult that deliberately shuns the facts of his life, by spinning speculations and opinions not based on the facts of the case.

Speculations and opinions are clearly based on a person's *never-questioned* me-centered conditioning. That makes speculations and opinions not worthy of paying attention to—let alone making them the foundation for "explaining" K.

In order for a critical opinion about this to have any weight at all, it must explain all of the above, and it must do so with full documentation and showing facts. Otherwise, silence on this matter is the best course of action—though that silence implies a lack of understanding K, and the insights expressed through him.

If there were no perennials in charge of the process, then the process remains, indeed, "a mystery"—incomprehensible, unknowable. But in that case, the process would turn into something that could *and would* be used to exploit the gullible and the intelligence-challenged, for the purpose of inventing and creating a new, K-centered religion and ideology, as K's warning to the KFA staff in 1972 quoted above pointed to.

On the other hand, if what K said from when he first experienced the process in 1922 until his death in 1986 is accepted as true—that the process was conducted by the perennials—then the experiences connected with it can be explained and need no longer remain "a mystery" (in the "unknowable" sense of the word).

By spelling this out—as is done in the present exploration—it would hopefully be less likely that this information might be misused in order to create a cult around it. That is what has happened before in history, through the creation of me-centered religious ideologies.

Some of K's students consider the process to be a mystery that "should not" be looked into. Or else, they fear that acknowledging K's rich inner life would contribute to the creation of a new religion around K—something not at all in keeping with K's insights and observations, and thus inappropriate, possibly even dangerous.

But these *unresearched opinions* ignore the fact that "only the truth shall make you free." If the truth is that K was consciously involved in the work of the perennials—as he stated numerous times, from the beginning and through to the end of his life—we must accept this fact and adjust our understanding accordingly. Not doing so would imply having the arrogant and intelligence-challenged, superstitious attitude of assuming that—based on one's ignorance of these issues—one knows better than what actually took place.

Such intelligence-challenged arrogance would further imply that one assumes that one knows better than what K himself said regarding his personal experiences. I submit to you, wise reader, that it is from such mere unresearched *opinions* based on people's ignorance and me-centeredness, that a cult or religion—in the "bad" sense—is bound to be created around K, perhaps inevitably.

Mystery-mongering

Ever-increasing research—not only my own—suggests that there have always been some exemplars of the perennial wisdom who have not been known publicly.[16] Given the horrific societies that we have created throughout history, it seems eminently plausible that a sensitive person—such as a perennial— might prefer to remain isolated from such circumstances.

In that sense, there is nothing particularly quaint about anonymous perennials having inspired America's founding documents and the creation of the theosophical movement. Nor should there be anything particularly strange about some perennials using the development of that movement as a springboard for giving to all human beings everywhere a message of universal sanity and mutual care and support.

That is especially true at this inflection point in human societies everywhere, when the regressive forces of backwardness and appeals to autocracy are more intense than ever before.

The present is the unprecedented time when embracing the perennial dimension in our personal lives has turned into either life or death—and not only for societies that have been trying to do their best to be more borderless and just.

In our time, even the meaningful survival of the planet itself is on the line.

---

[16] For a bibliography, consult paradigmshift.network.

CHAPTER 15
HPB, K, and Perennials

HPB MADE THE WORLD AT LARGE AWARE of the now known to be historically very real secret schools of perennial wisdom that have existed through the ages. Once the word was out about this revelation, zealotism joined hands with mercantilist enterprise—and a cottage industry of New Age "occult" schools was born.

It should be clarified that some of the "schools" that have some pedigree in HPB's work have been moved by a spirit of research and a sensible approach. Manly Palmer Hall's (1901-1990) Philosophical Research Society and Edgar Mitchell's (1930-2016) Institute of Noetic Sciences are two such institutions.

But a great many others—actually the lion's share of such groups—while broadcasting popularized versions of the perennial wisdom in one form or another, have also promoted their own *concepts* and *beliefs* regarding who "the Masters" are—and regarding what the presumably "real *teaching*" of those would-be "Masters" is. It is these notions that are largely responsible for the rise of misunderstandings regarding the perennials—as well as of their philanthropic efforts on our behalf throughout the ages.

Thus, what started out as a presentation of the borderless wisdom turned quickly into its *popularization*. Unfortunately, as the movement grew, popularization turned into *vulgarization* of the perennial wisdom. It is thus not surprising that most sympathizers of K—among many others—have shunned the "notions" of perennials and the perennial wisdom, altogether.

G.I. Gurdjieff (1872?-1949) also claimed to have been in contact with exemplars of the perennial wisdom. It would be interesting to examine whether evidence suggests that "his" perennials were the same as those who helped HPB with her work.

If nothing else, such a confluence between HPB and Gurdjieff might explain why at least some of the major early leaders of the Gurdjieff movement—P.D. Ouspensky (1878-1947), A.R. Orage (1873-1934), and Thomas (1885-1956) and Olga de Hartmann (1885-1979)—had come to Gurdjieff from the theosophical movement.[1]

In Gurdjieff's work, the perennial wisdom emphasizes "self-remembering." Similarly, in the origins of the theosophical movement self-understanding and transformation were the very core of what was "taught." Later beliefs were *invented* by people who should have known better, but who unfortunately didn't. Their intellectual heirs still don't, more than a century later.

HPB never promoted a cult-like worship of her perennial mentors—as if they had been something like the saints and gods of some religious cults. Yet she was surrounded by enthusiastic Victorian *exoterics*. Even as early as her lifetime, HPB's perennial mentors tended to be regarded by Victorian exoteric TS members and others as "gurus"—and even as objects of worship, much like Christian saints or Hindu gods. This purely Victorian-exoteric trend continued throughout the history of the TS, to this day.

Unfortunately, that trend has contributed to the erroneous perception of "theosophy" as a new-fangled cult that has appropriated and syncretized teachings from all over the world, particularly from Asia—as briefly noted in Chapter 10, "The Perennial Explosion."

But whatever misconceptions may exist about these perennials, the fact remains that HPB's perennial mentors were intent on bringing about major transformations on the planet, and that a spiritual-psychological mutation of individuals lay at the core of their work—as I have fully documented in *Muse* and the soon-to-be-published *Insights for a New Era*.

---

[1] For full documentation of the theosophical foundations of all Gurdjieff and Ouspensky work, see Webb, *The Harmonious Circle* (1980).

HPB, K, and the perennials

HPB and a handful of her esoteric colleagues always described the perennials as men and women of flesh, blood, and bone who find no enticement whatsoever in the life of the world, and who seek a life of relative peace, away from mainstream "civilization."

Perennials have been said to live often in communities with others like themselves, whose primary interest is the pursuit of insight and compassion and research into the nature of *what is*—all in the context of aiding humans to live more in tune with the borderless dimension, which is the source of unconditioned love, fairness, beauty, and truth-seeking-truth-finding.

The lifestyle, insights and interests of perennials inspired best-selling works of fiction that sometimes turned into influential films, such as H.G. Wells' (1866-1946) *The War of the Worlds* (1897; film adaptations 1953, 2005), and *The Shape of Things to Come* (1933; film adaptation 1936); Aldous Huxley's (1894-1963) *Brave New World* (1932; film adaptations 1980, 1988); Somerset Maugham's (1874-1965) *The Razor's Edge* (1944; film adaptations 1946, 1984); James Hilton's (1900-1954) *Lost Horizon* (1933; film adaptations 1937, 1973, 1997); and George Orwell's (1903-1950) *Nineteen Eighty-Four* (1949; film adaptations 1956, 1984).

All of those works point to the destructiveness personal and global that takes place as a consequence of humans moving away from borderless values.

Some of those works—and many others of similar content and intent—refer to perennial-like communities, often in the Himalayas. Such communities are much like the ones HPB and Gurdjieff spoke of often, as the place where they communed with perennials.

In Hilton's novel, that place is called "Shangrila"—a word that has become a permanent part of vernaculars, all over the world. Pursuits such as those moving such a community cannot be carried out uninterruptedly in the midst of "civilization," where the majority of humanity do not have such interests—and where the "monkey mind" rules, and the tyrant Little Caesar within reigns supreme.

According to HPB, the lack of seriousness as well as the intrinsic violence of the majority of us are the main reasons for surrounding perennial schools and communities with secrecy. This is also the case for anonymous perennials who choose to live incognito.

At the end of the day, it is the brutish fickleness of most people, and their focusing on me-centered activities in their daily lives, that mostly keep any aspect of the perennial wisdom an unlikely possibility in our collective as well as personal experience. *That* is what prevents the majority of us from even being aware of the very real existence of the perennial wisdom—let alone having anything to do with its exemplars and agents.

At the same time, however, the perennials hold the promotion of human welfare at heart, and so they are also interested in coming in contact with similarly philanthropic people who are nevertheless living in the mundane world, with all its pitfalls. As one of the perennials said to CWL in one of the letters addressed to him:

> Our cause needs missionaries, devotees, agents, even martyrs perhaps. But it cannot demand of any man to make himself either.[2]

HPB's description of the activities of the perennials is in fact not unlike a description of the activities that K engaged in. Throughout his long life, K spent a great deal of time alone, often in communion with nature, intensely engaged in research into *what is*—"reading from the book of life," as it were.

Those who attended K's talks or read his books were and are also often people interested in creating a better society by focusing on bringing about transformation in their personal lives. Thus the followers and sympathizers of K form a group similar

---

[2] Pedro Oliveira, compiler, *CWL World, Letters from the Master,* austheos.org.au.

to the secret transformative perennial schools that have existed throughout history, for the same ends.

K's work seems to be, in fact, an appropriate continuation—and even a culmination—of perennial work that has gone on throughout the ages. HPB's work was a component of such more recent efforts—and she was K's immediate major precursor.

Authors such as Carl Jung (1875-1961), Alan Watts (1915-1973), Aldous Huxley (1894-1963), Joseph Campbell (1904-1987),and Ken Wilber (b. 1949)—among a cast of thousands—have documented that the perennial wisdom has been a very real factor throughout history, and that therefore its represent-atives and agents are just as real.

There is no mystery nor mystification about any of this. As the evidence and context presented in what follows suggest, K's inner life could have taken place if—and only if—there is a per-ennial wisdom and there are living representatives of it, whether known or anonymous.

In fact, the richness of his psychic and spiritual life—not to mention the eminently beneficial, revolutionary nature of K's researches—can itself be regarded as the very best evidence to date for the existence of this ancient yet ever new wisdom, and so for that of its representatives, the perennials.

PART THREE

A NEW PERSPECTIVE

CHAPTER 16
A New Language

MORE THAN A CENTURY AFTER HPB's PASSING, the existence of an energy field in and around every physical living thing, including human beings, has become more widely known and accepted, thanks to research in a variety of related areas. The awareness that various forms of subtle energy not only flow through—but make up—all physical living organisms has also been gaining currency.

This has been made possible, to a large extent, as greater awareness of quantum physics and other factors have come into play. Energy flows in the body—aspects of which have been known in India for millennia as *kundalini* and the *chakras*—can now be described, instead, in terms of "subtle, ultra-subatomic energy-matter."[1]

Kundalini and *chakra*

Kundalini and *chakra* are Sanskrit words that indeed have been used for millennia throughout Asia, and more specifically in the schools of yoga and tantra. However, all major civilizations have recognized, depicted, and made use of these subtle energy patterns, though they have understood and described them in different ways. Such references are found, for instance, in the cultures of Tibet, China, Japan, ancient Egypt, ancient

---

[1] See, for instance, Bendit and Bendit, *The Etheric Body of Man* (1957); Edmunds, *Psychism and the Unconscious Mind* (1968); Regush, *The Human Aura* (1974); Puharich, *Beyond Telepathy* (1973); Karagulla, *Breakthrough to Creativity* (1969); and Judith, *Wheels of Life* (1987). For earlier expositions, see Kilner, *The Human Aura* (1911); and Powell, *The Etheric Double* (1925) and *The Astral Body* (1927). The best more recent exposition is Kunz, *The Personal Aura* (1991). The classic that started all this literature and that created the language that is now widely used is Leadbeater's illustrated *Man Visible and Invisible* (1902), which was preceded by *The Astral Plane* (1896).

Greece, Africa, Polynesia, and pre-colonial North and South America, as well as in Renaissance Europe.[2]

Those two words have turned ubiquitous and pervasive in practices and writings on this subject. Proof of this is the very fact that those two Sanskrit words have now become part of the vernaculars of all European and other languages, to the point that both have now been added in the respective dictionaries. Such facts regarding the pervasiveness of these words at the very least suggests that perhaps we need to consider seriously the possibility that these energies are indeed present in the human organism.[3]

The psycho-physiological perspective that results from looking seriously into these issues seems to hold answers to problems in what the European philosophical tradition (as taught at present in universities around the world) calls "the philosophy of mind."[4]

Clearly, this is of interest not only to researchers in fields like physiology and psychology,[5] but also to philosophers—and therefore to *all* academics. After all, the university as an institution was historically created as an offshoot of philosophy—and all university disciplines are, in many important ways,

---

[2] For references to the chakra-kundalini energy patterns (under different names and conceptual frameworks) in all the major civilizations, see, for instance, Bruyere, *Wheels of Light* (1994); see also Yu, *Taoist Yoga* (1976). For ancient Egypt, see the very extensive work of Schwaller de Lubicz, such as *Sacred Science* (1958); see also Leadbeater, *The Hidden Life in Freemasonry* (1926); for North America, see Waters, *The Book of the Hopi* (1972). For the Mayas, see Argüelles, *The Mayan Factor* (1987). For sixteenth and seventeenth-century Europe, see Leadbeater, *The Chakras* (1927), which also includes the first ever full-length borderless exposition of the subject.

[3] Unfortunately, the subject of the reality of kundalini and the chakras has been obscured and confused by the rampant gullibility and exploitation connected with this and related subjects. Christopher Hills addresses this issue most eloquently in his sobering "Is Kundalini Real?" in *Nuclear Evolution*, reprinted in White, *Kundalini, Evolution, and Enlightenment* (1979). White's anthology is essential reading for anyone interested in exploring these issues.

[4] For a comprehensive primer on the subject of the philosophy of mind, see William Jaworski, *Philosophy of Mind: A Comprehensive Introduction* (2011).

[5] See, for instance, Ritberger, *Your Personality, Your Health* (1998).

specializations within the grand, comprehensive field of philosophy.[6]

After all, the subtle energy patterns are said by *trained* clairvoyants to be the material basis of daily-life psychological phenomena such as emotions and thoughts.

The expression "trained clairvoyants" was used by C.W. Leadbeater (CWL) to refer to people who had been tutored in some way by the perennials, even when they had been born somewhat clairvoyant or had developed clairvoyance in some other way. CWL used this expression to distinguish such perennially "trained" candidates from other "clairvoyants."[7]

Crucially in the present context, a "trained clairvoyant" refers to someone *working with perennials*—and who *therefore* lives daily life in the process of ending me-centeredness and conditioning. There is great danger in developing what analyzers *assume* to be "psychic powers" without being first in the process of engaging daily in the ending of the me.

The result of such practices is making the me more arrogant, more powerful—while at the same time *assuming* recklessly that one is, somehow, "more spiritual." This goes to the very heart of discerning what is of true value, and what is dangerous—what is perilous to the clueless individual with newly-acquired "psychic powers," as well as to all his relationships, to the community he lives in, and globally.

The wisdom on kundalini, chakras, and related matters—as understood in differing areas of the world—is largely unavailable, in some cases because the literature is known incompletely, in others because it has not been made public or has been substantially destroyed (often by invading "civilized" conquerors). Tantra and yoga, on the other hand, are still iving traditions whose practitioners now include people from all over the world, thanks to the perennial explosion—which is unique to our times.

---

[6] For philosophy being the origin for all university faculties, see *The Analytical Fallacy.*
[7] For subtle material patterns of thoughts and emotions as seen by "a trained clairvoyant," see, for instance, Besant and Leadbeater, *Thought Forms* (1901). The subject of "trained clairvoyants" is addressed in most of Leadbeater's works dealing with these issues.

The fact that the perennial explosion has opened this up means that at least significant portions of knowledge of these subjects are—for the first time ever in history—out in the open, and easily available worldwide, regardless of their original source. Thus, tantric terminology has become particularly useful.

Nevertheless, one should be aware that this terminology tends to bring with it the particular conceptual frameworks of traditional tantra and yoga. Such regionalist frameworks ignore other ways of understanding these energies and energetic processes. As a result, regionalist approaches miss some connotations that are important to other ways of understanding the significance of these subtle energies for all human beings.

A specialist language

The available original Indian and Tibetan sources that refer to these psycho-physiological energy patterns use language that would be meaningful only to a tantric scholar, or to practitioners. The *Sat-Cakra-Nirupana*—a tantric work that, according to its translator, is meant to *clarify* our understanding of kundalini—provides an excellent example of this problem. That text begins with the following statement:

> At the right, are the two Siras, Sasi and Mihira. The Nadji Susumna, whose substance is the threefold Gunas, is in the middle. She is the form of Moon, Sun, and Fire; Her body, a string of blooming Dhatura flowers, extends from the middle of the Kanda to the head, and the Vajra inside her extends, shining, from the Medhra to the Head.
> . . . Over [the Svayambhu Linga] shines the sleeping kundalini, fine as the fibre of the lotus-stalk. She is the world-bewilderer, gently covering the mouth of Brahma-dvara by Her own. Like the spiral of the conch-shell, Her shining snake-like form goes three and a half times around Shiva, and Her lustre is as that of a strong flash of young strong lightning. Her sweet murmur is like the indistinct hum of swarms of love-mad bees. She produces melodious poetry and Bandha and all other compositions in prose or verse in sequence or otherwise in Samskrta, Prakrta and other languages. It is She who maintains all the beings of the world by means of inspiration and expiration, and

shines in the cavity of the root (Mula) Lotus like a chain of brilliant lights.[8]

However useful to practitioners or enlightening to scholars such convoluted, poetical presentations may be, the style and the specialist language used in such ancient texts—which, let us recall, were meant to "clarify" everything related to the subject— make them inaccessible to those outside the intimate and small circle of tantra's serious students. To non-experts, that passage reads as if it were a creative form of pig Latin—a prankish and playful form of double-talk, if you will.

Also, all of the ancient texts that relate to these subtle energies—in all cultures—tend to emphasize their psychological dimensions. That is, they usually consist of poetical attempts at describing what it feels and is like to sense and work with these energies. Generally, minimal or no attempt is made at trying to objectify these energies by describing their *material* properties, the way it is done now, almost universally—thanks to CWL's unprecedented manner of presenting these subjects.

In any case, because of the bewildering nature of this literature to outsiders, the wisdom of tantra had remained largely unrecognized outside of the secret world of practitioners—until the perennial explosion came about, largely as a result of the work of HPB and of those who have been inspired or influenced by her.

One of the great contributions made by the early disciples of HPB was the creation of a conceptual framework that made it possible to speak about kundalini and the chakras (and related factors) in universally meaningful and accessible ways.

Thus, although the existential, living quality of the ancient ways of speaking of these energies was lost to some extent, the new way of articulating our understanding and speech about these issues has made it possible to have that which could never have been, before our time: We now have a universally

---

[8] Avalon, *The Serpent Power* (1919), 326, 346-47.

understandable manner of conceptualizing and speaking about these matters.

That had been impossible, everywhere in the world, until HPB and her disciples—most of all, by far, CWL—created such a new way of speaking and understanding.

Making public all these formerly hermetically-sealed insights on the nature of being human is but one of many ways of seeing that the American Age involves a transformation of human consciousness, everywhere. What used to be reserved for "initiates" in secluded practices throughout the world, was now to be owned by all humanity. The use of one single language to capture what used to be regionalisms is part and parcel of that major transformation.

Tantric teachings would never have become as popular as they have become, without the efforts of HPB and her colleagues to demythologize and make more widely accessible the meanings of arcane ancient texts. They achieved this by using—*for the very first time ever, in human history*—a borderless language that anyone in the world could understand.

Thus, we find ourselves in an intriguing situation—a situation whereby even Indian and Tibetan scholars and practitioners have increasingly made use of the more universal, borderless language that was created in HPB's milieu.

This fact suggests not only the logical and historical priority of the perennial wisdom over the many regional versions of these issues found throughout the world.

It also suggests that HBP's "theosophy" is most emphatically not a syncretistic system built up and culled from regional "teachings"—as has been claimed recklessly and without evidence by some authors.

Instead, her work and that of her colleagues and disciples refer to the universal source of all those diversified descriptions, as she and her perennial mentors had stated, all along.

CHAPTER 17
Chinese Energy Wisdom

THE ANCIENT CHINESE DEVELOPED a research approach that was perhaps—according to our present collective memory—the earliest clearer explanation of the subtle energies that our bodies are made up of. The ancient Chinese also provided elaborate and careful descriptions and mappings of the physical energy flows.

These Chinese explanations are often more universally understandable by anyone in the world. For this reason, they stand—at least in that respect—in stark contrast to the mostly incomprehensible poetical and mythical presentations found in tantric literature.[1]

Such descriptions still form the core of Chinese medical diagnosis and therapy today.[2] In fact, there are numerous reports of relatively simple cures of chronic diseases, such as cancer and arthritis, brought about by Chinese physicians and other practitioners working with the subtler energies.

The Chinese presentation of the subtler energies began to come into its own worldwide only in the last quarter of the twentieth century—like so many other developments in every major area or human concern—largely as a result of the HPB-spearheaded ongoing perennial explosion.

In addition, and without question, the Chinese approach contributes importantly to our understanding of what a human being is. The fact that these energies can be manipulated successfully for health, as well as for martial arts purposes, tells us that they are not visions nor "mythical" teachings—let alone super-

---

[1] For excellent expositions of the Chinese understanding of subtler energies (using the language and conceptual frameworks that had been created mainly by CWL, but without referring to him), see any of the many works by Bruce K. Frantzis, especially *Opening the Energy Gates of Your Body* (1993), *Relaxing Into Your Being* (1999), and *The Great Stillness* (1999); see also Lewis, *The Tao of Natural Breathing* (1996).
[2] See, for instance, Porkert and Ullmann, *Chinese Medicine* (1990); see also Beinfield and Korngold, *Between Heaven and Earth* (1992).

stitions. Instead, they are as real as other forms of equally and powerful invisible energy, such as electricity and nuclear energy.

In fact, it has been becoming increasingly obvious that Traditional Chinese Medicine (TCM) in general, and the Chinese energy arts in particular, are in consonance with developments in contemporary physics, such as quantum and string theory, wherein the human body is perceived as an energy system within the grand energy system that the whole universe is.

By contrast, most contemporary medicine, especially in the US, is based on nineteenth century *conceptual* systems—which are now mostly thoroughly outdated. Incidentally, US medicine is an unprecedented system, in that it depends—for the first time ever in human history—primarily on the profit motive and on using poisonous drugs, not on the health or the well-being of humans.[3]

Downside

Yet despite its relatively analytical and descriptive components (which include very precise mapping of the energy flows throughout the body), the regionality of the Chinese approach to the healing arts—and its exclusion of "foreigners"—had kept it from being universally available to all, up until the last quarter of the twentieth century.

That is when Chinese-based medical and martial arts applications of the energy arts exploded on the international scene,

---

[3] For the effectiveness of Chinese healing where medicine based on European nine-teenth-century metaphysics (such as that practiced in the US) has failed, see the works of Dr. Dean Black, such as *Health at the Crossroads* (1988), which includes good additional references; see also Mendelsohn, M.D., *Confessions of a Medical Heretic* (1979). For the healing efficacy of the Chinese energy arts, see Frantzis, *Dragon and Tiger Medical Chi Gung Instruction Manual* (2008). Dragon and Tiger is a chi gung set that has been usefully found to cure or bring improvements to conditions such as cancer, among many others. I address the issue of the inefficiency and dangers of US medicine—in health-related areas in which other approaches have been successful—in "Tumor-Growing in America"; this is one of the many un-published book-length manuscripts that I will eventually publish. A precis of it is provided online at paradigmshift.network.

as one of the numerous expressions of the perennial explosion phenomenon, world-wide, in the American Age. That wisdom explosion phenomenon—of which TCM is only an aspect—is addressed more directly in Chapter 3, "The American Age," in Chapter 18, "American Agers," and throughout this exploration.

It is important to emphasize that different regional approaches describe the subtle energies differently. For instance, differing from the relatively arcane schools of tantric yoga, in the Chinese Taoist approach kundalini and its flow through the chakras are not described the way they are in tantra—and in K's experiences.[4]

The perennials who were in charge of K's "process" are said to have lived for millennia in what has been called "the roof of the world"—mountain ranges including the Himalayas, the Karakorum, and the Kuen Lun.

Those perennials are also said to be past-masters in *all* the energy arts, *borderlessly*. My take is that everyone cognizant of the "process"—including K—spoke of K's "process" using a language familiar to the Indian subcontinent. They spoke that way also because that is what they knew, at the time.

This may explain why people who are knowledgeable of tantra and yoga have been bewildered by some of what took place during K's "process." This is a big subject in itself, and I'll address it separately, as circumstances permit. I am only mentioning it here in order to bring awareness to the fact that approaches other than tantra and yoga—as they are understood in the Indian subcontinent—may have been employed in K's process.

The perennials—qua perennials—are neither Indian nor Chinese nor Nigerian. They are borderless.

Another factor to consider is that in order to benefit fully from the healing art as it has been known and practiced in China for millennia, it used to be essential to accept a number of

---

[4] For Taoist yoga, see, for instance, Yu, *Taoist Yoga* (1999); see also the numerous works by Mantak and Maneewan Chia, such as *Chi Nei Tsang* (1990); see also the brief yet powerful exposition of TAO yoga in Frantzis, *The Chi Revolution* (2008).

principles of Taoism and Chinese culture. There is nothing intrinsically wrong with this, of course. But adopting a Chinese/Taoist perspective—like adopting any other regional perspective, such as Tantra—may not appeal to everyone and will be more difficult to understand by "outsiders."

By contrast, the perennial wisdom's explosion in our times—which expresses itself in the *planetary* transformation of consciousness, everywhere on the planet—is multidimensionally borderless, and makes all such systems eminently accessible to everyone on Earth. This is yet another way in which the borderless perennial wisdom can be seen for the very real phenomenon it has always been—especially since it is in fact the source for the many diversified schools of internal energy work, throughout the world.

Throughout its history, the Chinese energy arts, then, have been able to develop to a considerable extent. Unfortunately, they have also limited themselves by being attached to that particular region of the world. In doing that, its practitioners from before the American Age wisdom explosion shut the gates to their "inner sanctum" from "outsiders."

Frantzis

This important limitation in the Chinese energy arts has now been largely overcome, thanks in no small measure to the formidable presence of Bruce Kumar Frantzis (b. 1949), beginning in the last quarter of the twentieth century.

I now proceed to explore this phenomenon, partly because it illustrates significantly a number of pointers I have shared with you, careful reader, in the process of referring to the perennial explosion. A more attentive exploration of this development in the Chinese energy arts also provides some documentation for the reality of energy circulation in human bodies—which anyone in the world can test. This energy circulation *must* be experienced in order to be "understood" in any significant sense of the word. In that sense, this is not something that can just be found in some book or that one can "agree" or "disagree" about.

Importantly, Frantzis reveals ways in which *anyone* can learn to use and manipulate these energies in our bodies for the purpose of healing, as well as for martial arts. Simultaneously, this is a very different approach to meditation from those originating in the Indian subcontinent, which have come to be better known, internationally.

In addition, I personally find most intriguing a number of connections between the work that Frantzis has been engaged in, and the sources for HPB's work—and therefore for K's inner life. One of these connections comes from Frantzis' main teacher, Master Liu Hung Chieh (d. 1986). After having been declared "enlightened" in Mahayana Buddhism by the relevant Buddhist authorities in China, and as Frantzis explains it,

> Liu now turned toward the Tao. He traveled to the sacred mountains of Western China, where for ten years he devoted himself to intense study with a number of those meditation masters who head the esoteric branches of Taoism that extend back to antiquity through an unbroken line of lineage masters.[5]

The "sacred mountains of Western China" that Liu went to in order to learn from perennials the deeper side of Taoist energy arts, are located in the roof of the world—where perennials have lived and operated for millennia, as just noted.

The careful reader will take notice of how Liu went seamlessly from Buddhism to Taoism—but without "converting" from one to the other. This shows ineffably that there is a universal wisdom behind both, and that it is such borderless wisdom that Liu was after.

---

[5] Frantzis, *Relaxing Into Your Being* (1999), 43.

HPB connections

HPB's perennial mentors had referred to those very same mountain ranges as an important part of what could be called "the perennial domain"—a kind of perennial "headquarters," wherein many perennials actually have lived, presumably since time immemorial.

Importantly, in the "controversial" and incomplete 1897 third volume of *The Secret Doctrine* (HPB's *magnum opus*), her perennial mentors had begun to provide the Chinese background for much of what they had obviously intended to share, all along. *Isis Unveiled* (1877) had focused on the perennial wisdom as it appeared in "the West"; the first two volumes of *The Secret Doctrine* (1888) focused on the Indian subcontinent background; and the third (incomplete) volume of *The Secret Doctrine* began to focus on the Chinese dimension of the perennial wisdom.

Unfortunately, the process of HPB's perennial mentors expounding on the Chinese approach ground to a sudden halt because HPB died in 1891. Therefore, only a few papers on the Chinese dimension turn up in that third volume. As a result, this unfortunate development left an important gap in the perennials' intended presentation of the borderless wisdom through HPB's *Secret Doctrine.*

Now that Frantzis is teaching formerly secret Taoist practices that were previously unavailable to "outsiders," some of that vital Chinese perennial component has finally become available—beginning a century after *The Secret Doctrine* was originally published.

Importantly, Frantzis is a lineage holder of a lineage going back to Lao Tse (c. 6th to 4th century BCE). This means that—despite his being an American, and not Chinese—his presentation of this ancient lineage is as genuine as it can be.

Chinese energy arts

There is another aspect of this development that is relevant to our better understanding of K's psychic and related experiences as directed by the perennials.

Frantzis shows how it is possible for any of us to use the mind to guide the energies in our bodies (called "chi" in the Chinese approach). He also shows how by guiding and directing this chi flowing through our bodies it is possible to make changes in our health. In fact, in China there are TCM practitioners who can manipulate the chi in other people, as an approach to help heal them. Such a "mind over matter" possibility would otherwise tend to seem "miraculous" to the uninitiated in these energy arts—and that includes anyone and everyone involved in health care, everywhere in the world.

This aspect of the Chinese internal energy arts, incidentally, is helpful also in getting us to understand better how the perennials in TS early history were able to do things that some might consider to be "miracles," in various ways.

For instance, they were said to be able to "materialize objects" or "teletransport" them—and there is some evidence for the reality of at least some of these abilities. They could also communicate with people "wirelessly" from many miles away. All of these—and other similar faculties—have been formerly associated with abilities that practitioners of certain forms of "higher" yoga are said to develop. For instance, Patañjali's *Yoga Sutras*—the central text of yoga—shows how to develop such faculties.

It must be emphasized once more that reading books will not do. You must experience these energies—and that takes a great deal of work and serious meditation. This is not for the fickle.

In the past, the use of such abilities had been considered by many outsiders as a kind of "trade secret" exclusive to Indian schools. Frantzis' revelation of these former "secrets" simultaneously makes them readily available to anyone who applies herself to practice diligently, while at the same time making it very clear that there is no "mystery" or "miracle" involved in any of it.

Rather, finding out about these abilities—which we all can develop—is merely part of the process of learning things about ourselves and the world we live in, things that we may not have known, at least not with this level of accomplishment.

It all can begin—as we learn this approach—with being sensitive to the flows of energy in your own body. Then, it becomes possible to guide those energies, to dissolve any blockages thereof, and to expand further possibilities.

Much later on, it becomes possible to do the same in other people's bodies. That, in turn, could eventually lead to mastering energies flowing throughout all that is. So the process is not "miraculous," nor is it "a mystery." It does take a great deal of determination and patience and sensitivity. But it is there, for anyone to at least begin to put into practice.

It is true that beginning at the end of the twentieth century there have been a number of authors and teachers (many of them Chinese or of Chinese descent) who have been speaking and writing about "chi" and "chi gung" and "tai chi," and other Chinese energy arts components. Some readers might then question why I emphasize and feature an American rather than others who have the advantage of knowing Chinese culture from within—and that is clearly a fair question.

That question also goes to the very heart of a main point being made in this exploration, regarding the borderlessness and non-regionality intrinsic to the perennial wisdom. That question is addressed more directly in Chapter 18, "American Agers."

Liu

To begin with, it should be understood that Frantzis is the current, living representative of a lineage in the internal energy arts that goes back directly to Lao Tse, the author of the *Tao Te King*. That small text is a foundation text for Taoism.

Lao Tse was also the founder of an esoteric school that has specialized for the past two and a half millennia in the internal energy arts. Though I had previously studied the *Tao Te King* and had had discussions with others about it, I had never even heard of this text having anything to do with the internal energy arts—until I encountered Bruce Frantzis.

In fact, I consider this to be such an important matter, that I asked Frantzis personally whether he had thought of publishing a new translation of the *Tao Te King* with commentary, to show the internal energies dimension of that foundational text. He said that he would, but only if he could find a world-class translator with whom to work. It would be wonderful if such a translator were to show up at Frantzis' doorstep, while there is time.

Frantzis' mentor Liu Hung Chieh had been the holder and living representative of that lineage—until he died in 1986. Liu would have been the last of that lineage, had it not been for a vision he'd had, in which he is said to have seen Bruce Kumar Frantzis coming into his life.

For quite a number of years before meeting Frantzis, Liu had been concerned about whether he would find someone with the multi-dimensional skills, understanding, and wisdom that would qualify that person for receiving the transmission of the lineage. He certainly had not found anyone in China who fulfilled the requirements, and he could not responsibly pass on the baton to an unqualified candidate—Chinese or not.

As a result, he must have resigned himself for many years—which included the entirety of Mao Zedong's (1893-1976) "cultural revolution." Mao's cultural revolution went from 1949 through his death in 1976. Given the destructive tenor of that period in China, Liu had been contemplating the likelihood that he would be the last of such a venerable ancient lineage.

Then, shortly before he died, he had the vision of Frantzis coming into his life. They met, soon after. They worked together intensely, and Liu could see that he had finally found the right person to whom to pass on the lineage. And so he did.

That, by itself, would be "reason" enough to feature Frantzis—rather than one or several of the many authors and teachers of related subjects, many of whom have Chinese ethnic roots. But his very clear connections to the perennial wisdom—and his important place in the perennial explosion—put Frantzis in a unique position that goes far beyond that of being "just" another martial arts teacher with a bag of tricks.

CHAPTER 18
American Agers

APART FROM EVERYTHING STATED in the previous chapter, it strikes me as appropriate that a non-Asian is Lao-Tse's lineage holder within the wisdom explosion that defines the present American Age.

Indian possibilities

Intriguingly, the perennials who were responsible for founding the TS could have selected an Indian to spearhead the theosophical movement—given that Indian culture still retained living examples of the perennial wisdom, as well as a bewildering number of perennially-inspired texts.

Instead, the perennials chose a Russian noblewoman turned American citizen and a Yankee-born colonel from the American Civil War—an unlikely duo in the eyes of the perennially uninitiated. Yet the perennials obviously found them to be perfect for what the situation called for—which turned out to be just right, given what this odd couple did get to accomplish. They made important contributions to help bring about the worldwide perennial explosion that we are all now benefiting from.

In fact, the two most prominent Indians visibly involved in the TS in the early days—Damodar K. Mavalankar (1857-?) and T. Subba Row (1856-1890)—would not have been able to implement the clearly internationalist tenor of the theosophical movement that the perennial agenda required.

Damodar was too mystical and detached from the practical work that such a delicate mission required. In fact, he ended up retiring from "the outside world," and finally exited that mundane world, and went off to live with the perennials in the Himalayas.[1]

---

[1] See Sven Eek (comp.), *Dâmodar and the Pioneers of the Theosophical Movement* (1965).

For his part, Subba Row was too deeply involved in Advaita Vedanta. In fact, for some time he had been concerned that HPB had been revealing too much of what he considered to be "initiatory secrets." He was still holding on to the hermetically-sealed notions of the old regionalisms. He didn't realize that we are indeed in a new, planetary era—an era in which the borderless wisdom that informs Advaita Vedanta is what must be emphasized, in order to produce a grand transformation in human consciousness, planet-wide.

It was only shortly before he died that he realized that it was the perennials—under whom he had been working, and by whom he had been initiated—who were responsible for the many previously hermetically sealed revelations made by HPB.[2]

Subba Row had understood everything he had learned from his main perennial mentor—who happened to be also HPB's—as if it only had meaning from an Indian perspective, from the Advaita Vedanta perspective.

But he began to realize only too late in his life that the perennials had indeed a borderless agenda in connection with the beginning of the grandest human-related worldwide cycle ever. Whether he got to see this clearly or not, the fact is that such a mission was difficult for *an Indian*—even an initiated one—to comprehend and accept.

American Agers

An Indian at the head of the theosophical movement would have been more likely to rely heavily on Indian culture. Such an Indian would have behaved much like Sri Aurobindo—who transmogrified the perennial wisdom into just another Indian cult.[3]

In the same way, a Chinese-born person would have been more likely to stick to his own culture, if the Taoist lineage had gone that way. If that had been the case—more probably than

---

[2] See Theosophy Wiki entry "T. Subba Row."
[3] For Aurobindo, see Part Four, "Mutation."

not—a Chinese-born lineage holder would have been more likely to have missed out on the borderless, international nature of the perennial explosion in the American Age.

If a Chinese-born person had been the lineage holder—rather than Bruce Kumar Frantzis—it's quite likely that there would not now be the kind of widespread knowledge and understanding of the internal energy arts, worldwide.

Importantly, the American Age perennial explosion is by, of, and for all humanity. It is absolutely not some "tradition" that belongs exclusively to some specific region or culture.

Founding documents

The present is a unique period in world history. We are living in a time in which the most important cycle ever in *human* experience is in the process of unfolding—and it is happening right before our eyes. It is a planetary cycle affecting *all* of humanity and not just a group here or there.

The present is a time for what could be called "American Agers"—people and leaders who whole-heartedly embrace the whole planet, and not just a region or culture thereof.

It should be clarified that America's founding documents address all human beings and are meant to instill a moral-psychological revolution in all of us, at this unprecedented moment in human history. The most important components of those documents are not related to politics at all, nor to a specific "country." This is addressed further in Chapter 27, "American Age."

The deeper import of America's founding documents is clearly meant for all humanity: "All men are created equal," and "justice for all," is what those documents stand for. America's two mottos—which are an intrinsic component of its founding documents—tell us that "a new age now begins," and that the whole planet is "a unified plurality"—"out of many, one," and "out of one, many."

Those documents also direct us to respect all religions and ideologies based on universal morality—and all such religions and ideologies (including Buddhism, Taoism, and Advaita Vedanta) are inspired by the *borderless* perennial wisdom. America's founding documents thus inspire *all of us* not to feature any one religion or ideology in particular, in contradistinction to all others.

America's founding documents are unambiguously perennial documents—just as much as any scriptures or texts from the past, from any and all world religions.

America's founding documents exhort us—though without using those precise words—to form a nucleus of the universal brotherhood of humanity, without distinctions based on race, creed, caste, gender, color, nationality, or any other prejudice-prone segregations. That, precisely, is what the first object of the Theosophical Society states. And the TS was the main springboard for the ongoing perennial explosion, despite its important deficiencies.

Nothing human is "perfect."

In the perennial explosion—which is the fountainhead and inspiration for *all* humanity at this unprecedented time of major planetary transformations—everyone involved in it must be beyond creating or enabling or accepting prejudicial distinctions of any kind among humans. Those divisions could be related to nationality, or geographical location, or to ethnicity, or to culture, or to standing in society—or to any other prejudicial distinctions.

I submit to you, sensitive reader, that the perennial tenor of the grand revolution that we are all witnessing is at the core of why one sees so many "crossover" elements in the perennial explosion. That, I submit, explains "crossovers" in the founding leadership of the TS. That also explains Bruce K. Frantzis being the Taoist lineage holder.

The Role of a Flower

Incidentally, if you have not met him but wish to see what Frantzis looks like, all you have to do is watch the K video called *The Role of a Flower*, which you can see on *YouTube*. This is a documentary made in Brockwood Park, England, and it includes a poignant excerpt from a talk K gave there in 1985, a year before his death.

At one point in that video, the camera pans through the audience, and then lingers on one man, Bruce Kumar Frantzis. After a while, he was visibly annoyed by the camera being trained on him, and he gets up and walks out of camera range.

Frantzis' interest in K was shared, incidentally by "the other Bruce." According to Bruce Lee's (1940-1973) widow, K was the central inspiration for the most famous martial artist of all times. It was K's insights and observations that inspired Bruce Lee to perceive the martial arts in the revolutionary, internationalist way that he did—and which inspired so many others around the world. It is an intriguing fact that early on in his career as a martial artist, Frantzis sparred at one point with Bruce Lee—exchanging each other's energies, one might say.

Like Frantzis, Lee—who was an American citizen—also followed "the water-course (Taoist) way." Since that happens to be the perennial approach, it is poignantly akin to K's presentation of it—except for the fact that K's message was more clearly borderless, and so was of so much interest to Bruce Lee.

I should clarify that none of the comments above are meant to suggest any connection between Frantzis and K—or with the TS, or with HPB. To my knowledge, Frantzis has no connection with any of them.

My take on this is that it makes sense that Frantzis should have been interested in K, as part of his own education—just as he spent some time in India, learning diverse yogic approaches. But his presence in various places should not be interpreted as meaning anything more than their being part of his "continuing education"—which is to be expected from any serious truth-seeker-truth-finder.

In Frantzis' many books and in the programs that I've been able to attend, he never once refers to K. In addition—to the extent that I'm aware, and despite his being clearly a creative innovator—Frantzis largely adheres to the traditional understanding of Taoism, whereas there is nothing traditional about K.

I should also clarify that my only connection with Frantzis is as a participant—among many thousands, worldwide—in a few of his programs, and as a careful reader and student of his books. In fact, my mentioning him in the present context may be, if anything, a source of annoyance to him.

Perennial explosion

In any case, in the process of becoming more pervasive throughout the world, the Chinese approach has taken full advantage of the receptive milieu created by the perennial explosion of our times. Much like Indian and Tibetan yoga or tantra scholars and practitioners, those involved in the Chinese approach—including Bruce Frantzis—have borrowed some of the terminology and conceptual structures they use from the writings of HPB and her colleagues, particularly those of CWL.[4]

For the above and related additional reasons (discussed more thoroughly elsewhere, such as in *Muse*), the perennial perspective remains invaluable as the source of a borderless universality not available in any regional tradition.

Perennial expositions on subtle energies can and do incorporate the wisdom of the Chinese system as well as that of tantra and other energetic systems from around the world. It is this universality, this borderless quality, that has appealed to people

---

[4] See, for instance, Mantak and Maneewan Chia, *Chi Nei Tsang* (1990), and other works. See also the works by Bruce Frantzis cited above. All of those—and many other titles related to the Chinese energy arts—use CWL's manner of presentation of the body's energy currents and his unprecedented use of language whenever he refers to the subtle energies. Such books tend towards even taking advantage of CWL's illustrations (or a derivation thereof)—but without giving CWL credit.

everywhere. It is also that universality that has made the work of HPB and her colleagues—and even more so K's—unique in world history.

CHAPTER 19
Victorian Exoterics

EARLY TS MEMBERS WERE VICTORIANS. It should be clarified that Queen Victoria (1819-1901) had relatives sitting on the thrones (or being close to thrones) of most European countries. So when I refer to "Victorians," I am referring to all Europeans—and their descendants in many colonies—who lived during Queen Victoria's reign (1837-1901), particularly in the last two decades of it. I am speaking about that period in European and world history, not about the UK alone.

It is important to keep in mind that the terminology and descriptions used publicly by Victorians for their perennial gleanings were cast in the language of their era. Later observers of their work often forget—or fail to see—that some of those Victorians were true pioneers in uncovering and broadcasting these insights, and that they could not but express those insights in terms of the language and perceptions typical of their milieu.

This means in part that perennials—who have always been borderless—had a bewilderingly enormous challenge, in trying to convey borderlessness to deeply committed racist-colonialist-imperialist and highly opinionated Victorians.

Conversely, it was a similar and even greater challenge for TS-connected Victorians to come even close to understanding what the perennials were trying their best to communicate to those Victorians. This was clearly an immensely difficult task, on both sides. It was much like trying to match square pegs with round holes—or maybe even like a Mexican standoff. This seemingly unsurpassable chasm needs to be kept in mind, when considering this issue.

Popularizing *knowledge* of the esoteric

There is in addition an even more important factor to keep in mind—especially in the context of the present research into what is, by far, the most critical phenomenon in perennial as well as TS history. Despite its importance, this factor regarding the Theosophical Society (TS) has been consistently ignored— *by friends and foes alike.*

The TS has always been—from its beginnings, and through to the present—*an exoteric organization.*

The main function of the TS has always been (to put it in the words of the Mahachohan, who was a senior perennial) to "popularize" a *knowledge* of the esoteric.[1] Popularizing *knowledge* of the esoteric is nowhere near being the same thing as *engaging* in the esoteric—let alone *being* an esoteric. Having merely *knowledge* of the esoteric is profoundly and totally unrelated to *understanding* what the esoteric is about.

Merely having knowledge of the esoteric is totally incompatible with the daily act and process of being an esoteric.

Unfortunately for those who have ignored this, actually living the esoteric life is an essential prerequisite for having even the most basic understanding of anything having to do with HPB— *according to HPB and to her perennial mentors.*[2]

This popularizing TS factor is, and has always been, an extremely important function: Without the TS, it would have been impossible for the perennial explosion to have flowered—at least to the extent that it has.

On the other hand, living the esoteric life has never been popular, historically. For millennia, the vast majority of us have usually preferred the nostrums and authorities and hierarchies of conventional religion, rather than living borderlessly. Borderlessness implies caring deeply for all that is, including all human beings—and *that* has *always* been unpopular. It's been

---

[1] Chin, *The Mahatma Letters, Chronological* (1993), Appendix II, 477; Jinarajadasa, *Letters From the Masters of the Wisdom, First Series* (1923), 1.

[2] The requirement of *being* an esoteric in order to understand even the simplest thing about what HPB and her perennial mentors were communicating has been documented in the two-part paper "Transformation: Vital Essence of H.P. Blavatsky's *Secret Doctrine*," which was read at the Third Symposium on *The Secret Doctrine*, in Oklahoma City in May 1998—and it's available onn paradigmshift.network. That paper has been incorporated in the soon-to-be-published *Muse*, which provides a more thorough background and documentation of this all-important fact.

"unpopular" in terms of what people actually do—though not in terms of what they *believe* that they do, and what they say.

The most racist and divisive people I have personally met have been members of group-thinks or congregations who assume themselves to be "the salt of the earth," on the grounds that they belong to such groups.

The importance of popularizing the universal wisdom is not difficult to see. For instance, without the TS, it would have been extremely unlikely that words used initially in a perennial context would have come into the international mainstream vocabulary.

I am referring to words and expressions such as "karma," "Masters," "esoteric Christianity," "shifting of Earth's poles," "Shamballa," "thought forms," "esoteric" "Illuminati," "life on other planets," "avatar," "Zen," "akashic records," "Atlantis," "thought power," "secret societies," "Lemuria," "laws of attraction," "trained clairvoyant," "new age," "aura," "initiation," "chakra," "reincarnation," "yoga," "angels" (in a non-sectarian sense), "meditation," "vegetarianism," "astrology," "cremation," "Kabbalah" (or "cabala"), "Buddhism," "feminism," "without distinction of race, creed, sex, caste, or color," "extra-terrestrials," and so many, many more.

The majority of us today (even within the TS itself) take for granted those and many other words—as if they had always been there, internationally. Even people born in Asian countries (where some of these words have been common for ages) have often come to use such expressions in a more universal sense, and not as a merely regional belief.

Popularization of the perennial wisdom is important.

Also—lest we forget—without the TS, it would have been impossible for the most important phenomenon of the twentieth century to have taken place. The presence in that century of K's insights, researches, and observations—which can now be seen more clearly as *essential* for creating a good society, everywhere on the planet—is an unprecedented phenomenon in the history of the planet, as laid out in Part One, "Krishnamurti."

Obviously, the subject of the importance and relevance of the TS for the present era is immense and multidimensional. It is also beyond the scope of the present exploration—which focuses on the perennial explosion in general, while emphasizing K's insights and inner life as being at the heart of that explosion.[3]

The point I am making is that the significance and relevance of the TS as a perennial popularizer cannot be exaggerated.

At the same time—and despite the vital role that the TS has had in the creation of planetary culture (such as we now have it)—it is also true that the TS has always been *an exoteric organization*. No relevant TS-connected leader has ever claimed otherwise. This is why HPB's writings—and those of her perennial mentors—were invariably peppered with comments regarding the lack of deeper understanding on the part of TS members.

The ES

HPB's perennial mentors, in particular, addressed constantly in their correspondence *the necessity* for the actuality of a major switch in our whole way of perceiving and being. They identified this transformative switch by referring to what they usually called "initiation"—in order to understand even relatively "simple" perennial-related factors.

Unfortunately, TS members have always tended to assume that they already understand ("rather well, thank you very much")—*without being initiated*—everything that came from HPB and her perennial mentors. In other words, TS members and other New Agers have always had the astonishing impudence of assuming that HPB and her perennial mentors did not know what they were talking about. That's just how it is now. That's also how it's always been.

In fact, HPB and her perennial mentors were so appalled and dismayed by the lack of a deeper understanding on the part of

---

[3] The TS influence is addressed briefly in Part One and throughout this study, in various papers at paradigmshift.network, and more thoroughly in the soon-to-be-published *Insights for a New Era*, and *Muse*.

TS members, that in 1888 they created the Esoteric School of Theosophy (EST, or simply ES; the name has changed more than once).

The ES was reluctantly created by the perennials in order to provide an opportunity to the very few TS members who were more serious, to make explorations into the depths of the esoteric life—which is the life within, not the life of reading or writing books and giving lectures and believing in this or that.

Though there have always been TS critics of the very existence of the ES, the founding and existence of the ES is a well-known fact among TS members, and so is not disputed by them. So no one should complain about that *fait accompli.*

But what some TS members may balk at is *the fact* that *the TS is an exoteric organization.*

They tend to assume that being a TS member and believing in what they *arbitrarily* think is "Theosophy" is one and the same with being "esoteric." Unfortunately—and despite this transparent *wishful thinking—the fact* remains that, in founding the ES, HPB and her perennial mentors were stating, through their actions—unambiguously and as plainly as it can be stated—that they considered the TS an exoteric organization.

I should make clear that, in saying that the TS is an exoteric organization, I am merely a messenger. I am just quoting what HPB and her perennial mentors said *alarmingly*, all along—however uncomfortable or inconvenient that *fact* may be for exoteric TS members and New Agers, as we speak.

The exoteric nature of the TS is made clear by HPB and her perennial mentors in a document issued when they created the ES. In that document, they said,

> It is through the Esoteric Section alone, *i.e.*, a group in which all the members, even if unacquainted with one another, work for each other, and by working for all, work for themselves—that the great *Exoteric Society* [emphasis added] may be redeemed and made to realize that in union and harmony alone lie its strength and power.[4]

---

[4] Blavatsky, "The Esoteric Section of the Theosophical Society," in *The Original Programme of the Theosophical Society* (1888), 67.

HPB and her perennial mentors are clearly calling the TS "the great *Exoteric* Society." The language and conceptual structures that have been believed in by TS members—to this day—have been largely and almost exclusively *exoteric*, and usually sourced from Victorian perspectives. This is true also of the many books and articles that have been written—and the even more lectures that have been given and listened to by TS members and New Agers.

Please understand: This is not a criticism of the TS, nor of its members. It is merely a description of facts.

Esoteric texts

To my knowledge, in all the literature that has come out of the TS, only three texts are purely esoteric in nature: *Light on the Path* (1885), *The Voice of the Silence* (1889), and *At the Feet of the Master* (1910).[5] Significantly, the central subject of all of those small yet powerful inspirational books is the ending of the conditioned, ever-analyzing me—and *that* is what the esoteric is and has always been *exclusively* about, as addressed and documented more thoroughly in *Insights for a New Era* and in *Muse*.

Unfortunately, in my experience of six decades as a TS member, I have met precious few members who take this esoteric literature—let alone the esoteric life itself—to heart *in their daily lives*. Yet in the act and process of *putting into practice* these three esoteric texts can be found the best source there is for *being a beginner* in the very ancient yet ever new perennial wisdom.

---

[5] *The Stanzas of Dzyan* is also a purely esoteric text. But this work has been so distorted and misunderstood by Victorian-minded readers and commentators, that I have not included it here as being such a text. I have tried to point to this deeper, truer meaning of the *Stanzas*, by showing how it could be called *"The Stanzas of Zen."* But Victorian-minded exoterics will have none of that, unfortunately. For a fuller discussion and documentation, see *"Transformation: Vital Essence of HPB's Secret Doctrine"*—at paradigmshift.network—and the upcoming *Muse*.

Lamentably, that can be discovered only by the very few who are in earnest to be actual truth-seekers-truth-finders. Still, those small books—precious as they are—are only pointers. It's what you *actually* do daily that matters, not what you read, or even what you "practice"—or the organization that you belong to. That much ought to be obvious, even to the most recalcitrant exoteric.

Furthermore, the language and conceptual structures—and the (mis)understanding by exoteric TS members of the original texts authored by HPB and her perennial mentors, such as *The Secret Doctrine* (1888)—tend to have a Victorian twinge to them. Thus, one often finds bits of "Victorianese" language in subsequent books, and even in more contemporary presentations. Please keep in mind that being "Victorian" implies being racist-colonialist-supremacist.

But as K often said, the word is not the thing. The way something is expressed (whether in Victorianese or "new-paradigm" or any other literary style) is not as important as its substance. And its substance is nowhere nearly as important as being free of me-centeredness—without which freedom nothing one is exposed to means very much.

Perhaps the best way to read the early TS literature is to consider ourselves anthropologists who have just unearthed something from a foreign culture—even when that culture happens to be the one we were born into, or the one that we adhere to. We need to take from that literature only what we find of value for our own lives—in the act and process of being free from the known.

CHAPTER 20
A New Perspective

AS ADDRESSED IN PART TWO, K's inner life is inseparable from his insights, researches, and observations. The two are intrinsically interwoven. To the extent that you don't accept—let alone understand—either one, to that same extent you thereby deny yourself your capacity to understand the other.

I submit to you, attentive reader, that if one does not pay close attention to everything having to do with K's inner life, one is bound to misunderstand at least much of the intent and truer meaning of what he was addressing whenever he was sharing his insights, researches, and observations.

Trying to understand his insights independently of his inner life is tantamount to assuming that what he said is understandable by the analytical mind. That leads to making an ideology out of what he said. The moment that happens, one has transmogrified what he said into just another ideology—something to agree or disagree about—and that is the end of K's actual message.

In addition, given the fact that K spelled out the deeper significance of the borderless wisdom within each of us, this holistic understanding of K has a profound consequence for you, personally.

Inquiring into K's inner life together with his insights opens up a whole new panorama, for each of us. Doing so has the potential of us gaining a much clearer comprehension of life in general, and of our lives in particular.

Borderlessness required

Anyone inquiring into the inner life of K as well as his insights—and thereby the whole of K—would do well to keep in mind the material nature of the subtler energies flowing through our bodies. Such an inquirer would also need to note that these energies, like gravity, are borderless. That is, those energy flows are not culture- nor ideology-dependent. These energies are actually flowing through us, all the time. They are not mere beliefs—as we can corroborate, if we are serious.

Unfortunately, K's psychic experiences have often been discussed as if they were "just" part of "Indian" beliefs and practices—and so as if they belonged exclusively to the tantric or the yoga traditions of India. This is a major blunder, as noted in Parts One and Two.

But once K's experiences are understood not in terms of an "Indian" system of beliefs and practices, but simply as *human* experiences that do not belong to any culture, having a more accurate picture of what was happening in his life becomes possible. In other words, K's experience of the process was not merely or exclusively a result of cultural influences—not to mention "explanations" presumably sourced in *exoteric* "Theosophy," especially in its Victorian dimensions.

The language that has been used to describe many aspects of K's process includes expressions drawn from tantra and from Victorian "Theosophy." This is understandable, since the tantric tradition was the best-preserved perennially-inspired internationally-known school at the time. Also, the TS—within which K was "discovered" and through which he was first presented before the world—is historically associated intimately with India. So misunderstandings regarding K's inner life based on Indian traditions or on "Theosophical" (mis)interpretations of those traditions are quite understandable.

But no tantric text contains the science-inspired descriptions of the flow of subtle energy in K's "process." Such language is to be found, instead, in the literature of the perennial explosion. That unprecedented, borderless use of language—which is the one used to explain such phenomena—had not been possible, before CWL.

What are now widely accepted as the "true" meanings of words such as *chakra* and *kundalini*, for instance, were the *original* and *unprecedented* contribution of the perennial explosion.

That particular use of language—and its conceptual framework—had its source in HPB, and its culmination in CWL.

Another factor to keep in mind is that those who have written about K and his experiences have—more often than not—exhibited an intense prejudice against anything considered by them to be "Theosophical." This prejudice is to some extent also understandable, in part for the reasons stated in previous chapters. As already noted, both "friends" and "foes" of "Theosophy" have misunderstood its very real *perennial* origins.

Nevertheless, the anti-Theosophical prejudice is unquestionably there. This prejudice rears its ugly head in various ways—such as misrepresenting "Theosophical" teachings, and even TS history. The disparaging prejudice also appears in the form of demeaning references to the character of the movement's leaders—who were all individuals of unusually high integrity, and lived lives dedicated to serving humanity.

These anti-Theosophical prejudices are quite common in writings about K's life, even though none of their authors have provided good arguments or well-researched facts to fully justify their often unacceptably prejudicial and provincial attitude.

Credit Theosophists

Intriguingly—and ironically—the authors of these prejudicial views have invariably used theosophical explanations and terminology to discuss K's inner life while in the same breath denying or ignoring their theosophical source!

For instance, when Jayakar refers to "kundalini" and "the chakras" in references to K's inner life, she doesn't speak of "the spiral of the conch-shell," nor of "her shining snake-like form [going] three and a half times around Siva." Yet that precisely is what she needed to refer to—as she was attributing K's experiences to tantric lore, and that is what the actual tantric lore is like in writing, as quoted and discussed in Part Two.

Instead, she uses those terms in the ways presented and explained in *unprecedented language* by CWL—and by others following in his footsteps. Yet she doesn't credit CWL and Theosophy—as she had the obligation to do—for her use of that language. Instead, she recklessly criticizes CWL at every possible turn—while yet using CWL's language, *which had never been used before in human history.* Similar comments can be made by others who have discussed these issues, as related to K's inner life.

It is fine, of course, for anyone to criticize CWL or Theosophy. But honesty and integrity demand that critics absolutely never use the language and terminology that was uniquely created by CWL and by the Theosophical milieu—unless the critics give credit where credit is due. Yet none of the many critics have ever given credit to CWL—much less to HPB. That gigantic gap in their criticisms discredits profoundly, and perhaps totally, all such writings.

A New Perspective

An entirely new perspective on all this—a perspective based on facts and documentation, not on what amounts to malicious gossip—is obviously called for.

Clearly, a more open-minded, research-oriented, *borderless* attitude is needed when examining K's inner life. The present inquiry is an honest attempt at doing just that. The soon-to-be-published second edition of *The Inner Life of Krishnamurti* also addresses this borderless attitude called for in any discussion of K's inner life.

In the end, only posterity and further unbiased, presuppositionless, *honest research* could be a proper judge, of whether the present research has been successful in helping to unravel—at least to some extent—K's otherwise very strange inner life.

Let's first look briefly at how CWL almost single-handedly revolutionized the language we now use, to refer to energy flows in all human bodies. His language is so easy to follow, that it's become widely used—even in the mainstream. This CWL-created language has made it possible for us now to express in universally-understood terms what had formerly been incomprehensible to all but scholars and practitioners of tantric and yogic lore.

CWL

Among the early TSers, CWL was the pioneer who made a detailed clairvoyant study of the subtle energies. He provided the language and the conceptual and aesthetic images that have now become commonplace in discussions of these energies in the relevant literature—even in the mainstream. CWL's clairvoyant research made a considerable impact on the worldwide understanding of psychic elements in all of our lives—elements that are implicit in the borderless wisdom, which is within each and every one of us.

But importantly in the present context, CWL also played a critical role in K's early development. For these and related reasons, it is appropriate and even necessary to look at his research—even if it is done ever-so-briefly—and to consider some of its perennial implications.

During his lifetime, and particularly while he was more active as a writer and speaker internationally, from 1895 to 1934—and for several decades after his death—there was heated debate over the accuracy, and even the reality, of CWL's clairvoyance. Thus it is of value to see how his psychic ability has stood up to the more rigorous scrutiny of researchers, decades after his death.

CWL did clairvoyant research in numerous areas. Some—such as his investigations into K's previous incarnations, and related factors—are extremely difficult to assess.[1]

Apart from that difficulty, it is a fact that people's opinions about books of this sort are—more often than not—based on whatever prejudices they bring to their reading. Still, there is an extensive literature consisting of either accepting blindly or

---

[1] Leadbeater and Besant, *The Lives of Alcyone*, 2 vols (1924); see also Leadbeater and Besant, *Man: Whence, How, and Whither* (1913).

denying recklessly researches such as CWL's. Authors of such all-accepting or totally-denying books tend to ignore phenomenological principles of research—in which one must "bracket off" one's prejudices before one can claim to be truly *researching* anything.

Other areas of CWL's clairvoyant explorations, however, are more amenable to a more fair and balanced assessment. In some of these other areas, CWL's remarkable abilities appear unquestionable.

For instance, beginning in the 1880s or early 1890s until shortly before his death in 1934 (about four decades), CWL did extensive clairvoyant research into the structure of the 92 elements that were then said to make up all physical matter.[2] Though he was the senior researcher, he did much of this work with AB—up until 1913, when she decided not to continue using her clairvoyance for such investigations.

The main reason AB gave for cutting herself off from clairvoyant researches is that she considered it wiser to focus all of her energies on engaging rigorously on social change—largely, though not exclusively—through education.[3] Among numerous other activities, she worked ceaselessly on bringing about India's independence.

CWL and AB called their careful researches into subatomic particles "occult chemistry." To subsequent inquirers into these clairvoyant investigations, their researches seemed to have been either the subject of unquestioned belief, or touted as mere fantasy, for nearly fifty years after their deaths.

The most important assessments of CWL's occult chemistry investigations were made by the British Theosophical Research Centre Science Group, several members of which were highly respected scientists who belonged to the internationally

---

[2] Besant and Leadbeater, *Occult Chemistry* (1908); but consult the much expanded and better illustrated third edition (1951). There were 92 known elements in CWL's lifetime. Other elements have been identified since—but most of these have been man-made, in the process of researching atomic energy.

[3] For AB's intense work for social change, see Agarwal and Oliveira, compilers, *Annie Besant in India* (2021).

prestigious British Royal Society. As late as the 1950s, these scientists—who as TS members were willing to look into the issue with an open mind—had come to inconclusive findings. As they put it:

> In some few cases the occult structures seem better suited than the orthodox to explain the facts of organic chemistry, but in others there is difficulty in reconciling the occult structures with the available data.
>
> . . . Our brief comparison of the occult and orthodox theories of atomic structure clearly reveals one fact at least—that much work remains to be done before the rapprochement which we believe to be eventually, is actually realized.[4]

However, in 1980 Cambridge physicist Stephen M. Phillips (n.d.) published the results of his own subsequent research into CWL's psychic abilities in this field.[5] In summary, he wrote:

> In conclusion, the clairvoyant description of matter appears to have very close contact with chemistry, nuclear physics and the quark structure underlying the physical universe.
>
> . . . At present one can with a measure of confidence claim that quarks were observed by Annie Besant and C.W. Leadbeater, using yogic techniques, 69 years before scientists suggested that [quarks] existed.[6]

Phillips' assessment shows poignantly at least one critical fact regarding CWL's clairvoyance related to occult chemistry: The reason why previous investigators had assessed CWL's occult-chemistry-related clairvoyance either negatively or inconclusively is that CWL had been describing quarks and their behavior. But quarks were discovered by physicists only decades later. This underscores the reality of CWL's clairvoyant abilities in that area of research.

CWL could not have gotten the information from scientific sources, because there were none in his lifetime. Nor was the

---

[4] Smith and Slater, *The Field of Occult Chemistry* (1954).

[5] Phillips, *Extrasensory Perception of Quarks* (1980).

[6] Phillips, *The Theosophist*, October 1978.

notion of quarks even speculated about in the scientific literature, during CWL's lifetime.

Moreover, CWL's observations were not a set of casual or imprecise or vague remarks. Rather, his descriptions were the result of extensive and careful, meticulous research conducted
over a period of four decades. Out of his research he provided
specific descriptions, with very clear drawings of the subatomic
structure of all physical elements.

The aura

Another area that has been researched intensively since
CWL's death is the aura. It is CWL who popularized the use of
the word "aura," which is now commonly used. The aura can be
said to refer to the psychic field around all living things. More
often, it refers specifically to that field as it interpenetrates and
surrounds the human body.

Here again, much of what CWL had stated on the subject had
been a matter of belief or disbelief, for decades after his death.
However, a number of subsequent researchers have discovered
remarkable similarities—even identity—between CWL's descriptions and their own findings. Drs. J. Moss and K.L. Johnson of the Neuro-Psychiatric Institute of California, who conducted research on the human aura, commented in 1974:

> We are amazed at similarities between our photographs and the
> drawings and descriptions of human auras by psychics Annie Besant
> and C.W. Leadbeater.[7]

Although these findings point strongly to CWL's clairvoyant
abilities in areas amenable to rigorous scientific investigation,
they do not guarantee that he was equally accurate in other aspects of his clairvoyant work. They do suggest, however, that his
work should be considered seriously. For instance, professor of

---

[7] Moss and Johnson, *Communion*, September 1974, 2. For more recent research into
the aura, see the bibliography in Kunz, *The Personal Aura* (1991).

physics P. Krishna relates the following anecdote, told to him by Mr. B. Shiva Rao, who had known K since he had been "discovered" by CWL. As professor Krishna relates:

> Being a scientist I was very skeptical about occult powers, so I asked Mr. Shiva Rao whether he had any direct evidence of the occult powers of Mr. Leadbeater. He told me that he had direct evidence of it because one day in 1912 he was with CWL when suddenly the latter said, "Shiva Rao, I see a dreadful thing happening. A large ship is sinking. People are running helter-skelter but no one is able to save them." He closed his eyes and lay down on the couch, and described the whole scene in detail. The next morning the papers reported the sinking of the Titanic! Apparently, CWL was seeing it all happening from thousands of miles away.
>
> His selection of Krishnamurti in 1909 is also evidence of his occult powers.[8]

Apart from his "discovery" of K, CWL also conducted extensive clairvoyant investigations in connection with K. In fact, *The Inner Life of Krishnamurti*—and much that is addressed in the present study—is in part an inquiry into some of the most debated claims made by CWL regarding K.

Pioneer

Scholars and researchers of the subtle energies who lived prior to CWL were limited to speaking of what they knew about such energies using the arcane terminology and concepts of their particular traditions. As already noted, tantric descriptions of kundalini and the chakras, for instance, were given in poetical, mythological, private terms meaningful only to tantric practitioners and academic specialists.

CWL demythologized the subject through his unique, unprecedented way of articulating his clairvoyant explorations conducted in a scientific spirit, and through his subsequent expositions using borderless language informed by science.

---

[8] Krishna, *A Jewel on a Silver Platter: Remembering Jiddu Krishnamurti* (2015), 127.

CWL made this research available to an international audience by describing what he saw in terms of the perennial wisdom as he understood it, while yet using (like K was to do later, in psychological areas of human experience) a language that was simple and easy to understand by anyone in the world. He was thus following in the footsteps of HPB—but using declarative sentences instead of mythical jargon expressed poetically. He also used a purely descriptive language that was his unique creation.[9]

CWL's unique use of language—as well as his conceptual framework—may on occasion seem dated. He was after all a Victorian—though most of his work was published after the Victorian era died with Queen Victoria in 1901. So it is through the filter of the verbal and even conceptual mannerisms of that subculture that we receive his perennial insights. Nevertheless, it is possible for anyone in the world (even those who disagree with him)—in any culture—to understand CWL when he writes:

> In ordinary superficial conversation a man sometimes mentions his soul—implying that the body through which he speaks is the real man, and that this thing called the soul is a possession or appendage of that body—a sort of captive balloon floating over him, and in some vague sort of way attached to him. This is a loose, inaccurate and misleading statement; the exact opposite is the truth. Man is a soul and owns a body—several bodies in fact; for besides the visible vehicle by means of which he transacts his business with his lower world, he has others which are not visible to ordinary sight, by means of which he deals with the emotional and mental worlds.

---

[9] For an example of the worldwide appeal and pervasive influence of CWL's unprecedented way of explaining these subtler energies, see, for instance, Shroff, *Khvarenaugh Khoreh Aura,* from *What Every Zarathustrian Should Understand* (1980). This work—as well as others in the series—includes actual reproductions of CWL's drawings to represent the aura, as well as CWL's explanations of the subtler energies, while making comparisons with non-Zoroastrian ways of describing those energies, such as the Chinese and the Hindu. The Parsees (as Zoroastrians are called in India, due to their Persian pedigree)—like the Hindus and the Buddhists—began to experience an ongoing explosion of activity at the end of the nineteenth century, as a result of the work of HPB and of those who followed in her footsteps, as addressed in Part Two.

. . . Students of medicine are now familiar with [the body's] be-wildering complexities, and have at least a general idea of the way in which its amazingly intricate machinery works.

. . . Naturally, however, they have had to confine their attention to that part of the body which is dense enough to be visible to the eye, and most of them are probably unaware of the existence of that type of matter, still physical though invisible, to which in Theosophy we give the name of "etheric." This invisible part of the physical body is of great importance to us, for it is the vehicle through which flow the streams of vitality which keep the body alive, and without it as a bridge to convey undulations of thought and feeling from the astral to the vis-ible denser physical matter, the ego could make no use of the cells of his brain. It is clearly visible to the clairvoyant as a mass of faintly-luminous violet-grey mist, interpenetrating the denser part of the body, and extending very slightly beyond it.

The chakras or force-centres are points of connections at which energy flows from one vehicle or body of a man to another. Anyone who possesses a slight degree of clairvoyance may easily see them in the etheric double, where they show themselves as saucer-like depres-sions or vortices in its surface. When quite undeveloped, they appear as small circles about two inches in diameter, glowing dully in the or-dinary man; but when awakened and vivified they are seen as blazing, coruscating whirlpools, much increased in size, and resembling min-iature suns. We sometimes speak of them as roughly corresponding to certain physical organs; in reality they show themselves at the surface of the etheric double, which projects slightly beyond the outline of the dense body.[10]

Before CWL, absolutely no one, in any of the worldwide cul-tures, ever spoke or wrote of these matters in such a clear, bor-derless, easy-to-understand way. It was CWL who created a manner of speaking of, and describing, specific aspects of our psychic anatomy and physiology. CWL's *unprecedented* and unique way of speaking and illustrating these energies has be-come an integral component of language everywhere, even in the mainstream.

Buddhists, Hindus, Taoists, Parsees, and others whose writ-ings refer to these energies and processes began to use CWL's borderless approach to refer to them—*but without ever giving*

---

[10] Leadbeater, *The Chakras* (1927), 1-4.

him credit for this all-important contribution, without which it is impossible to speak of the subject at all to an international, mainstream audience.

Despite the fact that CWL was clearly the pioneer and creator of this manner of speaking and conceptualizing, it is a fact that the vast majority of people who speak or write of these subjects—including scientific researchers—invariably either ignore its source in CWL's writings, or deliberately *choose* to ignore it.

Significantly, CWL originated a whole genre of worldwide literature on the subtle energy patterns in the human aura—what he called "thought forms," the "chakras," and "kundalini." Because of the descriptive, scientific-sounding literary style in which he wrote about these formerly arcane and even inscrutable subjects, he made it very easy for others subsequently to write or speak about them, including academics and even practitioners of all religions and methodologies in the world—not to mention advertisers and writers of TV sitcoms and of screenplays of feature films.

Unfortunately, the overwhelming majority of those others have never given him credit for his extraordinary contributions—without which none of them would ever have been able to say anything at all in this area.

It was CWL who gave all of them a voice with which to communicate to others. Whatever one may think of CWL himself— or of the topic—his manner of presenting it represented a genuinely creative effort, and an achievement unprecedented and unique in world history.

That is not an opinion. It is an easily verifiable fact.

Moreover, from the time CWL publicized his clairvoyant research (1895-1934) until the 1970s, no comparable works on the aura, or thought forms, or the chakras—or any kind of human energy flow—were published. During those decades, the writings of CWL—and to a lesser extent those of his colleagues and disciples in the TS, such as Geoffrey Hodson (1886-1983), Phoebe Bendit (1891-1968), and Dora van Gelder Kunz (1904-

1999)—were the only universally accessible and understandable sources for clairvoyant expositions of these subjects.

Pervasive influence

CWL's influence has been considerable. Apart from the direct impact implicit in creating a whole genre of literature and scientific research, CWL's clairvoyant work inspired a number of artists whose work is highly regarded. Among artists whose work was importantly influenced by CWL are, for instance, Wassily Kandinsky (1866-1944) in Europe and Agnes Pelton (1881-1961) in America.[11]

The most comprehensive documentation to date of the pervasive and even formidable influence of the perennial wisdom (mostly through theosophically-derived channels) on the birth and development of modern and contemporary art, is the massive and meticulously researched work by Marty Bax (b. 1956).[12]

Bax's reviewer—Thomas Ockerse (b. 1940), professor of graphic design at the Rhode Island School of Design—poignantly remarks on how Bax shows "[H]ow artists shared Theosophical ideas among themselves and how these ideas manifested through individuals and groups," and points out how this is "a book that looks into the fusion of Theosophy and art from an author who has substantial knowledge of both."[13]

Importantly in the present context, HPB in general, and CWL in particular, were central to the radical move in all art forms that took place primarily in the quarter-century before and after

---

[11] For CWL's influence on Kandinsky, see, for instance, Kandinsky, *Concerning the Spiritual in Art, and Painting in Particular* (1912). For Agnes Pelton (as well as some of the major figures in twentieth-century art), see Levin and Lorenz, *Theme and Improvisation: Kandinsky and the American Avant-Garde 1912-1950, An Exhibition Organized by the Dayton Art Institute* (1993). See also Regier, *The Spiritual Image in Modern Art* (1987).

[12] Bax, *Het Web der Shepping (The Web of Creation: Theosophy and Art in the Netherlands, from Lauweriks to Mondrian* (2006); see also Bax, *Piet Mondrian: The Amsterdam Years 1892-1912* (1994); see also Bax, *Complete Modrian* (2001).

[13] Ockerse, review of Bax, *Het Web der Shepping, Quest,* November/December 2008.

1900, which was the seminal period of this important cultural development.

Corrections

As a "trained clairvoyant," CWL certainly made it clear with regard to his research that he did not consider his perceptions to be "the final word"—as "ordinary" clairvoyants tend to do. He often said that he was doing pioneer work in an extremely difficult to convey aspect of human experience—and that therefore other researchers should take pains either to corroborate or correct his work. This has been done. Other trained clairvoyants have corroborated much of what he said, and have also corrected some of it on finer points.[14]

I should add here that clairvoyant research in the manner of CWL is not an easy thing to do. According to him, reporting on what the researcher sees is made extremely difficult by a number of features encountered by the viewer. Among other things, CWL points out that the "astral" world is not a three-dimensional world, and that there are more dimensions to it—so objects and events do not happen in the same way they do in 3-D.

That—in and by itself—makes it extremely difficult to convey to non-clairvoyants what is being perceived. The researcher is forced to speak in a manner that does convey to 3-D people what he is seeing, while yet being as true as possible to the reality actually seen—which is not in 3-D.

That is only one of many difficulties involved in conveying to others what CWL was perceiving clairvoyantly. But it is sufficient to understand what CWL meant, when he said that further research by others was necessary.

---

[14] For trained clairvoyants subsequent to CWL who have corroborated substantial aspects of his perceptions and expanded on others, see the numerous works by Geoffrey Hodson, including *The Miracle of Birth: A Clairvoyant Study of Prenatal Life* (1929), *The Kingdom of the Gods* (1952), and *Music Forms: Superphysical Effects of Music Clairvoyantly Observed* (1976). For more recent research, see works by Dora Kunz, such as *The Chakras and the Human Energy Fields* (1989, co-authored with Dr. Shafica Karagulla).

Incidentally, this may also help explain why tantric literature uses poetical and quite convoluted language to refer to non-clairvoyants the nature of that psychic world. This is not an easy thing to do—and it goes directly to showing that what CWL achieved in this regard is truly monumental, however much we may just take it for granted now.

The pioneering work of CWL—both clairvoyant and literary—has opened doors even for scientific researchers to make investigations into the nature of kundalini, and for a more universal idiom to be employed when speaking of these formerly arcane and cryptically-expressed subjects. For instance, in his introduction to what could be considered a definitive anthology on kundalini, editor John White explains:

> Kundalini is the personal aspect of the universal life force named *prana* by the yogic tradition. This primal cosmic energy is akin, if not identical, to *ch'i* (Chinese), *ki* (Japanese), the Holy Spirit, and various other terms from cultures that identify a life force that is the source of all vital activity.
>
> Prana has not yet been identified by modern science, but ancient wisdom maintains that it is the means for raising human awareness to a higher form of perception, variously called illumination, enlightenment, cosmic consciousness, *samadhi*.
>
> Kundalini, often referred to as the "serpent power" because it is symbolized by a coiled snake, can be concentrated and channeled through the spine into the brain—a process likewise not yet identified by modern science. The systematized process for accomplishing this upward flowing of energy is known as kundalini yoga.[15]

Such a clearly expressed exposition—which anyone can understand—would never have been possible, had it not been for the pioneering literary and research efforts of HPB and her colleagues, foremost of all CWL.

The impact of CWL's work in the context of the present study—as well as in *The Inner Life of Krishnamurti*—needs to be especially acknowledged. A main reason for the dire need to acknowledge CWL's stunning contribution to world culture, is

---

[15] White, *Kundalini, Evolution, and Enlightenment* (1979), 21.

that most authors who have written about chakras, auras, kundalini, or similar matters either ignore CWL altogether, or criticize him in terms of their own preconceived notions.

Such authors have shunned CWL despite the fact that they would never have been able to write such books, if it hadn't been for CWL having given them first the language and the conceptual structures and the clear illustrations that made their work possible at all.[16] This is true despite the fact that all of these authors draw on CWL's linguistic and conceptual framework, since he was the pioneer in this field.

More significant for the present exploration is the fact that authors writing about K have also questioned CWL's clairvoyance without providing evidence for their claims against him on this point—hence my present clarification regarding CWL's massive and unacknowledged influence on present-day worldwide culture.

CWL, the process, and kundalini

All of the above—and much more that I haven't gone into—shows clearly how very critical it is to have as thorough an assessment as possible of CWL's abilities, in order to better understand what was going on in K's process. Otherwise, K's inner experiences can—and have been—arbitrarily labeled as "hallucinations," "mysterics," "visions"—and even "delusions." Or else—which is just as bad—they have to be described in the specialist language of a particular sect.

It was the rise of kundalini up K's spine—but even more, its active, painful action in his head—that held center-stage in the psycho-physiological aspects of the process. In fact, most of what the process consisted of was focused on several centers *in the head*, not on the conventionally accepted chakras, as noted

---

[16] For examples of such usage without crediting CWL, see, for instance, Bruyere, *Wheels of Light* (1994), and Judith, *Wheels of Life* (1987), neither of whom give credit to CWL, despite their use of his terminology, his style of presentation, his conceptual framework, and his way of illustrating with drawings many such psychic phenomena related to the more subtle human anatomy and physiology.

in the second edition of *The Inner Life of Krishnamurti*. It is in large part this perennial focus on the centers in the head that differs totally from the conventional understanding of "kundalini" and the "chakras."

In any case, and as the following shows, the word "kundalini"—as it comes up in K's process—is used in a non-cultural, borderless sense, much like the borderless sense ascribed to the word "gravity."

With that understanding, we may proceed. I have found it helpful to look at kundalini not so much as if it were exclusively a kind of "mysterious force" that happens to be intrinsically connected to Indian lore *exclusively*. Rather, it has helped me to look at it in terms of energy flows such as those addressed in quantum physics.

Concerning the serpent fire—as kundalini is often called—CWL goes deeper than ancient scriptures in the process of explaining its nature and significance. As he put it:

> This force . . . exists on all planes of which we know anything; but it is the expression of it in etheric matter with which we have to do at present. It is not convertible into either the primary force already mentioned or the force of vitality which comes from the sun, and it does not seem to be affected in any way by any other forms of physical energy.
>
> On attempting to investigate the conditions at the centre of the earth we find there a vast globe of such tremendous force that we cannot approach it.
>
> . . . The force of kundalini in our bodies comes from that laboratory of the Holy Ghost deep down in the earth. It belongs to that terrific glowing fire of the underworld. That fire is in striking contrast to the fire of vitality which comes from the sun, which will presently be explained. The latter belongs to air and light and the great open spaces; the fire which comes from below is much more material, like the fire of red-hot iron, of glowing metal.
>
> There is a rather terrible side to this tremendous force; it gives the impression of descending deeper and deeper into matter, of moving slowly but irresistibly onwards, with relentless certainty.
>
> . . . We hear much of this strange fire and of the danger of prematurely arousing it; and much of what we hear is undoubtedly true. There is indeed most serious peril in awakening the higher aspects of

this furious energy in a man before he has gained the strength to control it, *before he has acquired the purity of life and thought which alone can make it safe for him to unleash potency so tremendous* [emphasis added].

But kundalini plays a much larger part in daily life than most of us have hitherto supposed; there is a far lower and gentler manifestation of it which is already awake within us all, which is not only innocuous but beneficent, which is doing its appointed work day and night while we are entirely unconscious of its presence and activity.

We have of course previously noticed this force as it flows along the nerves, calling it simply nerve-fluid, and not recognizing it for what it really is. The endeavour to analyse it and to trace it back to its source shows us that it enters the human body at the root chakra.

Like all other forces, kundalini is itself invisible; but in the human body it clothes itself in a curious nest of hollow concentric spheres of astral and etheric matter, one within another, like the balls in a Chinese puzzle. There appear to be seven such concentric spheres resting within the root chakra, in and around the last real cell or hollow of the spine close to the coccyx; but only in the outermost of these spheres is the force active in the ordinary man.

In the others it is "sleeping," as is said in some of the Oriental books; and it is only when the man attempts to arouse the energy latent in those inner layers that the dangerous phenomena of the fire begin to show themselves. The harmless fire of the outer skin of the ball flows up the spinal column, using (so far as investigations have gone up to the present) the three lines of Sushumna, Ida and Pingala simultaneously.[17]

Like other expounders of the perennial wisdom, CWL used terminology from various religions and philosophies in his expositions. The careful reader may note how that terminology gains a different, more universal, borderless meaning when put in the perennial context, the way CWL does.

Another aspect of CWL's exposition that the alert reader will notice, is his attempt to express what he saw in scientific terms. That is, he was making direct observations. He was not merely following the language of some culturally-dependent tradition. In doing this, he was inviting others to make further observations—he was proposing that one follow the scientific method,

---

[17] Leadbeater, *The Chakras* (1927), 27-31.

whereby numerous investigators would make observations, and then correct and tweak whatever had been gathered before.

CWL's approach is always one of being very careful in his painstaking observations, while at the same time being tentative in his expression to others. He never once claims anything like omniscience regarding any of his clairvoyant investigations, no matter what the subject. He always emphasized that others needed to update or clarify or explore further whatever he had observed.

That scientific attitude of CWL's is not to be found in any prior literature on these subjects. Subsequent authors in the TS line—clairvoyants such as Dora Kunz and Geoffrey Hodson—have followed CWL's approach of treating those types of observations as scientific investigations—not dogmas to be believed in devotedly.

Unfortunately, authors outside of that line have often gone back to expressing themselves with a sense of authority about their expositions—and that makes their assertive (and therefore me-centered) approach kindred to the way ancient literature is often (mis)understood. This is an extremely important point to keep in mind, whenever one is delving into these subjects.

Not all "clairvoyants" are alike. *Caveat emptor.*

CWL and K

CWL's clairvoyant findings are not only relevant to better understand K's "process." They are also in accord with K's researches into *what is*, in an interesting and perhaps unexpected way. CWL consistently described emotions and thoughts as composed of ultra-subatomic particles of energy-matter. In this, he was following in HPB's footsteps, though he was expressing it, again, in his unique manner.

This means that—according to CWL's perceptions—there is no clear demarcation between the observer and the observed. This implication of his work is in agreement with K's insights regarding human psychology. It is also in accord with quantum physics, which—despite its being "discovered" in the 1920s—did not really come into its own until long after CWL's death.

Having a non-authoritarian and even hesitant or tentative perspective is the very heart of the perennial wisdom. Not coincidentally, it is also the approach of any true scientific research. And—lest we forget—this non-assertive spirit of tentativeness is at the very core of K's insights, researches, and observations. Such is the nature of truth-seeking-truth-finding.

This is yet another way of saying that CWL's humble attitude is critical, and not just because it is precisely the attitude of any true scientist. The very core of the perennial wisdom is about the ending of the me—while authority and unquestioned assertiveness epitomize and glorify the me.

K himself knew and confirmed the value of CWL's work.

In the late 1970s, after Mary Lutyens' first volume of memoirs on K had been published in 1975, academics and other professionals met with K on various occasions. More than once in these meetings, as well as in private—and based on what they had read in K's biography—CWL and AB were criticized by these academics and others, as having been misguided in many ways.

In every one of these various occasions, K found himself defending CWL and AB, pointing out that "these were very serious people."[18]

---

[18] K's biographies make references to K defending CWL and AB, as addressed more pointedly in *The Inner Life of Krishnamurti*. But K's attitude towards CWL and AB also was referred to by several of those present in those conversations. Among the participants in such conversations was Dr. David Bohm—who confirmed this to me in personal communications.

CHAPTER 21
Discovery

CWL IS A CENTRAL FIGURE IN ANY STUDY or consideration of K's life. After all, it was he who "discovered" the boy Krishna on Adyar Beach in early 1909. Immediately upon seeing him for the first time ever, and not even knowing who K was, CWL confided to a few close colleagues that he had never seen an aura so free of selfishness. Later, CWL created puzzlement and unbelief in many who knew Krishna, when he stated unequivocally that the boy would turn into a great speaker.

One of CWL's colleagues, the educator Ernest Wood (1883-1965)—about whom more is detailed in Part Four, "Mutation"—was astonished at CWL's words. He knew Krishna and his brothers very well, as he had befriended them in the process of tutoring them—and he was certain that CWL was wrong.

In Wood's estimation—and apart from the fact that the boy did not know English, there were other factors. Wood was teaching him and his younger brother Nityananada (d. 1925), and he thought that Krishna was "retarded" and would probably die at a young age, as some of his siblings actually did. In fact, everyone else who knew Krishna at the time perceived him much the way Wood did—even including Krishna's father. As it was, all of his siblings were dead by the early 1950s, while K lived until 1986. As Mary Lutyens wrote in her memoir of K:

> It could not have been Krishna's outward appearance that struck Leadbeater, for apart from his wonderful eyes, he was not at all prepossessing at that time. He was under-nourished, scrawny and dirty; his ribs showed through his skin and he had a persistent cough; his teeth were crooked and he wore his hair in the customary Brahmin fashion of South India, shaved in front to the crown and falling to below his knees in a pigtail at the back; moreover his vacant expression gave him an almost moronic look. People who had known him before he was "discovered" by Leadbeater said there was little difference between him and his ["retarded"] youngest brother, Sadanand.

Moreover, according to Wood, he was so extremely weak physically that his father declared more than once that he was bound to die.[1]

Later, CWL looked more closely at K's aura, and eventually got to study clairvoyantly some fifty of the boy's previous incarnations.[2] These researches convinced CWL that not only would K develop into a much greater speaker than AB—who was a legend in her own time as a very accomplished orator, even among non-sympathizers. CWL also made declarations about K based on what the perennials who founded the TS—and with whom CWL was in constant contact—had told him.

According to CWL, those perennials told him that the Buddha Maitreya—whose incarnation as the successor Gautama Buddha is expected by Buddhists within this time period—would "overshadow" K. Based on what the perennials had told him, CWL declared that the "Lord Maitreya"—who is known as "Krishna" in India, and as "Christ" in Christianity—would give out, through Krishnamurti, the keynote teaching for the new era that HPB had referred to in her writings.

AB was later to confirm all of CWL's claims in regard to K. She declared that her perennial mentors—as well as HPB—had told her that K would be "overshadowed" by Maitreya.

A critic's dilemma

Needless to say, CWL's declarations, which were supported and restated by AB, created a huge uproar in the TS. After all, the TS had never been millenarian, in any way—and the organization was split many ways as a result. In fact, this issue became the *cause célèbre* that generated many splits in the TS, thereby creating some of the central groups that eventually became what later came to be called, collectively, the "New Age" movement.

---

[1] Lutyens, *Krishnamurti: The Years of Awakening* (1975), 21.
[2] These researches—which were originally published in *The Theosophist*—resulted in Leadbeater and Besant, *The Lives of Alcyone*, 2 vols., 1924. Further details about the previous lives of "Alcyone" (the name given to "the reincarnating entity") are related in Leadbeater and Besant, *Man: Whence, How, and Whither* (1913).

Given the fact that both AB and CWL were deeply committed to the work and success of the TS, the resultant turmoil in the TS had to affect them negatively quite intensely, on a daily basis.

Furthermore, these declarations of theirs caused an immense amount of trouble personally for both AB and CWL. It is a fact that the remainder of their lives (a quarter of a century) would have been far simpler and happier if they had not made such momentous declarations.

In addition, CWL stated many times that he personally would never have pushed the onslaught of notoriety on the extremely shy and sensitive boy, but that he and AB made these declarations at the behest of the perennials. They both affirmed numerous times that—in making such declarations—they were merely doing what the perennials had requested them to do, and that they were but doing "the Masters' work."

If CWL and AB had invented all this—as a number of authors have asserted, without any evidence and based on their prejudiced predispositions—it was a most unintelligent and self-defeating thing for them to have done. Essentially, they got only an immense amount of grief in return, and their theosophical work suffered tremendously, as well. Yet no one has ever accused either of them of having lacked in acumen—nor accused them of being frivolous regarding the TS.

Anyone looking seriously into this *must* answer the question: Why did CWL and AB make such declarations? They said all along that they thought it wrong to expose the shy and sensitive boy to all the notoriety. They got no personal benefit at all from doing so, but suffered immensely and personally, instead. The declarations put the whole TS—whose work they were deeply committed to—in bewildering turmoil.

Why would they do such a thing? Any would-be critic must *answer that question.*

In fact, this issue is without question the most difficult in theosophical history for later TS members to explain, to this day. One must also look very carefully at the fact that CWL and AB spent more energy on promoting "the Coming of the World

Teacher" than on any other project they undertook throughout their very long and superactive lives.

If they were mistaken—given their prioritizing "the Coming" far more intensely than anything and everything else they were involved in—suspicion must be cast on much of the rest of their work, as well. Any serious person *with integrity* must answer this.

Why was this, *by far,* the most important thing for both of them to do?

Why?

In subsequent decades—and up to the present—many TS members have chosen to "look the other way" on this issue, and have stuck determinedly on a "don't ask, don't tell" attitude, while avoiding making any references to this subject, or even to CWL and AB. That strikes me as a multidimensionally shallow and fickle attitude—considering that this is unquestionably the most central and important issue in the history of the TS—and in the history of the whole New Age movement. After all, this was the one and only reason that "the New Age movement" is called "New Age."

This attitude is not only shallow and fickle: It is positively immoral—to the extent that it implies undermining the work of perennials throughout the ages, not to mention that it is a clear violation of universal morality, which is within each of us.

At the same time, such TS members almost universally have disagreed about this with AB and CWL—not to mention HPB and her perennial mentors, who had declared in 1888, upon founding of the Esoteric School, that there would be "an avataric manifestation" in the twentieth century.

TS members and New Agers who deny the claims made by CWL and AB are in total disagreement with HPB and her perennial mentors—insofar as they stated in print that there would be "an avataric manifestation" in the twentieth century.[3]

---

[3] In fact, this declaration of "an avataric manifestation" appears in more HPB publications than anything else she ever wrote. Yet in my experience, the vast majority of TS members are totally oblivious to this fact. Please do yourself a favor, and check

Many TSers have gone out of their way to disavow any connection whatsoever with anything having to do with these declarations—and with CWL in particular.

Their antagonistic attitude towards CWL's and AB's declarations put these critics (in and out of the TS) in the unenviable position of largely accepting the metaphysical and clairvoyant presentations and writings of CWL and AB—though usually not acknowledging them by name—while at the same time rejecting the one component of it all that CWL and AB both considered most important, by far. These critics clearly give the strong impression of wanting to keep the cake, but eating it, too.

To this day, such *exoteric* TS members have *never* explained this profound incompatibility between their professions of faith, and their practice. It has always seemed to me that exoteric, Victorian-minded TS members have absolutely no explanation for their K-related prejudices, and that their only option—in order to sustain such prejudices, at all costs—is to ignore anything and everything having to do with K. They seem to feel that all they have to do is pretend that these *well-documented* realities never happened—and that those realities will go away, somehow.

Whenever these would-be critics do speak of K (usually only because they are pushed into doing so), they often will refer to K as "a great teacher"—meaning by that expression that K was "one of many." Also, in saying that K was "a great teacher," they make the absurd assumption that they thereby wash their hands of the whole issue, given that they have acknowledged "something good" about K.

Once they have done that, they then proceed to change the subject to something they find "more palatable"—subjects of Victorian interest, such as Western "Traditionalism," with its intense and purely me-centered interest in "psychic powers," or in "life after death," or in "fairies," and other New Age subjects. If

---

carefully Blavatsky, *Esoteric Instructions* (1888), 74,75; *The Secret Doctrine* (1898), V 465, 466; *Collected Writings,* XII (1888), 600, 601. This supremely important fact of TS history is addressed more thoroughly in the upcoming *Muse.*

you don't believe this, please pick up *any* issue of *Quest* magazine, which is the official organ of the TS in America—and you will confirm that those are the dominant subjects covered in that publication.

Dora Kunz

A statement on this subject by Dora Kunz is eminently relevant, at this point. Dora had been one of the most visible leaders of the TS throughout most of her life, and was elected President of the TS in America, from 1976 to 1987. Not only did she know CWL personally, since she had been CWL's disciple as a girl and then as a young woman. She was also herself a born clairvoyant, and as a mature woman became a well-known *"trained* clairvoyant." CWL—under perennial supervision—had undertaken most of her tutoring on clairvoyance, beginning when she was a child.

Also, and for several decades, she worked with medical doctors to help them—through her clairvoyance—arrive at otherwise difficult diagnoses.[4] In other words, her clairvoyance, though rigorously tested, has never been questioned by anyone, especially the many doctors with whom she worked—not to mention the patients, who benefitted from her work personally.

In addition—though she was born clairvoyant—Dora was further tutored in her clairvoyance by CWL, like her brother Harry. The many successful tests of her clairvoyance that she was subjected to by these diagnoses provide indirect yet very powerful additional evidence for CWL's own very real clairvoyance. After all, CWL was Dora's teacher in showing to her the meaning of

---

[4] I was a personal witness of Kunz's research with doctors, throughout the 1960s. This work consisted mostly of her being invited to look clairvoyantly into cases that doctors had been unable to diagnose accurately, or at all. By looking into patients' energy flows, Dora was able to clarify for the doctors what was actually going on in the patient's body or psyche, and thus determine a more accurate diagnosis. Clairvoyance ran in her family, for generations. Her brother—Harry van Gelder (1905-1995), a D.O. and naturopath of Ojai, California—diagnosed his patients by seeing their energy flows clairvoyantly. See also Karagulla (with whom I also had a number of discussions on all this research), *Breakthrough to Creativity* (1967), wherein Dora is called "Diane," to protect her privacy.

what she was seeing clairvoyantly. It was CWL who guided her and tutored her. He could not have done that, except by being himself an accomplished clairvoyant.

It is critical to note the fact that she was extremely well aware of all the clairvoyant work that CWL had engaged in, in numerous areas of research. And yet—from her personal perspective—according to her, the most important application of CWL's clairvoyance had been his "discovery" of K. As she put it (emphasis added):

> [CWL] was without a doubt clairvoyant. *The best known and impressive demonstration of his clairvoyance was his "discovery" of Krishnamurti.* Leadbeater was walking on the beach by Adyar when he saw two brothers also walking there. They were very poor and badly fed, not much to look at. But he saw their auras and he recognized a tremendous potential in one of the boys, Krishnamurti.
>
> CWL never had much money, but he helped to support the boys from his own income, and he interested Mrs. Besant in them. She adopted the boys and sent them to England, and Krishnamurti turned out to be a unique person. Whatever CWL saw in that starving boy's aura, he picked him out, and Krishnamurti has made his own contribution to modern society.[5]

Kunz is careful here about not stating specifically the actual claims CWL made regarding K—which she was absolutely totally aware of. One must keep in mind that that very subject was overwhelmingly the one subject that reigned supreme in TS circles, as she was gowing up in its midst in the 1910s and 1920s.

It must be kept in mind that this subject is still "controversial," even decades after Dora's death. In fact, the subject of K and the claims made about him by CWL and AB has been even taboo in TS circles—whenever TS members are even aware of it, in the twenty-first century.

Furthermore—and given Dora's status in TS history—it is understandable that she was careful in the way she expressed what

---

[5] Kunz, "The Early Leaders of the Theosophical Society," *The American Theosophist*, Late Summer, 1995.

she did say, so as to not get embroiled in a K-related "controversy" within the TS at the end of her life.

Yet this is a remarkable statement coming from someone who was thoroughly acquainted with CWL personally, and with all of his work. This is someone whose own clairvoyance is undisputed, and who was not connected with K's work once he was barred from the TS in 1933.

In other words—much like CWL and AB had done before—in making such a statement Dora had nothing to gain or ax to grind. In fact, in making this statement she had, if anything, much to lose—given K's unpopularity in exoteric-minded TS circles. Yet *she considered CWL's revelations regarding K the most important of all his clairvoyant work—and that must be looked at very carefully by anyone who is serious and who has integrity.*[6]

Whatever one may think of his claims regarding the Telugu boy, CWL's impact on people's attitudes toward extrasensory perception and other paranormal abilities, and what may be possible through them, has been indubitably phenomenal. He was the first person to speak of the subtler realms in those terms, using a language that would be meaningful to a worldwide public, for centuries to come.

Anyone since his time who has spoken of energy patterns, chakras, psychic fields, auras, centers of force, kundalini, or vibrations (or "vibes," a term whose theosophical origins few people are even aware of), has been following in CWL's footsteps—however unbeknownst that fact may be to them, or however much they may want to disassociate themselves from him.

Any and all critics of CWL and/or of K must *explain—clearly and with documentation* and with integrity—*what precisely is the foundation for their criticism.*

My research of six decades of looking borderlessly into this very issue shows that such would-be critics have absolutely no credible foundation for their criticisms. None. Zero.

---

[6] See *Insights for a New Era.*

Yet on the basis of such ignorance, critics believe themselves to be the proper authorities, and judges—and executioners—of these issues.

* * *

When her husband Fritz died in 1972, Dora was surprised to receive a call from K. She and Fritz had not been in touch with K since the 1920s. Neither of the two had had anything to do with K's work, nor with him personally, for many decades. In addition, very few people were aware of Fritz's passing. Yet there was K, expressing his condolences to her.

When she communicated this to me at Olcott, in 1976 (when I was a volunteer at the TSA headquarters), and she had just been elected President of the American Section of the TS, she told me that she was astonished and deeply touched by K reaching out to her.

The significance of this is that Dora was not one to be astonished easily. She had always been proud of being "a tough cookie," as she expressed it often. She told me that, to begin with, K had no "normal" way of knowing of Fritz's death. But also, for K to call her to express his condolences after more than four decades of not having had any contact at all—that was "too much," she said.

From the way she said it, it was obvious that she was overwhelmed with emotion, when she got that call from K.

CHAPTER 22
TS Mission

THE TS HAS MOVED VERY FAR AWAY from what CWL and AB had been telling its members regarding the deeper purposes that the perennials had when they founded it. In many ways—as addressed in previous chapters—CWL and AB were but restating what HPB and her perennial mentors had said on the subject of the TS's mission.

As a result of pervasive ignorance about the intent of the actual perennial wisdom, most TS members—and most New Agers and others—are now unaware of the deeper mission of the TS. They are unaware of what they all should consider to be the central work and the vision for the TS in particular, and for the resultant New Age movement in general.

Importantly, both CWL and AB had not only been disclosing privately, since 1895, that the main mission of the TS had been, all along, to prepare the way for the coming of the next "avataric manifestation" (as HPB and her perennial mentors had put it).[1] Significantly, they had started making these statements, as it happens, in the year in which K was born, and therefore long before he came to be known widely, after he was "discovered" by CWL fourteen years later, in 1909.

It was expected, all along, that many TS members—being Victorian-minded exoterics as they were (and still are), *according to HPB and her perennial mentors*—would be likely to reject that manifestation, once it finally came. On numerous occasions, both CWL and AB warned the members (even before K began his work as a speaker and writer in the 1920s) that the presentations made by the mouthpiece of the new era would—more likely than not—be rejected by TS members.

One of the most poignant of these many warnings by CWL and AB came in a talk that Mrs. Besant gave to a London TS audience on White Lotus Day, May 8, 1909. She made this

---

[1] Blavatsky, *Esoteric Instructions* (1888), 74, 75; *The Secret Doctrine* (1898), V 465, 466; *Collected Writings,* XII 600, 601

statement barely days after K had been "discovered" in India, and before she had even met him:

> Some of you think, but you think mistakenly, that you would recognise, say, a Master, or even a Christ, if He appeared. Are you so sure? They never have been recognised by the people of their time, save by a small minority, and why should we be different?
>
> The Christ was not recognised when He came last; His Messengers have not been recognised since, save by a minority. They are so different from the people of their time that there is much to get over before you can recognise them.
>
> . . . If you would recognise them when they come, try to cultivate the power which answers to greatness without, by cultivating greatness within, remembering that spiritual recognition is the recognition of all those who are kindred to yourself. If you have the virtue in you of the spiritual man, you will know spiritual men when you meet them; but if you cannot answer to Him, then He will pass you by unknown, and probably disliked.
>
> . . . Now our work is clear before us: to try to change the public opinion of the world into the attitude which is sometimes called disparagingly hero-worship, which is essentially the thing we need at the present time—the power to know the hero when we see him.
>
> "No man is a hero," it is said, "to his valet." And people think that that means that he is small when seen close by. Not so; but that the small soul which is typified by the word "valet" cannot appreciate the greatness of the hero near whom he stands. The servant soul does not recognize the greatness of the hero, and therefore the hero is no hero to him. Only the heroic recognise the hero; *and if you can develop that in yourself which is like a Master, then, and then alone, will you know a Master when He comes* [emphasis added].
>
> . . . Seeing the God in them, and loving and trusting, that will help them to grow out of the limitations, of the blunders and errors that are hindering the divine manifestation. And remember that is what is wanted now, not for yourselves only but for every one around you, so that when the Teachers come, They may be able to remain in the world amongst us.
>
> *They dare not come yet, because even in the Theosophical Society They would not be welcomed* [emphasis added]. A Master who came amongst you now would not for the most part be very much liked by you; His way, His views, His thoughts would be so different, He would raise suspicion and dislike. We saw it in the earlier days when They came out more, and were met by judgment and criticism, until one of Them said, in the fashion in which They look at ignorant

criticism: "The standard of the Adept is not kept at Simla [where A.P. Sinnett (the recipient) lived], it is kept at Shamballah, and I try to accommodate myself to that."

There is a great lesson in that for all of us. The standard of those who are passing onward into the higher life is not the standard of the judgment of the people around them, but the standard that the Masters hold up before them, to which they are ever trying to conform.

Think of that in your attitude to the people around you; remember that on you, and on people like you everywhere, depends the success or the failure of the next great manifestation of the divine life on the earth; that this Theosophical Society, spread everywhere over the world, is literally the John the Baptist to prepare the way for the coming of the Christ; to fill that part is your work and duty—and need I say, your privilege, your highest honour?[2]

TS members who turn their backs on K's unprecedented, multidimensionally beneficial and transforming message for mankind, are thereby turning their backs on these words of wisdom—and on Mrs. Besant herself, as well as on CWL, who often spoke along the same lines—not to mention HPB *and her perennial mentors.*

Yes, exoteric Victorian Theosophy does have a value—a *great* value, I might add. Its value is in spreading the word concerning numerous issues of concern to mankind in general. But wisdom *and integrity* dictate that it should *never* be forgotten that exoteric Victorian Theosophy gets its deeper value from representing *esoteric theosophy* as clearly and thoroughly as each TS member is capable of.

Traditionalists, especially, need urgently to pay attention to this fact.

Even more seriously, turning one's back on K is one and the same with turning one's back on the central mission of the TS—and on HPB and the perennials who founded the TS. Yes, the baby's bath water (exoteric Victorian Theosophy) is precious for grooming and cleansing the baby (esoteric theosophy).

But it would be far more than foolish—a crime of the most horrible nature possible—to throw away the baby of initiation,

---

[2] Besant, *The Changing World* (1910), 291-295.

of *daily dying to the known* (as K most aptly put it, using the simplest words). Those who do discard the baby of initiation, do so for the sake of *preserving* and even *worshipping* the soiled bath water of mere "teachings."

Importantly, "teachings" are clearly changeable and time-bound—and even discardable, at the end of the day—regardless of how "fascinating" or "valuable" or even "sublime" they may be, in certain contexts.

The survival of the living "baby" of daily dying to the known is precious—*and it's not negotiable.*

Mutation is the subject of Part Four.

PART FOUR

MUTATION

CHAPTER 23
Unlikely Yogi

PUPUL JAYAKAR'S DESCRIPTION OF K'S PROCESS quoted at the beginning of Chapter 7, "Perennials," seems to assert that K was an accomplished yogi in 1922, when the process began. Her statement suggests that—as yogis do—K was someone who had spent many years engaging arduously and daily in subtle and elaborate "yogic" practices, to the exclusion of much else.

The fact is that K, however, had actually been doing no such thing. Jayakar's statement is so critical for the purpose of seeing clearly the falseness of unsupported assertions such as hers, that it is worth repeating, at this juncture. As she put it (emphasis added),

> In August 1922 Krishnamurti was to be plunged into the intense spiritual awakening that changed the course of his life. *In the Indian tradition*, the yogi who delves into the labyrinth of consciousness awakens exploding kundalini energies and entirely new fields of psychic phenomena, journeying into unknown areas of the mind. *A yogi* who touches these primordial energies and undergoes mystic initiation is recognized as being vulnerable to immense dangers; the body and mind face perils that could lead to insanity or death.
>
> *The yogi learns the secret doctrines* and experiences the awakening of dormant energy *under the instruction of the guru.* Once the yogi becomes an adept, *these transformations* of consciousness on the playground of consciousness *are revealed in a mystical drama.* The body and mind must undergo a supremely dangerous journey. *The adept is surrounded and protected by his disciples;* secrecy and a protective silence pervade the atmosphere.[1]

Dolce far niente

From 1911 through 1921, K lived in England. During that period, he spent much of his time studying under tutors to enter Oxford—though he never passed the exams. Unlike his younger brother Nytia, K didn't have the intellectual capacity required

---

[1] Jayakar, *Krishnamurti: A Biography* (1986), 46-47.

for passing the exams. AB had left K under the care of wealthy friends, and he spent most of his time learning about mundane things of interest to the wealthy.

Biographical accounts show that he was involved with Theosophy—or anything that could be construed as "spiritual" practice—only in the most peripheral way. His remarks at the time about Theosophy—other than his communications with AB and CWL to keep them updated about his life and activities—show, if anything, a lack of interest on his part in such matters in general, or in meditation in particular. An uninitiated onlooker might have called this period in K's life "the lost decade."

Mary Lutyens (1908-1999), who knew K intimately from 1911 when he first went to England at the age of sixteen (and she was two years old), wrote:

> The boy Krishna I had known had been quite vacant, childish, almost moronic, interested really in nothing except golf, and mechanical things such as cameras, clocks and motorbicycles.[2]

Her speaking of K as "the boy Krishna," though he actually turned twenty in 1915—when Mary Lutyens was eight years old—underscores the point that he was clearly not an accomplished yogi in the Indian tradition—as Jayakar asserts without any evidence—especially given his mundane interests, and his disregard at the time for yoga or any other similar practice.

In addition, though AB was K's legal guardian between 1911 and 1921, she was in India throughout that decade; the European war (1914-1919) had made travel extremely difficult. But also, she was deeply involved in India's independence movement and in creating a number of cultural and educational organizations in India.[3] Those activities put her at odds with the British government—and that made the possibility of travel for her even more unlikely.

---

[2] Lutyens, *Krishnamurti: The Years of Fulfilment*, 225.
[3] For AB's activities during this period, see C.V. Agarwal and Pedro Oliveira, compilers, *Annie Besant in India (2021)*.

Significantly—especially regarding K—AB never pushed others into sharing her beliefs. For her, theosophy was not so much a belief system as a path to transformation.[4] In other words, *AB practiced esoteric theosophy more* than she was interested in exoteric Victorian Theosophy, in her personal life. As K expressed it, shortly after she died:

> Dr. Besant was our mother, she looked after us, she cared for us. But one thing she did not do. She never said to me, "Do this," or "Don't do that." She left me alone. Well, in these words I have paid her the greatest tribute.[5]

In addition—according to K's biographers—AB conveyed to K's tutors that they should not attempt to mold his mind in any way, outside of the conventions of his academic studies, such as those were. According to her, this advice actually came from the perennials, and AB was merely passing that advice on to those who turned out to be in charge of K for fully a decade. These were his formative years.

As documented in the biographies, K's great passions in the 1910s were playing golf and volleyball, finding out as much as possible about cars—an avocation he never fully abandoned—and racing them, and learning how to dress well. Meditation was not on his list of daily activities. His life was that of a wealthy young man—a dandy, if you will. He was surrounded by rich, wealth-minded people who were teaching him by example their manners and perspectives. His life could best be described as having consisted of a seemingly never-ending *dolce far niente*.

K was not a yogi—as Jayakar recklessly asserts, strictly out of her Indian-conditioned imagination, and totally without any facts or documentation to support her fantasy assertions.

---

[4] For AB on transformation, see Newcomb, *Personal Transformation in the Tradition of Annie Besant* (1990), which also includes an extensive bibliography.
[5] Krishnamurti, *Collected Works*, 19 vols., vol. 1 (1933-34), 172.

Overwhelmed

The available documents show that K returned to "the work" in 1921 more out of a sense of duty and out of gratitude to AB—whom he called *"Amma"* (mother)—than anything else. The biographies show that he was, if anything, weary of much of what he had seen in TS circles since his "discovery" in 1909.

Some of the remarks he made in 1921-22 (in letters, or recounted by others in anecdotes) suggest a sense of guilt on his part for not having adequately fulfilled the expectations connected with what people around him believed to be his mission. Apart from that, he seems to have been bewildered, because he had no forethought at all about what he might be expected to say or do, after "the Coming" that everyone around him was anticipating. It must have been very difficult for him—to say the least—when AB returned to England in 1921.

The partying was over.

Lutyens shows that his mind was truly vacant, all along. So this was generally a period of inner struggle for K. On one hand he was unhappy with the predominant understanding of Theosophy in the TS—which was almost exclusively exoteric, as addressed in Parts One and Three.[6] On the other hand—especially towards the end of this tough period (despite its *dolce far niente* aspect)—he knew that the time was near for him to begin to fulfill the grandiose expectations held by those who were aware of AB's and CWL's declarations made concerning the "Coming" of "the World Teacher."

Given all of those circumstances, Krishnaji may have been, if anything, overwhelmed by those expectations about what he was supposed to do, "when the time came"—and that moment was fast approaching. According to documentation provided by Lutyens, he had absolutely no forethought—let alone understanding—regarding "the Coming," or anything having to do with it.

---

[6] For the exoteric tenor and history of the TS, see also *Insights for a New Era*.

Those actualities in K's life at the time point clearly to one very pesky fact: Statements made by Jayakar regarding K being "a yogi"—especially one that had been under the tutelage of "a guru" (in the Indian tradition) seems to be absolutely something coming out of Jayakar's imagination, and has zero relationship to the facts.

So much for trusting *everything* affirmed by a K "biographer."

CHAPTER 24
The Process

THE FIRST MANIFESTATIONS OF THE PROCESS began shortly after Krishnaji and his brother Nitya (d. 1925) had arrived in Ojai from Australia in the summer of 1922. While still in Australia, a message for K was "brought through" by CWL from one of the perennials connected with TS work, Koot Hoomi (KH). That message read:

> Of you, too, we have the highest hopes. Steady and widen yourself and strive more and more to bring the mind and brain into subservience to the true Self within. Be tolerant of divergences of view and of method, for each has usually a fragment of truth concealed somewhere within it, even though oftentimes it is distorted almost beyond recognition. Seek for that tiniest gleam of light amid the Stygian darkness of each ignorant mind, for by recognising and fostering it you may help a baby brother.[1]

This message had "a profound effect" on Krishnaji, according to Lutyens. Shortly thereafter, he settled in Ojai—where the two brothers would find themselves in solitude, in the midst of an expanse of nature and silent tranquility such as they had never experienced before. In that new, rural environment, K began to meditate daily—something he apparently had not done since he had first arrived in England in 1911. This was so unexpected, that he wrote to Lady Emily Lutyens (Mary's mother, whom K called "Mum"):

> All this is rather surprising you, isn't it? I am going to get back my old touch with the Masters and after all that's the only thing that matters in life and nothing else does. At first it was difficult to meditate or to concentrate, and even though I have been doing it for only a week. I am agreeably surprised.[2]

---

[1] Lutyens, *The Years of Awakening,* 147.
[2] Lutyens, *The Years of Awakening,* 152.

K started meditating for roughly fifteen minutes to half an hour daily only fourteen days prior to when the process commenced on August 17, 1922. Again, it should be noted that half an hour of daily meditation—especially by a beginner—does not an accomplished yogi make.

Just a few days after he started meditating, he began to practice a form of meditation in which he was trying to fathom who or what was "the Lord Maitreya," and what was "the Buddhic plane" of consciousness—which is the insight-compassion dimension within all of us. Outsiders might perceive that type of meditation as having triggered the process.

Perhaps a main reason why K and Nitya were sent alone to Ojai—all by themselves, with no "chaperons" of any kind—was that they would be experiencing a solitude that they had never known before. Perhaps such solitude was a requirement for the process to come about.

From those tentative beginnings in meditation, it seems that the process was not something he initiated consciously. Nor was the process the result of anything he did intentionally. In fact, even as late as 1961, at the age of 66—four decades after the process first began to manifest—he wrote in his journal (later published as *Krishnamurti's Notebook)* about the process in terms that leave no room for the possibility that he did anything to induce it.

> The pressure and the strain of deep ache is there; it's as though, deep within, an operation was going on. It's not brought on through one's own volition, however subtle it might be. One has deliberately and for some time gone into it, deeply. One has tried to induce it; tried to bring about various outward conditions, being alone and so on. Then nothing happens. All this isn't something recent.[3]

From his own comments—in which he was trying to describe the process—it is clear that (unlike a yogi) K had little intentionally to do with the tremendous mutation of the brain that he was soon to begin to experience in the summer of 1922. Yet it is from

---

[3] Krishnamurti, *Krishnamurti's Notebook,* 16.

such mutation that the unprecedented insights that he became uniquely known for came from. That is, this mutation would in turn—through the insights and observations that came through him as a result—get to have a transforming effect on intelligent people, worldwide. As K was to say often throughout his life, what comes from the depths always comes "uninvited, unexpectedly."

In other words, throughout the process there was an element of what Christians might refer to as "grace." K's contribution to the process seems to have consisted exclusively of two factors:

- The vacancy of his mind. This could be described as the kind of emptiness spoken of in many schools in which transformative meditation has a central role. Examples of such schools are yoga, where it is called *sunya* (emptiness), and Zen Buddhism, where it is called *sunyata* (emptiness).

  This empty mind may also be described as being an autistic mind—much as many in our stressed and fast-moving society may think of autism as "an illness."
- K's predisposition to be of unconditional service in the work of the perennials.

Put simply, this was an inner goodness, a predisposition on K's part to "do the right thing" at deep levels, without preconditions, and under all circumstances. That quality is far more rare than some might think. It certainly impressed CWL when he first saw Krishnaji clairvoyantly, and perceived in the boy someone who was *uniquely* "selfless." However, it is highly unlikely that these two qualities—excellent as they are, in themselves—would have been sufficient for the process to take place, let alone for his insights and observations.

Outsiders or critics may want to rule out the possibility that an outside agent initiated and conducted the process—as K, CWL, and all other witnesses to it said was actually the case. A few other "explanations" have been given by sundry authors, in various attempts to "explain" the process. Among those other "explanations" are—prominently—the following:

- K went through periods of severe hallucinations through-out his life.
- Kundalini was somehow awakened in him spontan-eously.
- There was deception of some kind involved.

Critics of the reality of perennials have favored these latter explanations. But before looking carefully at these various pos-sibilities in the next chapter, however, the process itself should be examined in some detail, so that there's clarity regarding what was involved in it—before jumping to uninformed conclu-sions, as so many have unfortunately done.

Krishnamurti's Notebook

Krishnamurti's Notebook is a diary that K kept from June 1961 through January 1962—though it was not published until fourteen years later, in 1976, soon after Lutyens' first book of her memoirs on K's life was published. Throughout that diary—which focuses on the process—he says in many different ways that "the purification of the brain is necessary." He spoke of this in the context of the excruciating physical pain that generally came along with the psychological-physiological-transformative process that he underwent.

In fact, it seems as if K wrote this journal in order to docu-ment his own impressions and descriptions while the process was going on. It is as if he intended for this document to be pre-served, for the specific purpose of noting how the process made up a wholeness, together with the insights that flowed through K, as an intrinsic aspect of it.

Crucially, *Krishnamurti's Notebook* also contains some of the clearest and deepest expositions ever of his insights, researches, and observations. This is an example:

All night it was there, whenever I woke up. The head was bad going to the plane [to fly to Los Angeles]. The purification of the brain is necessary. The brain is the centre of all the senses; the more the senses are alert and sensitive, the sharper the brain is; it's the centre of remembrance, the past; it's the storehouse of experience and knowledge, tradition. So it's limited, conditioned. Its activities are planned, thought out, reasoned, but it functions in limitation, in space-time. So it cannot formulate or understand that which is the total, the whole, the complete.

The complete, the whole, is the mind; it is empty, totally empty and because of this emptiness, the brain exists in space-time. Only when the brain has cleansed itself of its conditioning, greed, envy, ambition, then only it can comprehend that which is complete. Love is this completeness.[4]

The careful reader will note how K connects directly the physiological mutation of his brain to the process—*and to his insights, researches, and observations*. This is eminently important, obviously. If the excruciatingly painful process that K went through is at one with the insights, researches, and observations that K is known for, this clearly points to the insight that the process did not consist of hallucinations, "visions," or deception.

I also find intriguing that the connection that K makes between process and insight points to something critically important. Evolutionary biology now tells us that mutation in one member of the species opens the door for that mutation taking place in other members of the species.

In other words, K's process is what made it possible for borderless insights to take place. Those insights touch deeply anyone who listens attentively to what they point to. Then, that act of listening attentively and borderlessly to K's insights triggers a possibility of transformation in the brain of the listener.

That is precisely the process of evolutionary mutation.

---

[4] Krishnamurti, *Krishnamurti's Notebook*, 9.

The wheels of Ooty

The last quoted passage was written on June 19, 1961. K had been experiencing the process recurrently since at least April of that year, and continued to do so throughout the writing of the journal. On May 12 (which happened to be K's birthday) he had written about it to Mrs. Jayakar's sister Nandini Mehta (b. 1917?). At the time, he was in England giving talks and holding meetings. He wrote to Nandini:

> The wheels of Ooty are working, unknown to any, and other things are taking place. It is so extraordinary, and words seem so futile. Days are too short and one lives in a day, a thousand years.[5]

His phrase "the wheels of Ooty" refers to the period in 1948 when the two sisters—shortly after they had met him for the first time—had been with him in the Indian hill station of Ootacamund. At that time, they had been bewildered by being witnesses to manifestations of the process.

"Wheel" is the English word for the Sanskrit *"chakra."* Clearly, K was saying to his Indian friends that during the process, he could sense his chakras being vivified.

This awakening of the chakras is widely recognized in the literature as what happens when the serpent fire of kundalini rises up the spine. Even a treatise meant for the general public, such as the *Sivananda Companion to Yoga*, includes a brief discussion—which uses without attribution CWL's unique language and conceptual structures—of the movement of kundalini from the lowest, or *muladhara* chakra at the base of the spine, to the highest, or *sahasrara*, chakra at the crown of the head:

> As kundalini passes through each of the various chakras, different states of consciousness are experienced. When it reaches the Sahasrara, the yogi attains samadhi. Though still operating on the

---

[5] Jayakar, *Biography*, 242.

material plane, he has reached a level of existence beyond time, space and causation.[6]

K's Indian correspondents—and others who have referred to K's experiences during the process—made the understandable assumption that whenever he spoke of "the wheels of Ooty," he was referring to the chakras as understood in conventional literature.

But if one reads carefully the accounts described by K and by close witnesses, *the "chakras" that he was referring to were all in the head,* and were not the "chakras" that are usually described as appearing from the base of the spine to the top of the head. This is addressed more carefully in the second edition of *The Inner Life of Krishnamurti*, which I intend to publish as close as possible to the publication of *Dawn of a New Era*.[7]

K continued to make references to the "wheels of Ooty" in subsequent letters. On June 1, for instance, he wrote that "The wheels of Ooty are working furiously and painfully."[8] The day after he left England (to fly to Los Angeles, as mentioned in the *Notebook* passage quoted above), his friend Doris Pratt, who at the time was apparently not fully aware of the perennial nature of these experiences, wrote about his visit in a letter:

> [T]here were some very strange and difficult times when all life and energy seemed to be drained from his body and when he became "weak and ill" to an alarming degree. These occasions only lasted a few moments in their essence, but necessitated rest afterwards. On quite a few occasions he cried out aloud at night and on one or two occasions Anneke [Korndorffer] heard him and was very troubled. On other occasions he would mention at breakfast that he had been calling out and that he hoped he had not disturbed us. Similarly on several occasions at meal times he suddenly dropped his knife and fork and appeared to be kind of transfixed for a moment or two, and then to go limp and faint so that one thought he might drop to the floor.
>
> I questioned him about it because I wanted to know whether there was anything at all the onlooker could do. He replied there was

---

[6] Lidell, *A Companion to Yoga*, 71.
[7] For updates, consult paradigmshift.network.
[8] Jayakar, *Biography*, 243.

nothing we could do except keep quiet, relaxed and not worry, but also not touch him at all. I pressed him a bit, and he said while he himself knew exactly what was happening, he was unable to explain it to us. He said it was linked with the happenings [related to the process] which were alluded to in the unexpurgated book by Lady Emily [Lutyens].

During the eight weeks I was living in the same house I felt on many occasions that I was an onlooker at a most profound and tremendous mystery.

. . . There was the man who during his own morning meditation period, spread a mantle of intense quietude over the house which even a rhinoceros like myself could feel. Then there were those mysterious attacks and some equally mysterious healings.[9]

"Mysterious healings," incidentally, refers to K's ability to heal others, which—like his clairvoyance, singing of mantras, and private performance of certain rituals—is generally played down, or not even mentioned, in books about his life or among his would-be non-followers.

Perhaps the authors of such books preferred to avoid acknowledging the perennial implications of these abilities and practices. Or perhaps they wished to avoid possible associations with any "messianic" notions, given that K (like Jesus), had the ability to heal the sick by imposition of hands—plus there had been a messianic mystique surrounding him, throughout his life.[10]

When K referred to the head being "bad," as in the passage quoted above, he was speaking of a painful physical aspect of the process, whereby kundalini presumably burned through the synapses and various centers in his brain. In that sense—as addressed more carefully in *The Inner Life of Krishnamurti*—some aspects of his very painful experiences were historically unique to K.

---

[9] Lutyens, *The Years of Fulfilment*, 107-108.
[10] For a personal, intensely poignant account of K's abilities as a healer, see Vimala Thakar, *An Eternal Voyage;* see also Krishna, *A Jewel on a Silver Platter,* which is peppered throughout with specific instances of K healing others, in different parts of the world.

Doris Pratt also said in the quote above—referring to his process-related behavior—that "[K] said it was linked with the happenings [related to the process] which were alluded to in the unexpurgated book by Lady Emily [Lutyens]." This refers to a book that Lady Emily Lutyens (1874-1964) had written in the 1950s. She was the mother of Mary Lutyens, K's biographer.

Lady Emily's book *Candles in the Sun* (1957) initially included her own description of the process, as she had witnessed it many times. Initially, K had given her carte blanche regarding all the many details involved in those experiences—as she witnessed and understood them. But at the eleventh hour, he recanted, and said the book should not be published, even though the publisher already had made a large investment on it. So a compromise was reached, whereby the book was published—but without passages that detailed the process, as perceived by Lady Emily. In the passage quoted above, Pratt was referring to the original manuscript of this book, not to the later, heavily edited version that got to be published.

A critical insight to consider is that, as just noted, the very same process that was so excruciating to him personally—according to K—relates directly to profound changes that each of us must make in order for our brains to be cleansed from the confusions and oppressions that are inevitable, to the extent that we persist in living me-centered lives.

Passages such as the ones quoted above from the *Notebook*—which are frequent—make a clear connection between the process that K was undergoing, and the psychological and even physiological mutation that is at the heart of his insights, researches, and observations. Those insights are, in turn, meant to apply to *any* human being, including you and I.

This points intriguingly to the way evolution is considered to proceed, according to recent evolutionary theories. If these speculations are correct, presumably, one individual in a particular species has a kind of "ah-ha!" moment, which results in a change of perception and behavior from what had been the norm. That new way of perceiving and behaving is said to induce a biological mutation. Then, other members of the species somehow "resonate" with that mutation—and the new way of being spreads throughout the species, eventually becoming a dominant trait of survivors.

K's mutation, as a result of the process, has resonated with a relatively few members of the human species—and that mutation-in-the-making has been spreading, ever since.

K's "process"—and some of its implications—is the central subject of *The Inner Life of Krishnamurti*. In its second edition, I delve deeper into this matter than I had been able to do in the earlier, 1999 version.

In any case, mutation is clearly not an easy matter *for anyone*.

Mysterium tremendum et fascinans

It is intriguing to note that the psychological dimension of K's experience of mutation has a family resemblance to Rudolf Otto's (1869-1937) *mysterium tremendum et fascinans*, which was mentioned briefly in Part Two. This kind of transmutation takes place at deep levels and affects all aspects of one's life. Shifts in behavior or experiences that bring about changes only in limited areas of human experience (such as "conversion" from one religion or ideology to another) are not of this type and are not transformation—at least not in K's integral, borderless sense of that word.

The mutation that K spoke of was not a mere "conversion" from one system of thought or behavior to another. Rather, it is more a total, profound shift in consciousness—a shift in which the me-centered way of perceiving and being ceases to be, thereby making it possible for an all-comprehensive way of perceiving and being to come about.

Such an all-comprehensive way of perceiving and being is unconditional love.

CHAPTER 25
Mutation

FROM THE BEGINNING OF HIS PUBLIC WORK in the 1920s, K spoke of the need for radical transformation-mutation—though early on he used expressions such as "initiation" and "the path," instead.

But the word is not the thing.

In fact, even *At the Feet of the Master*—which was published in 1910 and first catapulted him into the public eye—is about the transformation that we all must go through, as we move away from the me-centered world of confusions, divisions, conflicts, and dangers for us all.

Simultaneously, as me-centeredness retreats, there is a shift within us towards the dimension of wholeness—the dimension of universal morality, borderless truth-seeking-truth-finding, comprehensive love, excellence, insight, creativity.

Without such borderless psychological mutation humanity would not have a meaningful future—and perhaps it would have no future at all, given the planetary as well as personal consequences of me-centeredness, which we can now see all around us, and within us. After all, a me-centered way of being—whether individually, in relationship, in a community, or planet-wide—is intrinsically destructive.

K had addressed this kind of comprehensive mutation from the beginning.

But it was primarily during the last years of his life that he came to articulate this far-reaching insight in a more powerful way.

Late in his life, K came to elucidate more carefully that this mutation was not only psychological-moral—which is the way his audiences had mostly, or even exclusively, understood it. He also intended that we bring about a *biological* mutation of the brain—much like what HPB had addressed (though only as a description), throughout her public life.

David Bohm

Perhaps the clearest exposition of this mutation came up in a series of dialogues that took place in the early 1980s—particularly the one that was published later as *The Future of Humanity* (1983). In that dialogue, K and renowned physicist David Bohm (1917-1992) explored the question of whether humans can change radically their pervasive self-destructive patterns of behavior.

Bohm was one of the seminal physicists of the twentieth century. Among other accomplishments, as a young man he had worked with Albert Einstein (1879-1955) on the so-called "unified field theory." That theory attempted to bring together relativity and quantum physics, which would otherwise remain incongruent theories about the foundations of the universe. Einstein was of course the discoverer of relativity, and Bohm was to become one of the world's foremost exponents of quantum—so theirs was a perfect partnership. According to biographers and statements that he made, Einstein considered Bohm his intellectual heir.

All along—but especially in later years—Bohm had the insight that consciousness had to be a component of the way the universe is put together. In fact, this is something that Einstein had also intimated in numerous ways, and particularly in a statement that he repeated often, as a terse criticism of quantum, if taken by itself to explain all that is. From the 1930s until his death in 1955, Einstein often said that "God does not play dice." That often-repeated statement clearly implies that consciousness must be a factor in any credible explanation of the way the universe is put together.

So Bohm and Einstein were of one mind, when it came to the understanding that consciousness—intelligence in all that is—had to be a factor in any credible all-embracing physics theory of everything. Hence their attempt to come up with a unified field theory.

A few quotes from Einstein make this harmony between him and Bohm rather obvious:

> [T]here are moments when one feels free from one's own identifi-cation with human limitations and inadequacies. At such moments, one imagines that one stands on some spot of a small planet, gazing in amazement at the cold yet profoundly moving beauty of the eternal, the unfathomable: life and death flow into one, and there is neither evolution nor destiny; only being.[1]
>
> A human being is a part of the whole, called by us "Universe," a part limited in time and space. He experiences himself, his thoughts and feelings as something separate from the rest—a kind of optical delu-sion of his consciousness. This delusion is a kind of prison for us, re-stricting us to our personal desires and to affection for a few persons nearest to us. Our task must be to free ourselves from this prison by widening our circle of compassion to embrace all living creatures and the whole of nature in its beauty.[2]
>
> The finest emotion of which we are capable is the mystic emotion. Herein lies the germ of all art and all true science. Anyone to whom this feeling is alien, who is no longer capable of wonderment and lives in a state of fear is a dead man. To know that what is impenetrable for us really exists and manifests itself as the highest wisdom and the most radiant beauty, whose gross forms alone are intelligible to our poor faculties—this knowledge, this feeling . . . that is the core of the true religious sentiment. In this sense, and in this sense alone, I rank my-self among profoundly religious men.[3]
>
> The true value of a human being is determined primarily by the measure and the sense in which he has attained to liberation from the self.[4]

Einstein's perceptions—as just quoted—point rather clearly to a view of the world strikingly similar to that of Bohm and K. In fact, such perceptions are rather similar to the sorts of in-sights that came out of the Bohm-K dialogues.

---

[1] Jeremy Bernstein, *Einstein* (1973), 11.
[2] Walter Sullivan, "The Einstein Papers: A Man of Many Parts," *New York Times,* March 29, 1972.
[3] Peter Barker and Cecil G. Shugart, eds., *After Einstein: Proceedings of the Einstein Centennial Celebration at Memphis State University* (1981), 179.
[4] Albert Einstein, *The World As I See It* (2011), 10.

K and Bohm

Learning about Krishnamurti in the late 1950s—and meeting him shortly thereafter—turned out to be an inflection point in Bohm's life, as well as in his understanding of how the universe works. That initial encounter with K led to investigations with him into *what is* until he died in 1992.

Bohm got to work intimately and intensely with the two most formidable geniuses of the twentieth century.

Rightly or wrongly, Bohm's learning journey can be summarized in a few short statements. He began by trying to understand *all that is* in terms of quantum physics. That was incomplete, because quantum could not account for insights about the universe that came from relativity—which seemed to be incongruent with quantum. So he then pursued an attempt to explain how quantum and relativity could work together, in the work he did with Einstein. Unfortunately for their efforts—and try hard as they did—they were never able to find a satisfactory unified field theory.

Perhaps the attempt to understand the universe in analytical terms is a quest much like that of Don Quixote. Perhaps a comprehensive understanding of all that is comes from the perennial dimension—and there is zero analysis in that dimension.

In any case—in the midst of the disappointment that came from not having found a unified field theory—Bohm encountered K, shortly after Einstein's death. That serendipitous meeting of world-class minds led to Bohm eventually developing the theory of the "implicate order" of the universe.

Bohm's journey could thus be summarized by stating that the theory of the implicate order began by going from Bohm by himself, to Bohm and Einstein; from there it went to Bohm and K, and finally ending back to Bohm alone, again.

His psychological researches with K were paramount to Bohm. They were so vital to him, that he came to consider seriously abandoning his work in physics altogether, with the intention of engaging instead exclusively in K's psychological-moral investigations. Those psychological-moral researches with K implied the actual mutation of humanity, which in the end is what matters most to all of us.

Theoretical concerns—whether in physics or in any other field—are secondary to whether humanity as a species has the capacity to evolve truly, which in the end is one and the same with its capacity to survive. That insight—which came to him in context of his history-making dialogues with K—is what came to move Bohm, for the rest of his life.

These dialogues into *what is* were a meeting of two world-class minds engaging in *transanalytical* research—a type of research not to be found anywhere else in world history.[5] There were several series of such dialogues, most of which are available on video and/or audio, and some of which were later edited, and turned into books. One of those series of dialogues is available on video and audio, and is summarized in the book *The Future of Humanity*.

Early on in their inquiry, K and Bohm noted that knowledge and thought are not adequate to make us move away from self-destructive patterns of behavior and on to more creative and harmonious relationships with each other and with *all that is*. In the preface to the book—and more relevant to the present exploration of mutation—Bohm outlined the content of the discussion, and remarked:

> But if knowledge and thought are not adequate, what is it that is actually required? This led in turn to the question of whether mind is limited by the brain of mankind, with all the knowledge that it has accumulated over the ages. This knowledge, which now conditions us deeply, has produced what is, in effect, an irrational and self-destructive program in which the brain seems to be helplessly caught up.
>
> If mind is limited by such a state of the brain, then the future of humanity must be very grim indeed. Krishnamurti does not, however, regard these limitations as inevitable. Rather, he emphasizes that mind is essentially free of the distorting bias that is inherent in the conditioning of the brain, and that *through insight arising in proper*

---

[5] I refer to the uniqueness of this type of research ever-so-briefly in Part One, "Krishnamurti," and address it more thoroughly in *The Analytical Fallacy* (2002).

undirected attention without a center, it can change the cells of the brain and remove the destructive conditioning.[6] If this is so, then it is crucially important that there be this kind of attention, and that we give to this question the same intensity of energy that we generally give to other activities of life that are really of vital interest to us.[7]

Evolution and brain plasticity

Mutation of the brain cells within a human lifetime would have been unacceptable in conventional academic circles earlier—and even at the time when K and Bohm were having these discussions. Until very recently, brain cells were thought by experts to be the only human cells that do not undergo significant change.

In fact, when I was writing *The Inner Life of Krishnamurti* in the late 1980s and early 1990s, I looked for scientific corroboration or refutation of what K had been addressing for decades, in this regard. Poignantly, the best I could find was remarks that Deepak Chopra—who was well-aware of K's insights and observations—made in a mass-market book written for a general audience. As Chopra put it,

> It was long thought that we are born with a set number of brain cells that never divide to form new ones, yet recently it has been found that the DNA in neurons is active, which may lead to new conclusions.[8]

As Sharon Begley documented regarding the state of neuroplasticity research at the end of the twentieth century:

> As late as 1999, neurologists writing in the prestigious journal *Science* admitted, "We are still taught that the fully mature brain lacks the intrinsic mechanisms needed to replenish neurons and reestablish neuronal networks after acute injury or in response to the insidious loss of neurons seen in neurodegenerative diseases."[9]

---

[6] Emphasis added.
[7] Krishnamurti and Bohm, *The Future of Humanity*, 2-3.
[8] Chopra, *Ageless Body, Timeless Mind* (1993), 244.
[9] Begley, *Train Your Mind, Change Your Brain* (2007), 6. The quote cited is from Lowenstein and Parent, "Brain, Heal Thyself."

This means that in 1999—the year that *The Inner Life of Krishnamurti* was published—brain researchers were still holding onto non-researched beliefs that hailed back to nineteenth century speculations which assumed the rigidity of brain physiology. This is why I could not find any up-to-date scientific references related to the plasticity of the brain cells and larger brain components. There were no such references—at least no easily available ones—as there are today.

Further, it was only in the late twentieth century that scientists even began to note that evolution in nature does not take place gradually—through very small changes and adaptations over long periods of time. Such gradualness in evolution had been at the core of the thesis proposed by Charles Darwin (1809-1882) in his landmark and highly influential work *On the Origin of the Species* (1859).

Ever since that book came out, it seems as if "everyone and her sister" had assumed that evolution takes place in an exceedingly slow gradualness, over millions upon millions of years—one micro-mutation at a time. That is, it had been thought previously—since the publication of Darwin's seminal work—that evolution is a painstakingly slow matter.

This is eminently relevant in this inquiry, because K had been saying—beginning at least in the 1930s—that there is no time at all involved in mutation.

As K put it, mutation is what happens when there is insight, and insight is instant, not gradual. There is no time at all involved in mutation.

Intriguingly, it is only late in the twentieth century that evolutionary biologists and other scientists began to consider that Darwin may have been mistaken on the issue of evolution being ultra-slow and gradual.

Rather than being gradual, evolution is now largely understood as being more likely to occur in sudden spurts of biological mutations that take place—for reasons not yet known to science—after long periods of relative lack of change that often last millions of years.

As biologist James Lovelock (1919-2022) summarized it, "[T]he evolution of the environment is characterized by periods of stasis punctuated by abrupt and sudden change."[10]

HPB and K on evolution

Interestingly and importantly, long before scientists came upon this notion, HPB and her perennial mentors also had said that evolutionary mutations take place abruptly, not gradually. Further, HPB's perennial mentors had said that such mutations occur at the endings and beginnings of "major cycles."

That is, they not only had stated *in the 1880s* what came to be accepted in biology only more than a century later. They also provided an explanation for it—in connection to cycles—which conventional science has not yet done.

Part of what's involved here is that—throughout HPB's lifetime, and even a century after her death—conventional science never gave particular significance to cycles, and scientists were convinced in Victorian times that evolution was a drip-drip-drip gradual process.

So in spite of the perennial explosion's influence in the more creative and avant-garde fringes of science, this critical insight had been largely ignored in academic circles.[11] Significantly, K was to say precisely—and more concretely—the same thing that had been stated more generally by HPB and her perennial mentors.

Recent developments in the biological sciences seem to confirm K's insistence—which predated scientific acceptance and even serious consideration—that psycho-biological human mutation takes place immediately, not gradually. As John White expressed it:

> [N]ew research indicates that even in old age, the neural cells of the cerebral cortex respond to an enriched environment by forging

---

[10] Lovelock, *The Ages of Gaia* (1988), 153.
[11] For modern research into cycles, see, for instance, Luce, *Body Time;* see also Ward, *Living Clocks;* and Gauquelin, *Cosmic Clocks.*

new connections to other cells. (The cerebral cortex is the "thinking" or "intellectual" part of the brain.) In other words, the brain can grow nerve cells at almost any age in response to novelty and challenge. A study of rats showed that neurons increased in dimension and activity, glial cells (which support neurons) multiplied, and the dendrites of neurons (branches of neurons which receive messages from other cells) lengthened. The dendritic increase allows for more, and presumably better, communication with other cells.

. . . There is nothing firmly conclusive in this intriguing research, but it reminded me of something I wrote in the introduction to *The Highest State of Consciousness* (1972). There I suggested that enlightenment involves a repatterning of the brain's neural networks. Integration or unification is a primary aspect of the mindstate called enlightenment.

Since mind and brain are obviously closely related, it seems clear that whereas before enlightenment the brain's nervous system had unconnected or "compartmentalized" areas (the neurological analog of a "fragmented" understanding), in enlightenment there is a breakthrough resulting in an integration of the nerve pathways through which we think and feel.

Our multiple "brains" become one brain. The neocortex (the "thinking-intellectual" part), the limbic system and thalamus (the "feeling-emotional" part), and the medulla oblongata (the "instinct-unconscious" part, at least according to Carl Jung) attain a previously nonexistent but always possible mode of intercellular communication.

A threshold is passed, probably explainable in terms of both cellular electrochemical change and growth of new nerve-ending connections. However it may be accomplished in neuro-physiological terms, the result is intimately associated with a new state of consciousness, a new mode of perception and feeling associated with the discovery of nonrational (but not irrational) forms of logic—forms which are multilevel/integrated/simultaneous rather than linear/sequential/either-or.[12]

It should be noted that White not only had dialogues with K. He had also been well aware of HPB's work—which included discussions of the plasticity of the brain (its capacity for change, and even for mutation).[13]

---

[12] White, *The Meeting of Science and Spirit* (1990), 13,14.
[13] For White's acquaintance with HPB, see White, *Pole Shift*, 1988 [1968].

Brain plasticity

To my knowledge, HPB was the very first person ever to refer to the capacity of the brain to undergo mutations. Following in HPB's footsteps, William James (1840-1910)—who is universally acknowledged as being the "Father of Modern Psychology"—was the first person ever to use the word "plasticity" in connection with the brain. James used that word to refer to the brain's and the brain cells' ability to change and mutate.

What is almost universally ignored is that James was a student of HPB's work, and that he became a member of the TS in 1882. Therefore, the course on Psychology that he taught at Harvard *about a decade later,* and which provided him with the foundation for his seminal, two-volume text on psychology (which is still in print), was informed by HPB's discussions of the process of brain plasticity, even though she didn't use that word. As Sharon Begley put it:

> No less a personage than William James, the father of experimental psychology in the United States, first introduced the word *plasticity* to the science of the brain, positing in 1890 that "organic matter, especially nervous tissue, seems endowed with a very extraordinary degree of plasticity." But James was "only" a psychologist, not a neurologist (there was no such thing as neuroscience a century ago), and his speculation went nowhere.[14]

James, and HPB before him—and K since at least the 1930s—were pioneers in making statements concerning the plasticity of the brain.

Plasticity would not be even considered by neuroscientists until more than a century after HPB's original pronouncements in that regard. These recent developments are in fact central to Deepak Chopra's landmark work as an M.D., particularly as it applies to aging in the context of the possibility of physiological regeneration. Chopra summarizes much of this research, and

---

[14] Begley, *Train Your Mind, Change Your Brain,* 5; James, *Principles of Psychology,* 110.

makes connections between physiological changes and the possibility of transformations in the brain cells:

> We are the only creatures on earth who can change our biology by what we think and feel.
> ... It would be impossible to isolate a single thought or feeling, a single belief or assumption, that doesn't have some effect on aging, either directly or indirectly. Our cells are constantly eavesdropping on our thoughts, and being changed by them.
> A bout of depression can wreak havoc with the immune system; falling in love can boost it. Despair and hopelessness raise the risk of heart attacks and cancer, thereby shortening life. Joy and fulfillment keep us healthy and extend life.
> This means that the line between biology and psychology can't really be drawn with any certainty. A remembered stress, which is only a wisp of thought, releases the same flood of destructive hormones as the stress itself.
> Because the mind influences every cell in the body, human aging is fluid and changeable; it can speed up, slow down, stop for a time, and even reverse itself. Hundreds of research findings from the last three decades have verified that aging is much more dependent on the individual than was ever dreamed of in the past.
> ... The biochemistry of the body is a product of awareness. Beliefs, thoughts, and emotions create the chemical reactions that uphold life in every cell. An aging cell is the end product of awareness that has forgotten how to remain new.
> ... Impulses of intelligence create your body in new forms every second. What you are is the sum total of these impulses, and by changing their patterns, you will change.[15]

It should be kept in mind that, according to Chopra, "In my own life, Krishnamurti influenced me profoundly and helped me personally break through the confines of my own self-imposed restrictions to my freedom."[16]

There is an important point to note in this discussion regarding the primacy of HPB and those who followed her—including James, Annie Besant (AB), and K:

Perennial science has always preceded academic science.[17]

---

[15] Chopra, *Ageless Body, Timeless Mind* (1993), 4-6.
[16] Blau, *Krishnamurti: 100 Years,* 233; see also Rezamusic.com.
[17] See Sanat, *Insights for a New Era.*

Perennial Science

Mutation of the brain cells was a pivotal component of perennial insights shared by HPB, her perennial mentors, and her colleagues—*beginning in the 1880s*—fully more than a century before this had even been considered by neuroscientists (the word "neuroscience" itself was coined in 1963). Even those few neuroscientists at the end of the twentieth century who began to consider this were "at the leading edge" of their field. Yet HPB and her perennial mentors had discussed this *explicitly* more than a century earlier, thus inspiring the Father of Modern Psychology to speak of "brain plasticity."

This should come as no surprise to anyone who has *researched* this subject, as just noted and as discussed further in *Insights for a New Era.*

Throughout her writings, HPB often spoke of how "in the course of natural evolution our 'brain-mind' will be replaced by a finer organism."[18] In any case, HPB and her perennial mentors had said that the twentieth century would mark the beginning of several major world cycles. That is, they were saying that the time that you and I are living in would be a very critical period for humanity, and that human mutations of evolutionary proportions involving mutation of the brain cells would begin to become more common.[19]

Given its intimate connection with the core of early disclosures by HPB's perennial mentors, the creation of a new human type and a new age of mankind was an issue discussed with great passion among early HPB students and colleagues. For instance, in *A Study in Consciousness*—her seminal work published at the

---

[18] Blavatsky, "Problems of Life," *Collected Writings,* XII 411-412.

[19] For HPB on new and important cycles beginning in the twentieth century, see, for instance, Blavatsky, *The Secret Doctrine,* I, 64-65; II, 335-337; V 465-466. See also her *Collected Writings,* VIII, 174 fn; XII, 384 and 600-601; see also *The Original Programme of the TS,* 71. See also Chin, *Mahatma Letters Chron,* 308, Letter 93B, and Humphreys and Benjamin, *Mahatma Letters,* 145-146, Letter 23B, and numerous other references. Also, consult paradigmshift.network.

turn of the twentieth century—AB spoke of brain cell mutations in terms of the innate potential in all human beings for moving on to new horizons in consciousness. As she put it:

> [The] enlarging of waking consciousness is accompanied with development in the atoms of the brain, as well as with the development of certain organs in the brain, and of the connections between cells.
> . . . So long as these physical developments remain unaccomplished, Self-consciousness may be evolved . . . but . . . its workings do not express themselves through the brain and thus become part of the waking consciousness.[20]

Basic to the perennial understanding of some of these early HPB colleagues was the notion, implied in AB's words, that for a faculty to become a reality it must be part of waking consciousness in the physical brain—not merely "an interesting intellectual theory" or even "an accomplishment by the mind" on "the inner planes."

For the reality of mutation to come about, the individual must engage in a transformative lifestyle conducive to such physical and psychological mutations.

If and when they took place, such mutations would usher in a new human type, a new humanity, a new age. This is the point that would be insisted on later by K—as the Bohm quotation above states. Significantly, K grew up in that HPB-inspired environment.

These insights also point directly and unequivocally to the fact that the TS was founded specifically with the intention to help bring about such mutation in humanity. Because early TS members did not respond adequately—or at all—to this intent on the part of its founding perennials, the perennials reluctantly founded the ES, as addressed in Chapter 28, "The TS."

In other words—AB is telling us—even though evolutionary mutations take place at critical times determined by world cycles, they do not happen willy-nilly or mechanically, at some "appointed time"—according to some linear, super-slow-mov-

---

[20] Besant, *A Study in Consciousness* (1904), 171.

ing clock. "The world" is us. So the expression "world cycles" refers to cycles that we each participate in, together with all other living entities. We are—each and all, and in conjunction with all other entities—co-creators of *what is*, including all cycles.

Such critical evolutionary developments require engagement on the part of a few pioneering members of the species, who actually engage in a way of being that makes it possible for us as a species to undergo mutations.

This is in fact the way biological evolution is now said by researchers to take place. According to such researchers, only a few members of a species undergo evolutionary mutations, whenever mutations do happen. Then, other members of the species follow in the footsteps of those who had initially undergone such mutations. That is, other members of the species resonate with those who engage in mutation, and before they "know" it, they have themselves mutated.

The process is similar, in the creation of a new human type: Mutation in the brain cells of a few individuals would be enough, to get the evolutionary developments moving.

Early Theosophists—who, let's recall, were Victorians—believed that the proper way to bring about such mutations in the brain was through engaging in "the (spiritual) path" outlined in Theosophical books—*as they understood it.*

They also took this "path" to refer to *what they understood* to be the "esoteric" components of the major religions and other traditions. The "path" that they believed in implied a linear progression—which was presumably accomplished through a series of mechanical algorithms. The "path" that they believed in consisted of a sequence of linear "steps" that would presumably lead to perennial "initiation" in the context of that "Path."

Despite such misunderstandings and misrepresentations, it seems that what has been called "initiation" throughout the world for millennia, and even in the early Theosophical milieu, is the process whereby this actual mutation is accomplished—with the profound clarification that *perennial* initiation involves the mutation of the brain, as just discussed briefly.

MUTATION

The process of mutation—which has clearly been the very foundation of the perennial wisdom throughout the ages—can now be understood in a far, far clearer way than was ever possible, before. We all owe that clarity, depth, and power to insights that have come from the likes of HPB, William James, and recent scientific researches.

No one has expressed this more clearly and powerfully than J. Krishnamurti.

CHAPTER 26
Aurobindo

AMONG THE VERY MANY WHO WERE ENERGIZED early on by HPB's insights was Sri Aurobindo (1872-1950). Though this has never been pointed out before—at least to my knowledge—it is a fact that Aurobindo's "integral yoga" was picked up by him from HPB, and then elaborated on.

In the process of appropriating and adopting the *unprecedented* language and conceptual structures that had been created by HPB and her colleagues and followers (primarily CWL and AB), Aurobindo was following a pattern of behavior that was to be repeated numerous times, all over the planet.

That is, in fact, the main way in which the wisdom explosion of our times—including the so-called New Age movement—flowered everywhere on Earth, as addressed in many ways in the present exploration, and more so in *Muse*.

Wisdom explosion

Very many throughout the world—such as Aurobindo, G.R.S. Mead (1863-1933), Aleister Crowley (1875-1947), Nicholas Roerich (1874-1947), Carl Jung (1875-1961), and Edgar Mitchell (1930-2016), among "a cast of thousands"—would pick up on some aspects of HPB's insights that were of particular interest to each. Then, they would express those insights—*particularly the* unprecedently b*rand new manner of presentation and of conceptualizing those insights*—in a slightly different way, thereby addressing unique audiences with differing interests.

They would also always elaborate further on the aspects that they personally considered of more interest. Importantly, every single one of those (mostly furtive) HPB followers would always retain the basic language and conceptual structures that were historically *unique* to HPB and company.

Some of those HPB copyists would almost always proceed to claim credit for the insights—but without ever mentioning her name. Examples of this—among many others—are Richard Kieninger (1927-2002), founder of com-munities in Stelle, Illinois and Adelphi, Texas; L. Ron Hubbard (1911-1986), founder of the Church of Scientology; and Ken Wilber (b. 1949), knower and understander of "all and everything," according to him.

For full disclosure, it should be mentioned that both Kieninger and Hubbard were at some point in trouble with the law, for fraud of some sort. None of them—and many others like them—ever acknowledged their debt to HPB (which was greater than that to the IRS), despite the fact that it was she who provided the fundamental insights and unique language that buttressed their differing expositions.

Others took the different path of *mentioning* HPB in their work—but then would proceed to claim, without evidence, that theirs was a "better" insight, somehow. Among these are some of the main leaders of the New Age movement, such as Alice Bailey (1880-1949), founder of the Arcane School; Rudolf Steiner (1861-1925), founder of the Anthroposophical Society; and Guy Ballard (1878-1939), founder of the I AM Activity.

Others still would also have their start with HPB, but then would go on to renounce her and even attack her. The most glaring example of this is René Guénon (1886-1951). What makes Guénon "the most glaring example" is his enormous influence worldwide and to the present, especially among academics.

Guénon is unquestionably the main source for what came to be called the "Traditionalist" understanding of history in general, and of the universal wisdom in particular. The second book he published was *Theosophy: History of a Pseudo-Religion* (1921). This book in particular—and much of his work more generally—consists largely of a sustained attack against HPB. Intriguingly, everything else he ever wrote—and even much that is found in this book itself—is based on HPB's insights, while using her *unprecedented* language!

Guénon thus provides a far more clear example than probably anyone else, of how an enormous, multi-faceted movement—usually called "New Age"—came about, worldwide, based on HPB's *unprecedented* insights and approach.

It pays to take note of the fact that all such early leaders—mentioned and unmentioned—have continued to have a history, beyond their deaths. For instance, in the case of Alice Bailey, for a long time—into the 1970s and 1980s—her followers were over-whelmingly simply readers of her books. Then—slowly but surely—many of these readers began to gravitate towards the TS.

Given that TS members did not have a unifying vision of what the TS mission was, it turned out to be a perfect place for Bailey followers to drift towards, and find a niche—and settle in.[1] By the 1990s, an ever-increasing number of TS members were ac-tually Bailey followers. They assumed that "Theosophy" con-sisted of what they had found in Bailey's books—not so much in the writings of HPB, CWL, or AB (let alone Krishnamurti), which they tended to shun.

Followers of Nicholas Roerich's Agni Yoga Society followed a totally different tack from that of Bailey-ites. Today, the most visible leaders of that movement are Zinovia Dushkova (b. 1953), and Ricardo González (b. 1974). Though both are well-known internationally, Dushkova—who, has created a kind of renaissance of interest in HPB—has been most successful in Slavic countries, including her native Moldova.

González is most popular in the Hispanic world. But he's been a regular on GAIA TV, where he mostly speaks about his con-tacts with the Apunians—extraterrestrials whose teachings "happen to overlap" those of Roerich.[2]

---

[1] Respecting the "lack of vision" by TSers, I recall how, in the 1970s and 80s, promi-nent TS members and others discussed quite intensely—in *The American Theoso-phist* and elsewhere—the subject "What shall we teach?" They truly didn't know "what to teach," and were asking one another for guidance. The diversity of opinions on that subject was quite telling. No one in the TSA seemed to have a clue regarding what the TS mission was—at least that was my very strong impression, based on the evi-dence these discussions provided, as well as my personal experience with TSers.

[2] For the most insightful and science-based discussions on extraterretrials—espe-cially as that issue affects you personally—see Dr. Stephen Greer (b. 1955), *Hidden*

Despite Dushkova's focusing on HPB and González on extra-terrestrials, they both make it clear that they follow the path of Roerich's Agni Yoga—which originally had been inspired by HPB's insights.

G men

Apart from the above—which are actually but a tiny fraction of authors and leaders who had been initially inspired by HPB—there were also the main followers of G.I. Gurdjieff (1872?-1949), who was also known simply as "G."

The main G disciple—and credibly the most influential—was P.D. Ouspensky (1878-1947), who inspired the creation of several "fourth way" organizations. There were also Thomas (1885-1956) and Olga de Hartmann (1885-1979), who were close friends of poet and novelist Rainer Maria Rilke (1875-1926) and painter Wassily Kandinsky (1866-1944)—who were also similarly inspired. Thomas de Hartmann was a renowned composer, and became the compiler of numerous musical pieces that had been improvised by G; his wife Olga was a well-known operatic singer. The G music is available today.[3]

There have been and are many other G disciples, throughout the planet—such as the highly influential Sri Madhava Ashish (1920-1997), who co-authored with Sri Krishna Prem (1898-1965) their commentary on HPB's *Secret Doctrine* called *Man The Measure of All Things* (1969).

All of the above and other G followers who became leaders of groups had begun by being members of the TS and/or were very serious students of HPB's work.[4]

Truth, Forbidden knowledge, 2006; see also his YouTube channel; see also his series of interviews with Billy Carson (b. 1971) on GAIA TV.

[3] Cecil Lytle, *Seekers of the Truth: The Complete Piano Music of Georges I. Gurdjieff and Thomas de Hartmann,* three CDs.

[4] For a full account of the Gurdjieff associations and connections to the TS, see the well-researched *The Harmonious Circle: The Lives and Work of G.I. Gurdjieff, P.D. Ouspensky, and Their Followers* (1980), by James Webb.

Orage

Personally, I feel that the deepest and most psychological of Gurdjieff's disciples-teachers was A.R. Orage (1873-1934)—a genius who was at the leading edge in several fields.

Orage was mainly known for his deep commitment to literary criticism, liberal policies, and philosophy (particularly Nietzsche). All of his interests found a channel in the weekly magazine *The New Age*, which he owned from 1907 to 1923. Through that journal, he introduced to the world literary figures of the caliber of Ezra Pound (1885-1972) and T.S. Eliot (1888-1965). Orage also promoted "guild socialism"—which included what is now much discussed as a possible solution to economic snags internationally, and generally known as "universal basic income."

One thing that many G followers—direct or indirect, through G's immediate disciples—are unaware of, is that years before he even knew of G, Orage had been a prominent TS member. He'd been an international lecturer of the TS—which he gave up partly because of the intelligence-challenged element in the TS, and partly in order to focus on *The New Age*.

Subsequently, he became one of the premier teachers of G's "fourth way." In addition—and importantly—he was the "translator" of G's works. Given the unusual and creative use of the English language—particularly in one of those works, *Beelzebub's Tales*—it is practically a certainty that the real author of this literary masterpiece was Orage, not G. The style of writing in that work is somewhat reminiscent of James Joyce's (1882-1941) *Ulysses* (1922). Joyce had also been impacted by HBP. I consider Orage a co-author of G's books, not just a translator. In fact—for whatever it's worth—I consider him to be the senior author, at least in terms of their literary value.

Incidentally, in *Beelzebub's Tales to His Grandson,* Beelzebub is an extraterrestrial who comes back to Earth every few thousand years, each time assessing the very little progress achieved by humans.

Gurdjieff's English was famously broken, sometimes incomprehensible (perhaps deliberately). Given the unique and highly sophisticated literary style in which this very long, three-volume book is written—my take is that this literary masterpiece was actually written by Orage, based on descriptions given to him by G in broken English.[5]

G referred to the three titles that he published (at first only privately) as "legominism," meaning by that word "one of the means of transmitting information about certain events of long-past ages through initiates." It is intriguing to note that Orage's name does not even appear in any of G's works.

Late-blooming Victorians

Though the emphasis in the discussion above has been on leaders of culture influenced by HPB, I consider it important to take notice of the very many who "borrowed" from Krishnamurti, but without giving him any credit, either. There have been many of those, but I'll just emphasize a couple, who were once profoundly influential in worldwide culture, and whose legacy is still going strong.

I am referring to Baba Da Free John (1939-2008) and Sri Rajneesh (1931-1990)—two highly controversial exponents of aspects of the universal wisdom explosion in the American Age. Both of them had a strong background in the field of academic philosophy—which shows, in various ways, in what they each taught. Both had been clearly touched by HPB and/or her colleagues—either directly or indirectly, though of course, without mentioning her—since they made use of her unique language and conceptual structures, especially Da, who had studied HPB as a young man.

Though both of them "borrowed" from Krishnamurti with impunity—and like St. Peter famously did to his "Lord," three times—neither ever acknowledged that debt, either.

---

[5] G.I. Gurdjieff, *Beelzebub's Tales to His Grandson*, 3 vols. (1950).

Rajneesh (aka "Osho") was quite successful at taking insights "borrowed" from K, and combining them with libertine sexual practices "borrowed" from an exoteric understanding of tantra. The crowds of young people who followed him lapped it all up. They felt that with Osho, they got "the best of both worlds": They could engage in me-centered omnisex (everything goes), while at the same time would consider themselves "intellectually so-phisticated," on the grounds that they *talked* like K talked—even though they were not *walking the K walk, which implies a transformation away from anything me-centered.* I was privi-leged to get to know a number of them—often at K-related ven-ues.

They acted as if they were proud of being so clever that they could enjoy me-centeredness while being "transdimensional." From their perspective, the "bonus" was that they thought they were so astute, that they could fool Mother Nature, and live their daily lives without what to them seemed to be the "peskiness" of having to end the me, while at the same time being involved daily with a free-for-all me-centered lifestyle.

Like Osho's disciples, many of Da's also got involved in "for-bidden sex"—as well as using drugs and alcohol.

In fact, one general observation I feel I can make regarding the counter-culture movement in general, is that it was actually quite Victorian, at a very deep level. What I mean is that—just like Victorian Theosophists, whence counter-culturists got their mojo, by and large—they made the fateful assumption that "hav-ing the 'proper' scheme" (the "proper" *analysis*) is "where it's at."

Like the scout-father of the counter-culture—Alan Watts—Osho and Da (and by extension, their followers) assumed that so long as you gave a strong impression to others (and to your-self) of being "cool," you were surely the cat that everyone got high on. Being super extra cool led them all to a relatively early demise—Watts at 59, Osho at 58, and Da at 69, but Da was very sick for at least the last ten years of his life, which he spent mostly in semi-retirement.

To my mind, all three of them were brilliant—perhaps geniuses, in many ways. It strikes me as obvious that they inspired very many people to look more deeply into themselves—and thereby introduced the world at large to deeper aspects of the perennial wisdom explosion in the American Age. The Ayahuascans of today are very much like that group from a previous generation—and that, too, is a personal observation based on experience.

For some reason, this discussion of Osho and Da—and their many followers—makes me think of an extremely prosaic saying among cowboys in the US southwest: "Sometimes a blind pig finds an excellent truffle."

Yet—despite their unquestionable cleverness—there was a severely serious downside. Both Da and Osho were ridiculously narcissistic, and thought very highly of themselves—an attitude that is captured with precision in the hit song by Mac Davis, which was contemporary to them,

> Oh, Lord! it's so hard to be humble
> when you're perfect in every way!
> I can't wait to look in the mirror
> Cause I get better-looking each day![6]

Both Da and Osho claimed to be "the avatar of the new era"—knowing without a doubt that that very notion had been (rightly or wrongly) promoted decades before by HPB's colleagues AB and CWL, regarding K. In fact, AB and CWL had declared that K was "the World Teacher"—given that his message was said by them to be planetary, not one with borders, as all previous perennial messages had been.

Yet despite knowing that full well, Da had the impudence and gall actually to call himself "The World Teacher"—thus stealing without attribution from K not just K's insights, but also the putative title that had been given to K exclusively.[7]

---

[6] Mac Davis, *Hard to be Humble*, Casablanca, 1980.
[7] For Da calling himself "the World Teacher," see his autobiography, Adi Da Samraj, Da Free John, and Adi Da, *The knee of listening: The early-life ordeal and the radical*

Incidentally, I feel I should explain why the book just cited seems to have three authors and the title mentions a fourth and a fifth, and a sixth, and a seventh ("True Heart-Master," "Da Avabhasa," and "the Bright"), when Da was its only author—after all, it is an autobiography!

Franklin Albert Jones ended up having more monikers than any mafia person I've ever known of—which is reflected in the eight different sobriquets used by him in his autobiography. The grand shuffle of names began when Swami Muktananda (1908-1982) innocently gave to Da not one but two spiritual names, Dhyanananda and Love-Ananda. But that was before he became "Adi Da." For good measure, he later assumed the name "Bubba Free John"—and from there, it was off to the races. In Hawaii, he was Da Love-Ananda Mahal—followed by Da Love-Ananda, Dau Loloma, Da Kalki, Hridaya-Samartha Sat-Guru Da, Santosha Da, Da Avadhoota, Da Avabhasa, and Adi Da Love-Ananda Samraj (or just Adi Da, for short).

Why did he have such a predilection for "Da"? No one has explained that. Perhaps he had a strong affinity for the Dadaists of the early twentieth century. But that's just speculation.

It is worthy of note that both Da and Osho ended up being in trouble with law enforcers who did not appreciate the importance of being New Age cool—and were more interested in people being law-abiding.

In the case of Osho, many of his closest associates left him when he was investigated for allegedly committing many felonies, including arson, attempted murder, drug smuggling, and vote fraud. In 1985, he pleaded guilty to immigration fraud and was deported from the United States—and was then refused entry to 21 countries (to which he attempted to flee) before he was forced to return to India, which he had been avoiding because of trouble with the law there.

---

spiritual realization of the Divine World-Teacher and True Heart-Master, Da Avabhasa (the "Bright"), Middletown, CA: Dawn Horse Press, 1992 [1972].

Deconstructing Sadhguru

Of all the innumerable leaders of culture who have figured significantly in the American Age wisdom explosion, Sadhguru is unquestionably—at least to my mind—the most comprehensively representative of the era.

Differently from practically everyone else, he openly and humbly acknowledges the importance and relevance of H.P. Blavatsky, Annie Besant, and C.W. Leadbeater. Importantly, he could have sent his child to any of the best schools in India—yet he chose to invest her more fragile, formative years at the Krishnamurti school, in transparent acknowledgment of his respect for what K said regarding education.

In fact, he also openly acknowledges how it was K's inspiration that largely put him on the path that led him from being Jagadish Vasudev, aka "Jaggy" (b. 1957) to becoming the internationally renowned and widely respected Sadhguru.

You will find in Sadhguru no controversies resulting from misplaced cleverness—as seen in the likes of Da, Osho, and so many, many others in the present planetary wisdom explosion era. Nor will you find in him blatantly Victorian notions—such as with Alice Bailey, Rudolf Steiner, and the "cast of thousands" who followed them and others similarly placed.

In fact, what you do see—among other positive elements—is his passionate engagement in yoga and in environmental concerns—as witness his creation of organizations such as the Isha Institute of Inner Sciences, Project GreenHands, Rally for Rivers, Cauvery Calling, and Save Soil. In 2022, he spoke at the United Nations' Convention to Combat Desertification—and he has been involved in projects for saving the planet from an ecological disaster, and for world peace.

In many ways, I perceive him as promoting a kind of "perennial wisdom for the masses"—a new *popularization* of the borderless wisdom. He has a unique way of expressing otherwise complex issues of enormous importance to all of us—yet presenting them in simple terms that anyone can understand or relate to.

Unfortunately, he manages to achieve all that by assuming the hegemony of Indian culture. Despite its overwhelming and multidimensional importance for everyone on the planet, Indian culture is but one of many that could be assessed in a similar way—such as the Chinese and the Toltec, just to mention two out of a very large number.

All worldwide cultures—including the Indian—are the patrimony of all humanity. They don't "belong" with exclusivity to the people who happened to be born in each—let alone be "the one" that everyone on Earth "should" adhere to.

Anyone who promotes the superiority of any one culture is thereby denying the perennial wisdom—which is everywhere and within each of us, and is not confined to any particular venue.

Yet that, precisely, is what Sadhguru does. He is right, of course, in saying that the solution to our many problems is "yoga"; what we all need is transformamtive meditation—and yoga at its best is that, without question.

But one could just as well say that "the solution" is tai chi and the many Chinese energy arts—which include chi gung, nei gung, tui na, and many other modalities, comprehended in what is now called Traditional Chinese Medicine.[8]

In addition, even his name, "Sadhguru," includes the fateful word "guru"—which is addressed in Chapter 5, "Masters." That word stands for assuming falsely—much like Victorians did, as discussed throughout this exploration, but especially in Chapter 19, "Victorian Exoterics"—that there is such a thing as authorities in the field of universal morality. Lamentably, falsely assuming the efficacy and reliability of authorities in areas in which authority clearly does not belong—and is actually and unquestionably dangerous—is promoted implicitly and explicitly by Sadhguru.

---

[8] See Chapters 17, "Chinese Energy Wisdom," and 18, "American Agers."

So even by wearing his name, he is committing the analytical fallacy—as everyone has done throughout history, except for J. Krishnamurti, as documented in Chapter 1, "Krishnamurti."

So for all the goodness identified with his work, Sadhguru turns out to be just one more analyzer—a mere intellectual, a late-blooming Victorian—and this is immensely dangerous, especially in our times, when the human soul itself is at risk.

It is interesting to note that—despite the profound effect that K had on him personally, as related by him—Sadhguru criticizes K:

> Around Jiddu Krishnamurti, everyone could feel the man is special, but no one could get what he was talking about because he refused to play the role of a Guru. He refused to initiate anyone into anything or give any kind of method or process.[9]

That is, Sadhguru is assuming that the Indian approach of "initiating" someone in an Indian school of thought and practice is essential for anyone in the planet being able to understand anything. One *must* be immersed in Indian culture—says Sadhguru—in order for anyone to have anything of value to say.

He is also asserting—without any evidence at all and against all the evidence, as discussed and documented throughout this exploration—that we all *"need* [a] method or process." That is, he is stating unequivocally that unless there is an *analysis* of some sort, understanding or self-realization is impossible. Yet that, precisely, is the definition of committing the analytical fallacy—and therefore of making oneself a cripple, when it comes to truly understanding anything at all.[10]

With his actions and statements, he is telling us that we need to ignore that we are all in the midst of the most formidable wisdom explosion in history in the whole planet. With his actions and statements, he is telling us that we all must *regress* to "the good ol' days" when we all committed the analytical fallacy right

---

[9] "Sadhguru on Jiddu Krishnamurti," isha.sadhguru.org.
[10] See Chapter 2, "The Analytical Fallacy."

and left with impunity, without regard for the very serious and dangerous consequences that such a path leads us to.

It is the act and process of committing the analytical fallacy that has been responsible for all humans being under siege and incapable of experiencing freedom, for as far back as our history goes, everywhere on Earth. Right now, we are at a point in which that challenge has become survival-defining, for each of us personally, and for humanity in general. We can no longer afford to continue playing that kind of spiritual-moral Russian roulette.

It is the act and process of committing the analytical fallacy that has led us to the extremely sad and dangerous place where we are all at, at present.

Yet Sadhguru is asserting—against the overwhelming evidence, as provided in part throughout this exploration—that we must *regress to tribalism*, and to all the inequities and problems implicit in doing that.

This is just cultural hubris. It is pure, unadulterated arrogance. It is a forceful denial of universal wisdom, which is borderless. And borderlessness—not tribalism—is what we all need, in the unprecedented, extremely difficult and challenging moment that we are all experiencing.

Sadhguru on K

Sadhguru declares—as if it were a matter of fact—that K was engaging in "just intellectual dissection" and that what K said was "pure Gnana Marga," clarifying that "Gnana means the path of the intellect."[11]

We are to believe that Sadhguru gathered these K-defining insights by having an astonishingly minimal exposure to K, and by not having looked carefully into what K was saying. Sadhguru clearly ignores that K's insights are without any precedent in human history, as documented in Chapter 1, "Krishnamurti," and elsewhere in this exposition. Yet Sadhguru treats those insights

---

[11] "Sadhguru on Jiddu Krishnamurti," *Ibid.*

disrespectfully—as if it were some piece of gossip one heard, and which one can accept or discard, without any consequences.

As Sadhguru relates, in the process of telling us what his total exposure to K was, some friends invited him to participate in K-related discussions:

> For five weekends, I went there every Saturday afternoon just for about an hour-and-a-half. They would play one half-an-hour video or audio and then get into a discussion.[12]

He further reveals his extremely limited exposure to K, when he says that,

> I did not do much reading but I heard a few audios and watched a few videos. I enjoyed him, but I was too wild to listen to anyone. Life was calling me all the time. I had no time to listen to my parents or my teachers or to Krishnamurti. I had no time for anything, so I left the study circle and went on.[13]

Despite Sadhguru's amazingly minimal exposure to K, it's intriguing and impressive to note the profound effect that K had on him. As he says,

> When I went to these five Saturday afternoons for an hour-and-a-half, on one of these days he spoke about education. It really gripped me because I had never thought of an alternative way of educating people. I was only thinking of how to dismantle all the education systems in my mind. I thought these education systems are the most horrible evil and I could grow up better under a mango tree—or upon a mango tree depending upon the season—rather than being in a school.
>
> When he spoke about education, suddenly it struck me that there is another way to do this. I was maybe 17 or 18 and I was living wild and I had dreams of running away somewhere. I just thought that I would like to put children into the kind of education he was talking about.
>
> It just so happened that when my daughter had to go to school, she got admission in some of the best schools in Ooty, which is where

---

12 "Sadhguru on Jiddu Krishnamurti," *Ibid.*
13 "Sadhguru on Jiddu Krshnamurti," *Ibid.*

everyone would want to go, but then it just flashed in my mind, "Okay, there is a Jiddu Krishnamurti school. Why not send her there?" She went to that school and she spent eight years studying there.

So those five Saturday afternoons of an hour-and-a-half each had that much impact on me, that I handed over my daughter to his care in one way or the other. My contact with Jiddu Krishnamurti was just seven-and-half hous and that is the influence he had upon me.[14]

Sadhguru tells us, regarding his perception of K, and how K impacted him, that

This man is straight. Too straight. Just the integrity of the person is spilling all over him. Just the sheer integrity of the man cannot be missed.

. . . Once, Jiddu Krishnamurti was at some place and Kahlil Gibran went to meet him. Gibran later said, "When I walked into the room, I walked into a wall of love."

You would never associate Jiddu Krishnamurti with love. He definitely does not look loving, but he is very loving. His energies are absolutely compassionate, but his words are like a knife.[15]

In sum, we learn from Sadhguru that K had an immense, beneficially transformative impact on his life. Yet from various comments he makes, it's obvious that he made the catastrophic mistake of falsely assuming that K was somehow "an intellectual." He criticizes K for not "initiating" anyone into an Indian school of thought and practice, and for not providing "a method" or "structure" that any analyzer could follow—especially one from India.

Against all the evidence, Sadhguru asserts that no one understood K. Yet the fact is that K had discussions with children at his schools throughout the world, for decades, and they clearly understood what he was saying—to the point that these discussions had a transformative impact on them.[16]

---

[14] "Sadhguru on Jiddu Krishnamurti," *Ibid.*
[15] "Sadhguru on Jiddu Krishnamurti," *Ibid.*
[16] For examples of K discussing with children who were transformed by these exchanges, see the video by Michael Mendizza, *Krishnamurti: With a Silent Mind*, 1989.

Perhaps Sadhguru might benefit from asking his daughter whether she had any trouble understanding K. After all, she spent eight years at a Krishnamurti school—and it's likely that she participated in K exchanges with children, in his periodical visits to all the K schools.

Importantly, Sadhguru based his assessment of the unprecedented worldwide phenomenon that K was, in the context of his being profoundly and multidimensionally ignorant of who K was, and of what K was communicating—as Sadhguru himself tells us. That is, his knowledge and understanding of K is based on seven and a half hours of audio and video exposure, and brief discussions thereafter. His assessment of such an unprecedented phenomenon in world history is based on that ignorance—and so he chastises K for being "different."

Popularization—in Kansas

Despite the severely concerning problems with Sadhguru's tribalist teachings, I feel that—like the very many gurus and other teachers who have had an international exposure in the HPB-inspired wisdom explosion in the American Age, he is unquestionably a great *popularizer* of the borderless wisdom, much like Victorian-minded TSers still are.

The problem that I perceive in emphasizing popularization, however, is that we are no longer in the nineteenth century—and not even in the twentieth—when "popularization" may have been a good, and even an excellent thing, in some respects.

Our actual present situation—as opposed to what Sadhguru pretends it to be, against overwhelming evidence—is reflected in a famous scene from the timelessly popular 1939 film *The Wizard of Oz*. As Dorothy poignantly said to her little dog, "Toto, I think we're not in Kansas, anymore."

Sadhguru behaves as if he's unaware that we are in the twenty-first century, when we are all facing possible extinction at the hands of analyzers—who see everything as "a subject" for having opinions "pro" or "con," and their analyses are based on some form or another of group-think—such as promoting the hegemony of Indian culture.

Like it or not, we are all faced, as we speak, with the most inconvenient reality that unless there is profound transformation in each of us, we are doomed to face consequences more horrid than anything ever witnessed by humans.

Popularization was wonderful in the nineteenth—and perhaps good even in the twentieth—century. But then was then.

But we're not in Kansas, anymore.

Right now, what the actual situation we find ourselves in requires is to move away from atavisms of any kind—including of course any kind of prejudicial cultural identifications. To my knowledge, no one in history has addressed that very situation with the clarity and strength that K did—as Sadhguru himself acknowledged happened to him, as a result of a handful of brief encounters with a virtual K.

I'm not saying that we all must abandon Sadhguru or whomever, and become K-ites. Nothing could be furthest from what I'm pointing out. What is required of each of us is to be no one's follower, to be truly free, to be truly responsible for one another, to love one another—all of which K addressed in a most impactful way, as Sadhguru revealed in his personal experience with K.

I am merely pointing out that—to my knowledge—no one in history has expressed that reality so unambiguously, the way K did. It is not a question of being anyone's follower. It is a question of you and I actually engaging in a transformative way of-living daily life—a borderless, transdimensional way that alone can help transform the planet, and create a good society.

By his own words, Sadhguru is telling us all that we should not engage in borderless transformation, and that we should instead *regress to tribalism*—and deliberately ignore the profound crisis that the whole world is engulfed in, and that you and I find ourselves in the midst of.

Wisdom-Compassion-Morality

I feel compelled to clarify that it gives me no pleasure at all to deconstruct Sadhguru. In fact, that enterprise actually gives me a headache THIS BIG. I'll explain, attentive reader.

He is obviously a very sweet, loving, caring, insightful human. He obviously has been inspiring millions of people to replicate in their lives that wondrous way of being.

In fact, my perception—for whatever it's worth—is that such moral-spiritual qualities in him are what gives oomph to his evident charisma. People flock to him because they are attracted to such and similar qualities in him. They flock to him because their hearts resonate to that love and sense of responsibility towards one another and towards the planet that he exhudes.

His is a communication from heart to heart.

I submit most humbly to you, caring reader, that such is precisely what distinguishes theosophical (divine-like) states of awareness. That theosophical dimension is within each and every one of us. All the greatest spiritual-moral geniuses, throughout the ages, have been inviting us all to find that gem within (the jewel in the lotus)—and to bask in it, in our daily lives.

Unfortunately, some in the many audiences that perennials have had, since ancient times, have tried to "capture that"—and tried their best to "manufacture" it and "market" it (popularize it)—which is grossly absurd. The deepest "teaching" consists of being responsible for one another, of caring for one another and for all that is. It is from that state of comprehensive being that the great insights have always come.

Theologies won't help bring it about. Nor will rituals, uniforms, hierarchies, or institutions. That state of peace and caring is a law unto itself, and needs no "help" from the conditioned part of us—which is just as real as the unconditioned, theosophical, borderless state of being.

In that transdimensional state of being there are no Indians—nor Mexicans, nor Polynesians, nor Timbuktuans. In that transdimensional state, there is only that which is—but words are useless, and even dangerous.

The word is not the thing.

The great spiritual-compassionate geniuses have always communicated heart-to-heart—and that is all that's needed, in order to help create a good society. Yes, there does have to be planning, and there needs to be decision-making—and planning and decision-making are but forms of analysis, which is intrinsically me-centered, as shown in Chapter 2, "The Analytical Fallacy."

But when such analyses are inspired by the borderless dimension, they are properly used in the service of all of us—of all that is.

I submit to you, listening reader, that all the many teachers, gurus, authors, and "group leaders"—both within and without the New Age movement, in the American Age wisdom explosion—have shared some aspect of that deeper dimension.

There is something to be learned from everyone—"even" when they give the impression of being rascals, such as Osho and Da. Everyone has Buddha nature. Everyone is expressing the one and only mind there is (according Erwin Schrödinger (1887-1961), a pioneer of quantum physics—and according to all the great spiritual geniuses throughout the ages.

Problems arise only when some "clever bird" has what to him is the "brilliant" idea of trying to package the one mind, and market it—and thereby create a "religion" or a "philosophy," or some institution.

No less and no more than that is what K addressed for decades, throughout his long life—inspiring millions of people, much like he did Sadhguru. Very many in K's audiences were bewildered—Sadhguru being but one of millions—because K showed the urgent necessity for all of us to embrace the borderless dimension of wisdom-compassion-morality, but without the ever-divisive trappings of the analyzer.

But—to my knowledge—K is the only person in history who made it totally clear that it is critical not to make any attempt to "package" or to "market" that packageless-marketless border-less-transdimensional state of being. Very many have been bewildered by that, because they expected to be given some structure—some analysis—that they could then go on to be entertained with, much like children or like witless-clueless people.

It is precisely such a structure that Sadhguru expects—as if it were a given—according to him, as quoted above.

Is it possible for you and I to remain in that *autistic* state, without having any expectations that "there *must* be a structure"—despite the fact that structures make the dimension of compassion impossible to manifest? Is it possible for you and I to remain in that dimension, which is the dimension of intelligence?

All the geniuses throughout history have said, "Yes we can!" Our problem is that we have invariably migrated towards activities and people who are incompatible with intelligence-compassion—which is not organizable nor institutionable.

At the end of the day, Sahguru is only the latest version of numerous gurus that India has produced in the Blavatsky-inspired wisdom explosion in the American Age. Some of these popularizers of the perennial wisdom have been Swami Vivekananda (1863-1902), Ramana Maharshi (1879-1950), Paramahansa Yogananda (1893-1952), Maharishi Mahesh Yogi (1918-2008)—and Sri Aurobindo (1872-1950). All of them were touched—and even inspired—by the internationalist, borderless tenor of HPB's presentation of the perennial wisdom. But—before Sadhguru—that background is most obvious in Aurobindo.

Aurobindo

Aurobindo differed from European HPB surrogates only in that he was an Indian enamored of and committed to his culture. So he tweaked HPB's *borderless* insights into his own version of Indian schools, such as Advaita Vedanta and Yoga.

In fact, Aurobindo could be said to have been guilty of behaving strikingly similarly to the way Europeans had done—but with one major exception. While most Europeans had tended to claim that the *borderless* wisdom was actually "Western," Aurobindo presented it—as Sadhguru was to do a century later—as being thoroughly "Indian." Just as many "Western" HPB copyists were succeeded by others who followed their tack, there came to be a "cast of thousands" of gurus and swamis and Babas following Aurobindo's "Eastern" tack—though most of them never acknowledged their debt to Aurobindo, not to mention HPB.

In their prideful and very divisive and mistaken (mis)understanding, they were all missing the most central aspect of the one wisdom. They failed to comprehend the very simple fact that wisdom is borderless, and that the moment you understand it as being "Eastern" or "Western," you are thereby transmogrifying it, and making it out to be something that denies importantly that wisdom.

That's one of innumerable ways in which a person can be intelligence-challenged.

"East is East, and West is West—and never the twain shall meet," sayeth Rudyard Kipling (1865-1936). But "Wisdom has no walls, so Rudy really stalls," respondeth some fool disrespectful of quotable bromides.

Actually, that very famous quote has been misused horribly—which is obviously not Kipling's fault, despite his having been otherwise a Victorian-minded imperialist. In that poem, he goes on to state, quite accurately, something that contradicts that otherwise divisive expression. He said,

> Oh, East is East, and West is West,
>   and never the twain shall meet,
> Till Earth and Sky stand presently
>   at God's great Judgment Seat;
> But there is neither East nor West,
>   Border, nor Breed, nor Birth,
> When two strong men stand face to face,
>   though they come from the ends of the earth![17]

---

[17] Kipling, *The Ballad of East and West*, 1889.

Aurobindo's debt to HPB becomes rather clear, once one looks into what are universally accepted as being his two most visible and salient contributions. Those two bedrocks of Aurobindo's teaching are:

- His understanding of evolution.
- His "integral yoga."

The generally accepted opinion—not based on any actual research—is that these two contributions were original to Aurobindo. My research, however, has shown that it is a fact that both of these insights came originally from HPB's perennial mentors as seen in her writings—not from Aurobindo.

The brief brain plasticity discussion in the previous chapter shows with clarity that "spiritual evolution" was first taught—and rather thoroughly—by HPB, throughout the 1880s, the years when Aurobindo was still going through childhood and adolescence.

Furthermore, HPB was in India in the 1880s, and her presence was pervasively well-known and most impactful throughout the country—especially among the cultural, religious, and intellectual avant garde, of which Aurobindo would eventually become a main exemplar. In that context, Aurobindo is often credited with being the first to speak of "the evolution of the brain." But as just documented in the previous chapter, it was HPB who first spoke of this, and rather extensively—without any question.

Regarding the psychological evolution of humanity (including the evolution of the brain) Aurobindo's contribution consisted of elaborating on HPB's insights. In that respect, I find Aurobindo to be strikingly similar to Ken Wilber.

Aurobindo focused on presenting those same insights in terms of Indian culture—and in terms of establishing himself as a guru to be worshipped in his ashram, as is so common in India. But this commonality and association with a particular region of the world is precisely the great blunder in Aurobindo's presentation of the *borderless* wisdom—as addressed more pointedly in the discussion of Sadhguru.

Importantly, in the process of transmogrifying the border-less wisdom by making it out to be a merely Indian "teach-ing"—and a teaching that called for a wisdom-denying struc-ture of authority—he is telling us that he never understood what the ancient yet ever new actual wisdom is really about.

There is an uncanny similarity between Aurobindo's follow-ers, and TS members—especially regarding what they both be-lieve in. One outstanding difference between them is that Auro-bindo followers are beholden to and identify with Indian culture and background. TSers tend to be followers of a form of Tradi-tionalism, in which certain teachings from all over the world are emphasized. Other than that, both the Ashramists and the TSers misunderstand and fail to see the *borderless* nature of that which they respectively believe in.

Integral yoga

Apart from his rehashing of what HPB had said regarding the evolution of the brain, Aurobindo's other major contribution was what he called "integral yoga."

This expression is used by Aurobindo to summarize what HPB had taught about yoga, years before him. At the behest of her perennial mentors—who (lest we forget) *mastered* the his-tory and practice of yoga—HPB had emphasized that what most people identified as "yoga" was, at best, incomplete, and at worst, erroneous. In her times, as well as today, what most peo-ple have identified as "yoga" is *hatha* yoga—physical exercises meant to improve physical health.

HPB—as a mouthpiece of the perennials—spoke instead of how hatha yoga was just one of the various forms of yoga to be found historically in the literature. I should reiterate that most (perhaps all) of what was published under the name "HPB" can be said to have been authored by the perennials behind her work.[18]

For instance, "she" pointed out that there was mantra yoga—the yoga of using sound to help awaken and transform the psyche. There was bhakti yoga—the yoga of devotion to and love of the divinity, also meant to help bring about a psychological transformation. There was karma yoga—the yoga of doing good deeds for others and for the community at large, thereby helping create harmony within oneself and in all relationships. There was jnana yoga—the yoga of delving into the nature of reality through the mind, and hopefully transforming that mind through the union between the observer and the observed.

The Sanskrit word "yoga," after all, means "union"—referring to that non-temporal flash in which there is no observer and no observed, but just *what is*. As Patañjali put it at the beginning of his *Yoga Sutras*, "Yoga takes place upon the dissolution of dysfunctions in the psyche." In the *Yoga Sutras, asana* (postures) is just one of "eight limbs" that make up total yoga.

According to HPB's perennial mentors, yoga must be understood as incorporating all the many forms it has taken, over thousands of years. The important, central point of all yoga is for me-centeredness to come to an end, when there is a union (yoga) between the so-called observer and the so-called observed—as Patañjali expressed it, in the *Yoga Sutras*.

HPB's perennial mentors' insights into yoga were briefly summarized later—but before Aurobindo published his understanding of "integral yoga." Annie Besant (AB) presented HPB's summary in her *Introduction to Yoga*, which was an edited version of what she had been speaking of since the 1890s, and which was published in 1907.[19]

---

[18] For the perennial authorship of works attributed to HPB, see Boris de Zirkoff, *Rebirth of the Occult Tradition: How The Secret Doctrine of H.P. Blavatsky was Written* (1987); see also numerous references in Olcott, *Old Diary Leaves*, especially vol. I; see also Wachtmeister, *et.al.*, *Reminiscences of H.P. Blavatsky and the Secret Doctrine*.

[19] Annie Besant, *Introduction to Yoga*, 1907.

Incidentally, Aurobindo often followed closely AB's writings, in the sense that he would publish his own version of subjects covered by her. Quite often, Aurobindo would even use exactly the same title of books published by Besant—such as "Reincarnation," "Karma," and other matters related to what was then called "the ancient wisdom."

Importantly, Aurobindo used the language that was unique in the HPB milieu, and particularly AB's many works—in which she shared her own take on the borderless wisdom. Aurobindo then went on to say basically what AB had said—but giving it a nationalistic and culturally-biased Indian twist.

It should be kept in mind that there were also Indian authors who were TS members, and who spoke of various elements in Indian culture, but under the inspiration of the borderless wisdom, which they had learned from HPB. Perhaps the best example of these authors was T. Subba Row (1856-1890), who was discussed earlier. Some of what Aurobindo was to publish later—as if it were his own insights—can also be found in Subba Row's works.

It should be clarified that in HPB's published works she often gave the impression of favoring jnana yoga over all the others. But privately, she taught that raja yoga—the yoga better known from Patañjali's *Yoga Sutras*—is the "kingly" yoga, the one yoga that incorporates simultaneously all forms of yoga.

That single yoga—which includes hatha, mantra, bhakti, karma, jnana, and any others—is what Aurobindo was *later* to call "integral yoga." This integrality of all yoga is addressed in AB's *Introduction to Yoga*—which is actually a transcription of lectures she had given years earlier on the subject.

Vivekananda

While we're on the subject of "integral" yoga, it should be noted that Swami Vivekananda (1863-1902) was to teach—a few years after HPB, but also before Aurobindo—exactly the same thing that HPB had done at the behest of the perennials.

Vivekananda wrote a series of books on the various yogas, and on how the most complete yoga would be one that incorporated them all—an *integral* yoga. It is intriguing to note that Vivekananda's own "integral yoga" (though he didn't call it that) was much like what HPB had been teaching on the subject, before Vivekananda.

Where did this understanding of there being a union of all forms of yoga come from, at approximately the same time? Was this a coincidence?

However that may be, it is a fact that Vivekananda—like Aurobindo was to do *later*—proceeded to present his insights in the non-regional and non-culturally-attached borderless language and conceptual structures that HPB and her colleagues had created. Such borderless language and conceptual structures did not exist in Indian literature before HPB and her colleagues used them. As Elizabeth De Michelis put it, Vivekananda

> . . . capitalized on the interest in Indian religions generated by the academic study of religion and, even more so, by the popularization of Oriental ideas carried out by occultist groups such as the Theosophical Society.[20]

Precursors

It should also be kept in mind that much of what Vivekananda shared with others probably came—at least in some important ways—from his teacher Ramakrishna Paramahansa (1836-1886).

Of particular interest in the present exploration is that Ramakrishna—like HPB—understood all religions as having a common origin, and being but different expressions of the very same borderless wisdom.

That precocious insight on the part of Ramakrishna is remarkable in many ways, since he was born in a village and in a very poor family, so this borderless perception is not likely to

---

[20] Elizabeth De Michelis, *A History of Modern Yoga*, 154.

have come from any external source. So while Ramakrishna did not use the kind of language and conceptual structures that were unique to HPB and her colleagues, he did seem to have the insight that the borderless wisdom is prior to all external forms.

Like Soyen Shaku (1860-1919) and D.T. Suzuki (1870-1966) were to do in Buddhism, Ramakrishna had an internationalist understanding of the borderless wisdom. A major difference is that Shaku and Suzuki relied on the TS's planetary vision, which they became acquainted with as a result of Shaku staying at the TS headquarters and holding dialogues with Olcott (whom Buddhists living then considered "a bodhisattva") on international Buddhism, in 1888.

On the other hand, Ramakrishna had these perceptions years before the TS was even founded. Ramakrishna's lack of wider education prevented him from going much deeper into that insight—yet that is a truly extraordinary fact about his life and perceptions.

It is as if the borderlessness implicit in the brand new American Age was indeed "in the air," and that a number of people throughout the planet picked up on it—and each addressed it in some unique way, relevant to the time and place they found themselves in. It was the American Age zeitgeist. This phenomenon also points to the fact that while the TS was unquestionably at the forefront of the still ongoing wisdom explosion, there were precursors to it, in many ways.

A good example of this was Emanuel Swedenborg (1688-1772), whose insights were often strikingly similar to HPB's, though he shared those insights more than a century before HPB. There were many others—a number of whom are cited or quoted in HPB's voluminous works.

All this background shows that perennials had indeed been preparing for bringing about the present wisdom explosion, and that they had been doing so for centuries. There are numerous references to that effect in their correspondence, as well as in HPB's works.[21]

The "rush" to progress—as one of the perennials called it—has led to the wisdom explosion, which is still ongoing.

That "rush" is addressed briefly in the next chapter.

---

[21] Perhaps the most poignant of these references appears in Chin, *Mahatma Letters Chron.,* Letter 93B (Letter 23B in earlier editions), where the perennial KH explains to A.P. Sinnett the source for what Sinnett had sarcastically referred to as the "curious rush" in human progress over the previous 2,000 years.

CHAPTER 27
American Age

WHEN IT COMES TO HPB, I HAVE FOUND—through decades of careful borderless research—that there are far too many "coincidences" similar to that with Vivekananda, as noted in the previous chapter. I am referring to Vivekananda's "integral yoga" being much like what HPB had taught, and what Sri Aurobindo—who came to own the proverbial trademark "integral yoga"—was to teach, later.

My perception is that there have been numerous such "coincidences," in many different fields of human interest—not just in yoga, and definitely not just in Asia. I have found that a large number of New Age authors and prominent figures—including Indian gurus—have often claimed for themselves the credit for some contribution or another.

Yet upon careful research, I have found that they had actually been but restating—and "buttressing"—something that HPB's perennial mentors had said, mostly through her writings. In that sense, that plethora of authors and figureheads—"East" and "West"—turn out to provide part of the evidence for HPB's statement at the beginning of *The Secret Doctrine*, that "we are at the dawn of a new Cycle."

That is, the many "coincidences"—when viewed as a whole—point poignantly to the fact that humanity is indeed in the midst of what is, by far, the most species-transforming cycle in human history—at least within our present collective memory.

In fact, that "new era" is precisely what I am calling "the wisdom explosion"—which is a main focus of the present exploration. What I perceive is that perennials have been immensely active in the last few centuries, doing their best to make the borderless wisdom more accessible to everyone on Earth—more so than they had ever been able to do before, for millennia.

Yes, HPB's TS has been clearly the focus of much of this effort within this wisdom explosion—as documented partly here, and more thoroughly in *Muse* and in *The Secret Doctrine, Krish-*

namurti, and Transformation. But—apart from HPB—there have been many others who have been and continue to be thus inspired by the *universal* wisdom. That borderless wisdom—while it is within each and everyone of us—doesn't "belong" to anyone in particular nor to any specific institution, including the TS.

No institution can ever capture the borderless wisdom. "Truth" is indeed "a pathless land," as K expressed it in his 1929 seminal speech.[1]

In the present context, it can be said briefly that there are many examples of perennials having provided the scaffolding for the flowering and explosion of the universal wisdom in our times—beginning at least centuries before HPB. My sense of it is that such perennial efforts have never ceased, for millennia, and that the relatively recent "rush" has been due to many forces moving "from within" towards "the beginning" of the new cycle.

Perennial documents

An excellent example of this is the presence of perennially-inspired leaders of culture, such as Emanuel Swedenborg (1688-1772), Voltaire (1694-1778), and Benjamin Franklin (1706-1790), a century before HPB. They—and many others, in various cultures and in different parts of the world—contributed significantly to what is unquestionably the most important transformative development in history, such as we know that history at present.

My research has led me to see that the founding documents of the United States of America are—in many ways—the foundation texts for the ongoing worldwide wisdom explosion. For reasons that I discuss more thoroughly elsewhere, I call the setting for that wisdom explosion "The American Age."

---

[1] On August 3, 1929, K gave the speech that has since been identified as marking his "official" departure from Victorian "Theosophy"—and his initiating a purely borderless wisdom adventure beyond any and all institutions. That exact date marked seven years since he had begun the meditations that led to the process on August 3, 1922.

Insights such as "justice for all," and the attempt to create a pluralistic society—as in America's motto *E pluribus unum*—and in affirming that *every human being has the right* to expect to enjoy "life, liberty, and the pursuit of happiness," have always been crucially central aspects of the perennial wisdom throughout the ages.

In fact, the first object of the TS summarized with unequaled precision what America's founding documents express more vaguely: "To form a nucleus of the universal brotherhood of humanity, without distinctions of race, creed, sex, caste, or color." I am not aware of a better short summary of the essence of America's founding documents—which express the same insight and sentiment, but tend to do so in vague, or too abstract, or imprecise generalities.

Furthermore, America's founding documents promote the unprecedented creation of a society in which all religions are respected, in the context of not favoring any one religion or ideology in particular.

Given that all religions and ideologies based on universal morality owe their very origin to the borderless wisdom, it becomes clear that America's founding documents were but a new expression of that ancient-yet-ever-new borderless wisdom on which all such religions and ideologies are based.

In addition, America's founding documents address themselves to all of humanity. They state clearly and unambiguously that "all men are created equal." They don't say "all white people are created equal," nor do they say that "all Americans are created equal." All men.

In fact, that expression—"all men"—has the most unfortunate apparent connotation of seeming to exclude women. As is now universally accepted, the use of the word "men" used to refer to all humanity—and it is in that sense that it appears in America's founding documents.

Significantly, it is the grand, planet-wide revolution that those documents catapulted into existence that inspired feminism and related movements towards respecting individual rights *for all human beings.* So despite that important gaffe in the expression "all men," the hearts of the presumed authors of those documents were obviously in the right place.

After the founding

It is that perennial origin of America's founding documents that touched the hearts of some of its most prominent scions, beginning at least a century before HPB founded the TS, when those documents were drafted.

Subsequently—in the interim between the US revolution and the founding of the TS—there were many exemplars of the revolutionary tenor of America's founding documents. Such were the Transcendentalists, who tended to incorporate Asian insights into their perceptions of *what is.* Ralph Waldo Emerson (1803-1882) was the most prominent and influential of the group. But there were others, such as Henry David Thoreau (1817-1862) and Margaret Fuller (1810-1850).

It will be recalled that Emerson was the godfather of William James—who was "the father of modern psychology," a TS member, and "first" presenter of the insight of brain plasticity, as discussed in chapter 25, "Mutation."

It should be clarified that Transcendentalism was parallel to Christian Unitarianism—which was a "milder" version of it that still has followers today, and from which the more universalist Transcendentalism originated. Despite their Christian background, Unitarians have historically always had a borderless dimension that clearly points to the universal wisdom—just like all the major religions and ideologies based on morality without walls.

My perception is that Transcendentalism is the first—and the most eloquent—truly and purely American *philosophy.* As it happens, it is also perennial—and that, I believe, is not a coincidence. In universities, the young are (mis)taught, sadly, that the "only" and "first" purely American philosophy is pragmatism—which flourished in the first half of the twentieth century. I beg to disagree with that assessment, as everything said in this exploration suggests.

Further, I perceive Transcendentalism as preparing the way for HPB's work—which culminated with K's *transanalytical philosophy* (as I call it), which is the bedrock for the American Age, as addressed briefly here, and more thoroughly in *The Analytical Fallacy* (2002).

This means that—contrary to what is taught in universities—there have been three (not one) major philosophical "schools" that can be said to be "American." As it happens, the two schools that are never mentioned as such are, by far, the most important—Transcendentalism and transanalytical philosophy. Both of these are thoroughly perennial, especially the latter—so they both fulfill abundantly the contents, and the aims and hopes implicit in America's founding documents.

The third purely American philosophy—which is the only one invariably recognized in philosophy departments—is *pragmatism*. As it happens, the school of pragmatism is universally recognized as having been founded by William James—and James was following in the footsteps of his godfather Ralph Waldo Emerson. James was a TS member and an important promoter of perennial values. An excellent example of his broadcasting such universal values can be found in *The Varieties of Religious Experience* (1902)—a highly influential and purely perennial work, in which he quotes HPB at length.

Apart from Transcendentalists and Unitarians, there were other prominent Americans who also promoted the borderless wisdom at the same time that they provided us all with an "American" way of perceiving the world around us—a borderless way of perceiving based on America's perennially-inspired founding documents.

Prominent among these was Mark Twain (1835-1910)—whose *Innocents Abroad* (1869) reads like a borderless wisdom treatise, particularly the humorous way in which that wisdom is presented.

Humor is usually not identified with wisdom, even though humor *goeswith* wisdom. Without a sense of humor, it is *impossible* to have wisdom worthy of the name—and "wisdom" without a sense of humor is a travesty thereof. Those of us who didn't know it, can learn that important lesson from reading Mark Twain.

There have been many others, each of them pointing to a different aspect of what is often only implicit in America's founding documents. Examples of this are American leaders of culture such as Frederick Douglass (1817-1895) and Susan B. Anthony (1820-1906).

America's own HPB

HPB was also such a prominent American. She became an American citizen despite having been born to Russian nobility. Her family's ancestry went back to the Ruriks, founders of the country who gave to Russia its name, in the ninth century. I should clarify that HPB was actually Ukrainian by birth and Russian by pedigree.

The TS that she founded promoted exactly what America's founding documents are clearly after—"to form a nucleus of the universal brotherhood of humanity," without prejudicial distinctions of any sort.

The main difference between America's founding documents and HPB's works is that America's founding documents have been used, misused, and abused by a population (including its presumed "leaders")—who are clearly unschooled in the perennial values on which those documents are based. By contrast, HPB was central to the still ongoing wisdom explosion that came into being with the specific purpose—among others—of providing clarity and power to America's founding documents.

America and the TS are but two limbs of the same wisdom-explosion—"two birds on a tree"—leading to that explosion's grand expression in K's insights and observations.

Yes, it is true that TS members and others touched by HPB's works have adulterated the central insights in those works—often to the point of being unrecognizable as having a perennial source. But that body of work is still intact, and it does spell out what the borderless wisdom is truly about, in ways that don't even come up in America's founding documents—in which the perennial wisdom, while clearly present, is presented mainly in generalities.

HPB's works have no such limitations.

A new beginning

Just as the TS has had serious failings in terms of its hopeful beginnings, the United States of America has been, if anything, a dismal failure, as well—most sadly. From its beginnings, many US citizens have transmogrified the borderlessness of America's founding documents.

Just as TS members created from the beginning a fantasy "Theosophy" based on Victorian "values"—which (lest we forget) included imperialism, colonialism, white supremacist assumptions, and oppressions of various sorts—some US citizens have always been beholden to similarly provincial notions. Such notions are simultaneously dangerous to our common welfare, and are passionately opposed to the borderless nature of America's founding documents.

Such an outcome—horrific as it is—should come as no surprise. Every single previous perennial effort has encountered precisely the same passion to transmogrify it. It is in precisely such a way that all the major religions and ideologies originally based on the borderless wisdom had their beginnings. Despite their lofty beginnings, they all ended up being corrupted in one way or another—eventually turning into sworn enemies of the supreme sanity that the borderless wisdom is.

Yet despite this very serious and concerning development, the present American effort is different from all previous perennial attempts in a number of significant ways.

For one thing, the universal wisdom in us learned from previous failures that erecting hierarchies of authority is catastrophic to sanity and fairness. This time, in America, universal wisdom was presented in a deliberately ambiguous way, in that respect. Instead of erecting "a Church" or "an empire"—or some other such hierarchical structure—a "constitutional democratic republic" was created. That, in itself, provided a much greater possibility that intelligence-compassion might have a better chance for success.

Unlike what had been done before America, such a structure invites discussion among all participants. That implies that all enemies of sanity and wisdom would be compelled to justify their intelligence-challenged, me-centered expectations. If nothing else, that would make it more difficult for the enemies of wisdom to be able to trample over "justice for all" cavalierly and with impunity.

While admittedly not "perfect," such a structure is pure genius.

It is not perfect because it is a structure—and all structures are analytical, and all analysis is me-centered. But putting that which is not analytical—the borderless wisdom-compassion—in an analytical framework, as America's founding documents provides, that is pure genius.

Church and state

The "separation of Church and state"—which is fundamental to America's founding documents—has been driving the intelligence-challenged crazy, from the very beginning. This separation means that no particular "religion" can ever be the law of the land. If such a "religion" ever gets to gain hegemony over the US, it could only do it by violating that strict separation between religion and the state that America's founding documents *require*.

It is as if America's founding texts are proclaiming that "there is no ideology (including religious ideology) more important than truth-seeking"—to paraphrase the motto of the TS.

America's founding documents appeal to universal morality—not to a particular ideology, whether it be "religious," "political," or "philosophical."

In order for any such "religion" to pretend that it is "the one and only" that should rule over America, its defenders would have to justify it through dialogue—and dialogue is fatal for the intelligence-challenged.

This is pure, unadulterated genius.

In addition, every single "religion" is to be respected—or at least tolerated, *by law.* If anything, this principle in America's founding documents makes the intelligence-challenged go batty.

The intelligence- and morally-challenged have always—throughout history—made the assumption that theirs is "the only one religion." They have assumed that "the one religion" happens to be "mine." All other "religions" are "obviously" pure "shams." That's been the history of humanity, until America came along.

In such a belligerent environment as the one created by "religious" hegemonists, the borderless wisdom has no chance. So the notion of respecting all religions equally makes it extremely difficult for the intelligence-challenged and morally-challenged (which is the same thing) to impose their will over everyone else—in the kind of autocratic and theocratic ways that humans had always behaved like in the past—before America.

America's founding documents' appeal for all of us to respect all "religions" has clearly another dimension. By respecting all such ideologies—which are based initially on the perennial wisdom—those documents appeal to the sense of universal morality in each and every one of us.

America's founding documents stand for the best expression ever in history of universal morality—which is one and the same with borderless wisdom. It is the best ever in large measure because there is no attempt at all to institutionalize universal morality—which is an absurdity, yet it is precisely what had always been done, in the past.

Words fail me, to express the level of genius that this "principle" in America's founding documents implies. All the previous religions and ideologies based on universal morality have failed—as we can see all around us, by looking at the belligerent stances towards one another, and the chaos that they have thereby created.

But America's founding documents manage to convey that universal morality in its most pristine purity ever. They accomplish this not by appealing to any metaphysical principle nor to any scripture nor to any authority of any kind. They do not appeal to an institution.

America's founding documents accomplish this by appealing to our intelligence—to our sense of universal morality, which we all have.

America's founding documents are the platinum standard for universal morality—and that makes them stand for something far more comprehensive and true than any particular religion or ideology, no matter how otherwise "sublime" such a group-think notion may be.

Again, this may not be "perfect." But it's damn astonishing—a level of genius that one normally doesn't encounter in daily life, or in any other context, for that matter.

Checks and balances

From their contents, it is supremely evident that America's founding documents don't trust the intelligence-challenged and the morally-challenged (which, again, is exactly the same thing).

But America's founding documents go even further—much further. Those documents express categorically and in no uncertain terms that the intelligence- and morally-challenged must be treated as if they were criminals—which indeed they happen to be.

Yes, the US is constituted by those in government and those who are under that government. On the surface, that looks like much the same thing that humans had always experienced, going back to our days as cavemen and cavewomen. Somebody has always been "Top Dog"—and the majority of others have been subjugated to Top Dog's whims. That has been basically the structure of government since time immemorial. In that sense, the US looks no different—at least on the surface.

But this exploration is all about going under the surface, in an attempt to discover a deeper, more meaningful truth.

The US is the very first democratic constitutional republic in history. That, right there, implies a profound transformation in the meaning and the practice of "government."[2]

America's founding documents trust no one in "government." Those documents show that they have absolute trust in everyone being or becoming a criminal—or at least being criminal-minded—the moment they are given even a miniscule amount of power over others. So America treats *everyone* in government as if that person were a criminal.

Yes, the US has a president. But that president is not to be trusted. She is not a queen. She is not a dictator. She can't do whatever she likes. There is Congress. There is the judicial power. There is the free press. There is WeThePeople. There are elections.

Each of the three "official" powers—the executive, the legislative, and the judicial—are meant to be separate yet equal in power. Each of them has the obligation—mandated by America's founding documents—to assume that the other two are up to no good. Each of the three powers is to check up on the other two—to make as sure as possible that no person exceeds his power over others.

---

[2] A specific discussion of the notion of a "social contract"—which was the rage in Europe and America during the times of the Founding Fathers, would take me too far afield, so I don't mention it. So I just do my best to describe here what life under the social contract can be like. The social contract is a theme for another time.

The United States of America is based on checks and balances. Everyone checks up on everyone else, to make sure that justice will balance the outcome, so that no one ends up being Top Dog. That had never even been tried before. It is the most stunning social experiment in all of history.

Checks and balances don't end there. All of the US government is based on the strict principle that assumes that everyone in government is implicitly a criminal. So everyone must be checked as thoroughly as possible. And even then . . .

The president has a Cabinet—every member of which he nominates, and the Senate must approve of.

But every Cabinet member is first of all an American citizen—and therefore beholden to America's founding documents, above any loyalty to the president. This means that every Cabinet member has the legal and moral obligation to check up on the president. The president might be a criminal. The president might assume that he's Top Dog. So he needs to be put on a leash. He needs to be checked up on. That is part of what Congress—and not just the president's Cabinet—is for.

Congress is made up of two bodies—the House of Representatives and the Senate. The House has the obligation and duty—mandated by America's founding documents—to check up not only on the president. It is mandated by law to check up on the Senate, and the Senate must do the same with the House. Anyone and everyone might be a criminal, and they must be checked up on, as thoroughly as possible.

America trusts no one. They might all be criminals. Indeed, they all must be assumed to be criminals. That's checks and balances.

The analyzer is a criminal, at heart. If given the opportunity, he'll commit the crime—and justify it by some analysis or another.

There is no morality at all in the analyzer, as addressed in Part One.

All members of Congress—House and Senate—have a staff. Each staff member is first an American citizen, and must swear an oath of loyalty to the Constitution—not to the person they work for. So every single staff member has the duty to check up on the boss. She might be a criminal. She must be assumed by the staffer to be a criminal. It's in America's founding documents.

Checks and balances spread far and wide, and not just in the three powers of government. Every state in the US has a governor, a state Congress with two houses, and a judicial power. Every state has counties and municipalities, each with its own government. They are all entreated to watch out for the criminals—they are everywhere.

Every person involved in every aspect of state and county and municipal government is first of all an American citizen. Everyone has the duty—as mandated by America's founding documents—to check up on everyone else. Everyone must be assumed to be a criminal. State governments check up on the federal government, and vice versa.

Just as the executive and the legislative powers are to be checked, so is the judicial—which has as many divisions as the legislative. Everyone involved in the judicial power is to be considered a criminal—according to America's founding documents. Everything said about the executive and the legislative applies—if anything, even far more—to every aspect of the judicial power, from top to bottom.

On the surface, some may think that what has just been said contradicts the American texts notion that "everyone is innocent, until proven guilty." But there is no contradiction—none at all.

The presumption of innocence in America's founding texts is actually yet another means in those documents to protect us all from the me-centered, intelligence-challenged. By presuming innocence in everyone, America's founding texts are challenging any and all accusers who might make accusations based on some group-think, provincial notion, or some other me-centered motive. If someone is guilty of having committed a crime, then proof is required—and that proof would have to be acceptable to a jury and by the laws of the land and by the attorneys and judges involved in the proceedings.

America's founding texts defend us all from the potential criminal-mindedess of accusers who don't respect borderless morality.

Hocus pocus SCOTUS

Sadly, a serious gap in the Constitution's checks and balances has been discovered recently in the Supreme Court of the US (SCOTUS)—of all places.

SCOTUS members—also known as "Justices" or "Supremes" —have always enjoyed the unique privilege of having a lifetime tenure. In that sense, the Supremes are just like monarchs and dictators. For this reason, Supremes are not checked upon periodically, as is the case with elected officials—and everyone else in government, for that matter.

In fact, there are no checks and balances imposed on Supremes. That puts them outside of the very wise and indispensable notion—inscribed in the Constitution—that everyone is to be considered criminally-minded (as just noted), unless and until proven otherwise.

That privilege of not ever being checked on has come to be assumed by Supremes to mean that they are somehow "superior" to everyone else in government. "We are here for life"— they seem to say, with their actions—"no one can get rid of us. Regardless of what we do, we're here to stay."

Further—and far more seriously—no means have ever been established to put checks on SCOTUS members. This means that the Supremes are not subject to checks and balances—as is wisely the case for everyone else in government.

Given the criminally-minded nature of the analyzer—which is in every single one of us—this lack of checking on the Supremes is most worrisome, and even dangerous.

That stunning fact—which runs against the unambiguous spirit of America's founding documents—began to come to light as a result of the Supremes making a series of decisions that were severely opposed to the will of the American people, beginning in 2022.

In addition, some Supremes would fail to recuse themselves from cases in which they stood to benefit personally, in some way.

All other judges—and everyone else involved in the judicial power—are expected to recuse themselves from a case in which they have a personal interest. Even *an appearance* of personal interest is cause for recusal—*but only if there is integrity,* which is the whole issue. All other judges in the land recuse themselves whenever the case demands it.

Not the Supremes. They assume themselves to be above the borderless morality implicit and explicit in America's founding documents.

They act as if they are literally above the law—which they actually are, to the extent that they seek out to benefit personally from their decisions, and to the extent that they countermand the requirement of checks and balances *required* by the Constitution.

That is, the Constitution requires checks and balances from everyone in government—except for the Supremes. This means that the Supremes are not beholden to those checks and balances—and that they therefore may commit crimes against universal morality, with impunity.

Since there are no means for implementing checks and balances on the court, the Supremes are in a position to be above the law otherwise prescribed for everyone else in the country.

As of this writing, this is still very much a live issue. We all need to keep in mind that America is an *unprecedented* social-moral *experiment*, and that the revolution that it implies is still ongoing.

It remains to be seen whether changes are made, whereby Supremes are subject to the same checks and balances that everyone else is subject to. For as long as such constitutional measures are not taken, the Supremes are "Top Dogs" not beholden to anyone nor to any checks and balances—and therefore are in violation of the universal morality that is at the heart of America's founding documents.[3]

More checks and balances

As just noted, all the many checks and balances built into the very fabric of US government are not nearly enough.

There is a fourth power, beyond the three "official" powers mandated by the US Constitution. There is—on top of those three powers—the free press, also commonly called "the fourth estate."

Every journalist has the sacred duty of checking up as thoroughly as possible on every single aspect of every government official—from the President, all the way up to municipal government.

Of course, any person working for a news organization may go astray. All analyzers are criminals-in-the-making, at heart. But that is precisely the whole point of checks and balances. All journalists check up not just on all government. They also have the duty to check up on each other, as well as on private individuals up to doing something naughty—not to mention checking up on themselves, on a daily basis.

The ultimate checkers and balancers are what I call WeThePeople (one word, one people). If even after all the checks upon checks and counter-checks and triple-checks there are still bad boys doing mischief—which there always are—they can be voted out of office. Only WeThePeople have that power.

So the one thing that keeps the whole structure of checks and balances in place is the existence of elections by WeThePeople. Anyone who doesn't participate in elections is thereby giving power to the criminal-minded—and deciding thereby that we all return to the old system of having a whimsical Top Dog

---

[3] For the very serious issue of Supremes being at least questionable in their behavior, see Stephen Vladeck, *The Shadow Docket: How the Supreme Court Uses Stealth Rulings to Amass Power and Undermine the Republic* (2023).

disrespecting all of us and participating in all sorts of oppressions and inequities.

Elections matter.

Each individual still has, of course, the moral obligation to be responsive to universal morality in daily life. Such daily activity is in a way an act and process of applying "checks and balances" on oneself. Only when such checks and balances are applied at the individual level can a good society be created.

No one ever said that being a practicing American was easy.

All constitutional democratic republics in the world are beholden to the perennial principles first laid out in America's founding documents. Each country has its own set of documents and its own way of expressing what was first presented to the world in the American originals. Of course, there are bound to be relatively minor differences in each country, since circumstances and needs differ, in different parts of the world.

But the reality is that the whole planet is now beholden to the universal morality implicit and explicit in America's founding documents. That same universal morality is the bedrock of all the great religions and philosophies based on it, in history.

That includes America.

That includes all other nations on Earth.

Unchecked, imbalanced

As Thomas Hobbes (1588-1679) famously quipped in *Leviathan* (1651), if there are no checks and balances, our lives are bound to be "solitary, poor, nasty, brutish—and short."[4]

Yet even after all the bewildering number of checks and balances, the bad boys may triumph, in their never-ceasing efforts to wallow in a me-centered worldwide immoral miasma. Life does not come with an instruction manual—and it doesn't offer any guarantees.

If we collectively get to choose governments without checks— as America's founding documents alarmingly tell us that we

---

[4] Hobbes, *Leviathan*, XIII.9.

urgently need to do—then we'll all go back to living our lives in terms of the whims of some Top Dog. Our lives will then be supremely imbalanced—precarious, fearful, and more hopeless.

It is you and I who get to decide how this will turn out, by the way we live our lives.

America is a profoundly and multidimensionally fragile experiment—and it needs to be recalled that it is a planetary experiment. It is also an experiment perilous. Despite the many, many efforts to sustain it, it may end up failing, just as every other previous perennial attempt has done—wonderful as they each have been, in many ways. It is truly up to each and every one of us, whether this time sanity will prevail, rather than Top Doggism.

We each have now a challenge fall in our laps, whether we like it or not—and whether we ever acknowledge it, or not. We are all in the midst of the most formidable encounter between the me-centered provincial analyzer—that monstrous Leviathan that Hobbes referred to—and the universal wisdom-compassion that all the great religions and ideologies speak of, but whose followers sadly have not responded adequately to, in many ways.

However things may turn out, we can all see now that the ongoing worldwide wisdom explosion could be said to have had its visible origins in America's founding documents.

HPB's work could be said to have provided depth and context to the generalities in those documents.

But the most clear exposition of what it all means is to be found, unquestionably, in K's insights, researches, and observations. If you want to understand more deeply what America's founding documents—and HPB's whole corpus of work—are more deeply about, it is impossible to do any better than immerse yourself in K's explorations. K often referred to those insights as "the only revolution."[5]

---

[5] Krishnamurti, *The Only Revolution* (1970). To my knowledge, this is the best book there is on explaining what the grand wisdom explosion is centrally about—even

The only revolution

Without relationship, there is no "me." The "me" that we each identify with would not be—except for its being in relationship to someone or to something. As the Spanish philosopher José Ortega y Gasset (1883-1955) quipped, "I am I and my circumstances."[6]

What we call "society" is but the me—and all of its relationships—writ large. This is why there's no such thing as "society" independently of "me." "Society" and "me" are but two ways of looking at the same process.

The "history of humanity" is the history of oneself. At the end of the day, the only way to "change society"—politically, economically, religiously, ideologically, or in any other way—is to bring about a mutation in oneself.

Ideologies come and go—they always have. But the me is the ever-present factor in all human activity.

Like it or not, all of us are stuck with that reality. Being a member of "the purple party" as opposed to "the aqua party" will (by itself) leave things as they have always been, in "society" at large. The only thing that can ever make a significant dent on a true, meaningful change of any kind—hopefully a beneficial mutation—comes strictly from transformation in oneself. I fully realize that this is an extremely hard-to-swallow pill—but only from the perspective of the conditioned, me-centered analyzer.

Yet there it is. It is what it is.

Revolution begins with oneself, is either nurtured or destroyed in oneself, and is either ongoing or finished in oneself.

Revolution is not "political"—in the sense of being related to an ideology or way of analyzing things. The only revolution worthy of the name is the revolution in oneself. Anything else

---

though it never refers to "America," nor to "the perennial wisdom." In my estimation, this book is simultaneously the best exposition ever of what meditation really is.
[6] Ortega y Gasset, *Meditaciones del Quijote* (1914).

is purely reactionary—a way of perpetuating the old, while marking steps in the same place where one was, to begin with.[7]

An American revolution

In many important ways, our present world—even from a socio-political perspective—is a world based on America's founding documents.

Back when a handful of men created the United States of America in the late eighteenth century, they were thereby bringing about the very first constitutional democratic republic in history based on borderless values. At that time, tyrannies ruled over the rest of the planet, without exception. In Europe, those tyrannies took the outward form of monarchies, for a few centuries. Up to the American revolutionary moment, tyrannies had been the norm, everywhere and everywhen, for millennia. That is an easily confirmable fact.

All history—everywhere before America's founding documents came into place—can be said to have been a history of tyranny. Human history has been one of people trying their best to be free of any and all kinds of despotism. The vast majority of humans—everywhere and everywhen—had been yearning, for as far back as we can collectively recall, to be free of the oppressive shackles imposed by the privileged few. That, too, is an easily confirmable fact.

But the borderless wisdom that expressed itself through America's founding documents was clearly never meant to end tyranny in one particular place only. Apart from being silly, a "revolution" in just one region would be assuming that nothing else exists—and that is an absurdity. America's founding documents are unambiguously speaking to all of humanity, not merely to a fraction thereof.

They are still speaking. And they are speaking directly to you.

---

[7] See Krishnamurti, *The Only Revolution*.

In that sense—as well as in their actual contents—there is absolutely no difference between the source for those eighteenth century texts, and the source for the essential insights of Jesus, the Buddha, Lao Tse, Muhammad, and numerous other perennials throughout the ages. All perennial expressions—such as the ones just mentioned—have been of one voice, when it comes to what they each and all considered to be *indispensable* in the moral dimension of human life.

All religions and ideologies based on borderless morality—including America's founding documents—have affirmed, *without exception*, that me-centeredness must come to an end, so that the borderless wisdom can be *that which is*, in each and every one of our lives, everywhere on Earth.

A life lived in me-centeredness is a life lived in suffering—for oneself, and for everyone else. A life lived in terms of universal morality is a life full of love and fulfillment.

By contrast, me-centeredness has always been at the core of all tyrannical forms of government—including the "government" of "religious" or "ideological" institutions. It can be said that tyranny is an apotheosis of me-centeredness—a concentration of all power in one tyrant or in a cadre of tyrants. Those despots have always been served by the teeming masses—who thereby become slaves to their masters.

In such a soul-stultifying environment, it has always been extremely difficult—near-impossible, really—for the borderless wisdom to express itself. Whether it is socio-political, or religious, or ideological, or economic—or of whatever other sort—tyrannies have always stood in the way of the universal values that are implicit and explicit in the borderless wisdom.

There can be no universal morality or wisdom, anywhere, unless there is borderlessness.

Secret schools

An important part of the reason why there have been secret perennial schools and organizations for millennia, is that the establishment *du jour* has always opposed the freedom of individuals to think and speak and behave as they see fit.

While a word such as "occultism" has other connotations, one important reason for its use in HPB-related expositions is related to the fact that, before America, anyone interested in the freedom implicit in borderlessness had to hide—had to remain "occulted"—from authoritarian dictates, whether "religious," political, or of any other sort.

In any case, it is not a coincidence that most—if not all—of the many political revolutions since the American one have been inspired, and often crafted, by secret societies, most prominently (though not exclusively) Freemasonic ones.[8]

After the unprecedented triumph of a small band of humans against the specific tyranny of the king of England, the primordial yearning of all humans to be free, *everywhere*, was awakened. Once the small band of Americans were triumphant over socio-political tyranny, people everywhere began to realize that it is possible, after all, to do away with that kind of oppression.

What had always before seemed impossible—or, at least, extremely difficult—had now been accomplished, for the first time ever. It is as if humans everywhere began to say to themselves, "These Americans are basically creoles without the kind of social rank considered essential in European society. If a small band of such relatively unsophisticated people can do it, so can we."

It is based on America's founding documents that I use the expression WeThePeople (one word), to refer graphically to the fact that it is a wholeness that I'm referring to, not to a mere "group of (separate) people."

Borderlessness is a whole, not a collection of parts. To live in wholeness is to live in freedom—and there is no real freedom without wholeness. Without wholeness, there is no wisdom.

---

[8] See Robert Hieronimus and Laura Cortner, *Founding Fathers, Secret Societies: Freemasons, Illuminati, Rosicrucians, and the Decoding of the Great Seal*, which includes an extensive bibliography.

Wisdom wildfire

Indeed, hardly fourteen years after the triumph of WeThe-People against what was then the most powerful European kingdom, the age-old primordial human yearning for freedom from tyranny expressed itself again, in the form of the 1789 French revolution.

Very soon after that, Haitians—who had been part of the French empire before the French revolution—demanded the same freedoms for themselves. Intriguingly, the so-called "revolutionaries" in Paris fought the Haitians' quest for freedom. So a war of independence from France ensued in Haiti, and the Haitians were finally victorious in 1804.[9]

The word was out. Anyone in the world who wanted to be free of the nightmare of despotic regimes, had now permission to do so, if they wanted it. America's founding documents gave them not only permission to do so. It gave them an extremely deep insight into *the necessity* for all humans to be free of all forms of oppression. So long as there is oppression, it is impossible to have borderlessness, wisdom, justice for all—the pursuit of happiness.

The revolutionary spirit spread like wildfire, everywhere in the planet. Soon, there were revolutions in Latin America—beginning with the Haitian—each demanding freedom from their respective masters in Europe. That was followed by more revolutions in Europe itself, whereby the nations that we now recognize as being "the norm" were created, as old eugenics-obsessed fiefdoms and kingdoms crumbled down. The revolutionary spirit started by America's founding documents continued

---

[9] It should be clarified that the Haitian revolution was actually fought, in the end, against Napoleon Bonaparte (1769-1821). But Bonaparte was transformed—from being a political revolutionary into becoming a Little Caesar. Despite that, he saw himself as the exporter of "the revolution." He didn't recognize that the only revolution there is, happens when lovers of wisdom are transformed into kings, and kings are transformed into lovers of wisdom—as Plato taught in *The Republic*. But such a transformation can only happen in an enlightened democracy.

marching on in the twentieth century, when many African and Asian countries were created.

The whole planet came to be on fire—the fire of freedom from all sorts of oppression.

All of those many new countries had at least one important thing in common. They all recreated themselves—from being colonies to morphing into constitutional democratic republics. They were no longer ruled by tyrannies, as most countries in the world had been, before. They were clearly and unambiguously following America's model. Each and all of these brand new countries drafted a constitution—and with it, an appeal to all the borderless values found in America's founding documents.

It is fascinating to see how even the still-remaining dictator-ships today actually *claim* to be constitutional democratic re-publics. The message of America's founding documents is so powerful and so obviously truthful, that even Little Caesars want to have "some of that." In this way, what used to be quite com-mon and accepted as "normal"—tyrannies—now feel the need to justify themselves, by claiming cynically to be "just like Amer-ica."

That reality is immensely powerful. It goes to the heart of the truly colossal power of the perennial message of America's founding documents.

"There ain't no free lunch"

I just mentioned some essential points describing how the world in which we now live came about as a result of America's founding documents. Unfortunately—and as stated prosaically but clearly in a common American expression—"there ain't no free lunch."

One has to work for whatever one considers important. If you doubt that, please do yourself a favor, and ask any Ukrainian who was around in 2022 and beyond whether working hard for democracy is important.

The road towards achieving in society what America's founding documents lay out has not been an easy one. Even after almost three centuries, it is still a very rough road. Most democratic republics—*including, especially, the United States of America*—have found it extremely hard to live up to the borderless standards set by America's founding documents.[10]

The difficulties encountered by all nations today are one and the same as the difficulties that people everywhere have found in being true to the borderlessness of all major religions and ideologies based on universal values.

It all comes back to whether each of us is ready for the only revolution that truly matters, which is the revolution in oneself.

Without such a transformation in oneself, it is impossible for there to be a beneficial transformation in "society." Such a transformation can only happen as me-centeredness disappears from one's daily life, and borderlessness—wisdom, justice, love, and freedom—can shine through in each of us, and therefore in society at large.

K and America's founding texts

That revolution in oneself—which America's founding documents implicitly call for—is precisely what K's presence in the twentieth century was here to help bring about.

Expecting that "things will change for the better" by following some particular form of analysis—some "party" or some "religion" or some "ideology"—is not only silly and grossly inadequate for what is required. It is also immensely dangerous for each of us as individuals, as well as for all humanity, and for the planet itself. We all should see this as clearly as we can, since that, precisely, is what we humans have done throughout history—"rally 'round the flag"—and it is that divisiveness that has brought us to the present worldwide calamity.

---

[10] For a short yet very impactful expression of how difficult it is to sustain democracy, see Timothy Snyder, *On Tyranny: Twenty Lessons from the Twentieth Century* (2017).

Chaotic developments in societies around the globe in the twenty-first century should make that insight obvious to most of us.

Importantly, if one takes K's corpus of writings and talks as one single whole, that corpus stands as the most formidable presentation of the essence of America's founding documents. Everything that K said from the dais provides immensely far-reaching insights into America's founding documents.

K's insights are the most formidable, powerful, clearest exposition ever of what America's founding documents are about. No one before or after K has ever come even close to such a monumental achievement. This is one of many ways in which it is unquestionable that K's presence in the twentieth century marks a new beginning—a new era—for all mankind.

America's new beginning is asserted by that founding document which is its second motto, *Novus ordo seclorum*—a new age now begins.[11]

Yet it is only in K's insights—which came only about two centuries later—that one finds a clear, powerful, and passionate defense of America's founding documents.

One thing that is truly remarkable about this is that K never once even mentioned "America"—let alone its founding documents.

That is part of why—to my knowledge—no one has pointed out, ever before, the very real and absolutely crucial connection there is between K and America's founding texts.

It should be added, for completion, that K never made explicit reference to the perennial wisdom either, despite the fact that no one has ever expressed that wisdom with such power and passion and clarity.

If K had said something along the lines of "what I'm saying here is the perennial wisdom," or "my insights are about America," his listeners would have made the grossly mistaken

---

[11] The internationally renowned historian Charles Page Smith (1917-1995) provided this wonderful translation of America's motto from the Latin, in his widely acclaimed eight-volume *A New Age Now Begins: A People's History of the American Revolution.*

assumption that there was some "X"—some algorithm, some "set of rules"—to be followed mechanically, based on what K said. That is in fact what people have done, throughout the ages—every single time there has been a perennial message, as in the great religions and philosophies based on universal morality.

The knee-jerk reaction on the part of audiences of perennials throughout history has always been to ignore the *borderlessness* of what was being said.

Intelligence-challenged audiences have always identified that borderlessness with some institution. They have identified with some "X" that can be objectified, and with which people can identify. They then have used the segregation thus created artificially in order to shun others, who are not part of their self-created "X." That way, they can persuade those others to change—or fight them so as to *force* them to change.

K never made that divisive mistake, which has been extremely costly throughout history, in terms of personal and planetary pain.

In sharing this with you, sensitive reader, I realize that there is great danger, in that K's insights could be (mis)used for the purpose of defending some new ideology. On the other hand, this is a way for everyone to put our present dangerous situation in a historical as well as existential context. My hope is that intelligence will prevail—rather than something incompatible with intelligence.

All ideologies are intrinsically intelligence-challenged—and turn dangerous to our welfare, whenever they get to be implemented.

In any case, it is critical to keep in mind that K—just like America's founding documents and just like all religions and ideologies based on universal morality—was addressing the whole planet, and that there is no me-centeredness at all in any of his researches.

Speaking of "America" or of "a new age," or even of "the perennial wisdom," would have tainted severely what he was addressing—which is the mutation that we all need to be engaging in.

We need to be intensely attentive to that fact. What our situation calls for is not becoming "K followers." Becoming a K follower is one of many ways one can choose to be intelligence-challenged. What is required—alarmingly and urgently—is that wisdom prevail in our daily lives, and that me-centeredness and suffering be put in the rear-view mirror. If that does not take place, we are in deep, deep trouble.

This is not about K—not at all—as he made clear, constantly. It is, obviously, about mutation in you and I.

K's undistracted focus on this central issue is truly astonishing, especially when one considers that he was simultaneously articulating the perennial wisdom itself, when denuded of metaphysics, methodologies, hierarchies of authority, and other brick-a-brac that the misguided tend to identify the perennial wisdom with.

In sum, the revolution in oneself *must* come about—as K insisted, with a sense of intense alarm. *Please*, attentive reader, look at his writing on the wall.[12]

If that revolution doesn't come about, it looks like major destructive and even catastrophic changes will definitely take place in socio-political structures everywhere—not to mention in the planet itself.

Yes, we are in the midst of the beginning of a new era. But as in biological births, the beginning of a new era comes with growing pains, for all of us—and the baby is fragile and may die on the spot, or soon thereafter.

---

[12] See Krishnamurti, *The Only Revolution,* and *The First and Last Freedom.*

CHAPTER 28
The TS

REGRETTABLY, THE TS HAS NOT FARED MUCH BETTER than the planet's nations—nor the planet's population at large. We can now see how the clearly perennial message of America's founding documents has been transmogrified, in numerous ways—including in the United States, many of whose citizens ought to know better, but obviously don't, at least not yet.

For instance, anyone in the world who defends militantly any form of nationalism is obviously rooting for humanity to go back to tyranny.

Anyone in the world who assumes that a particular race or cultural group is somehow prejudicially "better," is obviously militantly opposed to America's founding documents.

Such divisive people are also militantly opposed to all the religions and ideologies based on universal morality—even though many of them are members of some "religious" congregation or another.

Anyone in the world who sets out to defend me-centeredness is unambiguously opposed to America's founding documents.

Sadly, millions of people—everywhere in the world, including US citizens—are passionately opposed to the clearly planetary, borderless defense of universal morality implicit and explicit in America's founding documents.

Corporations

In addition to such difficulties at present, there is now an intriguing and extremely worrisome development. Corporations have become the new and immensely powerful form of tyranny—far more powerful that any previous tyranny in history. Yet they have become the landlords of the US, in blatant violation of America's founding documents.

This is too big a subject to do it justice here, but it needs to be at least stated and addressed, however briefly.

MUTATION

First of all, it needs to be said that a corporation is a criminal enterprise whose leaders are protected from any crimes that they may commit—a protection from prosecution that comes from so-called "limited liability" laws.

A modern corporation is a dictatorship beholden exclusively to its me-centered investors, and has no moral obligation to anyone. It is not a moral enterprise—and does not pretend to be one. Its only object is to earn as much as it can, and to increase its power as much as it can.

A corporation is a purely me-centered enterprise, with no redeeming moral values—since, by its very nature, the power it seeks and implements is unrelated to (and actually against) universal morality.

Astonishingly, corporations are clearly criminal enterprises that have come to be identified with being what the US is now claimed to be about. It needs to be said that—contrary to such a widely-held assumption—the fact is that corporations are intensely me-centered enterprises that have zero responsibility for any harm that they may do to humans or to any thing, living or dead.

As long as there are corporations—such as we now know them—it is impossible to have democracy, anywhere.

The purpose of a corporation is to increase its own earnings and power—by any means necessary. It is impossible to have borderlessness in a corporate-dominated environment—such as the entire planet is, as we speak. This is not an opinion. It is just a description of the reality that we all find ourselves in.

So all nations—each and every one of us—have a lot of work to do, everywhere.

As noted throughout this exploration, the new era is meant to be the time when all regressive behaviors—such as those of criminally-minded corporations—begin to be put behind us. The New Age movement—and the TS that gave it birth—should then be expected to have a clear and achievable vision of how to bring about the major mutations required, in the midst of such a hostile environment as the one we find ourselves in.

The TS

Unfortunately, the whole New Age movement—including the TS—for the most part has responded severely inadequately to the very serious situation that the twenty-first century challenges us with. If anything, it can be said truthfully that New Agers have been largely oblivious and non-responsive to the multi-dimensional calamity that we are all in the midst of. The roots of this bizarre alienation is not too difficult to identify.

TSers in particular—and New Agers in general—have invariably and mistakenly assumed that the perennial wisdom is primarily an analytical enterprise. Such an analytical enterprise is much like a mirror image of what group-think followers have unfortunately done with previous perennial messages, such as the followers of religions and ideologies based on borderless values.

Included in the TSers' analytical enterprise have been such factors as entrenched beliefs, metaphysics, methodologies, hierarchies—and many other purely analytical elements, such as diagrams and graphic representations of what they staunchly believe is "reality."

Given the prominent place that its founding perennials had reserved for the TS, its having gone off on analytical (and therefore me-centered) tangents is extremely concerning. After all, without the borderless wisdom there doesn't seem to be any possible move away from stress, conflict, and confusion—and suffering—in the population at large. Let us keep in mind that me-centered analysis is the sworn archenemy of borderless wisdom.

I should clarify that everything I say here about TSers applies equally to all New Agers. This applies even more so to Traditionalists, who have invariably transmogrified the mutation that defines the borderless wisdom with mere rituals, metaphysics, mythologies, hierarchies of authority, and other paraphernalia, such as drugs—not to mention their assumption that somehow the "Western Tradition" is superior to everything and everyone else.

Some Traditionalists—such as Julius Evola (1898-1974) and Mircea Eliade (1907-1986) to mention just two of the most prominent Traditionalists—have even taken this me-centeredness to an extreme—as discussed briefly in Chapter 5, "Masters." They have transmogrified wisdom, and have become defenders of racist and fascist ideologies—which are unquestionably militantly opposed to the implicit borderlessness of the actual perennial wisdom-*compassion*, of which America's founding documents are the present champion.

The vast majority of TSers (and New Agers in general) have failed to recognize that without an actual switch away from me-centeredness—without the actual act and process of perennial initiation, which is emphatically not a ritual—there is no such thing as "divine wisdom" (*theosophia*).

This ignorance is what led the TS officially—and the lion's share of its members—to shun J. Krishnamurti after Mrs. Besant's death. This has happened despite the fact that it is in K that is found the most clear and powerful exposition ever in history of the actual perennial wisdom—and therefore a potential solution to the present worldwide catastrophe-in-the-making.

The TS "versus" K

There is a major difference between K's insights and observations on one hand, and early TSers' understanding of "initiation" on the other. That difference is K's insight that before a mutation can take place—and therefore before a new humanity (a new age) can be created—there *must* be a psychological "dying to the known," as he called it often.[1]

What K said is no more and no less than what HPB and her perennial mentors had said—as documented profusely throughout this exploration, and in *Insights for a New Era*. HPB and her perennial mentors were saying that in order to understand

---

[1] See Krishnamurti, *Freedom From the Known*.

even the simplest thing they were saying, *there must first be perennial initiation.*

This means, in part, abandoning one's identifications with a particular culture, system of ideas, or religion, and with the expectation built up over a lifetime full of me-centered conditionings of all sorts.

K addresses the urgent necessity for a complete, thorough dismantling of the me. This is an awesome prospect for many of us. Importantly, it is also an aspect of the supremely sobering *mysterium tremendum et fascinans*—which is the centerpiece of actual perennial initiation, not something that happens because one reads a book while sitting in an easy chair.

The act and process of dying to the known has always been the very heart of every single actual esoteric school in history—and it is such a dismantling that America's founding documents point towards, as addressed briefly in this exploration, and more fully elsewhere.[2]

At the end of the day, one must die to one's conditioning, in order to be true to the better angels of our nature in one's daily life, as required by being true to E pluribus unum.

In most esoteric schools in the past, this death of the conditioned me had often been referred to as "initiation." The word "initiation"—*when used in a perennial context*—refers to a profound *new beginning*, a true mutation in the life of the individual. It does not refer to rituals nor to hierarchies, nor to using drugs. Not at all.

This is to say that the very core of K's message consisted of what all the esoteric schools (and all the great religions and ideologies based on universal morality) in history called "initiation"—a new beginning.

Put in other words, K was inviting all of us to engage, in our daily lives, in the very marrow of that which has always been genuinely esoteric, which is the genuinely religious, the genuinely moral—and the genuinely American.

---

[2] See paradigmshift.network.

Popularizing "Theosophy"

Ironically, this difference between K and the TSers may have come as a misunderstanding that arose out of early Victorian TSers' attempts to communicate the ancient wisdom—as they (mis)understood it—to a wider audience, in their efforts to "popularize" what they *believed* was "Theosophy." In their zeal to make the formerly secret insights available to the public at large, they presented the perennial wisdom in the form of conceptual systems and methodologies of practice—and those systems and methodologies turned into mere *beliefs*, far more often than not.

This pattern of behavior is exactly the pattern found in all the great religions and ideologies based on universal morality, throughout history. So in this respect, TSers have *a lot* of company. It is because of this, in fact, that all previous perennial efforts have failed to bring about a true, major mutation in humans—as poignantly affirmed by the Mahachohan in what is universally considered the most important statement ever made by HPB's perennial mentors.[3]

The popularity of CWL's writings—and later of many others, such as Alice Bailey, Rudolf Steiner, and Ken Wilber—shows the successful component of this decision to "popularize" what Victorians initially understood by "Theosophy."

This conceptual approach was successful at least insofar as the *quantity* of people impacted by it is concerned. This "success" is much like the success of religions and ideologies based on universal values—whose membership is now counted in billions of people.

On the other hand, this conceptual presentation is clearly and unambiguously *exoteric.* One of its many limitations—apart from its generating numerous and mutually incompatible sets of beliefs and group-thinks—is that it diminishes profoundly the

---

[3] For the Mahachohan's theosophy-defining statement, see Chin, *The Mahatma Letters, Chronological* (1993), Appendix II, 477; Jinarajadasa, *Letters From the Masters of the Wisdom, First Series* (1923), 1.

quality of what is being presented, in terms of its *esoteric substance.*

In retrospect, then, popularizing "Theosophy" also ended up having had a detrimental effect—much as what has happened with previous perennial efforts. An important part of that downside, is that most people came to understand the perennial wisdom—erroneously—as if it were primarily a conceptual system and a series of robotically predetermined, repeatable practices, in the context of *inventing* hierarchies of authority—the way all tyrannies do.

Transformation and dying to the known—which is the actual perennial initiation and its mutation, as addressed in Chapter 25, "Mutation"—ended up being relegated to mere conceptual categories, where they clearly do not belong. After all, conceptualizing about "dying to the known" is as relevant to actual mutation as a mere menu is to a hungry person. What is required, instead, is *engaging* in *a true new beginning.*

Ideology and mutation

Many TSers and New Agers have assumed unquestioningly that any Tom, Dick, or Harriette is qualified—perhaps by just reading a book, or many books—even to begin to understand what "mutation" is. Thereby, they would further assume that they are "perfectly capable" of delving into perennial initiation. They would generally fail to see at all that it is such *initiation* that K's insights, researches, and observations were addressing—except that he was doing it in what is by far the clearest and most powerful manner ever in history.

This calamitous misunderstanding on the part of New Agers has led to a sobering reality—a reality that everyone must face: *A serious investigation into mutation requires actual mutation from the would-be researcher: "It don't mean a thing, if it ain't got that swing."*

The perennial wisdom is a jealous mistress. You can't BS yourself into what you may think are its graces.

Mutation—in a perennial context—is not just a concept that anyone can accept or reject according to a particular system of thought or methodology.

Of course, anyone can make that fateful, purely analytical (and therefore me-centered) assumption, the way so many Traditionalists do. But anyone who makes that assumption will find it *impossible* even to begin to scratch the surface of what the word "mutation" refers to—as in K's explorations.

Much the same can be said about assuming that the word "initiation"—when used in a perennial context—refers to mere rituals, hierarchies, and the paraphernalia and patinaed brick-a-brac that go with them.

Such assumptions are silly and dangerous—and can only be based on one's necessarily limited conditioning. To the extent that one insists on depending on concepts and algorithms, one makes it impossible to dig into deeper aspects of everything that K addressed in his researches—which were *transanalytical*, as spelled out in *The Analytical Fallacy*. Precisely the same can be said regarding the deeper aspects of the perennial wisdom—including America's founding documents—which amounts to exactly the same thing.

Unresearchers

Here is the problem: If one is gullibly committed and beholden to an ideology (such as a religion or a New Age groupthink) or to a guild (such as a profession or academic field) or to a particular culture's expectations—or to a system, or to a methodology, or to a mythology—it is inevitable that one's understanding of the would-be "research" will already be predetermined, to a defining extent, by one's prejudices, no matter what those prejudices might be.

In fact, one's commitment to such prejudices dictates, and tells us, that one is actually *an unresearcher*—someone who is intrinsically not interested at all in borderless truth-seeking-

truth-finding, but rather in interpreting whatever is being addressed in terms of the preciously-held prejudice.

That is propaganda—not truth-seeking.

The analytical approach to "research"—which is so dear to analyzers-unresearchers that it provides the very foundations for
what they assert, often against all evidence—is nothing more
and nothing less than a form of solipsism, and is therefore actually unrelated to the presumed subject of their sham "investigations."

This is a severely serious problem, and one that Traditionalists of all stripes clearly cannot surmount—given that the very
existence of a "Tradition" is ineluctably based on me-centered
analysis from a particular point of view, a particular "Tradition."

*Like characters in a play, analyzers-unresearchers—Tradi-
tionalists or not—are an inescapable result of their self-created
tragedy.*

This, I believe, is an important component of what K was referring to, when he said that "the observer is the observed." This
is an important aspect of why such a world-class mind as David
Bohm's was so powerfully attracted to the unique way in which
K was carrying out such researches.

That is, one may make the mistaken assumption that one is
trying to "understand mutation," for instance. But if one is looking into "mutation" from some predetermined—actually solip-
sistic—perspective, what one is in fact looking at is one's own
preconceived perception, as applied to what one thinks *the
word* "mutation" "ought" to refer to. The observer *is* the observed.

To the extent that one makes the fateful assumption that the
word "mutation" refers to a mere *concept* to be plugged into
one's already predigested—and perhaps inadequately questioned—expectations, to that extent one is merely playing games
with oneself.

The observer is the observed.

CHAPTER 29
Skeptics

LONG BEFORE K, OTHERS HAD POINTED OUT how our own me-centered limitations interfere severely with any would-be investigation into deeper aspects of our lives.

Kantian era

For instance, Immanuel Kant (1724-1804) had shown how our own predispositions are hard-wired into the way in which we (the observer) perceive everything (the observed). Kant showed how those predispositions predetermine *what we think we see* "out there." But there is no "out there." In other words, the way in which we perceive what we think we see "out there," is dependent on lively expectations already built into our psyches. The observer is the observed—that seemingly harmless sentence from K summarizes perfectly what Kant's *Critique of Pure Reason* (1781) is centrally about.

We tend strongly to make the assumption that "we" are in a position to inquire analytically into everything that is—into what we *assume* is the innermost nature of "reality." Such would-be "inquiries" were called "metaphysics" in Kant's time— and by some people uneducated in even conventional philosophy, to this day. There are still people who assume that any of us is in a position to inquire analytically into *what is*. In fact, Kant's pervasively influential work—*The Critique of Pure Reason*—could just as well have been called "The Critique of Predetermined Analysis" or "The Critique of Solipsism."

Ludwig Feuerbach (1804-1872)—who was following in Kant's footsteps—showed in *The Essence of Christianity* (1841), something truly remarkable. Feuerbach pointed out that in the area of religion (*any* religion or ideology claiming to be delving into *that which is*), our never-questioned predispositions (the presumed observer) is the actual subject (the observed) of all of our religious or ideological endeavors.

Many other researchers—such as Nietzsche, William James, Ludwig Wittgenstein (1889-1951), and more recently deconstructionists such as Jacques Derrida (1930-2004), and neopragmatists such as Richard Rorty (1931-2007), to name a few—followed up on these Kantian investigations further. All of them—and many other world-class minds, including practitioners of the science of physics—have made it increasingly clear, in a variety of ways: The observer *is* the observed—as K had been pointing out since the 1930s.

Asian Skepticism

In the academic field of philosophy, such questioners of the analytical mind are called "philosophical skeptics." Among them is Socrates—who is generally accepted to be iconic of the philosophical enterprise itself.

Yet despite the fact that philosophical skeptics have shown—in many and differing ways—that the analytical mind is a blunt, inadequate instrument for delving into deeper issues in our lives, professional "philosophers" today continue to persist in gullibly accepting and promoting that Aristotelian bromide.

In fact, that bromide—the acceptance of which consists of committing the analytical fallacy—is the very foundation of what is called "philosophy" in such quarters. Thus, philosophical skepticism—which is central to the actual act and process of engaging in *philosophia*—is ignored cavalierly, to the detriment of true education, of truth-seeking-truth-finding, and of the moral fiber of society.

This is not a merely academic dispute. Realizing the enormous damage to all society that committing the analytical fallacy is, is as serious as serious can get.

In Asia, this kind of skepticism regarding the presumed ability of the analytical mind to dissertate about *that which is*, is widely understood and accepted as being "obvious." This is considered so obvious in Asian approaches, that it is not even given a name, per se. Yet all major Asian approaches are saturated with such "philosophical skepticism," whether overtly recognized or not.

Let us recall that philosophical skepticism in the West was initially—and for many centuries—called "Pyrrhonism." From its beginnings, philosophical skepticism questioned thoroughly the capacity of the analytical mind for delving into the issues that most matter to us—as addressed more carefully in Part One, and even more so in *The Analytical Fallacy*.

Importantly, Pyrrho (360-270 BCE) learned his skepticism from the "gymnosophists"—as he called the "naked" monks (presumed to be either Buddhist or Jain) who taught him to "suspend judgment."

Philosophical skepticism originated in Asia—where there has always been clarity regarding the inadequacies and dangers of misusing the analytical mind for the purpose of delving into what matters most to us.

In fact, my perception is that this is an important component of why the TS was moved from New York City to India—a place where the analytical mind has always been perceived as the enemy of truth-seeking, not its ally, as has been largely and mistakenly assumed by Europeans and their colonists, up to the present.

One way of seeing this critical perennial insight in Asia, is to note its presence throughout history. For instance, Patañjali (3rd to 2nd century BCE) shared with all of us, in his *Yoga Sutras* (n.d.), that before there can be a deeper understanding of anything, *there must be sunya*—emptiness of *all* pre-dispositions, conditioning, and me-centered expectations.[1]

If there is not this emptiness (this lack of analytical me-centeredness), it is impossible—Patañjali tells us—for there to be any deeper understanding of *what is*. The *Yoga Sutras* is the foundation text for all yoga—and so its insights are at the core of all Indian culture, including all the many differing schools and sects of Hinduism.

---

[1] See I.K. Taimni, *The Science of Yoga*, which is the text and commentary on *Yoga Sutras*.

The ancient East is replete with perennial researchers who are totally skeptical of the me-centered analytical mind's capacity for addressing deeper issues—to the point that the analytical mind is often called "the monkey mind." Some of these researchers were the Buddha (6th century BCE), Lao Tse (6th century BCE), and Shankaracharya (8th century CE). To a man, they were all addressing—in different ways, each appropriate to a particular time and place—the dire need for there to be what Nagarjuna (150?-250?) referred to as *"sunyata."* Sunyata stands for the emptiness that *must* be present, before there can be any deeper explorations worthy of the name.

It is precisely this *sunya* or *sunyata*—this kind of emptiness at great psychological depths—that K was communicating to us, throughout his long life of sharing his insights and observations. In fact, *that* can be said to be what the word "mutation" refers to, in K's insights, researches, and observations.

One major difference between K and all other perennials and philosophical skeptics who had addressed this throughout history—everywhere on Earth—is that K never once relies on cultural atavisms, nor on systems or methodologies. That is, K is a far more thorough philosophical skeptic than anyone else in the history of mankind.

All other skeptics—from "the East" or from "the West"—have appealed to some form of analysis in the process of denying analysis. All previous skeptics relied on their cultural and other atavisms. Thanks to the presence of K in the twentieth century, it can now be seen with clarity that all such atavisms are themselves part and parcel of what needs to be left behind, if there is to be *sunyata.*

In contrast to all previous skeptics, K never appealed to any atavism of any sort. He was the purest Skeptic in the history of humanity. K was explicitly addressing himself to all of humanity, not to a mere fraction thereof—as all previous would-be philosophical skeptics had done.

Dawn of a new era

This difference between K and all other researchers in history is far, far deeper than unresearchers might think—to the extent that it points unequivocally to K's uniqueness in history. The presence of K in the twentieth century unquestionably stands for *a new beginning,* for all of us. This is as unprecedented as anything unprecedented can be.

Also, and just as importantly, K was clearly addressing all of us, and not just a group-think or particular region of the world—each with its own set of predispositions, prejudgments, and expectations based on me-centered conditioning.

As briefly noted in Part One, K is the first truly borderless, *transanalytical* researcher in history, and the first ever who taught the esoteric, and only the esoteric. That, too, is *a brand new beginning*—a mutation on a grand scale, if you will.

I submit to you, careful reader, that when HPB's perennial mentors declared that "we are at the dawn of a new era," it is mutation—with its implicit skepticism of all analysis of that which is—that they were referring to. What I have called "the American Age" is the Age of Krishnamurti, the age of potentially worldwide mutation.

Another critical point to keep in mind is the mutation of the brain addressed in Chapter 25, "Mutation." How to bring about the mutation of the brain had never been addressed before, anywhere in the world.

A few others—specifically HPB and her colleagues and popularizers, such as William James and Sri Aurobindo—had spoken of the reality of brain plasticity, or said that such plasticity is a requirement for human evolution—as addressed in Chapter 25, "Mutation."

But no one had ever described the process whereby such an evolution of the brain is brought about, before K.

Aurobindo was closest to doing that—but he spoiled his insight by attaching himself to group-thinks identified with Indian culture, including setting himself up as an authority figure—a mere guru.

This is yet another important way in which K was unique in world history, and stood for *a new beginning, a new era.*

Mutation, then, is an existential process that is either going on in oneself, or not.

Only the actual process of discarding all prejudices and ex-pectations—which are irrevocably entangled with a me-centered way of perceiving everything—can provide the kind of clarity without which it is impossible to address anything at all that truly matters to us, including mutation itself.

Mutation is not "a subject" for analyzers to talk about. The "mutation" that is talked or written about—as what is being done here—is unrelated to actual mutation. The word is not the thing.

"Mutation" is a name given—perhaps impertinently—to an ineffable process.

CHAPTER 30
Education

UNFORTUNATELY, THE VAST MAJORITY of the very few of us who are even aware of the urgent need for transformation seem to tend to assume that "mutation" is "a subject" that any one of us can "interpret" and talk about, "pro" or "con." The arbitrary assumption tends to be made that "mutation" is "a subject" concerning which one can have differing "views" or "opinions."

That indemonstrable assumption becomes highly problematic, when it comes to trying to understand what the borderless wisdom is about. The presumption turns even dangerous, when applied to K's *unprecedented* insights, researches, and observations.

Despite the implicit dangers in making such an assumption, it is quite common in TS and New Age circles. Thus, there is in that milieu a seemingly endless chatter about people's interpretations of what words such as "initiation" or "the path" or "Masters" mean. The same can be said about many who become interested in K, regarding words and expressions such as "mutation," or "dying to the known," which are often used by K to refer to the ancient perennial initiatory process. Opinions abound, regarding such "subjects."

Unfortunately for true-believers in misplaced analysis, there is a sobering fact that they need to consider: One might as well have opinions "pro" or "con" the sun being hot.

This self-centered, seemingly insurmountable stumbling block makes it impossible for any one of us to address anything that truly matters to us, at the end of the day. "Opinions" and "assumptions" clearly come from a universe of discourse that includes all of our many confusions, stresses, repressions, fears, fragmentations, and divisions.

Such a perspective—which is far more common than many of us would like to admit—prevents us from coming upon the all-comprehensive, presuppositionless truth-seeking-truth-finding dimension. Though we tend to shun that moral dimension with all our might, anyone can discover—upon researching this borderlessly—that the all-comprehensive, ineffable consciousness is within all of us. So it seems most proper and pertinent to address this by pointing to how critical it is for all of us to learn as well as we can about our limitations—as well as about our unlimited potential.

Education is the process whereby we engage in such all-important learning.

Midwifery

The word "education" comes from a derivation of the Latin *educere*—which is to educe, to draw out, in the sense in which a midwife draws out a fetus. It is thus that a fetus is "miraculously" *transformed* into a baby, at what we call "birth"—which is an initiation (a new beginning), into the physical world. This original meaning of the word "education" is directly related to words like "philosophy" and "esoteric"—in the sense that those words had at their origin, in the Pythagorean setting—as addressed in Parts One and Two.

The most famous and influential Pythagorean in history was Plato—whose teacher, Socrates, was often referred to as being "a midwife." According to Socrates, he had no *knowledge* to impart regarding *what is*. He specifically stated that he had no such knowledge. "I only know that I know nothing," he famously affirmed. Socrates was a philosophical skeptic—as addressed in the previous chapter.

Instead of sharing his opinions or "imparting knowledge"—as was common among "professors" of his time—Socrates considered his job to be that of *drawing out of others the wisdom that was already in them*. Unfortunately, most of us—including the many ancient Greeks who engaged Socrates in dialogues—seem to be unaware of wisdom being within us. I submit to you, attentive reader, that this ignorance on our part—this lack of *education*—happens as a result of our holding on to me-centered identifications. Many such identifications are fac-tors such as wealth, position, knowledge, cleverness, cultural background, ethnicity—or the lack of any such—and the like. But as Buddhists might put it, "everyone has buddha nature."

That is, there is wisdom-compassion within all of us, and it is the function of education to educe *that wisdom-compassion—which is already there—and bring it out into the open.*

That, precisely, is what was poignantly suggested by Maria Montessori's (1870-1952) expression encapsulated in the title of one of her many books on education, "to educate the human potential."[1] (Incidentally, Montessori wrote most of her pervasively influential books while she was a guest for several years at the international headquarters of the TS in Chennai, India.)

Importantly, this, too, is the essential function of philosophy—and of the esoteric, according to Pythagoras, who coined the word. The words "education," and "philosophy," and "esoteric" all refer to exactly the same existential process in oneself.

After all, Pythagoras was the creator of both of those words, "philosophy" and "esoteric." Plato certainly spoke of *philosophy* (the love of wisdom) as something that takes place exclusively when one dies every day of one's life to all the many worldly identifications. Such me-centered attachments make educing wisdom impossible.[2]

Training

So the word *"education"*—in its origins—has a deeper, perennial meaning. Maria Montessori based her educational work—which is now an important factor throughout the world—on that deeper meaning. In contrast to that original and true meaning of education is the me-centered practice carried out throughout the world on a daily basis, from kindergarten through postgraduate work. Rather than education, what actually goes on in

---

[1] Montessori, *To Educate the Human Potential* (1947).
[2] For *philosophia* as daily death, see Plato, *Phaedo*, 64a, Thomas Taylor translation.

most schools everywhere in our days should more properly be called *training*.

The intent of this training is not to *educe* the wisdom within all of us. Rather, its central purpose is to *train* the hapless clueless victim, the student—whether that disciple is a child or a young adult—into being a cog in the machinery of some institutionalized, me-centered leviathan. Then—very sadly—once they graduate at the presumably "highest" levels of *training*, they tend to become such institutionalized cogs.

It is as if the assumption is made, rather generally, that a student is much like a trained circus seal—not a human being with immense inner potential.

Historically, the leviathan's institutionalized universe of discourse—which is *always* intensely me-centered—has been mainly that of religious or political ideologies and institutions. In our times, that institutionalized me-centered universe of discourse tends to be, more and more, that of the new religious cult of Corporatism.

In the toxic environment of the Corporatist cult, the word "education" is clearly and cynically misused to refer to what is— unquestionably—*training and propaganda,* not *education.* The word "education"—as used in that grossly me-centered environment—is an important part of the *newspeak* of the religious cult of Corporatism—if I may appropriately borrow George Orwell's (1903-1950) neologism.[3]

This new religious cult is, by far, more in-your-face, blatantly me-centered than any previous ideology. The only thing that matters to this new *religious cult* is what it calls "the bottom line"—the wealth and power that accrue to the tiny minority who give their lives *and souls* to the corporate leviathan.

The new religious cult of Corporatism achieves this in the context of creating a level of worldwide oppression, abuse, repression and misery for the vast majority of humanity—misery such as the world had never seen before. The corporate creature

---

[3] For that and other neologisms related to tyranny, see Orwell, *Nineteen eighty-four* (1949).

also achieves its main purposes in the context of doing its best to destroy the biosphere in which all living entities (including all humans) live. The cult of Corporatism is a leviathan, indeed—a super-monster.

Training—whether that of a conventional religion, an ideology, or of the new religious cult of Corporatism—is intrinsically inimical to caring for *all* fellow humans or for fellow forms of life. Yet such *training* is what goes cynically by the name of "education."

In actual *education* there is an ever-developing sense of fellowship and care towards all human beings and towards all forms of life. Such a comprehensive sense of fellowship and responsibility towards all is at the very core of intelligence. Intelligence consists of being *educated* in that original, deeper sense of the word.

Education

Education could be said to consist of the awakening of intelligence.[4]

Education is not the stuffing of minds with self-enclosed, brutally-minded ideologies and institutionalized me-centered conditioning. Unfortunately, all that most of us have known throughout our history, everywhere on the planet, has been *training* in some form of brutality or another. *Education* has—unfortunately—*never* been a central component of any society, living or dead.

What K was addressing involves the creation of an entirely new kind of society—a planetary society with firm foundations in the compassionate and borderless truth-seeking-truth-finding that the-love-of-wisdom has always been. But in order for such a society to come into being—for the first time ever in the sorry history of mankind—*education* must have center-stage in our individual endeavors.

This, too, is a new beginning, at the dawn of a new era.

---

[4] See Krishnamurti, *The Awakening of Intelligence,* 1973.

Such education would be impossible, for as long as muta-tion—psychological *and* physiological—is not at the core of how we each live our lives, day-to-day. Engaging in such mutation on a daily basis marks the beginning and the continuation of the only actual solution to all of our woes and challenges—whether personal, in relationships, in the communities we live in, or planet-wide.

That is the urgency of mutation, as we speak. We are each faced with that urgency at the present unprecedented, cyclically-relevant moment in the history of our species.

CHAPTER 31
World University

EDUCATION WAS AT THE VERY CORE OF THE WORK of the TS, from its beginnings. After all, the borderless wisdom championed by the TS can be said to be all about us being *educated* on the urgent need to allow for wisdom to flow through us—rather than impeded by propaganda and other me-centered distractions.

TS education

Early on in TS history, it was *education* that propelled the work of Colonel Henry Steele Olcott (HSO) in Sri Lanka (then Ceylon).

HSO considered education so important, that he went to the length of taking a semi-sabbatical from being the founding international president of the TS. He took such an unexpected and revolutionary step in order to single-handedly help establish about 250 Buddhist schools. This was an immensely courageous act on his part. It was also illegal, given that it was in fact an act of civil disobedience to the British empire. The British were intent on "Christianizing" every place on Earth that was somehow under control of their empire.

HSO's intent was not to try to replace Christianity with *sectarian* Buddhism—as it might seem, on the surface. Rather—and as a true *practicing* American that he was—he was trying to appeal to the universal wisdom in all religions based on universal mora-lity, such as Christianity and Buddhism.

Borderless wisdom implies that no one ideology or religion—when it is true to its universal, borderless origins—shall ever supersede or have hegemony over all others.

What Olcott did is no more and no less than what America's founding documents have to say, regarding religion. In a way, his act of civil disobedience was a kind of continuation of the American war of independence from the British empire—which stood for the tyrannies of pre-America's past, throughout the world.

Any prejudiced ideology claiming superiority for itself is thereby being clearly me-centered—and turning its back on the better angels of its nature and origins. Those better angels of its nature are unquestionably borderless—and so are *never* prejudiced.

For her part, Mrs. Besant (AB) founded the seminal Central Hindu College in 1898, and implemented or inspired other related educational work in India—which the British government wasn't too happy about, either. In fact, AB's life throughout her TS tenure was a continuous act of civil disobedience, in the process of promoting borderless *education.*[1]

She was involved in such *civic-educational* work from the early 1890s (when she first arrived in India), until her death in 1933. Her intent in engaging in all this educational work—like Olcott's in his—was not to promote *sectarian* Hinduism.

Rather, AB was doing her best to bring awareness to the existence and reality of the universal wisdom in every system based on universal morality, such as Hinduism. Mahatma Gandhi understood this nature and intent of the perennial wisdom as mother of all religions—which he called "Theosophy"—until the day he died.

World University

For many decades (up until the 1970s) serious TS members—initially inspired by the perennials—had been keenly interested in creating what they called a "world university." This would be an institution of higher learning that would be more responsive to universal, borderless values.

Such a world university would be in contrast to the truly pitiful, even pathetic institutions that claim to be "educational," everywhere on Earth, up to the present. The latter "educational"

---

[1] For AB's work on education in India, see C.V. Agarwal and Pedro Oliveira, *Annie Besant in India* (2021).

institutions are in reality largely *training centers* in the service of a particular religion or political ideology—and the intensely me-centered religious cult of Corporatism.

What are euphemistically called "educational" institutions in our time exist for the explicit purpose of justifying self-centered—and therefore immoral—analyses. They thereby contribute, worldwide, to greater confusions, fragmentations, divisions, chaos—and suffering—at a time when real education is urgently needed. Existing institutions of "higher learning" achieve this chaotic situation either by being instruments of some form of group-think, or by being slavish servants to deeply me-centered and militantly immoral corporate power.

CIIS

Ernest Wood (1883-1965) was an educator and prominent TS member who was deeply involved in the TS's educational dimension. He had been prominent enough to run for international president of the TS in 1934, shortly after AB's death.

It will be recalled that Wood had been K's tutor in Adyar since before CWL had met the boy Krishna in February, 1909. In that sense, it could be said that it was Wood who "discovered" K. Wood continued to have a deep personal connection with K for the rest of his life. He certainly would never have thrown K out of the TS—if he had been elected TS President, in 1934.

In 1951, Wood became the president and dean of the then newly-created American Academy of Asian Studies (AAAS) in San Francisco. His tenure in that post was so brief, that it's usually not even mentioned in historical accounts of AAAS. It is tempting to speculate on why he changed his mind about participating in this project—which seemed to be intended to be much like the "world university" that TSers had dreamed of.[2]

Wood may have changed his mind about AAAS because businessman Louis Gainsborough (n.d.)—who was funding the

---

[2] The Theosophical World University was created in 1925, with Annie Besant at its head.

project—thought of it in part as a springboard for him to do business with Asian countries. It's easy to see how Wood would have seen AAAS as a purely educational project along the lines of the "world university" that TSers had been so very passionate about—not as something related to business in any way, shape, or form.

In any case, AAAS later merged with what is now called the California Institute of Integral Studies (CIIS). CIIS had been largely an academic expression of the "integral yoga" of Sri Aurobindo—who is addressed in Chapter 26, "Aurobindo."

After Wood's swift departure, Haridas Chauduri (1913-1975) and Alan Watts (1915-1973) headed AAAS. There is some evidence that Chauduri and Watts were able to convince Gainsborough—whose heart seems to have been in the right place—to focus on the educational dimension, and put aside other concerns. Wood's departure may have softened Gainsborough on the notion of mixing business with *education*—and that perhaps made it easier for Chauduri and Watts to convince him otherwise.

Chauduri was considered the foremost exponent outside of India of Aurobindo's "integral yoga" at the time—hence the word "integral" becoming part of the name of CIIS. Watts was even then well-known internationally for his books on Buddhism. Also, at the time he had just quit being an Episcopal priest and Chaplain at Northwestern University—which he had been, from 1944 to 1950.

Because of their international stature, Watts and Chauduri in turn attracted a number of internationally renowned scholars and teachers at the leading edge of various disciplines.

Though not connected officially at any time to the TS, CIIS has probably come closest than any other institution to the early TS dream of creating a "world university."

For one thing, CIIS has become the springboard and/or inspiration for a number of important developments in the worldwide wisdom explosion. Examples of this are the highly influential so-called "San Francisco renaissance," which included the birth and development of transpersonal psychology and the creation of the Esalen Institute—whose founders Michael Murphy (b. 1930) and Dick Price (b. 1930) had been enthusiastic CIIS students.

The TS connection

From its beginnings, CIIS has always looked much like what early TSers had dreamed would be a "world university." Apart from that, there actually are important factors tying CIIS and the TS—though such factors are never mentioned in any of the various accounts of its beginnings and history. For instance—and as just noted—prominent TSer Ernest Wood was the first head of AAAS.

To my knowledge, part of what is never mentioned (to my knowledge) in accounts of CIIS, is that Watts began his perennial education in the TS. When he was barely fourteen, Watts had become a TS member, attached to the Buddhist Lodge in London.

Following the suggestion of Annie Besant, the Lodge was later turned into the internationally influential Buddhist Society, headed by Christmas Humphreys (1901-1983). At the time when the TS Buddhist Lodge became the independent and internationally highly influential Buddhist Society, Humphreys was in his 20s—not much older than Watts. They were two bright kids, who ended up having worldwide influence as major components of the American Age wisdom explosion.

In addition—and importantly in the present context—Watts maintained a life-long mentoring friendship with K, much like Wood had done. In fact, every single time that Watts was about to take a major step in his life—such as becoming an Episcopalian priest and university Chaplain, and later moving away from those positions to work at AAAS—he first consulted K.

This very close connection between Watts and K can be seen only in his autobiography, *In My Own Way* (1972). His biographers—perhaps with the best of intentions—fail to point out his having been a TS member. Nor do they spell out the level of spiritual intimacy of his relationship with K. Apart from K's impact on Watt's perceptions—as reflected in all of his books—K impacted his life even more, on a personal level. When looked at carefully, their relationship might have even been one of Watts depending on K at crucial turning points in his life—including his untimely death at the age of only 59.

K's influence on Watts' understanding and presentation of Buddhism and Taoism was quite pervasive.

Importantly, it was D.T. Suzuki (1870-1966), Christmas Humphreys, Alexandra David-Neel (1868-1969), and W.Y. Evans-Wentz (1878-1965)—all of them TS members—who together with Alan Watts brought about a non-sectarian understanding of Buddhism that eventually turned into an altogether brand new, international version of it.

Such a borderless understanding and practice of Buddhism had never existed before, in the 2,500 years of Buddhist practice and study, in many countries. Anyone today who is a Buddhist or interested in Buddhism outside of Buddhist countries, owes an immense debt of gratitude to the TS. Even sectarian Buddhists ought to be thankful to the TS—though relatively very few of them have done so, thus seeming to show an apparent lack of integrity.

It should be added that—following in HSO's footsteps—Christmas Humphreys' Buddhist Society did not defend sectarian Buddhism. Instead, it promoted *the perennial wisdom in Buddhism*—which is borderless. To my knowledge, the Buddhist Society became the first institution ever in history to promote international Buddhism, for that very reason.

It was this perennially-inspired institution that was mainly instrumental in making the world aware of the work of D.T. Suzuki—who was unquestionably the most important *international* Buddhist scholar in history. It is largely through his many books—and those by Watts, David-Neel, Humphreys, and Evans-Wentz—that international Buddhism came to be popularized worldwide. It is largely thanks to those early pioneers that international Buddhism is what it is today—despite sectarian Buddhists mostly missing out on this critical dimension.

Suzuki had become a TS member in the 1880s. In an important way, he was following in the footsteps of his roshi Soyen Shaku (1860-1919)—whose astonishingly unprecedented internationalism in Japan Suzuki embraced. In Japan, sectarian Zen had always been hermetically sealed to all outsiders—until Soyen Shaku first opened it to the world at large. His internationalism—and Suzuki's—was based on the perennial understanding that they had learned from Olcott, HPB, and the TS.

Tyberg

Another important early participant at AAAS was Judith Tyberg (1902-1980)—though she is usually not mentioned in accounts of the beginnings of CIIS. She was born and raised in "Lomaland," Point Loma, California—at the headquarters of one of several splinter TS organizations, often called "the Point Loma (later 'Pasadena') TS."

In addition to her having grown up being immersed in Theosophy, Tyberg received several degrees—in mathematics and in classical languages such as Hebrew, Latin, and Greek, and several European languages—from the Theosophical University that had been created by the Point Loma TS, in a kind of competition with the one founded by Annie Besant, in 1925. Later, Tyberg became the most internationally renowned teacher of Sanskrit. I feel compelled to add that I am personally grateful to her in this respect, since I began to learn Sanskrit from her books, beginning in the 1960s.

Tyberg collaborated with Geoffrey Barborka (1897-1982) in the design and creation of the first ever ancient Sanskrit (devanagari) lynotype keyboard—which made it possible for her to use it in her many books on Sanskrit and its texts. Even in India there had not been such a keyboard before Barborka and Tyberg invented one.

Eventually, Tyberg became the Dean of Studies at the Theosophical University. This was the Point Loma TS version of the world university—which was far more successful in its implementation than the one from Adyar. Tyberg held this post from 1935 to 1945. She resigned from the Point Loma TS in 1946, due to internal divisions in the organization.

In this regard, it should be noted that schisms were common in the TS, from its beginnings. In fact, it is from such schisms that the New Age movement and the worldwide perennial explosion were largely built up. I have always perceived those divisions not as "problematic" in any way. I have always seen them, rather, as a very important way in which the wisdom explosion ended up being widely spread, everywhere in the world.

In Tyberg's case, it is a fact that her disagreements with the organization is what led eventually to her becoming a world leader in perennial education.

Diaspora

In a sense, I perceive such TS-related schisms as being similar to what happened to the discipline of philosophy, historically. Among the Greeks, especially after Plato's disciple Aristotle (384-322 BCE), philosophy was largely an attempt to comprehend all that is.

But Aristotle's analytical understanding of "philosophy" marked a serious departure from the Pythagorean-Platonic perception of *philosphia* as the act and process of mutation—as laid out in Chapter 30, "Education." As the centuries passed, Aristotelian "philosophy" turned into numerous "specializations." It is thus that the many disciplines that make up a contemporary university came about.

We can still find vestiges of that fact, in a number of ways. In some British universities, for instance, there is no department of "physics." What is called "physics" everywhere else in the world—and even in the UK—has been referred to as *"natural philosophy."* Sir Isaac Newton's (1642-1727) magnum opus is his *Philosophiæ Naturalis Principia Mathematica* (1697). Use of the word "physics" to refer to "natural philosophy" only came later.

All disciplines that make up a university now, began as branches from the tree of philosophy.

Despite how very recent the history of the wisdom explosion still is, I see the many splits that took place in the TS as being much like the multiplication of "philosophy" into numerous disciplines.

In any case, once Tyberg left the Point Loma TS, she spent a couple of years teaching and lecturing in various colleges and universities in the Los Angeles area—and then went to study at Benares Hindu University (BHU). Significantly, BHU was the new name for the Central Hindu College that Annie Besant had founded in 1897.

Having been immersed in the borderless wisdom since she was born, it is understandable that Tyberg wanted to write her thesis on her understanding that the Vedas contained a "deeper," non-sectarian dimension—a borderless dimension. She had been unable to find such a *theosophical* dimension in any of the extant Vedic commentaries, old and new.

No one at BHU knew how to help her, so she couldn't find a credible advisor there. It was thus, through her borderless search, that she discovered Sri Aurobindo's *The Secret of the Veda* (1956)—and Aurobindo himself.

Aurobindo and The Mother

It was a meeting of perennial giants—at least that is how I perceive it. Tyberg ended up spending a great deal of time at Aurobindo's ashram in Pondicherry, and getting to know and understand integral yoga from the inside out. She also secured a friendship with Mirra Alfassa (1878-1973), whom Aurobindo referred to as The Mother.

Tyberg received numerous accolades from Indian leaders of culture—such as internationally renowned philosopher and first

President of India Sarvepalli Radhakrishnan, among many others—for her important contributions towards deepening the understanding of Indian culture inter-nationally, and even within India itself.

Mirra Alfassa's quest for deeper matters—like Aurobindo's, as noted in Chapter 26, "Aurobindo"—had its start within the TS milieu, in Paris. Among these important contacts was TS member Alexandra David-Neel, who became a very close and even intimate friend, and with whom she had many discussions and soul-searching explorations.

But the central figure in Alfassa's life in Europe—in her pre-Aurobindo days in India—was unquestionably Max Théon (1848-1927), a Polish Jewish kabbalist and occultist. Though Théon credited his wife, Alma Théon (1843-1908) for most of what he taught, he was one of the most important exemplars of the wisdom explosion in the French-speaking world—and beyond, through what he and Madame Théon called "the Cosmic Tradition."

Théon's journal *Cosmic Review* had an international readership, and was an influence on the so-called "Russian Cosmists." Russian Cosmists have more recently gained visibility because of their very real connection to outer space rocketry and travel, and extraterrestrials. Internationally renowned NASA scientist and space travel pioneer Wernher von Braun (1912-1977) was inspired importantly by the Russian Cosmists, particularly Konstantin Tsiolkovsky (1857-1935), who pioneered astronautic theory and is considered the father of outer space rocketry.

Intriguingly, the first we know with any degree of certainty about Théon's life is that he was part of the group that HPB had started in Luxor, Egypt, in 1870, when Théon was just 23.[3]

The Mother's background in Europe—and later in Algiers, at Théon's "ashram"—is eminently relevant to any thorough exploration of CIIS. After all, Aurobindo always considered The

---

[3] For the Théons and their connection to HPB, see Christian Chanel, Joscelyn Godwin, and John Patrick Deveney, *The Hermetic Brotherhood of Luxor: Initiatic and Historical Documents of an Order of Practical Occultism* (1995).

Mother to be his equal in deeper matters—and she did indeed take charge of the ashram and its teaching after Aurobindo's death in 1950. So at about the same time that CIIS got its start, it was The Mother who had been in charge of the Aurobindo Ashram.

Unfortunately, her thoroughly TS-related background—in Paris and then in Algiers, before she met Aurobindo—is usually either not mentioned at all, or its overwhelming importance is minimized in accounts of her life, which understandably tend to focus on its Aurobindo phase.

CHAPTER 32
Paradigm Shift

GIVEN WHAT HAS JUST BEEN REVEALED ABOUT CIIS, I feel obligated to disclose my relationship to it—slight as it actually was—and given that it shows further TS connections in its history and development.

In early 1978, I was invited to be a kind of graduate assistant to Dr. Paul Herman (d. 2012), who had become the main figure at CIIS, after the deaths of Watts and Chauduri just a few years earlier. In 1973, Paul had designed and headed CIIS's transpersonal therapy program—which he called "Integral Counseling Psychology"—the first of its kind in the world. When I was there in 1978, CIIS was called California Institute of Asian Studies (CIAS).

The fact that I had just recently been working on a PhD in the philosophy of science figured into Paul's decision to invite me. My awareness (through Fritz Kunz) of the avant garde in the sciences at the time intrigued Paul.

As part of his pioneering work in transpersonal psychology, Paul was going to teach a graduate seminar in Theosophical Therapy. Through the TS grapevine, he found out about my being in San Francisco at the time. So he invited me—as well as TS in America (TSA) National Lecturer Bing Escudero (1926-2005) —to buttress that seminar, by providing alternate backgrounds on the subject.

Basically, Paul wanted for Bing and I to provide the class with our respective takes on theosophy that might be relevant to such a course. It was a prescient choice on Paul's part, in the sense that Bing and I represented two radically different ways of understanding theosophy—and therefore we complemented each other.

Bing was an excellent teacher of the conventional approach— what I have called here "the Victorian-minded" approach, which relies heavily on beliefs, diagrams, and other forms of analysis.[1]

---

[1] For the "Victorian-minded" approach, see Chapter 19, "Victorian Exoterics."

In contrast, my understanding of theosophy—going back to 1958—has always been mutation-centered. That approach accepts the Victorian-minded as useful for *popularizing* theosophy, but also considers that approach to be dangerously and ridiculously mistaken when it assumes that such Victorianism is *theosophy* itself.

Apart from the profound difference in the way we approached and understood theosophy, it was also very helpful for the success of the seminar that Bing and I were very good friends—which led to an element of joy in the classroom, since both of us had a sense of humor. There was a lot of laughter in that seminar.

At the time, Bing had been lecturing throughout the West Coast on behalf of the TSA. He visited CIAS three times during the semester, to give lectures to the class on his Traditionalist take on HPB's *Secret Doctrine*. In contrast, I shared with the class my psychological and transanalytical understanding that "theosophy is that which happens in theosophical states of awareness"—and which I have briefly and incompletely shared with you in the present exposition.

I was saying to the class that "theosophy"—in its essence—is a *psychological* process of transformation, not a system of thought and belief.[2]

theosophy versus "Theosophy"

I should clarify that—unlike Bing—I was there for every class. In addition—and as assisting graduate students often do in such settings—I taught several of the classes in the Theosophical Therapy seminar. I did so as an unpaid contributor not officially associated with CIAS.

I feel that I made two original contributions to that class—both of which are quite relevant to the present exploration.

---

[2] This is more fully documented in the two upcoming books, *The Secret Doctrine, Krishnamurti and Transformation*, and *Muse*.

The first is that my perception of theosophy is not at all about any analysis of "reality"—which is what one finds in most "Theosophical" books and articles and lectures, to date.

Actually, I have avoided the use of the word "theosophy," given that it tends to be associated—by friends and foes alike—with a cultish set of beliefs and practices. For many years now I have called it—as I have done in this exploration—either "the perennial," or "universal," or "borderless" wisdom. Or else, I simply say "wisdom" or "compassion" or "intelligence," or "universal morality," with no further qualifiers.

Wisdom is not a system of beliefs—especially beliefs that require diagrams, hierarchies, or anything else analytical—as is done in cultish "Theosophy." As I documented fully in *The Analytical Fallacy* (2002)—and more briefly here, in Chapter 2, "The Analytical Fallacy"—all analysis is me-centered, and based on one's conditioning.

This means that any and all analyses of the universally moral (or "perennial") dimension—including "Theosophical" analyses—are clearly me-centered. As such, they are enemies of actual wisdom-compassion-intelligence, despite "good intentions" on the part of uneducated people.[3] Importantly, such analyses of the borderless dimension are also immoral, since universal morality is a critical component of that perennial dimension—which is not analytical, and therefore not me-centered.

Rather than being analytical—I said to the class—"theosophy" is an existential, psychological, transformative *process*. Theosophy is what takes place while one is in divine-like *(theosophical)*, transanalytical states of awareness. There *must* be a transformation, a mutation, before one can call anything "theosophical." I have already addressed this in various places in this exploration, in works about to be published—such as *Insights for a New Era,* and *Muse*—and in papers on paradigmshift.network, so there is no need to say more about it at this point and in the present context.

---

[3] For "education," see Chapter 30, "Education."

At that time, and for many years—I have distinguished lower cased "theosophy" from capitalized "Theosophy." The latter—consisting as it does largely of being a system of thought and belief—is capitalized. But lower-cased "theosophy" is that which happens in theosophical states of awareness, and is the enemy of systems of thought—or of any and all analyses, for that matter.[4]

Paradigm shift

The other major and original contribution that I feel that I made in that graduate seminar requires a little explanation. In one of the classes I taught—and while Paul was sitting to my right, also facing the class—I said that the mutation that theosophy consists of can be seen as making a direct impact on the community that one is a part of—including the planetary community. Such individual transformation—I pointed out—can also express itself planetarily, in a unique way, at this juncture in human history.

After stating that, I stopped, and remarked, "Before I go on, I need to refer to Thomas S. Kuhn's (1922-1996) book *The Structure of Scientific Revolutions* (1962), and his notion of 'paradigm shift.' Are any of you aware of this book or of this particular insight? Have any of you heard the expression 'paradigm shift,' which is central to Kuhn's thesis?"

Like all other classes at CIAS—which were at the graduate level—the class I was addressing was made up of already well-educated adults who were mostly in their thirties and forties (none younger). At 33 at the time, I may have been the youngest person in the room. All the participants in that class were extremely well-read, particularly on any subject related to transpersonal psychology—which "paradigm shift" is clearly a part of. Yet, none of them had ever even heard of Kuhn—much less of the expression "paradigm shift."

---

[4] For "theosophy" and "Theosophy," see *Insights for a New Era*.

Given that it was Paul's class, and that he was unquestionably at the leading edge of transpersonal psychology at the time—and that I thought that having an understanding of "paradigm shift" was critical for making the point I intended to address—I felt that it would have been impudent of me to proceed, without asking Paul if he wanted to explain "paradigm shift" to the class.

So I asked him whether he wanted to do so. As a result, all of us in the class could see immediately that he, too, had never heard the expression "paradigm shift"—let alone its important relationship to transpersonal psychology. He was clearly blushing and embarrassed—which made me feel awful for having asked him. I naively had assumed that "surely" everyone knows about this, since it was a major subject intensely discussed by anyone involved with the philosophy of science—which I was.

The scene was as if taken from a sitcom. Paul simply said, while smiling with the class, "No, please go ahead; you explain it." At this, everyone laughed, including Paul—while it was I who was embarrassed, by having put him on a spot, innocently as I may have done it.

I proceeded to say that Kuhn's book suggests that we have all been very wrong to think that science "progresses" gradually, step by step—each new generation following in the footsteps of the previous one, and making small adjustments here and there. In other words, we tended to think, said Kuhn, that "progress" in science happens much like "evolution" was believed then to take place in nature—gradually, drip by drip by drip. That— Kuhn said—is totally mistaken. It is a false way of understanding how science "progresses."

In fact, I believe that it is in large part because of Kuhn's insight regarding "revolution rather than evolution" in scientific "progress," that many scientists in the life sciences began to look at evolution in nature in a radically new way.

What actually happens, Kuhn said, is that a new generation thinks of a totally and radically new way of understanding things, and rebels against "the old fogeys"—their teachers, predecessors, and people who wrote the books and promoted "established" notions that "everyone" in the field followed.

The new generation creates a *revolution*, in which sometimes very little is left of the old. Even then, whatever is left over of the old will be understood henceforth in a radically new way. An excellent example of this, I said, is how Sir Isaac Newton's (1642-1727) "celestial mechanics" is now understood—after Einstein's 1905 paper on relativity—as a kind of "special case" in a universe ruled by relativity and its radically new understanding of time, space, gravity, and other factors. Before relativity, Newton's celestial mechanics was simply "physics."

When Albert Einstein (1879-1955) presented the world with relativity, he started a radically new way of understanding the field of physics—a way that is incompatible in some important respects with Newtonian mechanics.

That is a paradigm shift. That sudden and radical shift from the old to the new is what Kuhn refers to as "the structure of scientific revolutions"—as in the title of his book. Kuhn shows how science "progresses" by means of such *revolutions* that break with past understandings. Science doesn't "progress" in a drip-drip-drip sort of way, as evolution in nature had been supposed to take place, ever since Charles Darwin's (1809-1882) *On the Origin of Species* (1859) was published.

K and revolution

I explained to Paul's class that the first time I read Kuhn's book in 1972—as part of my education in the philosophy of science, which was my academic specialty—I immediately saw in Kuhn's insight an important connection to what K had been saying, for decades.

K had been saying—at least since the 1930s—that evolution in nature and in our personal lives does not happen gradually, in a drip-drip-drip sort of way. Rather, evolution is actually a revolution, because it does not happen gradually—step by step—in time.

Time—said K—is intimately intertwined with the me, and the me is too puny to see anything truly new; there is no evolution possible in the me. To see the new, said K, there has to be a revolution—a major shift in consciousness that uproots "the old"—with no gradualness involved, none at all.

What is required for revolution to come about is not gradualness. What is called for, instead, is a mutation—and psychological mutation takes place when there is insight. But insight is outside of time—and time's gradualness and intrinsic me-centeredness.

I said to the class that we are living at a time in human history when conditions exist in which such a mutation—biological as well as psychological-moral—can take place in many humans, and that such a mutation would affect all human society and all its institutions.

In other words, we all need to engage in a paradigm shift—something along the lines of what Kuhn said, *but in the deeper context provided uniquely by K's insights.*

Copernicus, Kant, and Kuhn

The difference between what Kuhn said and my K-related take on it was and is profound. Kuhn was using the expression "paradigm shift" exclusively to refer to the way *science* "progresses."

But the expression "paradigm shift"—as I understood it then and understand it now—involves not just science and its "progress." It involves every aspect of our lives—as K had presciently pointed out.

On the surface, I said to the class, some may think that this is much like the "Copernican revolution"—which is about how we perceive the Earth and celestial bodies—or like the revolution in perception of our reality that Kant referred to, in *The Critique of Pure Reason* (1781).[5]

---

[5] Kant's *Critique* is briefly addressed in Chapter 9, "Nietzsche," and in Chapter 29, "Skeptics."

There is in a way a family resemblance between all three revolutions—except that a paradigm shift (as I understood it and as I was presenting it) is much more than either of the two earlier revolutions, immense as they were, in their own right.

The revolution that Nicolaus Copernicus (1473-1543) revealed implied that Earth is not the center of the universe—as most of his contemporaries in Europe assumed. Copernicus' contemporaries were mostly guided by geocentric notions gathered from Aristotle (384-322 BCE), from the astronomer-astrologer Ptolomy (c. 100-170 A.D.), and from Aristotle-inspired-Church dogmatic beliefs.

Au contraire—pronounced Copernicus—Earth is instead but one of several planets that revolve around the Sun.

That shift in perception—that "Copernican revolution," as it came to be called—had an immense impact on European society, with numerous and profound, unforeseen consequences. Even today, we are the beneficiaries of those consequences, in many ways. So this revolution—from a geocentric to a heliocentric perception of our place in the universe—was obviously important.

Kant's revolution consisted of his describing how we all assume that we are in a position to know and understand what we assume is "reality." Kant pointed to the similarity there is between that self-centered assumption, and assumptions made by geocentrists before Copernicus regarding celestial bodies all turning around Earth.

In fact, Kant noted that similarity at the very beginning of his *Critique*, referring explicitly to "the Copernican revolution." In short, Kant pointed out that the "reality" that we assume is "the world out there," is actually predetermined by the way in which we are made up, psychologically. We separate "the world out there" from "me"—and we have opinions about that "world of reality," which we assume to be outside of us.

Kant then pointed out that this universally-held assumption is completely mistaken. The fact, Kant said, is that all we can ever know is predetermined by our own expectations—which are hardwired into the way in which we perceive everything. Those expectations—which we are born with—consist largely of what he called "the categories of the understanding," and by our assuming that all experience must take place in "space" and "time," as we understand them.

We all seem to be born assuming the world to be that which is actually predetermined by the categories of the understanding and by "space" and "time." We assume, for instance, that events take place "in time and space," and that "everything that happens has a cause." Unfortunately, those and other assumptions are made by us only because we are born with those "categories of the understanding" built into us—and "causality" happens to be one the categories that we assume to be the case. But we have absolutely no way of knowing for certain what the world "as it is in itself" is like.

Those lively expectations predetermine the way in which we will perceive everything. It is thus that what we assume are our perceptions of "the world out there," are actually what he called "phenomena."

Kant pointed out that we are never in a position to know "noumena"—things as they are in themselves. The implication is that any and all theories about "reality"—all "metaphysics"—are but forms of intellectual masturbation (my word, not Kant's). As such, metaphysical notions and speculations are unrelated to the way things actually are.

The act and process of realizing that all we ever perceive are "phenomena" is critical for science—which Kant was a professor of—and for our being better acquainted with what actually is the case, in our daily lives. That realization of our actual limitations produces a major shift within us. Kant referred to this grand shift in our perceptions as being "a new Copernican revolution."

Kuhn's notion that what creates scientific revolutions is a radical "paradigm shift" was itself, indeed, a major, revolutionary insight—much along the lines of the Copernican and Kantian revolutions before him. Kuhn's insight made it possible for all of us to be more predisposed to be open to transformations in our way of perceiving "progress," as it is related to science.

K's *psychological* revolution

All of those three revolutions—important and magnificent as they obviously are—refer to major shifts in *our assumptions* regarding "the way things are."

In other words—and apart from the specific issues that they each were addressing—all those three revolutions leave our me-centered conditioning intact. From the perspective of our me-centered conditioning, we can come to accept that we live in a heliocentric system, that our perceptions of "reality" are but "phenomena" (and not "noumena"), and that scientific paradigm shifts are revolutionary, not "evolutionary."

Yet while accepting intellectually those shifts in perception, we would still continue to be me-centered, based on our personal conditioning.

I explained to the class that the paradigm shift that I was referring to—while it had a family resemblance to Copernicus', Kant's, and Kuhn's—was actually of a profoundly and qualitatively different nature. The previous revolutions had all been referring to a major shift *in the way we analyze things.*

In contrast to those three previous revolutions, I was referring to a shift in consciousness in which there is no analysis of any kind. None at all. The paradigm shift that I was referring to is what takes place when there is insight—when the borderless dimension overcomes all analysis, and thereby all me-centeredness.

I was referring to a true mutation—a biological-psychological mutation in which analysis has absolutely no place. There is no analysis in the act of love, nor in the act of experiencing beauty, nor in the act and process of borderless truth-seeking-truth-finding.

In fact, such a mutation can be said to be that which takes place upon the ending of "the analyzer" in us—"the analyzer" being an expression that K used quite often, usually to refer to the conditioned me, who analyzes and interprets *everything* from the perspective of his puny personal conditioning.

I proposed to the class that such a mutation is unquestionably something that must take place in oneself. It is a psychological as well as a biological transformation—I said that it is in the context of such a major mutation that anything that could be called "theosophical therapy" or "transpersonal therapy" can ever take place. "Theosophical Therapy" was, after all, the subject of that graduate seminar.

Importantly, I said, such a paradigm shift refers simultaneously to a mutation in the way all of our human societies are put together. As K pointed out numerous times, "life is life in relationship." Life in relationship is the life of our society.

Theosophical therapy, I said, involves both the individual and all the relationships and societies that such an individual is involved in. There is no escaping that profound consequence of mutation taking place in oneself.

This goes to the very heart of why education is central to everything that K ever said. K's passionate concern with bringing about "right education" was indeed at the heart of everything he ever said. It resulted, in part, in the creation of a number of "Krishnamurti schools," worldwide.

Central to this *revolutionary* approach to education is the need for both teachers and students to put behind them the "old" notions of promoting me-centered "success" in what is basically a highly immoral, and even criminally-minded society.

Instead, the new, truly revolutionary approach to education involved a constant search for excellence in everything that one does—and comprehensive excellence is impossible unless one actually dies to me-centered "values" based on people's never-questioned me-centered conditioning. That is, comprehensive excellence is impossible unless one dies to the known—unless there is *mutation*.

Transmogrification of "paradigm shift"

At the time when I shared these insights with that graduate class at CIAS, it never even occurred to me what might happen with the expression "paradigm shift."

But in the process of writing this book, I realized recently—after so many intervening years—that perhaps that was the first time ever that anyone had spoken of a "paradigm shift" to apply in the psychological and planetary way that I understood it, thanks to Kuhn—and to K. I say this not just for the shallow purpose of attributing credit to myself for the origin of the popularization of that expression—though that, in retrospect, might be what happened that day.

But I do feel that it is important to try to express in the present context, as clearly as possible, that there is what I consider to be a very serious problem with the way that expression has come to be popularized—and grossly misused.

Now that the expression has left the sophisticated halls of academia and of the nouveau enlightened—and that it has been *vulgarized*—I feel that it has turned into a monster. It has turned into a nasty bug of Kafkaish proportions.

I feel that what's happened to the expression is much like what happens with apparently *everything* that gets to be "popularized." The transmogrification of the expression "paradigm shift" seems to be, in fact, a lot like that of the word "theosophy"—as discussed throughout this narrative.

This expression—which I intended for it to refer to the most serious event that can take place in the lives of any of us—has been sillified and transmogrified beyond recognition, in the process of being popularized. People seem to use it now as if it refers to anything from a change of clothes to a move to a new place.

Now, one can presumably make a "paradigm shift" by switching from Coke to Pepsi, or vice versa. Some may even go so far as being clever enough—and even "revolutionary"—to the point of claiming that the "true" paradigm shift is to go "altogether away" from "Coke *and* Pepsi," to . . . Dr. Pepper?!

A mutation from the me-centered conditioning implicit in all analysis into a dimension of wholeness—a dimension where all values exist, where universal morality has its being—is what the expression referred to, in my comments to the CIAS class.

This paradigm shift is not at all like a conversion from one ideology or group-think to another—where both the "from" and the "to" are obviously me-centered analyses of what is. There is zero paradigm shift in switching brands, such as from being a Baptist to "converting" to Buddhism. One could also convert from being a Buddhist to being a Baptist. Given the therapeutic nature of most of Buddhism, some might find that odd.

But a paradigm shift? Not today.

CIIS and the TS

I would be remiss if I fail to mention one final fact regarding CIIS, and its apparently hidden—and perhaps unexpected—connection to the TS.

Paul Herman and I had many private conversations regarding not only theosophical therapy, but also about what we understood by "theosophy." Paul said to me that he was a member of the TS—that is, the "Adyar" TS. Before that, he had been a member of the "Point Loma" (later "Pasadena") TS. And before that, he had been originally a member of the Adyar TS. He had gone back and forth—but had never been completely happy with either, yet feeling a very strong pull by both.

Given his prominent position in CIIS history—as the main person to whom Chauduri and Watts passed the baton—I find it poignant that he, too, had a TS background.

I also learned from Paul something else—something that I haven't seen in any of the writings I have consulted regarding the history of CIIS.

In the spring of 1978, when I was there, Paul was working at the California Institute of Asian Studies (CIAS), located in what looked like somebody's big house, at the corner of 21st Street and Dolores, in San Francisco.

One day, Paul and I were looking out a window while engaging in our private conversations, and he pointed to a building catty-corner across the street, on Dolores. He told me that that was the California Institute of Integral Studies. He also said that the inspiration for the school across the street was Sri Aurobindo, whereas the inspiration for CIAS was TSer-turned-Anthroposophist Rudolf Steiner. In fact, there was a large portrait of Steiner on one of the walls at CIAS.

He added, with a kind of knowing smile, that he thought that the two institutions might merge, at some point—given the strong similarity of aims and vision between the two. Perhaps he already knew that a merger between the two institutions was coming, but he couldn't reveal it to me, as an outsider. The Steiner connection that Paul mentioned is one that I haven't seen in any of the accounts of the history of CIIS that I have consulted—but one that suggests yet an additional tie between CIIS and the TS.

All of the above references suggest very strongly that—despite CIIS having been all along its own institution, and totally independent of the TS—there have been critical connections between the two. Given the passionate determination to create a world university by people connected with the TS throughout its history—decades before CIIS came into being—I find these TS-CIIS associations quite intriguing. To sum it up:

- The first major leader of CIIS can be said to have been Haridas Chauduri. He was a dedicated student of Sri Aurobindo—whose "integral yoga" had been inspired by the TS, as I have discovered in my researches—and as addressed in Chapter 26, "Aurobindo."
- The Mother—who was central to Aurobindo's work—also had a very strong TS background, as noted in the previous chapter.
- Some of Chauduri's own books—such as *Integral Yoga* (1965)—were published by the Theosophical Publishing House.

- Alan Watts, who became a TS member as a young teen-ager, worked hand-in-hand with Chauduri—thereby helping create and develop what came to be known as "The San Francisco Renaissance"—which was highly in-fluential in worldwide culture, such as we now know it.
- Ernest Wood—also a prominent TS member—had ini-tially been the head of the original institution, but left "in a New York minute" with his wife Hilda (n.d.) to establish the first Montessori school in America, the School of the Woods, in Houston, Texas.
- Judith Tyberg had been critically important in the growth and development of CIIS—and also had been a prom-inent TS member.
- Paul Herman has been identified as the one taking charge of CIIS after Watts and Chauduri died—and he, too, was a TS member.
- According to Paul, CIAS was inspired by Rudolf Steiner, who had started his perennial work as a TS member.
- I met Paul as a result of his teaching a graduate seminar at CIAS on "Theosophical Therapy."
- It is my understanding that the Theosophical Therapy seminar was funded by the Kern Foundation—which is managed by the TSA.

Perhaps these are coincidences. But even if they happen to be, they are worth noting, given the profound impact that the TS has had over the whole planet's ongoing wisdom explosion—a subject that I address more fully in works in the making.

In any case, the TS was initially inspired by perennials with the intention of bringing about a paradigm shift in human con-sciousness, everywhere. Intriguingly, CIIS has been—through-out its history—a major force in helping to bring about such a paradigm shift.

A new beginning

Intriguingly, the way the whole New Age movement was created was by individuals initially being inspired by some aspect of the TS—and breaking off on their own. Sometimes such individuals would become authors and/or leaders or participants in a newly created group or movement. Or else, they would start their own group—each of such groups emphasizing one particular element implicit in what they had initially elicited from the TS milieu.

What I find quite poignant and intriguing about the history of CIIS is that it has proceeded precisely along the same lines as so very many authors, groups, and organizations—sometimes under the aegis of "the New Age," sometimes not.

In addition, CIIS strikes me as having been closest than any other educational institution of higher learning to fulfilling the aims that many prominent TS members had yearned for, in their efforts to create a theosophical university.

As has been noted in this exploration, leaders of culture such as Carl Jung, Joseph Campbell, Ken Wilber—and many, many others—have followed what I have called "the code of silence." That code refers to leaders of culture hiding the fact that their original inspiration either came directly from the TS, or at least from the environment created by the TS.

In this, too, CIIS has followed a course that many have taken, as noted in the present narrative. Given the prominent status of CIIS as a leader in higher education, so far it has made sense for it to stay clear of any association with the TS in general, or with HPB in particular.

But I say, then was then. We're not in Kansas, anymore.

For more than a century—and especially in the academic world—it has been the case that anything and everything relating to the TS in general, or to HPB in particular, has much too often been considered to be somewhat "hoakie," for reasons discussed in part in the present exploration.

I submit to you, attentive reader, that such perceptions may have been justified for many decades—given that human consciousness had not yet been transformed to the extent that it now has, towards being more planetary. I submit that the time has come for acknowledging that which a superabundance of facts and documentation support at the present time.

I submit to you that we are in the midst of a paradigm shift such as has never been witnessed before—despite the obvious reality that we have not yet "reached the promised land."

The time for disclosure is upon us.

Perhaps all of the above is just an annoying coincidence—however intriguing. Perhaps it is an inconvenient truth.

You be the judge.

CHAPTER 33
Dying To The Known

DYING TO THE KNOWN IS THE VERY HEART of the wisdom explosion in the American Age. But what *is* "the known"?

The known

The known is all the prejudicial attitudes and views that we humans have identified with, for millennia.

The known is the tyrannical structure of societies—since time unknown—that have divided us all into "the haves" and "the have-nots."

The known is the prejudicial inequities between us, based on class, ideology, skin tint, or regional culture considered "relevant" by some of us. Such prejudices—and many others—come mainly from "those in power," or from those who arbitrarily assume that they "know," and that they are somehow "the salt of the earth."

The known is the same prejudicial inequities, but as accepted by those who are prejudiced against—and who thereby create their own me-centered divisions.

The known is the tedious dogmas and hierarchies of those who set themselves up as "authorities" in relation to universal morality. Such "authorities" establish themselves despite the fact that universal morality is already within us, and requires no authorities at all.

The known is the very same dogmas, when they are accepted by anyone who thereby willingly becomes the victim of the dogma inventors.

Universal morality can breathe exclusively when there are no moral authorities of any kind—nor those who accept such moral authorities.

Most importantly—and in sum—the known is the little Caesar who thrives within each and every one of us, to the extent that me-centeredness dominates our daily lives. It is that tyrant within who's been responsible for all the mischiefs that we have all been victimized by, in so many, many ways.

Religion and ethics

All religions and ethical systems based on universal morality—without exception—have been centrally about dying to the known.

When Jesus exhorts us to "love your enemy," and to be "meek" and to serve others, he is clearly and unambiguously imploring us to die to the known—to let the tyrant within cease to be. Upon close observation, "enemies" are always those whom we *assume* to be opposed to our very personal attachments and expectations.

The Buddha urges us to move away from samsara—which is the world of constant stress, conflict, depression, and hopelessness. The universe circumscribed by samsara is the me-centered dimension of our experience—which is the dimension of never-ending suffering-frustration.

The coming about of nirvana upon the ending of samsara in our daily lives is precisely what dying to the known is about.

Socrates stated that philosophy consists of dying every single day of one's life.[1] He was clearly saying that philosophy consists of letting the Little Caesar within us die, on a daily basis. It is only then that wisdom—*philosophia*—is possible. That is dying to the known.

The Jewish Ten Commandments entreat us to die to the me-centeredness implicit in violating any one of those ten injunctions. That is dying to the known.

The five pillars of Islam are about a total rejection of the known (as described above), and about an absolute abnegation to the supreme being—which encompasses us all. The Muslim life is a life of constant dying to the known.

---

[1] Plato, *Phaedo,* 64a, Thomas Taylor translation.

As Kant lays it out, universal morality is about practicing the Golden Rule, "Do onto others as you would have them do onto you."[2]

Such universal ethics can only happen to the extent that the me-centered known is in the rear-view mirror. Ethics can only be when there is deep concern over *doing the right thing*, and when such a concern is present in our every action. That can only happen when there is no me-centeredness—and *that* is dying to the known.

Lao Tse's *Tao Te Ching*—which is the foundational text of Taoism—has been summarized by pointing out the immense importance of having three qualities in our lives. Those "virtues" are simplicity, patience, and compassion.

Simplicity is what happens when there are no me-centered prejudices and expectations—which are the main sources of "complications" in life.

Patience makes it possible to be one with the way things actually are, without the confusions brought about by me-centered speculations and expectations.

Compassion implies listening to everyone and everything, having empathy—rather than having a ready-made me-centered map of the way things "ought" to be.

Taoism is about dying to the known.

Hinduism—despite its bewildering diversity and many schools—may be summarized by saying that it consists of the ending of the outward "me," in the context of the coming about of atman, which is really brahman.

Hinduism is about self-realization. That can only take place when there is the ending of the me—*ahankara*—and the realization that one's true self is *all that is*, brahman.

Hinduism is about dying to the known.

Atheism is centrally about being ethical in all of one's actions—especially towards other humans—since there is no

---

[2] See *Groundwork of the Metaphysics of Morals*, 1785; and *Critique of Practical Reason*, 1788.

"God" to sanction what we do or not do. Being an atheist is about being responsible to others—perhaps including all forms of life.

Atheism is about putting universal morality into practice in everything one does. It consists of shunning all divisive attitudes and all prejudices.

Atheism is about taking responsibility for all of one's actions, rather than passing that responsibility onto anyone or anything else.

Atheism is about dying daily to all me-centered prejudices, dogmas, and expectations.

Atheism is about daily dying to the known.

All religions and ethical systems based on universal morality—and our own personal sense of "right and wrong"—point rather clearly to the fact that universal morality is within each and every one of us. If that were not so, we would be unable to respond to the various messages communicated by perennials—throughout history and everywhere on Earth.

Intriguingly, "dying to the known" is an expression coined by K. It is yet one more example of how he could capture the formerly complex and sometimes convoluted—and as it has turned out, divisive—by using a very simple, borderless expression that even a child can understand.

America

America's founding documents are but the most recent major presentation of the self-same universal wisdom to be found in all great expressions of universal morality—including the moral sense within each of us.

A major difference between America's and other expressions of universal morality in history is that its founding documents explicitly address themselves to the whole planet. That had never been even tried before—at least not specifically. After all, there has never before been a planetary culture such as the one that exists in the American Age—so far as our collective memory can remember.

All other such appeals to universal morality—while being borderless and universally moral—came to be identified with a particular ideology or region or culture of the world. All such systems and institutions came to be mistakenly assumed to be synonymous with ideologies that were arbitrarily spun from the original expositions. Even atheism has its "scriptures."

Sometimes the "interpretations" of universal morality have been identified with a particular ethnicity.

America's founding documents appeal to every single human being—regardless of race, creed, gender, caste, or color. They tell us that *all* of us "are created equal," and that there must be "justice for *all*."

They do not say that only "Christians" are "Americans" nor that only the United States matter nationalistically, above all other nations. People who hold such divisive and conflict-pregnant beliefs are *obviously* unacquainted with America's actual founding documents.

As noted in Chapter 27, "American Age"—and elsewhere throughout this exploration—America's founding documents address themselves to the whole planet and to all humans. The United States is but the place on Earth where it so happens that those documents first saw the light. The country that was thus created was the one that was first to be *challenged* by America's documents.

All countries and institutions and people subsequently touched by those documents—which are now all nations on Earth and all internationalist organizations, such as the United Nations—are *challenged* directly by the borderless morality that America's founding documents proclaim.

Exactly like all other major expositions of universal morality—such as all religions and ethical systems based on universal morality—those documents were always clearly meant to be a moral challenge to each of us. They are centrally a call for us— everywhere in the world—to do our best to see and understand the very real great dangers that always come with creating me-centered societies.

Those documents are centrally about dying to the known. They are about putting behind us the tyrannical, dogmatic, divisive, conflict-ridden past.

E Pluribus Unum

In an important sense, America's main motto, *E Pluribus Unum*, can be said to refer to something much deeper than what may appear, on the surface.

There is a sense in which the universe in its entirety is E Pluribus Unum—*a grand solidarity of all that is, an implicit oneness in the midst of absolute diversity.*

The word "universe" itself suggests this oneness, this solidarity. The universe is "uni," one. Yet at the same time it is "verse," many: *E Pluribus Unum.*

My sense of it is that all entities—"large" and "small"—that make up the universe have a sense of being part of that grand whole.

This is particularly significant, especially in the context of what was just stated. Namely, all of us have a sense of "right" and "wrong." Where does that universally moral sense come form?

Where does universal morality come from?

I suggest—and it's just a suggestion for you to look at, seriously and as deeply as you're capable of—that every entity in the universe somehow knows or senses itself to be a mere tiny component of the grand whole. We all somehow "know" or "sense" that we are each in solidarity with everything and everyone else in the universe.

I suggest that it is this sense of oneness with the all that makes us be attracted to the various religions and ethical systems based on universal morality.

My sense is that this is, in fact, where universal morality comes from. We each know or sense ourselves to be siblings of all other beings. We are—each and all—children of the one mother, the universe. In our mother's womb we live, and move, and have our being, and thrive.

To me, that "explains" our attraction to universal morality—an attraction that has always been there. Something within us propels us to care for others, to serve them or help them—or "just because."

God

Some of us give a name to that sense of oneness within. We may call it "God," or something similar. Some call it "Nature." Some call it "love" or "beauty" or "goodness." I suggest, if I may, that there is an important sense in which the word—and the conceptual and practical paraphernalia that go with the word—is not as important as some of us may think it is.

If the word "God" or a similar word is important to you, then by all means use it. However, if the use of that word implies segregation from others, then you are obviously misusing that word. As Wittgenstein put it, "the meaning of a word is its use in language.[3] What matters is what you actually do, not the words you use. Are you everyone's friend and sibling? That is what matters.

The word is not the thing.

Universal morality

What is important is that there be that sense within of the grandness of the oneness—and the solidarity with everything and everyone that goes with it. That is what acting ethically is about.

Such action is a blessing like no other.

When there is that sense of sacredness in daily life, me-centeredness has no place.

Such is the nature of dying to the known.

---

[3] Wittgenstein, *Philosophical Investigations*, §43.

Living our lives in terms of dying to the known is *essential* for ending all stresses, all confusions, all conflicts, no matter what they are. It is only upon dying to the known, at all levels of our experience—whether personal, in our relationships, in our communities, or planet-wide—that there can be peace and harmony in our personal lives, and in the societies that we live in.

Dying to the known is one and the same with all-comprehensive love.

Love is the true revolution.

EPILOGUE

THE PRIVATE GATHERING with K and David Bohm that I was invited to participate in by the Krishnamurti Foundation of America (KFA) took place in the last week of March, 1979. That was exactly one year after my ever-so-brief stint at CIIS, which is addressed in Chapters 31 and 32, "World University," and "Paradigm Shift."

There were about a dozen of us, coming to the KFA campus in Ojai, California, from different parts of the country and the world.

The gathering

There was an anthropologist from New Zealand, two German physicists, a philosopher from India, a housewife from San Francisco, a psychotherapist-turned-cab-driver from Seattle, and others. I thought it curious that three of us were from Cuba—Armando Verea, my wife Maria Teresa (both of them teachers), and I.

In every session, which began two hours before lunch, there were also present members of the KFA staff and board who'd drop in as listeners, though not every day. Two exceptions to staff participation were Booth Harris (n.d.), who recorded the event (and in whose house I stayed for one month), and Mary Zimbalist (1915-2008), who owned and lived in the house where the gathering took place.

In addition, there were daily evening sessions with Bohm—which took place in Arya Vihara, the house in which K lived initially, and in which the process began in 1922. The evening sessions with Bohm generally included about two to three dozen participants.

Apart from that, I had the opportunity to engage Bohm—usually one-on-one, but a couple of times with one or two others—in explorations in which we usually addressed not only mutation-related and social change issues, but also the philosophy of science, which was my academic field.

My contact with Bohm was further enhanced that summer, when he went to Berkeley (where I was living at the time) to lead a number of gatherings. During his visit, I became his point man—in the sense of helping organize most of these meetings, at different venues. One of those venues was UC Berkeley, where Bohm had been a student under famous physicist Robert Oppenheimer (1904-1967), as well as having been a teacher there.

The pregnant silence

Beginning in September 1966—when K had given a series of talks at the New School for Social Research in New York City—I got to attend a number of his public talks. In the 1970s, I became a permanent fixture in the Ojai talks at the Oak Grove, almost every year—and developed friendships with several KFA staff and board members.

All the K talks and discussions I ever attended had begun with a silence so pregnant that "one could cut it with a knife." That silence always put me in tune with a far more intense than the usual level of awareness.

The private gathering in Ojai was no different, in that respect.

I am reporting this from memory—and one's memory is only rarely a reliable source. What I am describing now is a personal recollection. There is a recording of the whole gathering, so a more precisely accurate description of this gathering is available. But existentially, what I relate here is accurate, as it affected me and as I recall it.

On the first day, and after a long pregnant silence, K looked around at each of us, and inquired, "Sirs, what shall we talk about, during this week?" He looked at us, waiting for an answer. After a long pause, someone made a suggestion, then there were a few others. Then, more deeply pregnant, high-energy silence in which there were no expectations. Yet there was full alertness.

K was looking intently at each of us, in a child-like inquiring stance. "Shall we talk about that, sirs? Do you wish to talk about fragmentation? Shall we address the corruption in our society? Shall we speak of *what is*?

You see, sirs, all of this, and the other suggestions made, tell us that we do live in a very corrupt society. It is a fragmented society. And is it possible to live rightly, in the midst of all that corruption? And where does that corruption come from? Are we not part of that society, and so part of that corruption? And is it possible to create a good society? Is that possible, sirs? Is it? Maybe that's what we'll go into. Is it possible to create a good society? Is that alright, sirs? Is that what we shall talk about?"

The silences at the beginning of talks, and the questions K was asking us were not a gimmick. For anyone who was there, it was obvious that this was not a studied, preconceived "setup." This was an honest-to-goodness straight-out, soul-searching, world-class *inquiry*.

Tabula rasa

As noted in the biographies, whenever K went before an audience, his mind was a tabula rasa. He had no idea or expectation regarding what was going to be said. In an important way, he was a spectator as much as the rest of the audience.

My perception is that it was from the audience that the subject matter came, not from K. The subject matter revealed itself to him, as he listened deeply to the inward chatter of all of those present. He would tune in to the audience before him, and what he received would determine the subject for the talk or discussion.

This is part of the nature of true *philosophical* research. It is also the nature of meditation, at its best. Meditation consists of listening borderlessly and in earnest—as if one's life depended on it. In such supremely alert listening, there cannot be any interference from the always impertinent monkey-mind analyzer—the analyzer being the conditioned me, who is ever ready to analyze everything in terms of his very small and limited past experience and cleverness.

When that Little Caesar within is completely silent, then—and only then—can there be listening. It is only in the emptiness from the analyzer that true philosophical or scientific research—or true meditation—can take place.

Anything else that one does is provincial, gossipy chit-chat—and is quite disposable.

Meditator

The baby had died in 1945. At the same time, there was a near-death experience. After that shock, the baby—and then the toddler, and then the infant—meditated throughout the day, for hours on end. This went on daily, until the child was four years old.

During those meditations subsequent to nearly dying, there was at the periphery an awareness of the body's physical surroundings and needs. But there was mainly an altogether different awareness—an awareness that was one with what could be called "the moral dimension." From then on—and as a result of what happened while the baby body was dead—the life of the physical entity became largely a search for what this entity's life "mission" would be about.

This sense of mission is nothing special or unique.

All of us are born with a mission, though many of us never get to realize that all-important fact about our lives. Some of us do get to know what that mission is, from early on. Some of us discover it later—sometimes even late in life. But we all have a mission, whether our conditioned brain is aware of it or not. We all each owe it to ourselves—and to *all that is*—to find out what that mission is.

The great mythologist Joseph Campbell (1904-1987) used to say, "follow your bliss." Clearly, "following your bliss" is precisely the same as finding out what your mission is. He was exhorting all of us to discover what our mission in life is—and to follow it.

"Follow your bliss"—which became a very popular expression, and is still used—was Campbell's version of something that K had been saying from the beginning of his work, "do that which you love." That is, find out what it is that you love doing more than anything else, and proceed to own up to that love. Such love is integrity in one's life.

It is not a coincidence that there should be such a conflation between "do what you love" and "follow your bliss." After all, Campbell began his work as a mythologist—instead of as an art historian, as he had planned—when he met K in 1924, and became K's friend for life. At least that is what Campbell stated in an interview with influential radio host Michael Toms (1940-2013).[1]

Mission

The inquiry into the life-mission was not some happenstance or something remembered only now and then. It was an intense, constant, daily yearning for finding out—exactly as if life depended on it, which it did. It is better not to say much about that quest—or of its origins—because if said, it is bound to be misunderstood and misinterpreted.

Let's just say that we all have a moral obligation to the universe, in whose womb we all live, and whose vital juices nurture us and give us life. That is actually a very paltry way of expressing something that is truly inexpressible.

There were several near-death experiences, later on—much like smaller tremors after a big earthquake. Each of those was much like a friendly reminder of what was at stake, from the beginning. It is that sense of urgency-without-tension that led to encountering various "forms of meditation," beginning in the summer of 1963, as noted in Chapter 6, "Disclosure."

---

[1] Michael Toms, *An Open Life: Joseph Campbell in conversation with Michael Toms* (1990).

In 1963, there was the discovery of Patañjali's *Yoga Sutras* through I.K. Taimni's (1898-1978) then recently published *The Science of Yoga* (1961). This intense study and practice led to years—to this day—of delving deeply into *what is*, from that perspective.

Beginning in 1963, there were years of Buddhist meditation, which included the *vipassana* meditation of Theravada Buddhism, then Mahayana Buddhism in the form of Zen meditation, and finally Vajrayana Buddhism in the form of a variety of unique approaches to meditation in Tibetan Buddhism.

There were explorations into Gurdjieff approaches, including sessions with internationally renowned author and philosophy professor Jacob Needleman (b. 1934)—who was near the top of the Gurdjieff Foundation's hierarchy at the time (1977-79)—and Kathy Riordan Speeth (b. 1937), a transpersonal psychotherapist who had met Gurdjieff in person as a child, and who taught meditation at the Nyingma Institute of Tibetan Studies in Berkeley, California.

There was Islamic Sufi meditation while dancing and singing communally as one being.

There was meditation during the holy eucharist celebration at mass.

This latter was surprising and extraordinary, because during meditation in the first four years after the near-death experience there were recollections of previous lives. These included a previous incarnation—a life in which a Christian bishop had been burned alive, by order of the Catholic Inquisition. That harrowing experience had created an intense aversion to the Catholicism that was pervasive in Cuba, as the child grew into adolescence.

So receiving all the minor orders in the Liberal Catholic Church in 1974 was in itself astonishing—a veritable transformation.

There was Taoist moving meditation, in the form of tai chi chuan, chi gung, nei gung, longevity breathing, and related practices.

Throughout, there continued to be meditation from moment to moment, while being in a crowded New York subway or BART in San Francisco, or while swimming, or while speaking with someone.

There was meditation while sleeping.

I still "practice."

Challenging K

I also discovered K in 1963.

But I was puzzled. What K was saying gave the impression of contradicting all traditionalist approaches. Yet what he said also struck me strongly as being true; it echoed my own perception, since the near-death experience. At the same time, it seemed to me, from the beginning, that "surely" there must be at least *some* value in traditionalist approaches from around the world.

Those insights and conundrums led to my beginning a years-long exploration—an exploration that consisted of getting deeply immersed in different systems and methodologies, as a way of *challenging* what K was saying, as a way of putting to the test of experience what his researches were pointing towards. At the same time, I was challenging my own perceptions, which agreed so completely with what K was saying.

All along—despite my recognizing his unique place in the history and practice of the universal wisdom—I have never been a K devotee, in the sense of being a blind follower.

At the same time, there was an appreciation of the value of various traditionalist approaches at first hand—limited as they are because of their self-imposed walls.

A major discovery that came out of the research is that it *is* possible to encounter deeper value in such approaches—*but only if and to the extent that the borderless wisdom is present, throughout.* It is particularly critical that one does not become prejudicially attached to any traditionalist approach.

That is easier said than done—especially given the psychological hegemony that traditional approaches *require* their respective practitioners to accept, in obeisance.

Following a tradition—even when informed by the borderless wisdom—can also lead very easily to self-deception. Engaging in a particular tradition is a lot like laying down next to a cobra— beautiful yet deadly. Alert awareness is required, every step of the way, when one decides deliberately to mix the borderless wisdom with a traditionalist approach.

Yes, it is possible to benefit from traditionalist ways. It is also important—if one does engage in such ways—to realize that one is walking on the edge of a precipice, in the midst of gale-force winds.

Caveat emptor.

Borderless meditation

What K was addressing is profoundly unique.

In absolute contrast, all traditionalist forms of meditation involve and imply asserting closed loops in the brain.[2]

Briefly, when one is attached to any form of conditioning— including meditation practices, such as the ones just mentioned—brain cells and organ components get to function in terms of "closed loops" in the brain. In traditionalism, the predetermined algorithms one is expected to follow are self-enclosed, and are meant to double-down on and reaffirm the group-think that the "meditation" *du jour* asserts—and expects practitioners to comply with.

Such predetermined "meditation" is in fact a perpetuation and even an enhancement of the most foundational problem we all have to face—which is the ending of the me in the context of the presence of the perennial dimension, which is within all of us.

---

[2] Closed loops are discussed more thoroughly in *The Inner Life of Krishnamurti.*

Traditionalist "meditation" hardwires us to a particular form of conditioning. As such, it is a reassertion of the me. It never is—nor can it ever be—the ending of the me.

There can be no true—perennial—meditation in traditionalism.

All traditionalist forms of meditation—and in fact, all traditionalism—implies the formation and the hardwiring of intrinsically me-centered closed loops in brain cells. The would-be meditator's activity incorporates mechanically-followed algorithms, and those algorithms "confirm" the presumed "reality" and "value" of the system that one is following.

In K's insights, researches, and observations there is *never* a moment when there is an algorithm of any sort to follow. There are absolutely zero algorithms involved. That had never been even suggested before, in the history of mankind—let alone in the history of the perennial wisdom.

Borderless research means that there is no pattern to follow. In such true research—which is also true research in science— there is no center from which to interpret everything encountered. Nor is there then a circumference for one to stay within the bounds of. In borderless research there is no "little box" within which one "meditates" and stays in.

Research and meditation have no meaning at all, unless they are borderless.

In borderless research—such as true *philosophical* or *scientific* inquiry—the brain cells are not functioning in a closed loop. The brain cells—and one's whole being—are then completely and totally open to whatever actually takes place. The brain cells are in an attitude of not accepting any self-enclosed, predigested pattern, and of being open to whatever happens. It is an attitude of profound listening—a kind of listening that meditators committed to any form of traditionalism *never* get to encounter, by the very nature of traditionalism as an intrinsically closed loop.

I can report that it is possible to enjoy the benefits of some traditionalist forms of meditation without being committed to the expectations that otherwise usually *gowith* all such systems.

It is possible to practice Patañjali's yoga, or various forms of Buddhist meditation, or practice nei gung, or even engage in the holy eucharist, while not being prejudicially committed to the system in question. But that calls for walking on the razor's edge—at least on occasion.

Alert awareness is critical, at all times, regardless of what one ends up doing or not doing—and that takes us back to K, and to *the actual* borderless wisdom.

Shock

On the third day of that week, something extraordinary happened.

At that point in my life, 1979, I had been deeply absorbed in what K had been saying—through his books, audios, videos, and personally in the many talks I'd been attending. I had been involved in K discussion groups, in different parts of the country. I had started several such groups. I had delved as deeply as I could into K's borderless explorations without a circumscribing center or circumference.

None of that prepared me at all for the shock that shook my whole being to its foundations that day. In a way, what happened resonated very strongly with what had happened upon the death of the baby's physical body. In important ways, what happened at the gathering was a kind of deepening of the earlier death—a new, deeper death, if you will. It took place at a moment when K was speaking.

Suddenly, I realized that—from the moment the gathering had begun—K had been communicating with us non-verbally.

Yes, what he was saying could be understood by the analytical mind. Yes, one could explore it analytically—which is what K discussion groups did, all the time.

But the realization at that moment of shock was that there was also a non-verbal, much deeper form of communication going on. I'm not trying at all to create some form of mystification regarding K. Perish that thought! I am trying to communicate to you, *listening reader*, that there is a great deal more to K than what he said—amazing as what he said is, in itself.

Because what I was receiving is non-verbal, it's obviously a waste of time—and a big mistake—to try to talk about it much. I'll just say that the wordless message can be summarized in this way: The borderless wisdom is saying to all of us, constantly, "Snap out of it! You know very well what you need to do! Shut up already, and just do it! Not a word out of you! Not a single word! Just do it!"

Every day, I'm still learning from that communication—44 years later, as I write this. It is as if it is still flowering and unfolding.

Importantly, this is not just "something coming from K"—as if K were behaving like the "spirits" who "channel" themselves through others. That would be a travesty and a gross misunderstanding of what I'm trying to convey here.

This is not at all complicated, so there is no need to try to complicate it. What is important here is that the borderless wisdom is telling *all of us*—with a sense of alarm and urgency—that we (each and all) need to heed its call to engage in unconditional love, justice, truth-seeking-truth-finding, courage, and everything else that *goeswith* the borderless wisdom.

You and I can look at that—and do so borderlessly. When we do, it becomes obvious that we—each and all—need urgently to heed that voice of wisdom. The "alternative" to doing that, is what we see all around us, as well as within our psyches—a world in chaos, in constant stress, in confusion, in conflict, in needless oppressions, in unacceptable inequities.

No person is telling you that you must do this or that. I certainly am not. I am simply saying that there is the high road of living in harmony with *all that is*—and that there is the low road of living our daily lives the way we always have, in the past. When you take the low road, you thereby choose to live life in a clearly immoral way—the way of divisions, prejudices, and constant battling with each other, and within ourselves.

And you know what? Like it or not, there is an inconvenient truth in all this—a truth that you may not like to hear, but which is looking right at you.

The ball is in your court.

.

www.ingramcontent.com/pod-product-compliance
Lightning Source LLC
Chambersburg PA
CBHW070015100426
42740CB00013B/2504